Augmented Reality

Augmented Reality

Principles and Practice

Dieter Schmalstieg

Tobias Höllerer

♦♦ Addison-Wesley

Boston • Columbus • Indianapolis • New York • San Francisco • Amsterdam • Cape Town
Dubai • London • Madrid • Milan • Munich • Paris • Montreal • Toronto • Delhi • Mexico City
São Paulo • Sydney • Hong Kong • Seoul • Singapore • Taipei • Tokyo

For information about buying this title in bulk quantities, or for special sales opportunities (which may include electronic versions; custom cover designs; and content particular to your business, training goals, marketing focus, or branding interests), please contact our corporate sales department at corpsales@pearsoned.com or (800) 382-3419.

For government sales inquiries, please contact governmentsales@pearsoned.com.

For questions about sales outside the U.S., please contact intlcs@pearson.com.

Visit us on the Web: informit.com/aw

Library of Congress Cataloging-in-Publication Data

Names: Schmalstieg, D. (Dieter), author. | Höllerer, Tobias, 1970–   author.
Title: Augmented reality : principles and practice / Dieter Schmalstieg,
    Tobias Höllerer.
Description: Boston : Addison-Wesley, 2016. | Includes bibliographical
    references and index.
Identifiers: LCCN 2016009049 | ISBN 9780321883575 (pbk. : alk. paper)
Subject: LCSH: Augmented reality.
Classification: LCC QA76.9.A94 S36 2016 | DDC 006.8—dc23
LC record available at https://lccn.loc.gov/2016009049

ISBN-13: 978-0-321-88357-5
ISBN-10: 0-321-88357-8
Text printed in the United States on recycled paper at RR Donnelley in Crawfordsville, Indiana.
1 16

Publisher
Mark L. Taub

Executive Editor
Laura Lewin

Development Editor
Susan Brown Zahn

Managing Editor
Sandra Schroeder

Full-Service Production Manager
Julie B. Nahil

Project Editor
Thistle Hill Publishing Services

Copy Editor
Jill Hobbs

Indexer
John S. Lewis

Proofreader
Anna Popick

Technical Reviewers
Reinhold Behringer
Doug Bowman
Kiyoshi Kiyokawa

Editorial Assistant
Olivia Basegio

Cover Designer
Chuti Prasertsith

Compositor
Shepherd, Inc.

To Ursula, Katharina, and Florian
—Dieter

To Julie, Clara, and Luisa
—Tobias

Contents

Preface

Over the past 20 years, the use of information technology has undergone a clear transition from stationary office and desktop computing—first to the web, then to social media, and then to mobile computing. Sales of smartphones and tablet computers have far outpaced the sales of conventional desktop PCs for years now, even if one places laptop or notebook computers within the desktop category.

While the predominant user interface style of today has not radically departed from the *desktop computing* of the 1990s (or the 1981 Xerox Star, for that matter), the way members of the young generation today attain computer literacy has changed: Apps and cloud computing are replacing the computer desktop in many cases. Computing has shifted from office or home office work to an anywhere-and-anytime activity.

Enter: Augmented Reality

As users move away from the desktop, it increasingly makes sense to include the physical world in our computing experience. Given that the physical world is not flat and is not composed of written documents, a new user interface metaphor becomes necessary. **Augmented reality** (AR) has the potential to become the leading user interface metaphor for *situated computing*. Augmented reality has the unique quality of providing a direct link between the physical reality and virtual information about that reality. The world becomes the user interface, leading to the familiar proclamation:

Back to the real world!

Virtual reality, the vision of immersing ourselves in artificial worlds, has propelled the development of game consoles with amazing 3D graphics and led to consumer devices such as head-mounted displays and gesture-tracking devices. Even so, a user interface metaphor such as virtual reality, which by definition monopolizes our attention, is not necessarily a good fit for everyday and spontaneous use of computing.

Instead, we increasingly rely on computer interfaces that make possible casual use and provide information in small, easily understood portions. We feel a need for **ubiquitous computing**. This can take the form of *calm* computing, which operates behind the scenes without the user intervening or even consciously noticing. If ubiquitous *interaction* is required, though, augmented reality excels as an appropriate user interface technology.

Why a Book on Augmented Reality?

Multiple overlapping research fields are contributing to the development of augmented reality, and the associated body of knowledge is growing fast. The authors of this book have been contributing to this body of knowledge as researchers since the 1990s. However, the main motivation for this book came from teaching classes on augmented reality at the authors' home institutions at Graz University of Technology and the University of California, Santa Barbara. In the preparation for these classes, it became evident that no single text is available that covers both the breadth and the depth of this rapidly evolving field. Some notes were available from tutorials at various conferences, several of which the authors were involved in, starting as early as SIGGRAPH 2001. A lot of ground has been covered since then, and the authors were motivated to assemble all this knowledge in a systematic way with an eye toward both novel concepts and practical information. Hence, this book was born.

What's in the Book?

As its title suggests, the book strives for a compromise between principles and practice. Our objective was to make it interesting and usable for both academic researchers and practitioners, especially engineers, who are interested in augmented reality applications. The book, therefore, is intended to be usable both as a textbook and as a reference. To get the most out of it, readers should have a basic understanding of computer science in general, and some knowledge of, and interest in, computer graphics and computer vision is helpful. We don't hesitate to refer to existing literature that explains specific aspects of the necessary background in more detail than we could within the constraints of a single volume. At the same time, we were careful to introduce and clearly explain any specific augmented reality concepts that go beyond basic knowledge, to make the book self-contained. Using the following structure, we present the technical and methodological foundations of AR.

Chapter 1, "Introduction to Augmented Reality," sets the stage by presenting a working definition of augmented reality, providing a brief history of the field, and then walking the reader through various application examples of this powerful real-world user interface technology. We conclude the chapter with a contextualization within the spectrum of related technologies and research fields.

Chapter 2, "Displays," deals with displays, a fundamental enabling technology for augmented reality. Based on some foundations of visual perception, various display technologies that are suitable for augmented reality are discussed—in particular, head-mounted displays, handheld displays, and projective displays. The chapter also discusses nonvisual displays, such as auditory and haptic devices.

Chapter 3, "Tracking," gives an introduction to tracking, one of the core technologies underlying augmented reality. We first discuss the characteristics that are necessary to understand how tracking—and measurement systems in general—work. We then discuss traditional stationary tracking systems and compare them to mobile sensors. Optical tracking as the most prominent tracking technology is given extensive treatment. The chapter concludes by sketching the principles of sensor fusion.

Chapter 4, "Computer Vision for Augmented Reality," picks up the issue of optical tracking from Chapter 3 and gives a detailed account of computer vision algorithms for real-time pose estimation, i.e. for determining a camera's viewing position and orientation from the observed imagery. To make this topic manageable and address readers with a wide variety of backgrounds, the chapter is structured along a suite of case studies. Every case study introduces only the knowledge necessary for it to be self-contained, so the reader does not have to accumulate in-depth knowledge of computer vision first. Moreover, advanced mathematical topics, which in practice are often used as a black box by relying on a software library such as OpenCV, are marked so that the reader can safely skip over them.

Chapter 5, "Calibration and Registration," deals with methods for calibration and registration of the devices used in augmented reality. Calibration of the digital cameras used for the optical tracking described in Chapter 3 is a necessary prerequisite to deliver repeatable, accurate behavior in augmented reality applications. Registration is the process that aligns the physical and virtual parts of the augmented reality experience geometrically, thereby giving rise to the illusion of a coherent mixed environment.

Chapter 6, "Visual Coherence," focuses on a family of computer graphics techniques that together produce a seamlessly blended view of real and virtual objects. It includes phenomena such as correct occlusion between virtual and real objects, or correct shadowing between virtual and real objects. We also explain diminished reality, or the removal of real objects from a scene, and examine the simulation of physical cameras.

Chapter 7, "Situated Visualization," is dedicated to visualization techniques. Visualization has the objective of making information comprehensible. In the context of augmented reality, this means that the computer-generated information that is geometrically registered to objects in the physical scene must be positioned and styled in such a way that it can be easily understood by its users. We deal with both two-dimensional augmentations (such as textual labels) and three-dimensional augmentations (such as synthesized views of the interior of objects, so-called "ghostings").

Chapter 8, "Interaction," examines the various interaction techniques and interaction styles that are relevant for augmented reality applications. The topics range from simple situated information browsing to full three-dimensional interaction. We specifically discuss props, widgets, and hand-based interaction, and the connection of augmented reality to tangible user interfaces of various forms. We also take a look at multimodal and agent-based interfaces for augmented reality.

Chapter 9, "Modeling and Annotation," is concerned with the topic of interactive modeling—that is, the creation of new geometric content through augmented reality. User interfaces that are embedded in a three-dimensional environment provide a powerful approach for re-creating a digital version of this environment. This capability is invaluable for all applications that deal with visual computing.

Chapter 10, "Authoring," discusses authoring approaches for augmented reality. The content of augmented reality presentations and information databases needs to be designed and created the same way that web content is authored today. Augmented reality content can be authored with conventional tools or in augmented reality itself. Authoring is concerned with aspects of the application that go beyond geometric and visual properties—in particular, establishing the semantics and the behavior of the application. Preferably, authoring should be content-driven and require no or only minimal traditional programming effort. We discuss various approaches to address this need, and also examine recent efforts to combine augmented reality authoring with emerging open web standards.

Chapter 11, "Navigation," deals with navigational guidance—a particularly relevant aspect of augmented reality as a user interface. Orientation in unfamiliar environments is an important application challenge involving mobile information systems. We present an overview of navigational guidance techniques implemented using augmented reality, and compare them to digital maps.

Chapter 12, "Collaboration," investigates collaboration. Augmented reality has strong potential as a medium that can be used for communication among individuals. This encompasses both co-located collaboration, which is enriched by the additional cues afforded by a shared augmented reality system, and remote collaboration, which can be significantly supported by augmented reality technology and, in the process, provide new forms of remote presence.

Chapter 13, "Software Architectures," analyzes the underlying architectures of augmented reality systems. Augmented reality has complex requirements, as it must combine aspects of real-time systems, multimedia systems, and often also distributed systems. Combining these requirements in a flexible way that can be mastered by an application programmer is a difficult endeavor. We discuss various architectural patterns such as distributed objects, dataflow systems, and scene graphs, and present a number of case studies.

Chapter 14, " The Future," reviews possible trajectories of augmented reality as it moves from a research field with demonstrated usefulness in prototype applications to potentially universal consumer adoption. As part of this effort, the chapter considers which roadblocks and unresolved issues remain to be overcome. It also summarizes trends and insights from all of the material presented in this book and sketches a future research agenda.

How to Use the Book and the Related Material

How you use this book will depend on your relationship to the field of augmented reality and the degree and focus of your interest. We discuss three types of roles that this relationship or interest might take.

If you are a developer: Professional developers can use the book for inspiration and guidance in the design, implementation, and evaluation of augmented reality applications. Readers with such backgrounds will find useful information on hardware setups in the display, tracking, and interaction chapters. They will benefit from the chapters on visual coherence, visualization, and authoring for the development of application content, and learn about appropriate registration technologies in the tracking, computer vision, and calibration chapters. User interface design is informed by the chapter on interaction and following chapters. Finally, the chapter on software architectures provides important information for actual implementation work.

If you are a teacher: The book is useful as a text for several different types of university-level courses. A graduate course on augmented reality can use it as the primary textbook. A course on computer graphics or visual computing could use the chapters on visual coherence and visualization as an introduction to graphical aspects of augmented reality. A course on computer vision can use the chapters on tracking and registration for teaching important real-time computer vision techniques. A human–computer interaction course can utilize the chapters on interaction, modeling, authoring, navigation, and collaboration to provide detailed coverage of augmented reality concepts.

If you are a researcher: This book can serve as a comprehensive reference guide for researchers interested in the development or evaluation of experimental augmented reality applications. The research agenda in the concluding chapter also provides researchers and students with a list of important questions to be addressed in the field.

Companion Website

The companion website to the book can be found at the following address:

> http://www.augmentedrealitybook.org

Augmented reality is rapidly evolving. To make this book a dynamic working document, this companion website provides additional information, including teaching materials. This site contains information and links related to the latest augmented reality research and applications. This is an open effort, so readers are invited to contribute to this collection. Your comments will help us to update the website, as well as future editions of this book.

Register your copy of *Augmented Reality* at informit.com for convenient access to downloads, updates, and corrections as they become available. To start the registration process, go to informit.com/register and log in or create an account. Enter the product ISBN (9780321883575) and click Submit. Once the process is complete, you will find any available bonus content under "Registered Products."

Acknowledgments

This book would not have been possible without the encouragement and expertise of many friends and colleagues. First, we offer our gratitude to the reviewers who provided invaluable insights and suggestions for improvements: Reinhold Behringer, Doug Bowman, André Ferko, Steffen Gauglitz, Kiyoshi Kiyokawa, Tobias Langlotz, Vincent Lepetit, Gerhard Reitmayr, Chris Sweeney, and Daniel Wagner.

Second, we want to thank our editors at Addison-Wesley: Peter Gordon, who believed in the idea of this book and helped us establish the publishing contract, and Laura Lewin and Olivia Basegio, who continuously encouraged us and provided us with great advice.

Third, we want to thank all colleagues that provided us with additional image materials: Aaron Stafford, Alessandro Mulloni, Alexander Plopski, Andreas Butz, Andreas Geiger, Andreas Hartl, Andrei State, Andrew Maimone, Andy Gstoll, Ann Morrison, Anton Fuhrmann, Anton van den Hengel, Arindam Day, Blair MacIntyre, Brigitte Ludwig, Bruce Thomas, Christian Pirchheim, Christian Reinbacher, Christian Sandor, Claudio Pinhanez, Clemens Arth, Daniel Wagner, David Mizell, Denis Kalkofen, Domagoj Baričević, Doreé Seligmann, Eduardo Veas, Erick Mendez, Ernst Kruijff, Ethan Eade, Florian Ledermann, Gerd Hesina, Gerhard Reitmayr, Gerhard Schall, Greg Welch, Gudrun Klinker, Hannes Kaufmann, Henry Fuchs, Hiroyuki Yamamoto, Hrvoje Benko, István Barakonyi, Ivan Sutherland, Jan Herling, Jens Grubert, Jonathan Ventura, Joseph Newman, Julien Pilet, Kiyoshi Kiyokawa, Lukas Gruber, Mark Billinghurst, Markus Oberweger, Markus Tatzgern, Martin Hirzer, Matt Swoboda, Matthias Straka, Michael Gervautz, Michael Kenzel, Michael Marner, Morten Fjeld, Nassir Navab, Oliver Bimber, Pascal Fua, Pascal Lagger, Peter Kán, Peter Mohr, Peter Weir, Philipp Descovic, Qi Pan, Ralph Schönfelder, Raphael Grasset, Remo Ziegler, Simon Julier, Stefan Hauswiesner, Stefanie Zollmann, Steffen Gauglitz, Steve Feiner, Taehee Lee, Takuji Narumi, Thanh Nguyen, Thomas Richter-Trummer, Tom Drummond, Ulrich Eck, Vincent Lepetit, Wayne Piekarski, William Steptoe, Wolfgang Broll, and Zsolt Szalavári.

Fourth, we want to thank all colleagues and students at Graz University of Technology and University of California, Santa Barbara, for the countless discussions on and off the topics in this book and for providing great working environments.

Finally, we would like to thank our families for supporting us and being patient during the not-so-short time of creating this book!

Dieter Schmalstieg
Graz, Austria, April 2016

Tobias Höllerer
Santa Barbara, California, April 2016

About the Authors

Dieter Schmalstieg is full professor and head of the Institute of Computer Graphics and Vision at Graz University of Technology (TUG), Austria. His current research interests are augmented reality, virtual reality, real-time graphics, user interfaces, and visualization. He received Dipl.-Ing. (1993), Dr.techn. (1997), and Habilitation (2001) degrees from Vienna University of Technology. Dr. Schmalstieg is author or coauthor of more than 300 peer-reviewed scientific publications. His organizational roles include associate editor in chief of *IEEE Transactions on Visualization and Computer Graphics*, member of the editorial advisory board of *Computers & Graphics* and of Springer's *Virtual Reality* journal, member of the steering committee of the IEEE International Symposium on Mixed and Augmented Reality, chair of the EUROGRAPHICS working group on Virtual Environments (1999–2010), key researcher of the K-Plus Competence Center for Virtual Reality and Visualization in Vienna, and key researcher of the Know-Center in Graz. In 2002, Dr. Schmalstieg received the START Career Award presented by the Austrian Science Fund. In 2012, he received the IEEE Virtual Reality Technical Achievement Award for seminal contributions to the field of augmented reality. He was elected as a senior member of IEEE, as a member of the Austrian Academy of Sciences, and as a member of the Academia Europaea. Since 2008, he has also been director of the Christian Doppler Laboratory for Handheld Augmented Reality.

Tobias Höllerer is professor of computer science at the University of California, Santa Barbara, where he co-directs the Four Eyes Laboratory, conducting research in the "four I's" of Imaging, Interaction, and Innovative Interfaces. Dr. Höllerer holds a Diploma in Informatics from the Technical University of Berlin, as well as an M.S., an M.Phil., and a Ph.D. in computer science from Columbia University. He is a recipient of the U.S. National Science Foundation's CAREER Award for his work on "Anywhere Augmentation," which enables mobile computer users to place annotations in 3D space wherever they go. He is an IEEE senior member and was named an ACM Distinguished Scientist in 2013. Dr. Höllerer is author or coauthor of more than 150 peer-reviewed journal and conference publications in the areas of augmented and virtual reality, information visualization, 3D displays and interaction, mobile and wearable computing, and social computing. Several of these publications have been selected for Best Paper or Honorable Mention Awards at such venues as the IEEE International Symposium on Mixed and Augmented Reality (ISMAR), IEEE Virtual Reality (VR), ACM Virtual Reality Software and Technology, ACM User Interface Software and Technology, ACM MobileHCI, IEEE SocialCom, and IEEE CogSIMA. Dr. Höllerer is an associate editor of *IEEE Transactions on Visualization and Computer Graphics*. Among his many organizational roles for scientific conferences, he served as program chair for IEEE VR 2015, ICAT 2013, and IEEE ISMAR 2009 and 2010; as general chair of IEEE ISMAR 2006; and as member of the steering committee of IEEE ISMAR.

CHAPTER 1

INTRODUCTION TO AUGMENTED REALITY

Virtual reality is becoming increasingly popular, as computer graphics have progressed to a point where the images are often indistinguishable from the real world. However, the computer-generated images presented in games, movies, and other media are detached from our physical surroundings. This is both a virtue—everything becomes possible—and a limitation.

The limitation comes from the main interest we have in our daily life, which is not directed toward some virtual world, but rather toward the *real world* surrounding us. Smartphones and other mobile devices provide access to a vast amount of information, anytime and anywhere. However, this information is generally disconnected from the real world. Consumers with an interest in retrieving online information from and about the real world, or linking up online information with the real world, must do so individually and indirectly, which, in turn, requires constant cognitive effort.

In many ways, enhancing mobile computing so that the association with the real world happens automatically seems an attractive proposition. A few examples readily illustrate this idea's appeal. Location-based services can provide personal navigation based on the Global Positioning System (GPS), while barcode scanners can help identify books in a library or products in a supermarket. These approaches require explicit actions by the user, however, and are rather coarse grained. Barcodes are useful for identifying books, but not for naming mountain peaks during a hiking trip; likewise, they cannot help in identifying tiny parts of a watch being repaired, let alone anatomic structures during surgery.

Augmented reality holds the promise of creating direct, automatic, and actionable links between the physical world and electronic information. It provides a simple and immediate user interface to an electronically enhanced physical world. The immense potential of augmented reality as a paradigm-shifting user interface metaphor becomes apparent when we review the most recent few milestones in human–computer interaction: the emergence of the World Wide Web, the social web, and the mobile device revolution.

The trajectory of this series of milestones is clear: First, there was an immense increase in access to online information, leading to a massive audience of information consumers. These consumers were subsequently enabled to also act as information producers and communicate with one another, and finally were given the means to manage their communications from anywhere, in any situation. Yet, the physical world, in which all this information retrieval, authoring, and communication takes place, was not readily linked to the users' electronic activity. That is, the model was stuck in a world of abstract web pages and services without directly involving the physical world. A lot of technological advancement has occurred in the field of location-based computing and services, which is sometimes referred to as *situated computing*. Even so, the user interfaces to location-based services remain predominantly rooted in desktop-, app-, and web-based usage paradigms.

Augmented reality can change this situation, and, in doing so, redefine information browsing and authoring. This user interface metaphor and its enabling technologies form one of today's most fascinating and future-oriented areas of computer science and application development. Augmented reality can overlay computer-generated information on views of the real world, amplifying human perception and cognition in remarkable new ways.

After providing a working definition of augmented reality, we will briefly review important developments in the history of the research field, and then present examples from various application areas, showcasing the power of this physical user interface metaphor.

Definition and Scope

Whereas virtual reality (VR) places a user inside a completely computer-generated environment, augmented reality (AR) aims to present information that is directly registered to the physical environment. AR goes beyond mobile computing in that it bridges the gap between virtual world and real world, both spatially and cognitively. With AR, the digital information appears to become part of the real world, at least in the user's perception.

Achieving this connection is a grand goal—one that draws upon knowledge from many areas of computer science, yet can lead to misconceptions about what AR really is. For example, many people associate the visual combination of virtual and real elements with the special effects in movies such as *Jurassic Park* and *Avatar*. While the computer graphics techniques used in movies may be applicable to AR as well, movies lack one crucial aspect of AR—interactivity. To avoid such confusion, we need to set a scope for the topics discussed in this book. In other words, we need to answer a key question: What is AR?

The most widely accepted definition of AR was proposed by Azuma in his 1997 survey paper. According to Azuma [1997], AR must have the following three characteristics:

- Combines real and virtual
- Interactive in real time
- Registered in 3D

This definition *does not require* a specific output device, such as a head-mounted display (HMD), nor does it limit AR to visual media. Audio, haptics, and even olfactory or gustatory AR are included in its scope, even though they may be difficult to realize. Note that the definition does require real-time *control* and spatial *registration*, meaning precise real-time alignment of corresponding virtual and real information. This mandate implies that the user of an AR display can at least exercise some sort of interactive viewpoint control, and the computer-generated augmentations in the display will remain registered to the referenced objects in the environment.

While opinions on what qualifies as real-time performance may vary depending on the individual and on the task or application, interactivity implies that the human–computer interface operates in a tightly coupled feedback loop. The user continuously navigates the AR scene and controls the AR experience. The system, in turn, picks up the user's input by tracking the user's viewpoint or pose. It registers the pose in the real world with the virtual content, and then presents to the user a *situated visualization* (a visualization that is registered to objects in the real world).

We can see that a complete AR system requires at least three components: a tracking component, a registration component, and a visualization component. A fourth component—a spatial model (i.e., a database)—stores information about the real world and about the virtual world (Figure 1.1). The real-world model is required to serve as a reference for the tracking

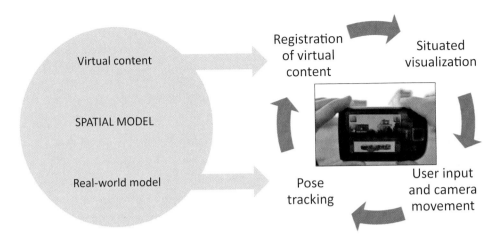

Figure 1.1   AR uses a feedback loop between human user and computer system. The user observes the AR display and controls the viewpoint. The system tracks the user's viewpoint, registers the pose in the real world with the virtual content, and presents situated visualizations.

component, which must determine the user's location in the real world. The virtual-world model consists of the content used for the augmentation. Both parts of the spatial model must be registered in the same coordinate system.

A Brief History of Augmented Reality

While one could easily go further back in time to find examples in which informational overlays were layered on top of the physical world, suffice it to say that the first annotations of the physical world with *computer-generated* information occurred in the 1960s. Ivan Sutherland can be credited with starting the field that would eventually turn into both VR and AR. In 1965, he postulated the *ultimate display* in an essay that contains the following famous quote:

> The ultimate display would, of course, be a room within which the computer can control the existence of matter. A chair displayed in such a room would be good enough to sit in. Handcuffs displayed in such a room would be confining, and a bullet displayed in such a room would be fatal. With appropriate programming such a display could literally be the Wonderland into which Alice walked.

Sutherland's [1965] essay includes more than just an early description of immersive displays, however. It also contains a quote that is less often discussed, but that clearly anticipates AR:

> The user of one of today's visual displays can easily make solid objects transparent—he can "see through matter!"

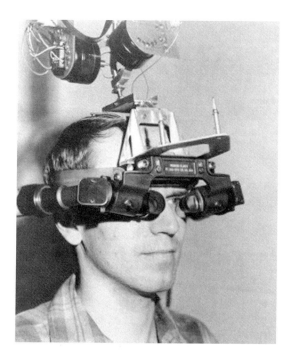

Figure 1.2   The Sword of Damocles was the nickname of the world's first head-mounted display, built in 1968. Courtesy of Ivan Sutherland.

Shortly thereafter, Sutherland constructed the first VR system. In 1968, he finished the first head-mounted display [Sutherland 1968]. Because of its weight, it had to be suspended from the ceiling and was appropriately nicknamed "Sword of Damocles" (Figure 1.2). This display already included head tracking and used see-through optics.

Advances in computing performance of the 1980s and early 1990s were ultimately required for AR to emerge as an independent field of research. Throughout the 1970s and 1980s, Myron Krueger, Dan Sandin, Scott Fisher, and others had experimented with many concepts of mixing human interaction with computer-generated overlays on video for interactive art experiences. Krueger [1991], in particular, demonstrated collaborative interactive overlays of graphical annotations among participant silhouettes in his Videoplace installations around 1974.

The year 1992 marked the birth of the term "augmented reality." This term first appeared in the work of Caudell and Mizell [1992] at Boeing, which sought to assist workers in an airplane factory by displaying wire bundle assembly schematics in a see-through HMD (Figure 1.3).

Figure 1.3   Researchers at Boing used a see-through HMD to guide the assembly of wire bundles for aircraft. Courtesy of David Mizell.

In 1993, Feiner et al. [1993a] introduced KARMA, a system that incorporated knowledge-based AR. This system was capable of automatically inferring appropriate instruction sequences for repair and maintenance procedures (Figure 1.4).

Also in 1993, Fitzmaurice created the first handheld spatially aware display, which served as a precursor to handheld AR. The Chameleon consisted of a tethered handheld liquid-crystal display (LCD) screen. The screen showed the video output of an SGI graphics workstation of the time and was spatially tracked using a magnetic tracking device. This system was capable of showing contextual information as the user moved the device around—for example, giving detailed information about a location on a wall-mounted map.

Figure 1.4   (top) KARMA was the first knowledge-driven AR application. (bottom) A user with an HMD could see instructions on printer maintenance. Courtesy of Steve Feiner, Blair MacIntyre, and Doreé Seligmann, Columbia University.

In 1994, State et al. at the University of North Carolina at Chapel Hill presented a compelling medical AR application, capable of letting a physician observe a fetus directly within a pregnant patient (Figure 1.5). Even though the accurate registration of computer graphics on top of a deformable object such as a human body remains a challenge today, this seminal work hints at the power of AR for medicine and other delicate tasks.

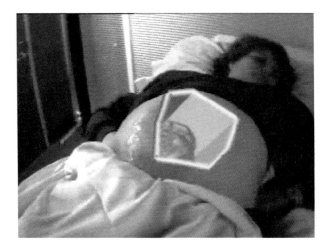

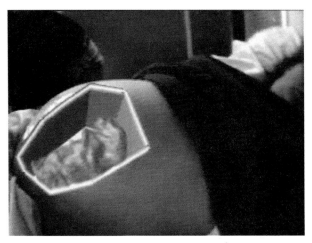

Figure 1.5   View inside the womb of an expecting mother. Courtesy of Andrei State, UNC Chapel Hill.

Around the mid-1990s, Steve Mann at the MIT Media Lab implemented, and experimented with, a "reality mediator"—a waist-bag computer with a video see-through HMD (a modified VR4 by Virtual Research Systems) that enabled the user to augment, alter, or diminish visual reality. Through the WearCam project, Mann [1997] explored wearable computing and mediated reality. His work ultimately helped establish the academic field of wearable computing, which, in those early days, had a lot of synergy with AR [Starner et al. 1997].

In 1995, Rekimoto and Nagao created the first true—albeit tethered—handheld AR display. Their NaviCam was connected to a workstation, but was outfitted with a forward-facing camera. From the video feed, it could detect color-coded markers in the camera image and display information on a video see-through view.

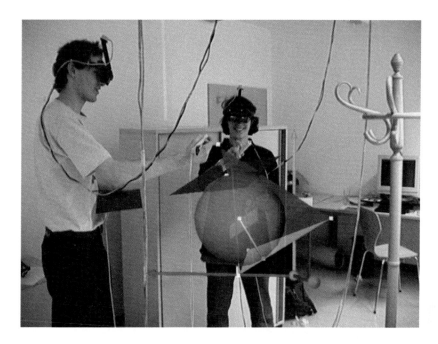

Figure 1.6   One of the applications of the Studierstube system was teaching geometry in AR to high school students. Courtesy of Hannes Kaufmann.

In 1996, Schmalstieg et al. developed Studierstube, the first collaborative AR system. With this system, multiple users could experience virtual objects in the same shared space. Each user had a tracked HMD and could see perspectively correct stereoscopic images from an individual viewpoint. Unlike in multi-user VR, natural communication cues, such as voice, body posture, and gestures, were not affected in Studierstube, because the virtual content was added to a conventional collaborative situation in a minimally obtrusive way. One of the showcase applications was a geometry course [Kaufmann and Schmalstieg 2003], which was successfully tested with actual high school students (Figure 1.6).

From 1997 to 2001, the Japanese government and Canon Inc. jointly funded the Mixed Reality Systems Laboratory as a temporary research company. This joint venture was the largest industrial research facility for mixed reality (MR) research up to that point [Tamura 2000] [Tamura et al. 2001]. Among its most notable achievements was the design of the first coaxial stereo video see-through HMD, the COASTAR. Many of the activities undertaken in the lab were also directed toward the digital entertainment market (Figure 1.7), which plays a very prominent role in Japan.

In 1997, Feiner et al. developed the first outdoor AR system, the Touring Machine (Figure 1.8), at Columbia University. The Touring Machine uses a see-through HMD with GPS and orientation tracking. Delivering mobile 3D graphics via this system required a backpack holding a

Figure 1.7   *RV-Border Guards* was a multiuser shooting game developed in Canon's Mixed Reality Systems Laboratory. Courtesy of Hiroyuki Yamamoto.

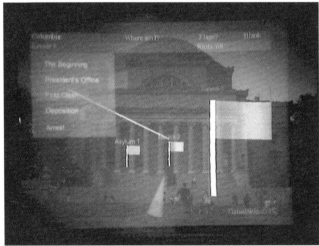

Figure 1.8   The Touring Machine was the first outdoor AR system (left). Image of the *Situated Documentaries* AR campus tour guide running on a 1999 version of the Touring Machine (right). Courtesy of Columbia University.

computer, various sensors, and an early tablet computer for input [Feiner et al. 1997] [Höllerer et al. 1999b].

Just one year later, in 1998, Thomas et al. published their work on the construction of an outdoor AR navigation system, Map-in-the-Hat. Its successor, Tinmith (few people know that this name is actually an acronym for "This is not map in the hat"), evolved into a well-known experimental platform for outdoor AR. This platform was used for advanced applications, such as 3D surveying, but is most famous for delivering the first outdoor AR game, *ARQuake* (Figure 1.9). This game, which is a port of the popular first-person shooter application *Quake* to Tinmith, places the user in the midst of a zombie attack in a real parking lot.

In the same year, Raskar et al. [1998] at the University of North Carolina at Chapel Hill presented the Office of the Future, a telepresence system built around the idea of structured light-scanning and projector-camera systems. Although the required hardware was not truly practical for everyday use at the time, related technologies, such as depth sensors and camera-projection coupling, play a prominent role in AR and other fields today.

Until 1999, no AR software was available outside specialized research labs. This situation changed when Kato and Billinghurst [1999] released ARToolKit, the first open-source software

Figure 1.9 Screenshot of ARQuake, the first outdoor AR game. Courtesy of Bruce Thomas and Wayne Piekarski.

Figure 1.10   A person holding a square marker of ARToolKit, the popular open-source software framework for AR. Courtesy of Mark Billinghurst.

platform for AR. It featured a 3D tracking library using black-and-white fiducials, which could easily be manufactured on a laser printer (Figure 1.10). The clever software design, in combination with the increased availability of webcams, made ARToolKit widely popular.

In the same year, Germany's Federal Ministry for Education and Research initiated a €21 million program for industrial AR, called ARVIKA (Augmented Reality for Development, Production, and Servicing). More than 20 research groups from industry and academia worked on developing advanced AR systems for industrial application, in particular in the German automotive industry. This program raised the worldwide awareness of AR in professional communities and was followed by several similar programs designed to enhance industrial application of the technology.

Another noteworthy idea also appeared in the late 1990s: IBM researcher Spohrer [1999] published an essay on Worldboard, a scalable networked infrastructure for hyperlinked spatially registered information, which Spohrer had first proposed while he was working with Apple's Advanced Technology Group. This work can be seen as the first concept for an AR browser.

After 2000, cellular phones and mobile computing began evolving rapidly. In 2003, Wagner and Schmalstieg presented the first handheld AR system running autonomously on a "personal digital assistant"—a precursor to today's smartphones. One year later, the *Invisible Train* [Pintaric et al. 2005], a multiplayer handheld AR game (Figure 1.11), was experienced by thousands of visitors at the SIGGRAPH Emerging Technologies show floor.

It took several years, until 2008, for the first truly usable natural feature tracking system for smartphones to be introduced [Wagner et al. 2008b]. This work became the ancestor of the

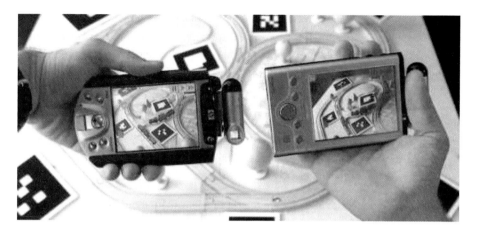

Figure 1.11   The Invisible Train was a handheld AR game featuring virtual trains on real wooden tracks. Courtesy of Daniel Wagner.

popular Vuforia toolkit for AR developers. Other noteworthy achievements in recent years in the area of tracking include the parallel tracking and mapping (PTAM) system of Klein and Murray [2007], which can track without preparation in unknown environments, and the KinectFusion system developed by Newcombe et al. [2011a], which builds detailed 3D models from an inexpensive depth sensor. Today, AR developers can choose among many software platforms, but these model systems continue to represent important directions for researchers.

Examples

In this section, we continue our exploration of AR by examining a set of examples, which showcase both AR technology and applications of that technology. We begin with application domains in which AR technologies demonstrated early success—namely, industry and construction. These examples are followed by applications in maintenance and training, and in the medical domain. We then discuss examples that focus on individuals on the move: personal information display and navigational support. Finally, we present examples illustrating how large audiences can be supported by AR using enhanced media channels in, for example, television, online commerce, and gaming.

Industry and Construction

As mentioned in our brief historic overview of AR, some of the first actual applications motivating the use of AR were industrial in nature, such as Boeing's wire bundle assembly needs and early maintenance and repair examples.

Industrial facilities are becoming increasingly complex, which profoundly affects their planning and operation. Architectural structures, infrastructure, and machines are planned using computer-aided design (CAD) software, but typically many alterations are made during actual construction and installation. These alterations usually do not find their way back into the CAD models. In addition, there may be a large body of legacy structures predating the introduction of CAD for planning as well as the need for frequent changes of the installations—for example, when a factory is adapted for the manufacturing of a new product. Planners would like to compare the "as planned" to the "as is" state of a facility and identify any critical deviations. They would also like to obtain a current model of the facility, which can be used for planning, refurbishing or logistics procedures.

Traditionally, this is done with 3D scanners and off-site data integration and comparison. This process is lengthy and tedious, however, and it results in low-level models consisting of point clouds. AR offers the opportunity to perform on-site inspection, bringing the CAD model to the facility rather than the reverse. Georgel et al. [2007], for example, have developed a technique for still-frame AR that extracts the camera pose from perspective cues in a single image and overlays registered, transparently rendered CAD models (Figure 1.12).

Schönfelder and Schmalstieg [2008] have proposed a system based on the Planar (Figure 1.13), an AR display on wheels with external tracking. It provides fully interactive, real-time discrepancy checking for industrial facilities.

Figure 1.12   AR can be used for discrepancy analysis in industrial facilities. These images show still frames overlaid with CAD information. Note how the valve on the right-hand side was mounted on the left side rather than on the right side as in the model. Courtesy of Nassir Navab.

Figure 1.13 The Planar is a touchscreen display on wheels (left), which can be used for discrepancy analysis directly on the factory floor (right). Courtesy of Ralph Schönfelder.

Utility companies rely on geographic information systems (GIS) for managing underground infrastructure, such as telecommunication lines or gas pipes. The precise locations of the underground assets are required in a variety of situations. For example, construction managers are legally obliged to obtain information on underground infrastructure, so that they can avoid any damage to these structures during excavations. Likewise, locating the reason for outages or updating outdated GIS information frequently requires on-site inspection. In all these cases, presenting an AR view that is derived from the GIS and directly registered on the target site can significantly improve the precision and speed of outdoor work [Schall et al. 2008]. Figure 1.14 shows Vidente, one such outdoor AR visualization system.

Camera-bearing micro-aerial vehicles (drones) are increasingly being used for airborne inspection and reconstructions of construction sites. These drones may have some degree of autonomous flight control, but always require a human operator. AR can be extremely useful in locating the drone (Figure 1.15), monitoring its flight parameters such as position over ground, height, or speed, and alerting the operator to potential collisions [Zollmann et al. 2014].

Figure 1.14 Tablet computer with differential GPS system for outdoor AR (left). Geo-registered view of a virtual excavation revealing a gas pipe (right). Courtesy of Gerhard Schall.

Figure 1.15 While the drone has flown far away and is barely visible, its position can be visualized using a spherical AR overlay. Courtesy of Stefanie Zollmann.

Maintenance and Training

Understanding how things work, and learning how to assemble, disassemble, or repair them, is an important challenge in many professions. Maintenance engineers often devote a large amount of time to studying manuals and documentation, since it is often impossible to memorize all procedures in detail. AR, however, can present instructions directly superimposed in the field of view of the worker. This can provide more effective training, but, more importantly, allows personnel with less training to correctly perform the work. Figure 1.16 reveals how AR can assist with the removal of the brewing unit of an automatic coffee maker, and Figure 1.17 shows the disassemble sequence for a valve [Mohr et al. 2015].

If human support is sought, AR can provide a shared visual space for live mobile remote collaboration on physical tasks [Gauglitz et al. 2014a]. With this approach, a remote expert can explore the scene independently of the local user's current camera position and can communicate via

Figure 1.16   Ghost visualization revealing the interior of a coffee machine to guide end-user maintenance. Courtesy of Peter Mohr.

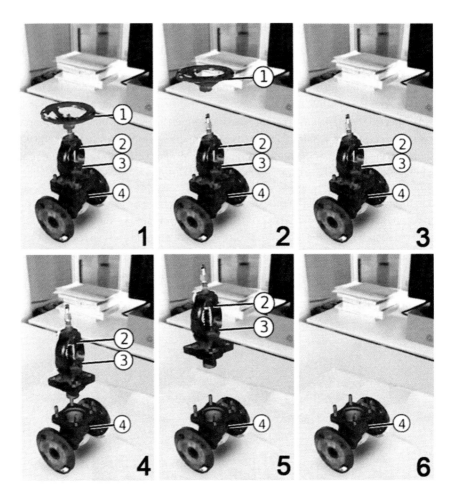

Figure 1.17   Automatically generated disassembly sequence of a valve. Courtesy of Peter Mohr.

spatial annotations that are immediately visible to the local user in the AR view (Figure 1.18). This can be achieved with real-time visual tracking and reconstruction, eliminating the need for preparation or instrumentation of the environment. AR telepresence combines the benefits of live video conferencing and remote scene exploration into a natural collaborative interface.

Medical

The use of X-ray imaging revolutionized diagnostics by allowing physicians to see inside a patient without performing surgery. However, conventional X-ray and computed tomography devices separate the interior view from the exterior view of the patient. AR integrates these

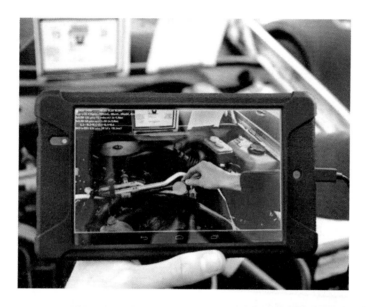

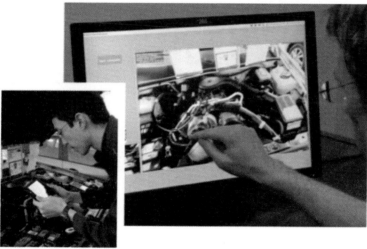

Figure 1.18   A car repair scenario assisted by a remote expert via AR telepresence on a tablet computer (top). The remote expert can draw hints directly on the 3D model of the car that is incrementally transmitted from the repair site (bottom). Courtesy of Steffen Gauglitz.

views, enabling the physician to see directly inside the patient. One such example, which is now commercially available, is the Camera Augmented Mobile C-arm, or CamC (Figure 1.19). A mobile C-arm is used to provide X-ray views in the operating theater. CamC extends these views with a conventional video camera, which is arranged coaxially with the X-ray optics to deliver precisely registered image pairs [Navab et al. 2010]. The physician can transition and blend

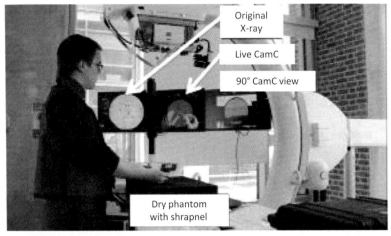

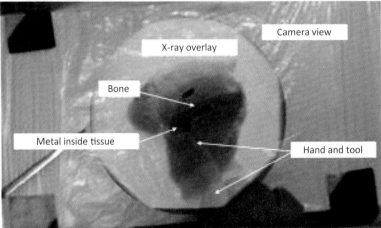

Figure 1.19   The CamC is a mobile C-arm, which allows a physician to seamlessly blend between a conventional camera view and X-ray images. Courtesy of Nassir Navab.

between the inside and outside views as desired. CamC has many clinical applications, including guiding needle biopsies and facilitating orthopedic screw placement.

Personal Information Display

As we have seen, several specific application domains can profit from the use of AR technology. But can this technology be applied more broadly to support larger audiences in completing everyday tasks? Today, this question is being answered with a resounding "yes." A large variety of AR browser apps are already available on smartphones (e.g., Layar, Wikitudes, Junaio, and others). These apps are intended to deliver information related to *places of interest* in the user's environment, superimposed over the live video from the device's camera. The places of interest

Figure 1.20   AR browsers such as Yelp Monocle superimpose points of interest on a live video feed.

are either given in geo-coordinates and identified via the phone's sensors (GPS, compass readings) or identified by image recognition. AR browsers have obvious limitations, such as potentially poor GPS accuracy and augmentation capabilities only for individual points rather than full objects. Nevertheless, thanks to the proliferation of smartphones, these apps are universally available, and their use is growing, owing to the social networking capabilities built into the AR browsers. Figure 1.20 shows the AR browser *Yelp Monocle*, which is integrated into the social business review app *Yelp*.

Another compelling use case for AR browsing is simultaneous translation of foreign languages. This utility is now widely available in the *Google Translate* app (Figure 1.21). The user just has to select the target language and point the device camera toward the printed text; the translation then appears superimposed over the image.

Navigation

The idea of heads-up navigation, which does not distract the operator of a vehicle moving at high speeds from the environment ahead, was first considered in the context of military aircraft [Furness 1986]. A variety of see-through displays, which can be mounted to the visor of a pilot's helmet, have been developed since the 1970s. These devices, which are usually called heads-up displays, are mostly intended to show nonregistered information, such as the current speed or torque, but can also be used to show a form of AR. Military technology, however, is usually not directly applicable to the consumer market, which demands different ergonomics and pricing structures.

Figure 1.21   Google Translate superimposes spontaneous translations of text, recognized in real time, over the camera image.

With improved geo-information, it has become possible to overlay larger structures on in-car navigation systems, such as road networks. Figure 1.22 shows *Wikitude Drive*, a first-person car navigation system. The driving instructions are overlaid on top of the live video feed rather than being presented in a map-like view. The registration quality in this system is acceptable despite being based on smartphone sensors such as GPS, as the inertia of a car allows the system to predict the geography ahead with relative accuracy.

Figure 1.23 shows a parking assistant, which overlays a graphical visualization of the car trajectory onto the view of a rear-mounted camera.

Television

Many people likely first encountered AR as annotations to live camera footage brought to their homes via broadcast TV. The first and most prominent example of this concept is the virtual 1st & 10 line in American football, indicating the yardage needed for a first down, which is superimposed directly on the TV screencast of a game. While the idea and first patents for creating such on-field markers for football broadcasts date back to the late 1970s, it took until 1998 for the concept to be realized. The same concept of annotating TV footage with virtual overlays has successfully been applied to many other sports, including baseball, ice hockey, car racing,

Figure 1.22 Wikitude Drive superimposes a perspective view of the road ahead. Courtesy of Wikitude GmbH.

Figure 1.23 The parking assistant is a commercially available AR feature in many contemporary cars. Courtesy of Brigitte Ludwig.

Figure 1.24   Augmented TV broadcast of a soccer game. Courtesy of Teleclub and Vizrt, Switzerland (LiberoVision AG).

and sailing. Figure 1.24 shows a televised soccer game with augmentations. The audience in this incarnation of AR has no ability to vary the viewpoint individually. Given that the live action on the playing field is captured by tracked cameras, interactive viewpoint changes are still possible, albeit not under the end-viewer's control.

Several competing companies provide augmentation solutions for various broadcast events, creating convincing and informative live annotations. The annotation possibilities have long since moved beyond just sports information or simple line graphics, and now include sophisticated 3D graphics renderings of branding logos or product advertisements.

Using similar technology, it is possible—and, in fact, common in today's TV broadcasts—to present a moderator and other TV personalities in virtual studio settings. In this application, the moderator is filmed by tracked cameras in front of a green screen and inserted into a virtual rendering of the studio. The system even allows for interactive manipulation of virtual props.

Similar technologies are being used in the film industry, such as for providing a movie director and actors with live previews of what a film scene might look like after special effects or other compositing has been applied to the camera footage of a live set environment. This application of AR is sometimes referred to as Pre-Viz.

Figure 1.25   The lifestyle magazine *Red Bulletin* was the first print publication to feature dynamic content using AR. Courtesy of Daniel Wagner.

Advertising and Commerce

The ability of AR to instantaneously present arbitrary 3D views of a product to a potential buyer is already being welcomed in advertising and commerce. This technology can lead to truly interactive experiences for the customer. For example, customers in Lego stores can hold a toy box up to an AR kiosk, which then displays a 3D image of the assembled Lego model. Customers can turn the box to view the model from any vantage point.

An obvious target for AR is the augmentation of printed material, such as flyers or magazines. Readers of the *Harry Potter* novels know how pictures in the *Daily Prophet* newspaper come alive. This idea can be realized with AR by superimposing digital movies and animations on top of specific portions of a printed template. When the magazine is viewed on a computer or smartphone, the static pictures are replaced by animated sequences or movies (Figure 1.25).

AR can also be helpful for a sales person who is trying to demonstrate the virtues of a product (Figure 1.26). Especially for complex devices, it may be difficult to convey the internal operation with words alone. Letting a potential customer observe the animated interior allows for much more compelling presentations at trade shows and in show rooms alike.

Pictofit is a virtual dressing room application that lets users preview garments from online fashion stores on their own body (Figure 1.27). The garments are automatically adjusted to match

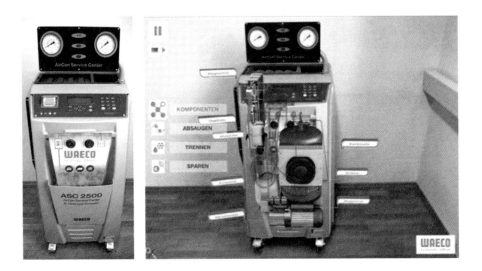

Figure 1.26 Marketing presentation of a Waeco air-conditioning service unit. Courtesy of magiclensapp.com.

Figure 1.27 Pictofit can extract garment images from online shopping sites and render them to match an image of the customer. Courtesy of Stefan Hauswiesner, ReactiveReality.

the wearer's size. In addition, body measurements are estimated and made available to assist in the entry of purchase data.

Games

One of the first commercial AR games was *The Eye of Judgment*, an interactive trading card game for the Sony PlayStation 3. The game is delivered with an overhead camera, which picks up game cards and summons corresponding creatures to fight matches.

An important quality of traditional games is their tangible nature. Kids can turn their entire room into a playground, with pieces of furniture being converted into a landscape that supports physical activities such as jumping and hiding. In contrast, video games are usually confined to a purely virtual realm. AR can bring digital games together with the real environment. For example, Vuforia SmartTerrain (Figure 1.28) delivers a 3D scan of a real scene and turns it into a playing field for a "tower defense" game.

Figure 1.28   Vuforia SmartTerrain scans the environment and turns it into a game landscape.
© 2013 Qualcomm Connected Experiences, Inc. Used with permission.

Figure 1.29 Using a TV-plus-projector setup, the IllumiRoom extends the game world beyond the boundaries of the screen. Courtesy of Microsoft Research.

Microsoft's *IllumiRoom* [Jones et al. 2013] is a prototype of a projector-based AR game experience. It combines a regular TV set with a home-theater projector to extend the game world beyond the confines of the TV (Figure 1.29). The 3D game scene shown in the projection is registered with the one on the TV, but the projection covers a much wider field of view. While the player concentrates on the center screen, the peripheral field of view is also filled with dynamic images, leading to a greatly enhanced game experience.

Related Fields

In the previous section, we have highlighted a few AR applications. Other compelling examples of applications only tangentially match the definition we have given of AR. These applications often come from the related fields of mixed reality, ubiquitous computing, and virtual reality, which we briefly discuss here.

Mixed Reality Continuum

A user immersed in virtual reality experiences only virtual stimuli, for example, inside a CAVE (a room with walls consisting of stereoscopic back-projections) or when wearing a closed HMD. The space between reality and virtual reality, which allows real and virtual elements to be combined to varying degrees, is called **mixed reality**. In fact, some people prefer the term "mixed

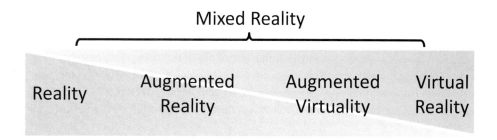

Figure 1.30   The mixed reality continuum captures all possible combinations of the real and virtual worlds.

reality" over "augmented reality," because they appreciate the broader and more encompassing notion of MR.

This view can be attributed to Milgram and Kishino [1994], who proposed a continuum (Figure 1.30) spanning from reality to virtual reality. They characterized MR as follows:

> [MR involves the] merging of real and virtual worlds somewhere along the "virtuality continuum" which connects completely real environments to completely virtual ones.

Benford et al. [1998] go one step further, arguing that a complex environment will often be composed of multiple displays and adjacent spaces, which constitute "mixed realities" (note the plural). These multiple spaces meet at "mixed reality boundaries."

According to this perspective, augmented reality contains primarily real elements and, therefore, is closer to reality. For example, a user with an AR app on a smartphone will continue perceiving the real world in the normal way, but with some additional elements presented on the smartphone. The real-world experience clearly dominates in such a case. The opposite concept, **augmented virtuality**, prevails when there are primarily virtual elements present. As an example, imagine an online role-playing game, where the avatars' faces are textured in real time with a video acquired from the player's face. Everything in this virtual game world, except the faces, is virtual.

Virtual Reality

At the far right end of the MR continuum, virtual reality immerses a user in a completely computer-generated environment. This removes any restrictions as to what a user can do or experience in VR. VR is now becoming increasingly popular for enhanced computer games. New designs for HMD gaming devices, such as the Oculus Rift or HTC Vive, are receiving a great deal of public attention. Such devices are also suitable for augmented virtuality applications. Consequently, AR and VR can easily coexist within the MR continuum. As we will see later, transitional interfaces can be designed to harness the combined advantages of both concepts.

Ubiquitous Computing

Mark Weiser proposed the concept of **ubiquitous computing** (ubicomp) in his seminal 1991 essay. His work anticipates the massive introduction of digital technology into everyday life. Contrasting ubicomp with virtual reality, he advocates bringing the "virtuality" of computer-readable data into the physical world via a variety of computer form factors, which should sound familiar to today's technology users: inch-scale "tabs," foot-scale "pads," and yard-scale "boards."

> Depending on the room, you may see more than 100 tabs, 10 or 20 pads, and one or two boards. This leads to our goal for initially deploying the hardware of embodied virtuality: hundreds of computers per room. [Weiser 1991]

This description includes the idea of mobile computing, which allows users to access digital information anytime and anywhere. However, it also predicts the "Internet of Things," in which all elements of our everyday environment are instrumented. Mackay [1998] has argued that augmented things should also be considered as a form of AR. Consider, for example, home automation, driver assistance systems in cars, and smart factories capable of mass customization. If such technology works well, it essentially disappears from our perception. The first two sentences of Weiser's 1991 article succinctly express this model:

> The most profound technologies are those that disappear. They weave themselves into the fabric of everyday life until they are indistinguishable from it.

Ubicomp is primarily intended as "calm computing"; that is, human attention or control is neither required nor intended. However, at some point, control will still be necessary. A human operator away from a desktop computer, for example, may need to steer complex equipment. In such a situation, an AR interface can directly present status updates, telemetry information, and control widgets in a view of the real environment. In this sense, AR and ubicomp fit extremely well: AR is the ideal *user interface* for ubicomp systems.

According to Weiser, VR is the opposite of ubicomp. Weiser notes the monolithic nature of VR environments, such as a CAVE, which isolate a user from the real world. However, Newman et al. [2007] suggest that ubicomp actually combines two important characteristics: **virtuality** and **ubiquity**. Virtuality, as described by the MR continuum, expresses the degree to which virtual and reality are mixed. Weiser considers location and place as computational inputs. Thus, ubiquity describes the degree to which information access is independent from being in a fixed place (a terminal). Based on these understandings, we can arrange a family of technologies in a "Milgram–Weiser" chart as shown in Figure 1.31.

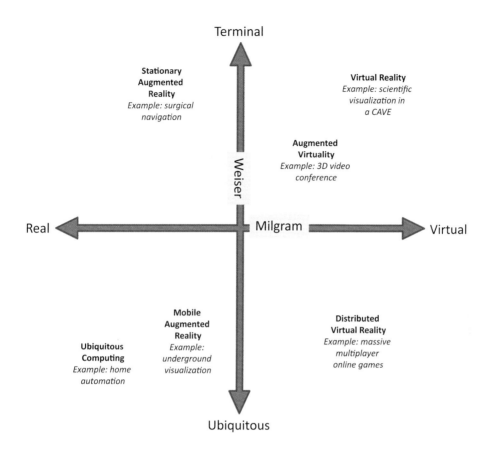

Figure 1.31 The Milgram–Weiser chart visualizes the relationships of various user interface paradigms.

Summary

In this chapter, we provided an introduction to the research field and practical occurrences of augmented reality. For a working definition, augmented reality relies on three key components: (1) the combination of virtual and real information, with the real world as the primary place of action and (2) interactive, real-time updates of (3) virtual information registered in 3D with the physical environment. Different technologies can be used to realize such a concept. The first part of this book provides an overview of technologies for displays (Chapter 2), tracking technologies (Chapters 3, 4, and 5) and graphics (Chapters 6 and 7). The second part of the book (Chapters 8 through 14) deals with interactive techniques.

We also presented a brief history of the field and then went on a whirlwind tour of AR application examples, with the goal of suggesting the enormous potential that AR holds as an interface metaphor to computing in the physical world (sometimes referred to as situated computing). While many specific application possibilities exist, such as AR for equipment maintenance or AR for surgery, one can also envision AR turning into a more general interface paradigm, redefining the overall browsing experience for computing in the physical world. Application examples from the domains of personal information display and navigation hint at that potential.

We concluded this chapter with a discussion of related fields. In doing so, we placed AR within the scope of Milgram's mixed reality continuum and contrasted AR with Weiser's concept of ubiquitous computing.

CHAPTER 2

DISPLAYS

AR displays differ from normal displays in that they must combine virtual and real stimuli. In this chapter, we investigate the various options for such displays. We start our discussion of AR displays with considering the nonvisual modalities. There has been significant work in the area of augmentations via audio, whereas our other nonvisual senses—touch, smell, and taste—have received comparatively less attention with regard to AR. Overall, the lion's share of AR interest and development to date has focused on the visual domain. While the authors have a keen interest in multimodal AR developments, this chapter reflects that reality by discussing visual displays in detail.

We will discuss desktop displays, head-mounted displays (HMD), handheld displays, projector-based displays, and stationary displays. Many of these display categories also integrate nonvisual modalities. Thus, before we focus on the visual domain, we will review AR-related work concerning sound and touch, as well as some cross-modal AR experiments regarding the remaining human senses.

Multimodal Displays

While AR is often assumed to be synonymous with the *visual* overlay of information onto a person's perception of the physical world, other sensory modalities can play an important role, too. The human experience of the physical world is intrinsically multimodal, so it makes sense for AR displays to support multiple augmentation modalities. Many modern AR products do cater to multiple senses, and some AR endeavors have focused on specific individual nonvisual modalities. In fact, an entire product line of *audio guides* or *electronic multimedia guides* presents audio information to visitors of museums and other sites oriented predominantly toward tourists. There is a rich history of audio AR endeavors, but research has also explored tangible and haptic AR as well as looked at other modalities. We will take a brief look at this work in the following subsections.

Audio Displays

Museum audio guides have been around since at least the early 1950s. For a long time, these audio tours made for a rather linear, nonpersonalized experience. Early systems broadcast taped narratives in different languages to visitors who checked out mobile radio receivers at the entrance desk. With the tapes running synchronized for any given group of visitors, the recipients of the broadcast walked and turned their heads in synchronized response to the broadcast [Tallon and Walker 2008]. Over the years, more playback flexibility, personalization, and multimedia support were added to the tour guides [Bederson 1995] [Abowd et al. 1997]. Today, at many indoor and outdoor tourist sites, electronic multimedia guides are available as standard rental equipment or for download to personal smartphones; they often include location-aware technology that enables them to provide on-demand audio describing nearby attractions [Tallon and Walker 2008].

A different application example of audio AR, assistive audio guidance systems for people with visual impairment, was prototyped as early as the late 1970s. "Talking signs" would broadcast digital voice recordings about objects at the transmitter via infrared signals, which could be picked up by mobile infrared receivers carried by the sight-impaired walking person within a range of 15 to 40 meters [Loomis et al. 1998]. Starting in the early 1990s, when the first handheld GPS receivers became available, Loomis, Golledge, and colleagues at the University of California, Santa Barbara, implemented and evaluated audio navigational support for the blind, using global positioning and geographic information system (GIS) resources, with voice synthesis and virtual acoustics displays communicating navigational information to sight-impaired pedestrians [Loomis et al. 1993] [Loomis et al. 1998].

Not all explorations of audio augmentation technology were targeted toward either special-purpose applications, as in the case of museum guides, or specific user groups, as with assistive navigational guidance. With needs related to general workplace communication and information browsing in mind, the Audio Aura system [Mynatt et al. 1998], for example, combines location-aware Active Badges [Want et al. 1992], distributed computing, and wireless headphones for the purpose of providing serendipitous background information via unobtrusive digital audio transmissions.

If a virtual audio source is to be registered with a physical 3D location, such that the listener on the move perceives the sound as emanating from this 3D location, spatial audio techniques [Burgess 1992] need to be employed. While sound propagation in complex environments is very challenging to model [Funkhouser et al. 2002], head tracking, spatial sound synthesis, and a carefully modeled person-specific *head-related transfer function* (HRTF) [Searle et al. 1976] can approximate spatial audio to a convincing quality. Over the years, there have been many demonstrations of audio augmented realities [Sawhney and Schmandt 2000] [Mariette 2007] [Lindeman et al. 2007]. Modern AR headsets, such as the recently announced Meta 2 and Microsoft HoloLens development kits, naturally support spatial audio. In fact, reviewers of the first public previews of the HoloLens spoke enthusiastically about the spatial audio experience, which is delivered via speakers embedded in the headset rather than conventional earphones. The necessity for end-user simplicity of use requires some compromises to avoid obtrusive measurements of person-specific transfer functions at some expense to 3D audio fidelity.

Haptic, Tactile, and Tangible Displays

In the real world, interactions with physical objects typically occur through touch. For augmented reality purposes, we can rely on specific physical proxy objects to passively provide touch feedback—as is the case with tangible AR (discussed in detail in Chapter 8)—or we can try to synthesize and reproduce convincing impressions of touch via devices and instrumented environments—the domain of *haptic* technology research. Providing a realistic sensory impression of touch is a difficult problem when no physical object is available with all the right attributes to impart this impression. While a great deal of research has investigated haptic feedback in virtual environments, the application to AR environments so far has been comparatively limited. AR applications, specifically mobile ones, require nonobtrusive technologies for the sense of touch. Bulky stationary force-feedback devices cover only relatively small workspaces, and it is unlikely that general audiences will be willing to wear conspicuous force-feedback devices, such as robotic exoskeletons, while going about their daily business.

One can attempt to reproduce a variety of touch phenomena in AR environments. Specifically, haptic feedback can be classified into kinesthetic and tactile feedback. Kinesthetic feedback is force feedback sensed by nerves in joints and muscles, whereas tactile feedback is surface-oriented touch feedback picked up by a variety of sensors embedded in skin and sub-skin tissue (responsible, for example, for the perception of skin contact, surface texture, vibration, and temperature). Thermal feedback can also be viewed as a separate type of sensation.

Bau and Poupyrev [2012] provide a good overview of approaches for haptic AR displays, categorizing them as either *extrinsic haptic displays*, which instrument physical environments, or *intrinsic haptic displays*, which augment the user's experience by altering tactile and kinesthetic perception. Extrinsic haptic displays commonly suffer from their coverage of only limited workspaces and from the obtrusive technology, such as mechanical robot arms (Figure 2.1) or nylon strings connected to (hidden) actuators [Ishii and Sato 1994]. Somewhat lower obtrusiveness is possible, however, as demonstrated by Disney Research's AIREAL prototype [Sodhi et al. 2013b]. This technology provides free-air touch sensations by generating directed compressed-pressure fields in the form of vortex rings. However, the types of touch sensations possible with AIREAL are limited to the frequencies, intensities, and patterns afforded by air vortices, and the system is currently not audio neutral (i.e., the vortex generation is accompanied by audible sounds).

An early example of an intrinsic haptic display in the form of a wearable tactile vest was demonstrated by Collins and colleagues in 1977 as a visual prosthetic for the blind [Collins et al. 1977]. Since then, many wearable haptic displays have been explored, including haptic gloves, shoes, vests, jackets, and exoskeletons [Tan and Pentland 2001] [Lindeman et al. 2004] [Teh et al. 2008] [Tsetserukou et al. 2010]. For creating the illusion of tactile sensations on arbitrary surfaces, one can inject weak electrical signals into the user's body [Bau and Poupyrev 2012]. Such wearable technologies can react to location sensing and, therefore, provide haptic stimuli for co-located

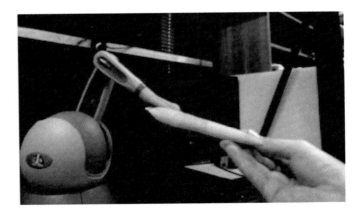

Figure 2.1   Example of visuo-haptic registration. The stylus of a Phantom Omni (now Geomagic Touch) haptic device is highlighted by visual augmented reality. Courtesy of Ulrich Eck and Christian Sandor.

visual or audio augmentations. Overall, the touch impressions that are possible with current technology are more suitable for symbolic notifications (taps or vibrations) than for realistic representation of specific virtual objects.

Jeon and Choi [2009] extend Milgram's mixed reality continuum (discussed in Chapter 1) to the haptic domain. *Haptic reality* includes the use of real tangible props as well as placeholders such as cardboard markers (see the discussion of tangible AR in Chapter 8). *Haptic virtuality* corresponds to environments with purely synthesized haptic sensations, which need to be registered with visual or audio augmentations. *Haptic mixed reality* uses combinations of real objects and synthesized actuation (such as virtual vibrotactile actuations of a tangible prop or tactile feedback on physical touchscreens).

Olfactory and Gustatory Displays

The idea of coordinating multiple sensory stimulations, including impressions of smell, date back to Morton Heilig's [1962] patent for the Sensorama simulator, a stand-alone movie console that he implemented and refined over the following decades. This device could present 3D cinematic experiences along with stereo sound, wind, and aromas [Heilig 1992]. Coordinated sensory stimulation was at the heart of Heilig's idea—and is also at the heart of multimodal AR experiences: "It is the cooperative effects of the breeze, the odor, the visual images and binaural sound that stimulate a desired sensation in the senses of an observer. For those instances where a sense of motion is desired, means is provided to induce small vibrations or jolts to simulate movement and, also, to simulate actual impacts" [Heilig 1962].

Delivering scents through the air in a natural but directed manner is not a trivial undertaking. While Heilig's machine simply released the aromas into air flow directed toward the viewer, SpotScents [Nakaizumi et al. 2006] utilizes vortex rings consisting of scented air. By coordinating two *scent projector* air cannons such that two air vortices collide and break up at a target location to release the scent impression, the system avoids hitting users with unnaturally strong airflow impulses. Smelling Screen [Matsukura et al. 2013] delivers scents to people sitting in front of a two-dimensional display screen by coordinating fans in the four corners of the screen. SensaBubble [Seah et al. 2014] delivers scented fog encapsulated in bubbles of specific sizes along directed paths. Additionally, bubbles are tracked and visually augmented with projected imagery. The visual augmentation persists only until the bubble bursts, at which point the scent is also released. The authors suggest that this mechanism could be used for playful notifications. All of these examples utilize extrinsic olfactory displays, in which odors originate in stationary environment locations. As examples of intrinsic displays, Yamada and colleagues [2006] demonstrated two prototypes of wearable olfactory displays and evaluated them in outdoor environments.

Coordination of haptic and gustatory (taste) modalities was the aim of the Food Simulator project, which demonstrated and evaluated a haptic interface for biting [Iwata et al. 2004]. Volunteers bit onto a force-feedback apparatus that simulated certain food textures. Simultaneously, the chemical sensation of taste was induced via small amounts of liquids containing combinations of substances representing the five basic tastes: sweetness, sourness, saltiness, bitterness, and umami. While this particular work did not make use of a visual representation of the simulated food item, other research projects have explored combined visual-olfactory augmentations.

For example, Narumi and colleagues [2011a, 2011b] have developed several incarnations of MetaCookie, in which AR markers are applied to plain cookies via a branding iron and a commercial food plotter with edible ink, respectively. An olfactory display and visual AR display are used to create the impression of differently flavored cookies (Figure 2.2). Evaluations have

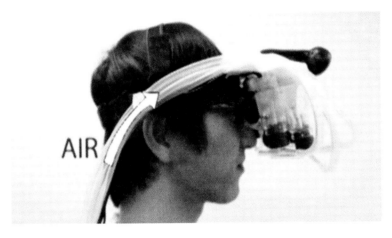

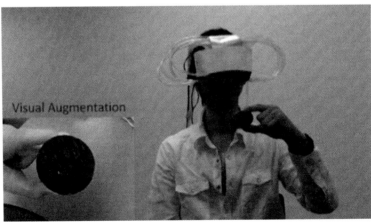

Figure 2.2 MetaCookie: An olfactory display is combined with visual augmentation of a plain cookie to provide the illusion of a flavored cookie (chocolate, in the case of the bottom image). Courtesy of Takuji Narumi.

shown that with several combinations of odors and visuals that emulate common cookie flavors, a convincing "pseudo-gustatory" effect can be achieved—that is, participants have reported a changed taste of the augmented cookie.

Now that we have briefly reviewed the history and state of the art of nonvisual AR displays, outlining the potential of multimodal augmentation, the rest of this chapter will focus mainly on the visual domain. We will preface our discussion of visual displays with a brief overview of visual perception. This sets the stage for an examination of the requirements and characteristics of different types of visual displays.

Visual Perception

Human vision is a highly sophisticated sense, responsible for delivering roughly 70% of the overall sensory information to the brain [Heilig 1992]. Consequently, AR has mostly concentrated on providing augmentations to a human user's visual perception. Before we discuss such visual AR displays, we will briefly mention important properties of the human visual system. For more detailed information on human perception, the reader is referred to general texts on the human vision system [Marr 1982] [Frisby and Stone 2010].

The human field of view, from both eyes combined, spans usually 200–220° horizontally, depending on head shape and eye position. The fovea (i.e., the area of best visual acuity) covers only 1–2°, with acuity peaking in the center 0.5–1°. Outside the fovea, the visual acuity falls off quickly with increasing viewing angle. Humans compensate for this effect by moving their eyes—in a range of up to 50°—and their head. High-quality AR, therefore, requires a viewing device that can present sufficient resolution in the area of high acuity.

By adjusting the pupil diameter, humans can control the amount of light that enters the eye. This allows us to accommodate a dynamic range (the ratio of maximum and minimum perceivable light intensities) of up to 10^{10}, covering viewing conditions from dim starlight to extremely bright sunlight. Thus, a truly versatile AR display will need to be able to adapt to a wide range of viewing conditions.

Their use of two eyes means that humans are able to perceive binocular depth cues. While monocular depth cues—such as size in the image, linear perspective, height in the field of view, occlusions, or shadows and shading—can be encoded in a single image by conventional computer graphics, binocular depth cues require display hardware that can present separate images to both eyes simultaneously. The most prominent binocular depth cue is stereopsis, the disparity between the left and right image. Stereopsis is very effective for conveying scene depth, especially for objects that are nearby. The closer an object is to the eyes, the bigger the angular offset, or parallax, of the object's projections in the two image planes.

Requirements and Characteristics

Before we discuss the different visual displays that have successfully been employed to implement AR, it is important to understand some of the requirements and varying characteristics of such displays.

An ideal AR system would have the capability of creating life-like 3D augmentations that convincingly populate actual physical spaces. AR designers might choose to have the augmentations appear as distinct from reality, but they would certainly appreciate the possibility of creating virtual content that is seamlessly integrated with existing physical reality. Both speculative science [Sutherland 1965] and science fiction, e.g., the *Star Trek* Holodeck [Krauss 1995], have featured visions of perfectly realistic displays, but rarely do such musings consider the inclusion of the actual real world. It would be amazing to be able to shift atoms around at will and generate virtual content as a true part of the real world in real time and to perceive these augmentations with all our senses. Clearly, most of that dream remains impossible to realize for the time being.

We will come back to the future in Chapter 14. For now, we will take a look at the characteristics and potential of actual visual AR technology. The design of a good AR display always involves some tradeoffs regarding its properties, and different types of displays have different pros and cons. We begin by reviewing the methods of augmentation that current AR displays employ.

Method of Augmentation

From the properties of the human visual system and the objectives of the AR application, we can derive requirements for AR displays. One obvious requirement that distinguishes AR displays from conventional computer-generated displays is that the real environment and the virtual environment need to be combined. When this combination of real and virtual content happens via a lens through which the user is viewing the environment, the result is described as a see-through display. There are two fundamental ways to achieve this result: an *optical see-through display* or a *video see-through display*. If the augmentations are projected onto actual physical geometry (be it dummy placeholder objects or natural parts of the real world), the technology is described as spatial AR, projection-based AR, or *spatial projection*. The following paragraphs briefly describe each of these three approaches.

Optical see-through (OST) displays commonly rely on an optical element that is partially transmissive and partially reflective to achieve the combination of virtual and real. A half-silvered mirror is a simple example of such an optical element. The mirror lets a sufficient amount of light from the real world pass through so that the real world can be viewed directly (Figure 2.3). At the same time, a computer-generated display showing virtual images is placed overhead or to the side of the mirror, so that the virtual images are reflected in the mirror and overlaid on the real image.

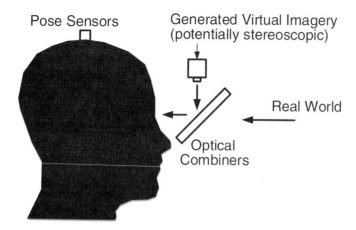

Figure 2.3 An optical see-through display uses an optical element to combine a user's view of the real world with computer-generated images.

Video see-through (VST) displays achieve the combination of virtual and real electronically. A digital video image of the real world is captured through a video camera and transferred to the graphics processor. The graphics processor combines the video image with the computer-generated images, often by simply copying the video image into the frame buffer as a background image, with the computer-generated elements drawn on top (Figure 2.4). The combined image is then presented using a conventional viewing device.

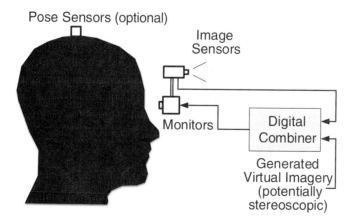

Figure 2.4 A video see-through display captures the real world with a video camera and electronically modifies the resulting image using a graphics processor to deliver a combined real and virtual image to the user.

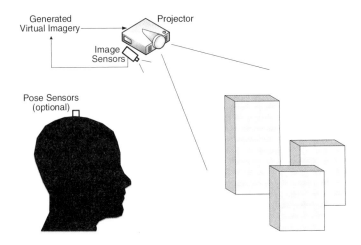

Figure 2.5 Spatial projection casts images directly onto real-world objects; no combiner unit is required.

With **spatial projection**, the virtual part of the AR display is generated by a light projector; instead of using a special screen, however, the virtual image is projected directly on real-world objects (Figure 2.5). This is also a form of optical combination, but here we do not need a separate optical combiner, and no electronic screen is involved. This display paradigm is an example of a *volumetric 3D display* [Blundell and Schwartz 1999], for which the points of light defining perceivable objects are physically distributed throughout a 3D volume.

Immersion factors of visual AR displays are key considerations in their development. While there has been a lot of research on immersion in VR [Pausch et al. 1997] [Bowman and McMahan 2007] [Cummings et al. 2012], the components and parameters of immersion and presence factors for AR are less well understood [MacIntyre et al. 2004a] [Steptoe et al. 2014]. In this book, we will apply Slater's [2003] distinction between immersion and presence. That is, immersion refers to the objective level of sensory fidelity a VR (or, in our case, AR) system provides, whereas presence refers to a user's subjective psychological response to such a system.

Ocularity and Stereoscopy

The question of monoscopic versus stereoscopic imagery arises with several see-through AR display technologies, such as near-eye displays and handheld magic lenses. If the physical world is seen through some kind of lens or mediated through cameras, two questions arise regarding scene dimensionality: (1) Is the three-dimensionality of the real world maintained? and (2) Are the augmentations displayed with stereopsis, exploiting binocular vision?

A **monocular** HMD presents images to only one eye. A monocular display can be used for AR, but this approach is not very popular, because it lacks immersion. A **bi-ocular** display presents the same image to both eyes, resulting in a monoscopic impression. This approach is some-times used for VST HMD, because only a single camera stream is required and sensing and processing requirements are minimized. Finally, a **binocular** HMD presents a separate image to each eye, resulting in a stereoscopic effect. Binocular displays obviously deliver the highest-quality AR among these choices, but have a significantly increased technical cost. They require two displays or, alternatively, a wide-format single display that can be appropriately split using two optical elements (Figure 2.6). Stereo augmentations can be rendered on top of a bi-ocular representation of the real-world backdrop coming from a single camera (such as the phone's camera in Figure 2.6, bottom row), but full-stereo VST requires at least two cameras for video input to provide a perspective similar to those obtained with two human eyes. Pairs of video cameras and pairs of displays must be synchronized to deliver the images at the same time.

Using near-eye displays, AR can be implemented with monocular or binocular viewing. When using binocular viewing, the real-world backdrop and the augmentations can be displayed with or without binocular disparity, which enables stereo vision. With OST displays, the real-world backdrop is viewed directly, and thus naturally exhibits binocular disparity. The augmentations can be rendered either with or without stereopsis. The design possibilities for see-through dis-plays in terms of stereopsis are depicted in Figure 2.7. Most example displays listed in this figure

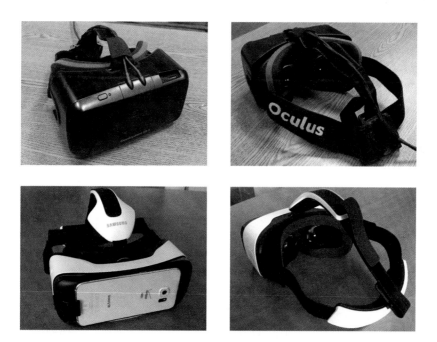

Figure 2.6   (top row) The Rift (here: DK2) is a binocular HMD intended for immersive computer games. It is under development by Oculus, which was acquired by Facebook in 2014 for $2 billion. This high-profile acquisition has raised the interest in HMD technology worldwide. (bottom row) The Samsung Gear VR is an example of an untethered virtual and augmented reality device that uses a smartphone (here: Samsung Galaxy S6) as the main I/O and computational engine.

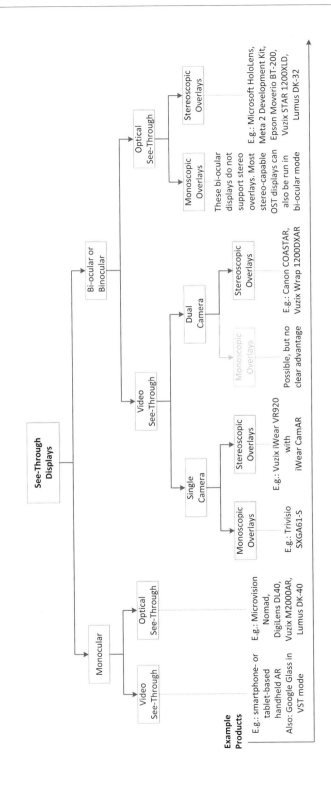

Figure 2.7 Categorization of see-through displays based on stereo capabilities.

are commercial HMDs (i.e., near-eye displays), but the monocular video see-through category also encompasses the common case of smartphone- or tablet-based handheld AR.

VST displays can employ either one or two cameras. A VST display with two cameras, aligned with the eyes' optical axes (see Figure 2.14 later in this chapter) can produce imagery that lets the user perceive the physical world under stereopsis. Unfortunately, it is notoriously difficult to give a realistic impression of a three-dimensional space using stereoscopic camera feeds. Humans are used to viewing the physical world unmediated and unencumbered and have high expectations for realism, especially regarding the interplay of varying depth cues. Unavoidable deviations from the ideal values for other immersion factors, such as field of view, resolution, and focus ability, will make for a slightly or even considerably unnatural experience.

Focus

Normal rendering of virtual objects with the pinhole camera model commonly used in computer graphics (where the camera aperture is an ideal point, and no lenses are used) will result in perfectly sharp images of all objects, irrespective of the focal depth. Our eyes and actual cameras have a certain aperture size and, therefore, have to cope with the problem of limited *depth of field*: Only a certain range of objects will be in focus, and everything outside this range will be blurred. Of course, our eyes can *accommodate* (focus) at varying distances.

Accommodation can occur as a reflex to *vergence* (independent rotation of eyeballs to fixate a point in space), but can also be consciously controlled. We accommodate at a certain distance by changing the form of the elastic lenses behind our pupils. Matters are not so simple when stereoscopic display screens are involved, however. Any display screen viewed with the naked eye or through a conventional optical system has a fixed focal depth. Consequently, images of virtual objects will always be displayed with this fixed focus, although the actual depth of the object (distance from the virtual camera) may be very different. In such a stereoscopic display, the object's actual distance is signaled to the human visual system via stereo parallax, resulting in a certain vergence response. The result is conflicting signals about focus and eye alignment—the so-called *accommodation–vergence conflict*. People get variable vergence information from binocular stereo cues in a virtual scene, which conflicts with the fixed accommodation needed for the display's focal depth. This phenomenon has been shown to reduce task performance and contribute to visual fatigue [Emoto et al. 2005] [Hoffman et al. 2008] [Banks et al. 2013].

The accommodation–vergence conflict occurs in VR as well as in AR, as long as stereoscopic displays with a fixed focal plane are used. For optical see-through AR with such stereoscopic rendering, however, there is an additional, related problem: Not only will viewing of the virtual augmentations suffer from the accommodation–vergence conflict, but the user will view the real world with correct accommodation cues, whereas to see the virtual annotations in focus, the user will need to accommodate to the display image plane. Thus, to read a textual label that is virtually positioned on the front plane of a building facade, the user must switch focus back and forth between the building facade plane and the display image plane. Looking at the facade plane, the user can see the architectural details in focus, but the textual explanation will be blurred, and vice versa. Any co-placement of virtual and real objects will suffer from this problem, unless the objects' depth happens to be at the display image plane. The magnitude of this problem has not been exhaustively assessed as of yet. People manage to adjust accommodation at will quite effortlessly, but increased visual fatigue and discomfort might ensue with medium- to long-term use.

One solution to this problem might be a display that can shift the focus plane in real time. With such technology, which researchers are currently investigating [Liu et al. 2008], one would need eye tracking to identify the objects the user is focusing on and then adjust the focus plane shift according to the user's attention.

Multifocus displays [Schowengerdt and Seibel 2012] present another possibility to avoid the accommodation–vergence conflict. Some promising technologies in this area are discussed later in this chapter, in the coverage of near-eye displays. Accommodation and vergence are naturally matched in the case of volumetric displays [Blundell and Schwartz 1999], where light emanates or reflects from actual points in a 3D volume. *Spatial projection*, a special case of this display modality, is described in the later discussion of projected displays.

If one sticks with stereoscopic displays that have a fixed focus plane, it may be possible to reduce the problems attributable to accommodation–vergence mismatch by clever use of other depth cues. For a review of depth cues, see the work of Cutting and Vishton [1995] or Chapter 1 of the book by Blundell and Schwartz [1999]. Depth of field effects, for example, can be simulated in computer graphics (see Barsky and Kosloff [2008] for a survey of techniques). In conjunction with eye tracking [Hillaire et al. 2008], the real-time rendering of realistic blurring effects outside the depth of field may alleviate the accommodation–vergence conflict [Vinnikov and Allison 2014].

In video see-through systems, the camera optics are responsible for delivering images that have the right focus. As mentioned earlier, VST displays can either employ a single camera or two cameras (Figure 2.7), with the latter allowing for stereoscopic display of the real scene. The focal dynamics of the cameras are likely very different from those for the human eye. Even if they were the same, it would be a big challenge to establish a link between the oculomotor cue of stretching and relaxing the eye lens and the focusing system of the camera. A camera could employ an auto-focus mechanism for automatically adjusting the focus to a central object. While such auto-focus settings are usually not available on the computer to which the camera is attached, the distance to the fixated object could still be determined from a scene model, which is either prepared offline or assembled live through methods such as SLAM, discussed in Chapter 4. With this information, an attempt can be made to render virtual objects with depth cues (e.g., depth of field blur) corresponding to the estimated focal depth, and even to perform image processing on the camera feed to approximate focus effects. Nevertheless, the VST experience in terms of depth perception in general, and focus effects in particular, likely will not be extremely realistic.

Occlusion

Occlusion between virtual and real objects is an important cue to convey the scene structure. While correct occlusion among real objects is naturally given, and correct occlusion among virtual objects is easily achieved by means of a z-buffer, achieving correct occlusion of virtual in front of real, or vice versa, requires special consideration. By using the z-buffer, a video see-through system can determine whether the virtual or real object is in front, if a geometric representation of the real scene is available. In optical see-through systems, where augmentations often appear as semi-transparent overlays, it is more difficult to make virtual objects appear as if they are truly in front of real objects. There are three alternatives:

- Virtual objects can be rendered very brightly relative to the intensity at which real objects are visible, so the virtual objects will be dominant. However, this may adversely affect the perception of the remaining portions of the real scene.

- In a controlled environment, the relevant part of the real scene can be illuminated with a computer-controlled projector, while the rest of the scene (in particular, real objects that are occluded by virtual objects) remains in the dark and, therefore, imperceptible [Bimber and Fröhlich 2002]. In these dark areas, virtual objects can be shown and appear to occlude real ones (Figure 2.8).

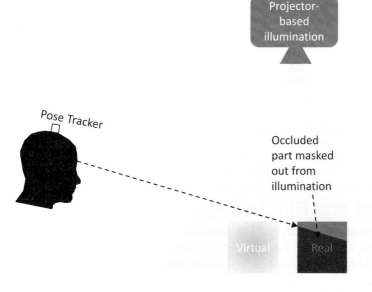

Figure 2.8   The occlusion shadows technique uses controlled illumination to blank out those portions of the real world where opaque computer graphics should be visible.

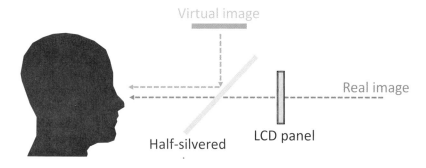

Figure 2.9   (top) The ELMO HMD uses an additional LCD panel between display and optical combiner for pixel-wise blocking of occluded real-world objects. (bottom) Prof. Kiyokawa with a prototype of ELMO. Courtesy of Kiyoshi Kiyokawa.

■   An optically transparent display can be enhanced with a liquid crystal screen, which allows for selectively making individual pixels transparent or opaque. The ELMO HMD [Kiyokawa et al. 2003] pioneered this approach (Figure 2.9).

Resolution and Refresh Rate

The resolution of the display has an immediate impact on the fidelity of the resulting image. Overall, resolution is restricted by the type of display and by the optical system. If a video see-through solution is used, the resolution of the real world is additionally restricted by the resolution of the camera. Usually, the computer-generated display will not be able to match the maximum resolution at which a human perceives the real world directly (Figure 2.10).

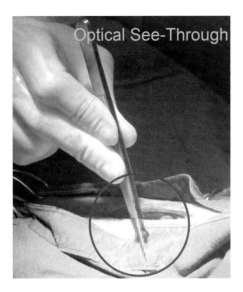 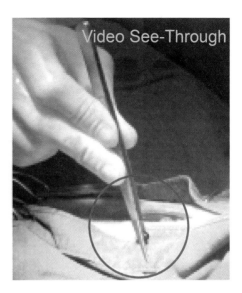

Figure 2.10   Image quality in optical see-through displays is higher for the real world, but generally inconsistent. The (normally occluded) tips of the pincers are rendered as augmentations. This illustrative mockup shows exaggerated resolution artifacts for the augmentation part on the left and the entire image on the right.

Nevertheless, a sufficient resolution is desirable to suppress disturbing artifacts of computer-generated images (such as pixelated lines or text) that stand out in comparison to the user's perception of the real world.

Apart from the spatial resolution, the temporal resolution—that is, the native refresh rate of the display—is important to minimize perceived flicker and to avoid image lag and ghosting. The flicker fusion threshold is the frequency at which an intermittent light stimulus appears to be completely steady to the average human observer. Many factors influence this threshold. While some human observers experience flicker in CRT displays with refresh rates of less than 75 Hz, newer display technologies with higher pixel persistence, such as some LCD displays, avoid flicker at refresh rates of 60 Hz or less. The refresh rate influences how displays render motion. For the purposes of presenting moving images, the human flicker fusion threshold is usually taken as 16 Hz, and TV cameras operate at 25 or 30 frames per second, depending on the TV system. For rendering fast motions without blur, higher frame rates (120 Hz and higher) can be advantageous, and for AR and VR, frame rates above 60Hz are commonly desired. Higher display refresh rates are also often used in VR and AR displays for time-multiplexing information transmission, such as alternating left- and right-eye frames in stereoscopic displays and field-sequential color displays that fuse colors by showing a single pixel in red, green, and blue in quick temporal succession.

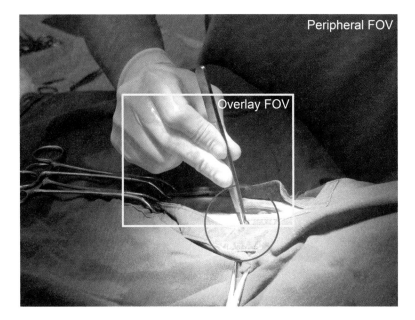

Figure 2.11 AR systems typically have a limited field of view, resulting in an "overlay FOV" area, in which augmentations are visible, and a "peripheral FOV" area, in which they are not.

Field of View

The field of view (FOV) is potentially even more important than the raw resolution. FOV and resolution are interrelated, as more pixels at the same density are needed to fill a wider FOV. A wider FOV means that more information can be shown to the user in a single view. In AR, we distinguish between an overlay FOV and a peripheral FOV. In the overlay FOV, computer-generated graphics are overlaid on the image of the real world. In contrast, the peripheral FOV encompasses the natural, non-augmented portion of the observed environment. If the overall shot in Figure 2.11 has a 62° FOV diagonally, the marked overlay FOV is approximately 30° diagonally. Such a relatively narrow FOV means that users will often have to put some distance between themselves and the virtual or real objects to see them fully, or move their head in a scanning motion to see the whole scene over time. FOV limitations are common in VR and, especially, AR displays, and the resulting reduction in immersion limits the user's presence in the displayed scenes and content.

In video see-through AR, it is actually the FOV of the camera rather than the FOV of the display that determines the amount of real-world information that can be presented. The camera often has a larger FOV than the display, so that the camera image actually appears compressed, similar to a fish-eye effect. When using smartphones as handheld AR magic lenses, for example, the camera on the back of the smartphone likely has a larger FOV than the angle subtended by the display, which, at arm's length, is quite small.

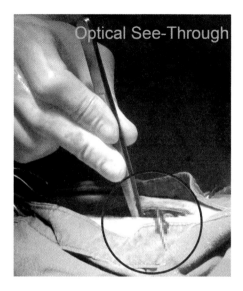 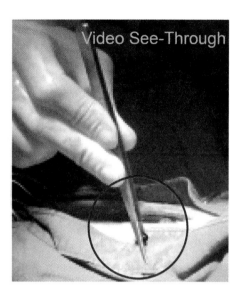

Figure 2.12 Insufficient eye-to-display calibration can lead to distracting offsets. In video see-through displays, pixel-accurate registration is easier to achieve.

For HMDs, the goal is to have as wide an overlay FOV as possible. To avoid having the HMD grow in size, then, we must either get closer to the eye (using retinal scanning displays or AR contact lenses; see the discussion in Chapter 14) or optimize the design of the involved optical elements. HMD manufacturers often specify a diagonal field of view rather than a horizontal and vertical field of view, which, conveniently, yields a higher number. When the distance of the eye to the display in an HMD is fixed, the field of view together with the spatial resolution of the display determines the angular resolution. A display with a very high pixel density can use rather simple magnification optics to present a wide field of view. This approach has been used in recent non-see-through displays such as the Oculus Rift, leveraging recent advances in flat display technology. With a fixed pixel count, however, it may be necessary to choose either a wider field of view or a higher resolution. For example, pilots may prefer a wider field of view, while surgeons may require higher resolution.

Viewpoint Offset

Optical see-through displays fuse the optical paths of the virtual and the real into one, so the resulting images are aligned by design. This outcome is desirable, as it corresponds to natural viewing. However, it requires **calibration** of the virtual camera, which is used to generate the virtual part of the AR display, to the eye of the user. If the calibration is not done carefully, an offset between the image parts will be the result. With video see-through displays, the camera frame can be used for computer-vision–based registration (see Chapter 4), leading to pixel-accurate annotations (Figure 2.12).

Video see-through configurations will often introduce a significant offset between the viewing direction of the camera and the viewing direction of the screen on which the camera image is presented. This offset may reflect restrictions in where the camera can be mounted (e.g., on an HMD), or it can be intended in the design of the AR workspace. For example, a workbench may present the augmented image from an overhead camera facing downward on a vertical surface in front of the user, so that the space where the user sees her real hands and the augmented view are separated in the field of view (Figure 2.13).

With miniaturized cameras, it is also possible to build an HMD with camera optics placed such that they are aligned with the viewing directions of the user's eyes (Figure 2.14). The first device of this kind was the COASTAR (Co-Optical Axis See-Through Augmented Reality) HMD, developed by Canon MR Laboratory [Uchiyama et al. 2002]. The design process for another such parallax- and distortion-free HMD is described by State et al. [2005].

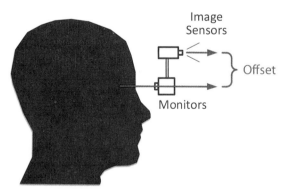

Figure 2.13   (top) A camera pointing diagonally downward from behind the display captures an AR interaction space centered on the user's hands. Courtesy of Morten Fjeld. (bottom) In general, an offset between the user's viewing direction and the camera's optical axis is not desirable.

Figure 2.14   COASTAR was the first commercial parallax-free video see-through HMD. Courtesy of Hiroyuki Yamamoto.

A special case of altered viewpoint is a mirror configuration. That is, AR can be delivered in a setup that is similar to a video conferencing configuration, with a camera facing the user being combined with an upright screen. In this case, it is advantageous to show a horizontally flipped camera image, with the resulting display resembling the conventional mirror with which humans are familiar.

The disadvantages of any kind of viewpoint offset are, of course, that the user needs to adapt to the viewing situation, and that the viewing is not entirely natural.

Brightness and Contrast

Achieving sufficient contrast in see-through displays is generally difficult. In particular, in outdoor situations or in situations with an abundance of natural light, most computer displays are not bright enough to achieve sufficient contrast. A common evasive measure is to reduce the amount of physical light that affects the viewing situation—for example, by using window blinds to control outside light influence on spatial projection indoors or by manipulating an adjustable visor on an HMD. An OST HMD allows a user to see the world directly. The maximum brightness of the display must compete with the brightness level of the real world, which makes is very difficult to obtain acceptable contrast levels, especially outdoors in direct sunlight. In certain cases, the optical system may also make the real world too dark (Figure 2.15).

In VST, no direct viewing of the environment is necessary, so the amount of natural light in the viewing environment can be more easily controlled. Unfortunately, the poor contrast achieved by conventional video cameras becomes more apparent. In addition, a VST HMD usually covers only a certain part of the user's field of view, and natural light may enter from the periphery. Additionally, VST is critically dependent on working electronic components. If the camera or the display fails, no meaningful image is shown at all (Figure 2.16).

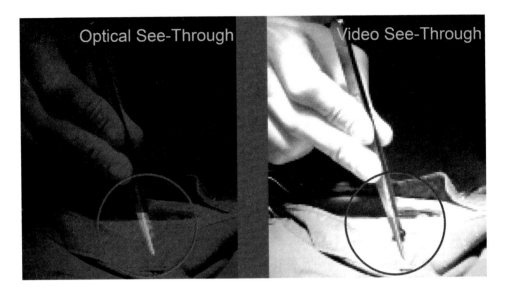

Figure 2.15 Optical see-through displays depend on the transparency of the optical combiner, while video see-through displays can change brightness and contrast arbitrarily, as long as the display itself can deliver sufficient contrast. On the right, the contrast limit is reached, and some real-world detail is lost.

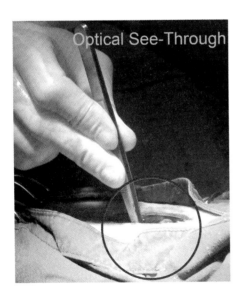

Figure 2.16 If the display fails, video see-through will not allow the user to see anything. This can be dangerous in critical situations such as surgery or piloting an aircraft.

Distortions and Aberrations

Every concrete display, be it OST or VST, will involve optical elements, such as lenses. These optical elements can introduce distortions, such as fish-eye effects—in particular, if a wide field of view is desired. In addition, the electronic imaging process can lead to sampling and recon-struction artifacts. For example, Bayer masks, which are widely used in electronic cameras, induce typical color aberrations. High-quality components and careful calibration can minimize these problems, albeit typically at an elevated cost.

Latency

Temporal errors can have a similarly detrimental effect as spatial errors. Just as insufficient spatial calibration can lead to offsets between virtual and real in the image, so insufficient temporal alignment between virtual and real can produce spatial offsets. If the virtual elements in an AR display are shown too late, perhaps, because the graphics generation takes too long to finish, the user may have moved in the meantime. As a result, the virtual elements will be displayed in the wrong part of the image.

Latency affects both OST and VST, as the virtual parts can be outdated in both cases. One potential advantage of VST over OST is the option of delaying the video so that it matches the virtual elements. The resulting AR display will be free from spatial misalignments, but at the cost of higher lag in the presentation. Such a lag may be acceptable only if the error is small.

High latency has been shown to contribute to the onset of cybersickness in VR and AR viewing scenarios. It is hard to give absolute numbers, because the data from various studies are very case specific, but the thresholds that have been studied in more depth lie somewhere between 20 and 300 ms. Predictive compensation can be effectively implemented to reduce apparent latency, resulting in a lower magnitude of simulator sickness [Buker et al. 2012].

Ergonomics

Obviously, users should be comfortable when using AR viewing devices. For stationary displays, this mostly requires a sensible arrangement of the workspace so that users can assume a con-venient standing or seated position while using the device. For mobile devices, there is a bigger risk of fatigue, and, therefore, acceptable ergonomic properties are much harder to achieve. Handheld devices that must be held at eye level quickly strain the user, and most HMDs subjec-tively appear heavy and cumbersome after extended periods of wearing.

Social Acceptance

How weird would you be willing to look? Mobile computers are in widespread use today, and wearing wireless audio headsets has just become acceptable. Even so, wearing an HMD in public is not yet fully acceptable in most social environments. This status may be primarily attributed to the fact that HMDs are still very bulky and cover the eyes and a large part of the face. Many users potentially interested in AR will, therefore, refrain from using HMDs, at least until they get less conspicuous. Researchers have made the point that nomenclature might contribute to limited user acceptance. "Head-mounted" displays might be less agreeable to the public than "head-worn" ones, and indeed several researchers prefer the latter term [Feiner 1999] [Cakmakci and Rolland 2006]. In this book, we will continue to use the more traditional "HMD" instead of the potentially more benign-sounding "HWD."

In contrast to HMDs, stationary AR displays are less immersive, but they trivially afford simultaneous viewing by multiple users and, therefore, are more social in a certain sense. Handheld devices lie in between the two extremes and may represent an acceptable compromise for the present and near future, even though they are fraught with their own ergonomic and social acceptance problems. Holding up a tablet or smartphone so that the user can look through it like through a lens may potentially tire out the user's arm. Likewise, looking at other people through the "lens" of a camera-equipped smartphone or tablet so as to see augmentations around that person's silhouette is likely to be perceived as rude. The perceived threat of being filmed by a worn camera has already resulted in a social acceptance problem for Google Glass [Hong 2013], and many researchers have pondered the problems of surveillance and privacy [Mann 1998] [Feiner 1999] [Michael and Michael 2013]. Less physically intrusive AR technology, such as that potentially enabled by AR contact lenses (see Chapter 14), might lead to higher user acceptance, but could bring with it a whole different set of social and societal problems [May-raz and Lazo 2012].

Spatial Display Model

Now that we have reviewed requirements and characteristics of visual AR displays, it is time to shed some light on the process of AR information display through the interplay of various coordinate transformations. As noted in the previous section, multiple indirections may be involved in a user's viewing of the augmented world. The viewing experience might be mediated through camera feeds and display screens. In AR, we rely on a standard computer graphics pipeline [Hughes et al. 2014] to produce overlays on the real world. Independent of the kind of AR display, this pipeline consists of a model transformation, a view transformation, and a projective transformation.

- **Model transformation:** The model transformation describes the relationship of 3D local object coordinates and 3D global world coordinates. The model transformation describes how objects are positioned in the real world.

- **View transformation:** The view transformation describes the relationship of 3D global world coordinates and 3D view (observer or camera) coordinates.

■ **Projective transformation:** The projective transformation describes the relationship of 3D view coordinates and 2D device (screen) coordinates.

The projective transformation is usually determined offline, but may need to be updated dynamically, if internal camera parameters, such as field of view, change (see Chapter 5). The other transformations can be static, and thus determined offline, or they must be determined by **tracking**, if they can change online. Tracking is discussed in great detail in Chapter 3.

Object tracking is required if we are interested in moving real objects in the AR scene, while static object positions can be measured once and need not be tracked. Object tracking is used to set the model transformation. If we want to augment only tracked objects (but not untracked static objects), we can give up a an explicit world coordinate system and can use one view transformation per tracked real object instead (e.g., in the case of independent AR markers; see Chapter 3).

Determining the view transformation can be more complex, because several components may be involved (Figure 2.17). If the user is moving relative to the display, **head tracking** and, potentially, **eye tracking** are necessary. If the display is moving relative to the world, **display tracking** is needed. If a VST display is used, **camera tracking** is required as well, because VST routes the user's perception of the real world through a camera, while OST lets a user see the world directly. A setup where user, display, camera, and object are all moving independently is conceivable, although typically a maximum of two simultaneous types of tracked entities are used. Nevertheless, a system may employ multiple instances of each component type (user, display, camera, object).

We will use the iconography of Figure 2.17 continuously throughout the later parts of this chapter to illustrate schematically various AR display and viewing configurations (Figure 2.23 and later figures).

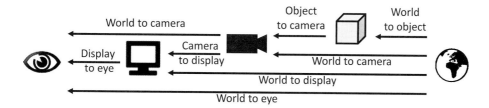

Figure 2.17   The spatial model of most AR displays can be defined as the spatial relationship of up to five components: the user's eye, the display, the camera, an object to be augmented, and the world. We depict the most important coordinate transformations here, each of which can be fixed and calibrated, tracked dynamically, or left unconstrained.

Visual Displays

To understand the technologies in today's visual AR displays in detail, a range of scientific topics must be considered. While it is beyond the scope of this book to review the physics of light, optics, and holographic principles, an excellent introduction to these topics as pertaining to display technologies is presented in the book by Hainich and Bimber [2011]. Here, we will briefly clarify the differences among the various 3D display technologies, as there are some common misconceptions, and as understanding is sometimes purposefully blurred by marketing materials. In particular, we will distinguish among the following classes of 3D displays: stereoscopic approaches, holographic displays, light-field displays, and volumetric displays.

We have already briefly discussed stereoscopy. Sending separate images to an observer's eyes has been the most common approach employed to bring 3D content to audiences. Binocular near-eye displays can naturally feed different images to a user's left and right eyes. When using monitors or large-size displays (potentially driven by projectors), different technologies are applied to enable stereoscopic viewing. Some require the user to wear active shutter glasses or passive filter glasses (color, polarization, or interference filters) in various configurations. Whether the left and right eye images are transmitted in a space- or time-multiplexed fashion, through synchronization or matching filters, the end result is always that the observer receives images with the appropriate perspective to their respective eye. Other, so-called autostereoscopic, techniques do not require glasses. Instead, they perform stereo-channel separation directly on or in front of the display, sending out the different perspective images into different viewing zones, which are smaller than the eye distance so that each eye can observe its own perspective. Examples include parallax barrier displays and lenticular displays.

Most of the time stereoscopic approaches rely on screens with fixed focal planes, but sometimes stereoscopy is combined with other imaging approaches [Halle 1994] [Huang et al. 2015]. At the other end of the spectrum are truly volumetric displays, where image formation occurs in 3D space; that is, light is emitted or reflected at the 3D coordinates where the imaged 3D object is perceived [Blundell and Schwartz 1999] [Kimura et al. 2006].

Holographic displays and light-field displays are closely related display categories, and the boundaries between them are sometimes blurred. Both approaches are concerned with recording (or generating) and replaying all the characteristics of light waves representing a certain scene. Ideally, there should be no difference between viewing an actual physical scene, a properly illuminated holographic recording, or a properly re-created light-field experience. In practice, each technology still has many limitations [Hainich and Bimber 2011] [Wetzstein 2015].

Holograms generally utilize coherent (laser) illumination for creation and viewing. Light-field displays usually function with incoherent light. Light-field displays can take many forms, including volumetric displays [Jones et al. 2007], multi-projector arrays [Balogh et al. 2007], and near-eye displays using microlenses [Lanman and Luebke 2013].

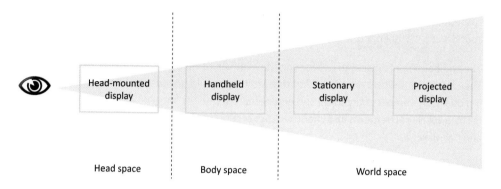

Figure 2.18   AR displays can be categorized according to the distance from eye to display.

The term "holography" originally referred to the phenomenon of encoding a light field as the interference pattern of a laser illumination beam and a scene's reflected laser light. It manifests itself in the form of variations in the opacity, density, or surface profile of a photographic medium. The terms *holography* and *holograms* have come into widespread use during the past few years, and have been (inaccurately) used to refer to any life-like 3D representation, including lenticular and other auto-stereoscopic and auto-multiscopic 3D displays, and the "Pepper's Ghost" stage illusion that operates with simple semi-transparent mirrors and clever content adjustment and lighting. While the generally accepted meaning of these terms is changing through their popular use, for the purposes of this book, we will stick with the terminology from the research literature.

Which displays do we need to present a convincing augmented reality? Hainich [2009] postulates that one would need just one type of well-functioning personal AR display—ideally, a nonintrusive, comfortable, high-resolution, wide-FOV, near-eye display with high dynamic range and perfect tracking—to emulate and replace all computer displays in the world. As compelling as this vision might be, it is pretty clear that in the near- to mid-term future, AR will happen on a combination of display technologies, including personal near-eye, handheld, and potentially worn displays, stationary large-screen and volumetric displays, as well as imagery projected onto physical environments.

Next, we review some of these display technologies relevant to AR. As proposed by Raskar [2004], we organize our discussion of visual AR displays in order of increasing distance from the eye (Figure 2.18). We start with HMDs, then progress to handheld displays, stationary displays, and projected displays.

Near-Eye Displays

The most prominent class of displays for AR is probably the HMD. The use of an HMD in an AR setup goes back to the seminal work of Sutherland. His "Sword of Damocles" HMD was suspended from the ceiling owing to its weight, and used CRT screens in an optical see-through configuration [Sutherland 1968].

The engineering of devices to be worn on the head is a complex endeavor [Kiyokawa 2007]. They must be unobtrusive and comfortable, yet they should provide the highest possible viewing quality. A number of technical and ergonomic parameters, most of which were discussed in the display requirements and characteristics section, are important for HMD design [Rolland and Cakmakci 2009].

Especially critical for near-eye displays are the ergonomics of the display to be worn. Obviously, an HMD should be as lightweight as possible, particularly to be suitable for longer periods of use. Apart from the electronic components and optics, the casing or mounting will largely determine the weight (Figure 2.19): Helmet-mounted devices are robust, but will mostly be appealing if the task already requires wearing a helmet, such as with pilots or firefighters. Clip-on designs can be attached to ordinary glasses or sunglasses, but result in a "see-around" effect where the display is out of the main field of view. Such a spatial arrangement, which is well known from the Google Glass device, is more oriented toward wearable information (text) displays, but is less appropriate for see-through AR displays. A display embedded in a visor is the most powerful approach, but requires careful design of the frame, because the weight of the display will tend to accumulate in front of the user's face and must be kept in place by appropriate fixtures. The frame or casing should be adjustable to different head sizes and comfortable to wear. It should also let sufficient amounts of air flow near the head to prevent sweating.

So what might an *ideal* near-eye display for AR look like? Suppose we have our sights set on binocular vision supporting 3D augmentations that are well integrated with the physical environment in front of us. A sizable overlay field of view would be beneficial in this case, as otherwise large 3D augmentations would be clipped and we would have to scan the environment to fully

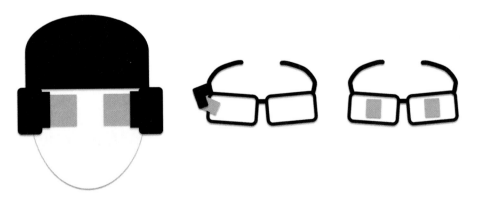

Figure 2.19   Different display mounting options. (left) Helmet-mounted display, like that used by Rockwell Collins SimEye. (middle) Clip-on display, like that used by Google Glass. (right) Visor display, like that used by Epson Moverio.

appreciate them. There are still a few more design decisions to be made. First and foremost is the question of method of augmentation: Should we go with an optical or video see-through display?

Optical See-Through Head-Mounted Display

An OST HMD requires an optical combiner to mix virtual and real. The standard approach, as implemented by the SONY Glasstron OST displays from the late 1990s, is to use a beam splitter to reflect the image from an LCD display into the viewer's eyes, while allowing a free view of the scene ahead (as shown in Figure 2.3 and Figure 2.20). A very challenging problem for OST AR displays is how to control the level of light that the display lets through from the outside world. The Glasstron series of OST displays placed an adjustable global LCD shutter mask in front of the beam splitter (farthest away from the eyes). Users could adjust the transparency of this shutter. Because of the high dynamic range of real-world lighting, even this shutter did not provide sufficient adjustability, though. In bright sunlight, a maximally darkened shutter could not keep enough light out to allow the user to see subtle details on the mirrored-in computer image. In indoor environments, a maximally transparent shutter did not afford a sufficiently bright view of the environment ahead. This experience highlights a major limitation of using simple beam splitters as optical combiners for OST HMDs. Kress and Starner [2013] review the state-of-the-art of HMD technologies and components and compare various optical combiner technologies used in the industry.

More recent OST display designs, such as from Lumus (Figure 2.21), make use of more advanced optics. Lumus's design feeds the output from a miniature projector into a special prism lens, where the light propagates via internal reflection and refraction.

An unresolved problem for near-eye OST AR is how to combine a wide field of view with a small, lightweight form factor. A larger viewing angle would naturally result from bringing a

Figure 2.20   Sony Glasstron LDI-D100B (retrofit on a custom mount as part of the Columbia MARS system). Courtesy of Columbia University.

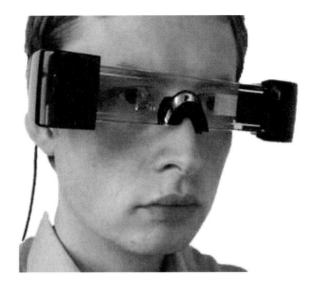

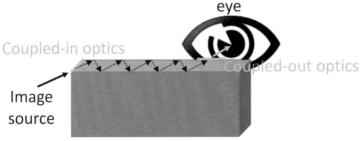

Figure 2.21   The Light-Guide Optical Element technology by Lumus propagates an image through a special optical prism. Top image: Courtesy of Jens Grubert.

(high-resolution) display closer to the eye. That prospect raises its own problems, however—for example, how to apply the necessary focus optics. One approach, demonstrated by Innovega Inc. with its iOptik platform, is to fit the optics onto a contact lens, with a central microlens enabling the viewer to focus on a glasses-based near-eye display. The central contact lens part uses polarization filters to ensure that only the light from the near-eye display is focused in this fashion, and not light from the surrounding environment. The outer part of the contact lens blocks light from the display, but allows environment light to pass through. In this way, the viewer can see the display in focus, while retaining natural accommodation on the ambient environment. It remains to be seen whether users will be willing to wear both a custom contact lens and a near-eye display for such a wide-FOV AR experience, but the glasses need not be much more bulky than normal sunglasses.

Pinlight [Maimone et al. 2014] is a novel OST HMD prototype that also addresses the problem of near-eye focus (Figure 2.22). It produces images using a novel kind of optical design, which

Figure 2.22 (top) Panel with a dense array of point light sources. (bottom) The Pinlight display prototype. Courtesy of Andrew Maimone, University of North Carolina–Chapel Hill.

resembles a densely packed array of projectors. This array consists of an LCD panel and an array of point light sources. The point light sources are generated by feeding light into an optical prism and letting it exit at precisely manufactured spots. The LCD panel is placed out of focus for the user, but the superposition of the projections generates an in-focus image on the retina. This display is currently a research prototype that has exciting possibilities, but some hurdles remain to achieve full practicality. To run the display with a reasonably high image resolution, the position of the eye relative to the display needs to be tracked. We expect future near-eye displays to incorporate eye tracking, but this integration of technologies, while demonstrated in early prototypes by some manufacturers, remains in its infancy. Truly mobile eye tracking solutions are currently still outside of the price range for consumer VR and AR.

Another recent development is a near-eye light-field display. Such a display holds the promise of relatively free eye movement and automatic focus adjustment, as its optics show a perspectively correct image from every viewpoint inside a supported area that a user can focus on at will. The NVIDIA prototype presented by Lanman and Luebke [2013] uses refractive microarray lenses and is not suited for OST. However, Maimone et al. [2014] point out that with sufficient pixel density, a pinlight display can also be manufactured as a light-field display, combining the advantages of an uncalibrated viewpoint with an OST property, and satisfying the eye tracking requirement. An "untracked light field configuration" of the pinhole display allows for limited movement of the eye within an *eyebox* region. However, this currently comes at the cost of some image degradation and significant loss of spatial resolution.

Recent announcements related to the Microsoft HoloLens project[1] and the secretive startup company MagicLeap,[2] which has received more than $500 million in funding from investors such as Google and Qualcomm, have triggered a lot of speculation as to the exact working principles of the respective technologies.

In Microsoft's case, a HoloLens development edition has been announced in the shape of a wireless optical see-through AR device, whose capabilities were demonstrated at the company's 2015 BUILD developers conference. Highly impressive achievements of the system include the integration of important AR technologies, such as custom tracking and depth sensing, spatial audio, and a state-of-the-art optical see-through display (albeit with somewhat limited overlay field of view), all in a wireless visor form factor. Microsoft uses the term "holographic computing" to describe this project and suggests that high-resolution holograms may be enabled via the company's HoloLens project. While the display optics may use holographic elements, early user experiences seem to indicate that the first prototype utilizes a stereoscopic display.

MagicLeap, in interviews and other communications by some of its stakeholders, and through the patents that have been published about the company's presumed technology, has indicated that it is working on "digital light field technology," claimed to address the accommodation-vergence mismatch problem discussed previously. The patents indicate a trajectory from research endeavors focused on scanning fiber displays at the University of Washington [Schowengerdt 2010] [Schowengerdt and Seibel 2012]. The most wearable version of these displays had suggested use of an array of optical fibers placed at different distances from a lens to form a superimposed multifocal beam. Stacked wave guide arrays for different depth planes of a 4D light field may also be part of the technology in the works.

---

1. http://www.microsoft.com/microsoft-hololens/
2. http://www.magicleap.com

Early commercial versions of *retinal scanning displays*, such as the MicroVision Nomad, did not find mass adoption in the marketplace. Retinal scanning displays work by drawing a raster image directly onto the retina of the eye, which is the only place where the image actually forms. Users perceive the image as floating in space in front of them. A mobile AR review from 2004 [Höllerer and Feiner 2004] mentions retinal scanning display technology as one of the very few candidates at the time that could produce augmentations with adequate brightness and contrast in direct sunlight outdoors. More recent commercial incarnations of retinal scanning displays include the Brother AiRScouter and the Avegant Glyph; they could give other technologies, such as holographic waveguide optics, a run for their money.

Whatever the actual technology, the hope is that novel displays can address some of the limitations of previous approaches, while maintaining as small and lightweight a footprint as possible. So many factors are important to ensuring an enjoyable and sustainable AR experience that it is difficult to predict which technologies will prevail. Ultimately, ergonomics and convenience of use (lightweight "wearability") need to be right for users to adopt AR and use it on a regular basis. For applications that require users to constantly focus both on the physical world and on virtual 3D augmentations, multifocus image formation (such as that enabled by light fields or holography) would be of some benefit, but may not be an absolute requirement for mass adoption.

In keeping with the spatial display model introduced earlier in this chapter, we illustrate display types with spatial relationship diagrams of their components, starting with OST near-eye displays. Certain parameters can be calibrated offline. They may be assumed to remain constant during operation, even though nonrigid mounting or material deformations may introduce small errors. In our spatial relationship diagrams, we depict such constant and calibrated transformations with an edge labeled **C**. Other parameters change in every frame and need tracking. Such transformations are depicted with an edge labeled **T**. The absence of an edge between two components depicted in a diagram implies that we do not know or do not care about their spatial relationship.

Optical see-through displays are relatively straightforward in terms of the spatial relationships among their fundamental components. Cameras are not necessarily involved. Of course, cameras can be and are often added for the benefit of performing vision-based tracking and scene understanding (as discussed in Chapter 4).

An OST HMD setup usually involves the display being placed at a fixed position relative to the eye. We can track the display relative to the world, while the eye-display transformation must be calibrated in advance or, better, right after putting on the HMD (Figure 2.23). Recent research [Itoh and Klinker 2014] has investigated the use of eye trackers mounted inside the HMD, such that a permanent update of the eye-display calibration is possible. This removes the need for manual calibration and is a robust defense against inadvertently moving the HMD on the head.

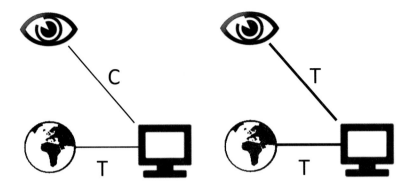

Figure 2.23 (left) Optical see-through head-mounted display. (right) Optical see-through head-mounted display with eye tracking.

Video See-Through Head-Mounted Display

A VST HMD adds one or more video cameras to a non-see-through HMD. With this technology, three components are organized in a rigid configuration: the user's eye, the display, and the camera (Figure 2.24). These components must be calibrated, while the transformation from the rigid assembly to the world must be tracked. This will usually, though not necessarily, be achieved using camera tracking. As with the OST HMD, we can extend this configuration with an eye-tracking device.

One difficulty that all VST HMD designs share is the challenge of a approximating a user's view of the real world, even though the world is now seen via the recordings of video cameras. Of course, it may be deemed acceptable or even advantageous for these cameras to use a field of view or line of sight different from those implied by the display's positioning in front of the

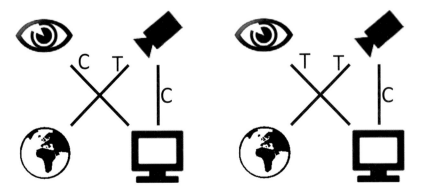

Figure 2.24 (left) Video see-through head-mounted display. (right) Video see-through head-mounted display with eye tracking.

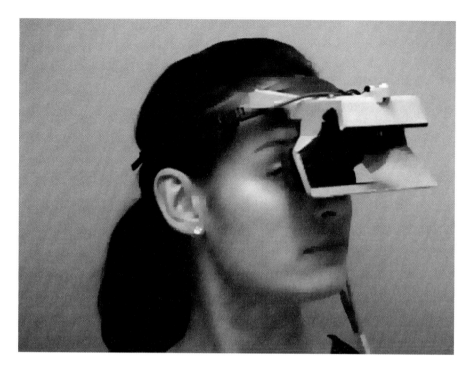

Figure 2.25   Example of VST HMD using cameras above the eyes with mirror optics. Design by Andrei State, 2005. Courtesy of Andrei State, University of North Carolina–Chapel Hill.

viewer's eyes. For example, if Google Glass (see Figure 2.19, middle) was used as a VST display, the display's camera FOV is much wider than the angle subtended by the small inset display window in the corner of the user's eye, so it makes sense to use this wider camera view as a backdrop for AR augmentations. Even in full-immersive experiences, a viewer will adjust readily to optical distortions (or even inversions), as early vision experiments demonstrated [Kohler 1962]. Nevertheless, a video view that is aligned with a user's unmediated view—a so-called parallax-free display—is probably the preferred AR experience, as it does not alter a user's perception of the world, and it emulates the seamless views an OST display would provide.

One design for a parallax-free VST HMD, proposed by State et al. [2005], places two cameras, one for each eye, above the head with a slanted mirror below it to achieve the correct line of sight and field of view of two near-eye displays to which the camera recordings are fed (Figure 2.25). A few years earlier, the Canon MR Laboratory had developed the first commercial HMD of this kind, the COASTAR [Uchiyama et al. 2002] (see Figure 2.14).

The AR Rift [Steptoe et al. 2014] (Figure 2.26) is a more recent example of a VST HMD. Its goal was not to provide exact parallax-free viewing, but rather to carefully align the viewing axes of cameras with the display screen of an Oculus Rift to create a wide-FOV AR display.

Figure 2.26   The AR-Rift, a modified Oculus Rift with two video cameras created by William Steptoe. Courtesy of William Steptoe.

The development of high-quality near-eye displays for VR and AR purposes was, for a long time, seen as a niche market endeavor. Apart from a few notable exceptions (e.g., the Sony Glasstron series from the late 1990s), the production of such displays was not focused on a potential mass market. A game changer regarding the possibilities for high-resolution near-eye displays was the remarkable development of more cost-efficient high-resolution LCD and OLED displays for the mobile device market (smartphones and tablets).

Realizing the general suitability of high-resolution handheld displays as near-eye displays with the addition of simple viewing optics, Mark Bolas and colleagues at the University of Southern California debuted a do-it-yourself cardboard stereoscopic VR viewer and software at the IEEE VR 2012 conference, dubbed the FOV2GO. This technology turned a smartphone into a VR headset, with split stereoscopic views provided by an app. Utilizing the back camera provided by most smartphones, this solution also functions as a VST AR display. Bolas had also developed the WIDE5 virtual reality HMD at Fakespace Labs in 2006, but its sales price of more than $30,000 meant that it was not suitable for the consumer electronics market. With the availability of increasingly affordable high-resolution displays, however, this work directly informed development of other VR and AR HMD endeavors, including the Oculus Rift, Samsung GearVR (see Figure 2.6), and Google Cardboard.

Now that we have reviewed both OST and VST displays, let us revisit our question about the *ideal* near-eye display. It clearly depends on the application and context: Is the use of AR fleeting or continuous over a prolonged period of time? Is it important that the AR device be taken off after use, or can it stay on? Is the location for AR use constrained, or can the AR interaction take place anywhere, indoors as well as outdoors? These are just some of the questions that may influence our answer. The answers may be easier to determine, if there are no technology constraints, and fewer or no tradeoffs must be made. In this case, we probably want an imperceptible (e.g., contact-lens form factor), comfortable (e.g., unnoticeable or even beneficial to eye comfort), convenient (always on and not needing charging or maintenance), optical see-through (not negatively impacting our real-world vision), high-dynamic range (working well in all possible lighting situations), eye-limited resolution (no pixels perceivable), full human visual field of view (no blinders and full overlay FOV) binocular display with true 3D depth (no accommodation–vergence conflict), true occlusion (no ghost-like transparent overlays unless wanted), and all the sensors needed to guarantee rock-solid and stable tracking, scene modeling, and AR application support. And did we mention that this device should cost less than $100?

For details on technical and perceptual issues with existing near-eye AR displays, see the book chapter by Livingston et al. [2013] as well as several survey reports [Kiyokawa 2007] [Rolland and Cakmakci 2009] [Hainich and Bimber 2011] [Kiyokawa 2012] [Kress and Starner 2013].

This concludes our discussion of near-eye displays. A display type of the head-mounted variety that we have not discussed yet is the head-mounted projective display (HMPD), which we will briefly describe when we talk about projection-based AR later in this chapter. But first, we will turn our focus to handheld displays.

Handheld Displays

The rapid development of smartphones and tablet computers has made handheld displays the most popular platform for AR to date. The back-facing camera captures a video for a VST experience (Figure 2.27). Given that the camera is usually pointing straight away from the back of the device, it is usually necessary to hold the device at least at chest height. This pose can lead to fatigue within a rather short period; in addition, it may be difficult to hold the device still enough in this pose to observe all the details. The fact that the display can be stored away when not needed is a mixed blessing. On the one hand, it circumvents the need to permanently wear an AR device, such as on the head. On the other hand, it impacts immediacy, because taking the handheld display out of the pocket may be too cumbersome for short-term usage.

A handheld display houses both the actual display and the camera rigidly mounted in a casing; the transformation from display to camera can be precalibrated. Tracking of the device's pose in the world will be performed through the camera in most cases, but other tracking modalities could also be used.

A recent development proposes user-perspective rather than device-perspective displays (Figure 2.28). That is, rather than showing an augmented video image purely from the camera perspective without any regard to the user's position, the user is also tracked [Hill et al. 2011] [Baričević et al. 2012]. User-to-device tracking can, for example, be performed with the front-facing camera built into many devices. Note that this configuration is considerably more expensive than the conventional device-perspective display. Not only are two separate tracking

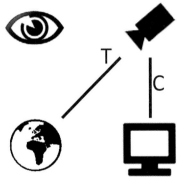

Figure 2.27 A handheld AR display can be built from an unmodified smartphone or tablet computer. Top image: Courtesy of Daniel Wagner.

systems required, but the system also needs to be able to render novel views from the backside camera footage. This can be done either by warping the video from the back-facing camera (which must have a wide enough field of view so that all viewing angles that a user may assume relative to the device are covered with imagery) [Hill et al. 2011] [Tomioka et al. 2013], or by reconstructing the 3D scene that the device is looking at—for example, via depth sensing [Baričević et al. 2012] or stereo reconstruction [Baričević et al. 2014].

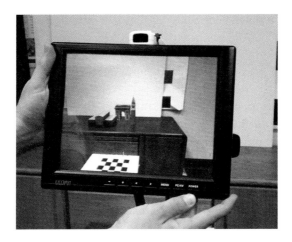

Figure 2.28 (top) Handheld display with device perspective. (middle) Handheld display with user perspective. (bottom) A user-perspective handheld display requires tracking both the camera and the user's viewpoint. Top and middle images: Courtesy of Domagoj Baričević.

With smartphones and tablets finding their way into ever-increasing numbers of pockets and households, and with those devices being key enablers for context-sensitive or "situated" computing, it is no wonder that handheld platforms are driving the vision of AR as a game-changing user interface to the physical world. We will see many more handheld AR application examples in the upcoming chapters. However, it remains to be seen if the video see-through magic lens AR viewing paradigm of handheld devices will truly be an interface that people will continually use, or if new display inventions, such as those in the near-eye or wearable categories, will be necessary to further bootstrap AR. Initial studies that have compared handheld and head-worn AR interfaces for specific tasks, such as visual search and selection [Wither et al. 2007] or mobile AR games [Braun and McCall 2010], have not reported any major advantages for the head-worn approach. In contrast, clear advantages have been reported for head-tracked AR over static instructions (either on a heads-up display or a fixed flat-panel display) in a maintenance and repair task [Henderson and Feiner 2009].

Stationary Displays

Earlier, we mentioned the possibility that with the right *personal* AR display, one could potentially emulate all other physical displays, by simply placing virtual displays at the corresponding locations in AR. Even in such a futuristic scenario, actual physical displays have some obvious benefits, such as their social function as group communication enablers that include non-AR audiences. Also, the world is currently full of displays of various kinds, so we might as well consider them for AR use. In this section, we briefly discuss desktop displays, mirror displays, display showcases, and window/portal displays.

Desktop Displays

The simplest AR display setup is a desktop display. For example, a desktop computer with a tethered webcam (Figure 2.29, top) or a laptop with a built-in webcam (Figure 2.29, bottom) is sufficient to build a VST display. This very economical approach is made possible by using the camera both as a source of video and as a source of tracking information. Therefore, the tracking system must be able to extract the pose of the camera relative to one or more real objects. Of course, the workspace supported by this approach will usually be rather small.

If the user holds the camera in the hand, this setup is sometimes called "eyeball in hand" [Robinett and Holloway 1992]. For convenience, the camera will often be placed on some sort of stationary point, such as a tripod or the monitor bezel. In the latter setup, the optical axis of the camera points in the opposite of the user's viewing direction, leading to a potentially awkward reversal of left and right.

Virtual Mirror

A virtual mirror uses a front-facing camera to take a picture of the user and display it reflected over the vertical axis, so that the impression of looking into a mirror is created. This type of setup is, of course, most appropriate for applications that augment the user in some way—for example,

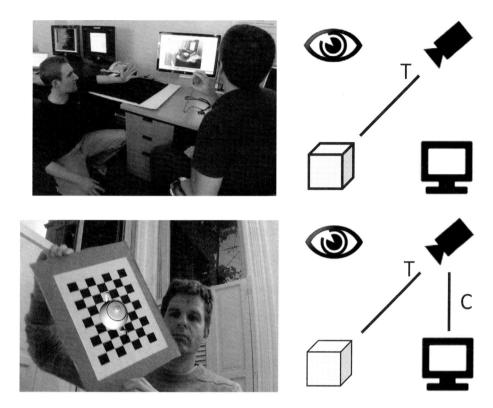

Figure 2.29   (top) A desktop AR display can be built using the eyeball-in-hand metaphor, in which the camera is tracked and its recordings are fed to the display. In the application depicted here, we are tracking the camera relative to an object (user's hand), which is recognized as a marker and subsequently augmented. (bottom) Often, the camera is stationary, covering a working volume, in which augmentations can occur. Again, we are tracking the camera relative to a moving object (checkerboard pattern).

allowing the user to try on virtual clothes or apparel such as eyewear. It can be conveniently implemented using computers that already have a built-in camera for video conferencing. To place objects correctly relative to the user, the user's body and head need to be tracked. This can be done with just one camera or with a multiple-camera setup, as shown in Figure 2.30.

When the screen simply depicts the tracked and augmented user, no matter what the spatial relationship between the user and the screen is, we do not need to track the user's viewpoint (head or eyes) specifically (Figure 2.30, left diagram). In contrast, if we want the display to truly behave like a physical mirror, reflecting the space in front of the display depending on the viewing angle, the user's viewpoint needs to be tracked (Figure 2.30, right diagram). Note that the tracking line from the eye icon in the diagram could also lead to the box, camera, or display icons. There are many equivalent graph representations for these spatial relationship diagrams.

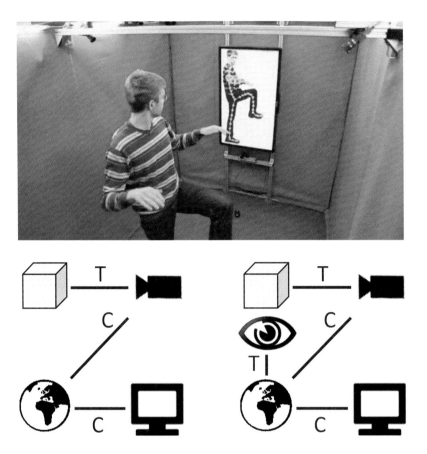

Figure 2.30   (top) Video see-through virtual mirror. Courtesy of Matthias Straka and Stefan Hauswiesner. (bottom) The schematics show that the user (here represented by the box icon, as the augmented object) must be tracked with respect to the camera. If the display always shows the user, independent of viewing angle, the diagram on the left applies. If the display is to emulate an actual mirror, the user's viewpoint must also be tracked, so the diagram on the right applies.

It is also possible to build an OST virtual mirror by combining a flat screen with a semi-transparent mirror (Figure 2.31). In this case, a video camera is not required, since the user's image is optically reflected. However, user tracking is still required.

Virtual Showcase

The virtual showcase [Bimber et al. 2001] is also a type of virtual mirror, but with a different configuration, resembling more a stationary variant of an OST HMD. A semi-transparent mirror separates the observer from the observed object (Figure 2.32). The mirror combines the reflection of a screen mounted above or below, so that the computer-generated image is reflected toward the viewer. A stereoscopic effect is achieved with active shutter glasses. Shutter glasses

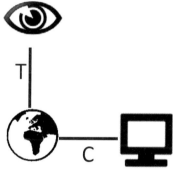

Figure 2.31 (top) Andy Wilson of Microsoft Research showing the HoloFlector. User tracking was done with a Microsoft Kinect. Courtesy of Microsoft Research. (bottom) Optical see-through virtual mirror schematics.

let left and right images pass through in a time-interleaved sequence, synchronized with the display, which presents the appropriate view for either eye.

The virtual showcase requires calibrating the position of the display and the mirror relative to the world, while the transformation from viewer to world (and hence to the mirror) must be tracked.

Window and Portal Displays

A similar set of component dependencies as in the last two cases (tracked user, positionally constant display) arises with an AR window or portal display. Figure 2.33 shows Samsung's 2012 Smart Window prototype; this transparent display operates as a window with a view to a (toy) city scene. Samsung did not actually demonstrate AR on this prototype, but simply provided some touch-operated apps (including virtual blinds). To annotate the city scene behind the

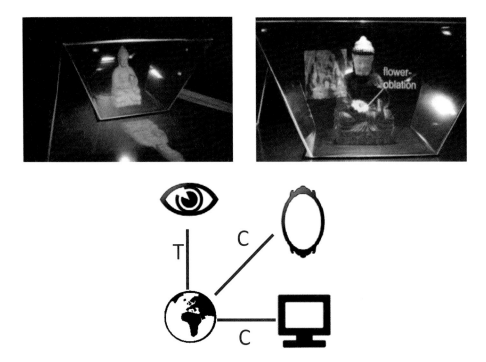

Figure 2.32   (top row) The Virtual Showcase is a stationary optical see-through display intended for exhibitions, museums, and showrooms. Courtesy of Oliver Bimber. (bottom) A virtual showcase requires a tracked user and a careful calibration of display and mirror optics.

window in the correct perspective for an onlooker, that person's viewpoint would need to be tracked. For an example application, Mark Weiser [1991] mentions the possibility of the windows recording the motion paths of people walking by during a day, and playing them back on demand as anonymized electronic trails.

Once the observer's viewpoint is tracked, one can augment the scene behind the window with arbitrary 3D augmentations using a simple portal rendering approach. The user could, for example, play AR video games in which giant monsters stomp around in the front yard.

A transparent display does not necessarily have to be an obstacle for reach-through or walk-through action. Figure 2.34 shows the interactive dual-sided FogScreen [Rakkolainen et al. 2005], which projects interactive imagery onto a dry sheet of fog that users can see and pass through. Using wands or hand tracking, people can interact with objects projected onto the screen from either side. With additional head tracking, content can be rendered from the perspective of the viewer, providing the impression of 3D objects floating in space. As first steps toward realizing a true volumetric fog display, Lee and colleagues [2007] explored this concept using multiple FogScreens and head tracking for a depth-fused 3D effect.

Figure 2.33   Samsung Transparent Smart Window display, showcased at CES 2012.

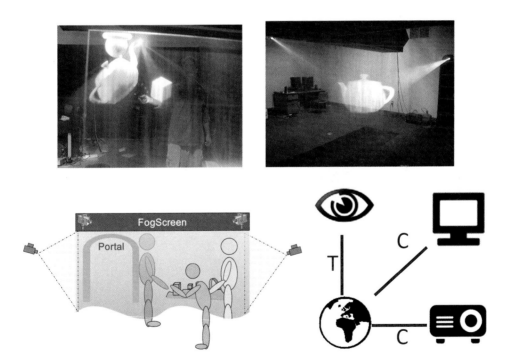

Figure 2.34   (top left) The dual-sided interactive FogScreen at SIGGRAPH 2005. (top right) Two FogScreens in an L-shaped configuration produce a depth-fused 3D rendering of a teapot for a tracked observer. (bottom left) People can augment each other and interact through the screen. (bottom right) Both the screen and the projector are at calibrated positions; the user's viewpoint is tracked (if perspectively correct 3D object rendering is desired).

Projected Displays

With the use of projectors in the FogScreen example, our discussion has entered the realm of projected displays. As projectors become increasingly powerful and affordable, they are breaking out of their traditional application scenarios (movie theaters, classrooms, and auditoriums) to find uses in personal setups and in novel public events involving the projection of special effects and interactive narratives onto outdoor architecture, such as building facades, or factory halls. The latter applications, which are sometimes referred to as *digital projection mapping*, exemplify the concept of spatial augmented reality.

In this section, we briefly review the concepts of spatial augmented reality, both view independent and view dependent. We will discuss the special cases of head-mounted projector displays, dynamic shader lamps, and the Everywhere Displays Projector.

Spatial Augmented Reality

Projectors can be used to create **spatial AR** [Bimber and Raskar 2005] without any explicit displays. With this approach, the projection is directly reflected from the surfaces of real objects, altering their appearance to the naked eye. The projection cannot change the shape of the object, but adds surface details, texture, shadows, and shading, and even the impression of dynamic behavior, if animated content is projected (Figure 2.35).

The success of this approach is obviously dependent on the surface material, which should ideally have a neutral bright color and diffuse reflection properties. Darker or textured materials can be used, but the achievable contrast will suffer. Similarly, the contrast will depend on

Figure 2.35   Spatial AR can be used to turn generic objects into textured models. Courtesy of Michael Marner.

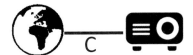

Figure 2.36 Simple spatial AR does not require any tracking, as long as the augmented scene is static.

the overall brightness of the environment. As long as the real world is static, spatial AR does not require any tracking (Figure 2.36). We just need to know the relative position of the projector to the objects, and the geometry of the objects themselves. Tracking is unnecessary, because the augmentations appear directly on the object surfaces, and we assume diffuse reflection.

View-Dependent Spatial Augmented Reality

With the help of active shutter glasses and user tracking (Figure 2.37), spatial AR can be made view dependent [Bimber and Raskar 2005]. This approach lets 3D virtual objects appear anywhere in space—not just on object surfaces.

Multiple projectors can be combined for better spatial coverage [Bimber and Emmerling 2006]. In this case, for every pixel, one can choose the projector delivering the sharpest image—that is, the projector with a focal plane closest to the considered surface point (Figure 2.38).

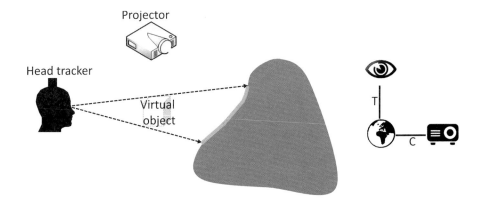

Figure 2.37 View-dependent spatial AR requires tracking the user, but can present free-space 3D objects.

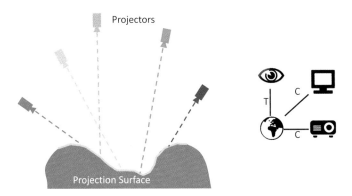

Figure 2.38 (left) Multiple projectors can be combined to minimize pixels projected out of focus. (right) The geometry of the projection surface needs to be known; it is represented here as a display calibrated to the world.

Related recent work has addressed the problem of limited depth of field for a *single* projector. Especially in dynamic situations, it is difficult to completely avoid situations where a single projector is responsible for covering projection over a significant distance along the projection axis. Because of the limited depth of field, this scenario leads to areas in the projection mapping that are considerably out of focus. To remedy this problem, Ma and colleagues [2013] propose "high-rank coded aperture projectors," employing high-speed spatial light modulators on the image plane and in the aperture of modified projectors. Iwai and colleagues [2015] place an electrical focus tunable lens in front of the projector's objective and perform a fast forward and backward sweep through the focusing distance range, at a speed imperceptible to a human observer. A single offline measurement of the point spread function for the projected pixels is sufficient to calculate and apply a focus adjustment within the sweep range.

Head-Mounted Projector Displays

As an alternative to placing the projectors into the environment, one might integrate them into a headset. This setup was demonstrated as early as 1997 [Kijima and Ojika 1997], and projector technology has been considerably miniaturized since then. This approach is often used in combination with retro-reflective screens. Retro-reflective materials are commonly used for traffic signs and high-visibility clothing, as they reflect the majority of an incoming illumination back to the illumination source, rather than scattering or mirroring it (Figure 2.39, top). When head-mounted projector displays (HMPD) are used in conjunction with retro-reflective material in the environment, this technology can produce personalized views and even separate views for each eye in case of 3D stereoscopic imagery [Inami et al. 2000] [Rolland et al. 2005]. Because nearly all of the projected light is reflected back to the viewer, the projection is invisible for onlookers at other viewing angles, and the projector's luminance is optimally used for a personal image.

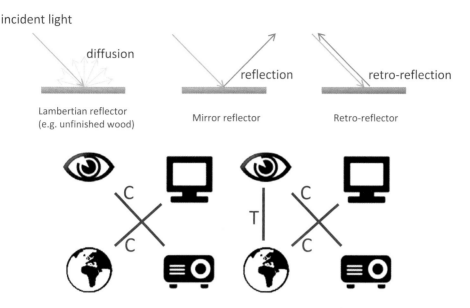

incident light

diffusion

reflection

retro-reflection

Lambertian reflector
(e.g. unfinished wood)

Mirror reflector

Retro-reflector

Figure 2.39   (top) Retro-reflective materials send incident rays back to the illuminating source, so they work well with head-mounted projector displays. (bottom) Spatial relationship schematics for HMPDs without and with head tracking. In the latter case (shown at right), virtual objects can be kept stable in space, while the viewer is moving.

Using this approach, it is also possible to camouflage objects, by projecting onto them a video representation of the scene behind the objects. This illusion works well as long as the video camera is aligned with the viewing direction [Inami et al. 2000]. The luminance of the head-mounted projectors can be adjusted such that projection onto non-retro-reflective surfaces is imperceptible to everyone, including the wearer of the display. This leads to the potential for correct occlusion effects. For example, the user's hands would correctly occlude a virtual object projected onto a retro-reflective surface behind the hand. 3D objects floating in space can be realized by using stereoscopy, with two projectors mounted on the viewer's head. To see such objects static in space while moving around, the user's head needs to be tracked (Figure 2.39, bottom right), and much of the environment needs to be covered with retro-reflective material to allow for arbitrary vantage points. Some occlusion effects involving such space-stabilized virtual objects would still be incorrect. For example, a non-retro-reflective interference object behind the virtual image, but in front of the retro-reflective screen, would break the illusion and incorrectly appear to occlude the virtual object.

Dynamic Shader Lamps

A variant of spatial AR with object tracking (Figure 2.40) rather than user tracking has been introduced under the name **dynamic shader lamps** [Bandyopadhyay et al. 2001].

The tracking information makes it possible to project dynamic content on a moving object. As shown in Figure 2.41, this can, for example, be used to "paint with light" or project convincing facial expressions on the head of an animatronic character [Lincoln et al. 2010].

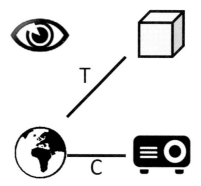

Figure 2.40   Dynamic shader lamps deliver spatial AR on tracked objects.

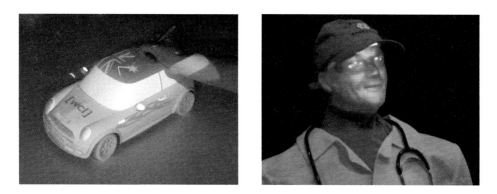

Figure 2.41   Two applications of dynamic shader lamps. (left) Painting with light on real surfaces. Courtesy of Michael Marner. (right) Animatronic character with animated facial projection. Courtesy of Greg Welch, University of North Carolina–Chapel Hill.

Everywhere Displays Projector

While spatial AR supports a moving user, and dynamic shader lamps support moving objects, we can also allow the projector to move. The Everywhere Displays Projector [Pinhanez 2001], which features this capability, is coupled with a tracked pan-tilt platform (Figure 2.42).

By changing the pose of the mirror, the system can reach every surface in an environment with its projection. This allows effects similar to spatial AR, but with a much larger working volume and the option of displaying augmentations that change position over time (Figure 2.43). Beamatron [Wilson et al. 2012], for example, combines a motorized projector with depth sensors to facilitate full-body tracking and display on the body.

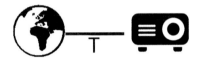

Figure 2.42   A steerable, tracked projector can display images anywhere.

Figure 2.43   The Everywhere Displays Projector is based on tracked, steerable projection and can deliver content on any surface. For example, navigational hints can be displayed on product shelves. Courtesy of Claudio Pinhanez (copyright IBM 2001).

Summary

This chapter explored displays for augmented reality. Such displays must be able to combine virtual and real, which can occur in different modalities. Most AR research has been pursued in the visual domain, but there has also been a research focus on audio AR. Our other human senses, particularly haptics, are playing an increasing role in realistic augmented experiences as well. State-of-the-art AR displays focus on visual augmentations, supported by spatial audio.

As part of our discussion of this topic, we reviewed the basics of visual perception and considered the main requirements for, and characteristics of, visual AR displays. Visual AR can be achieved either via optical see-through or video see-through approaches, or through spatial projection. Many immersion parameters are important for delivering a useful AR experience, including ocularity, field of view, brightness and contrast, occlusion, latency, focus mechanism, resolution, and the size and comfort of the display technology.

We organized AR displays based on their placement relative to the user—on the head, on the body (including handheld), or in the environment. The last class encompasses both stationary and projected displays. No single type of display can accommodate every possible use case. While handheld displays, through their sheer ubiquity and economies of scale, brought the idea and potential of AR technologies to everybody's awareness, head-worn displays, through advanced technological and ergonomic innovations, might represent the next wave of AR, but are still vying for widespread acceptance. In particular, light-field displays represent a promising new approach, taking advantage of the increasingly high pixel resolutions of contemporary microdisplays.

We introduced a spatial model to characterize the coordinate transformations and relationships implied by different display technologies. The schematic diagrams we provided for every new type of display summarize the main tracked or fixed coordinate relationships among the chief AR experience components—that is, user, display, camera, and world, and, with spatial AR, projector and object. These foreshadow the crucial topic of tracking technologies, which we will discuss in Chapter 3.

TRACKING

Tracking refers to the dynamic determination of spatial properties at runtime. Commonly, in the context of AR, tracking an entity means that the entity's position and orientation are measured continuously. One can track different entities: a user's head, eyes, or limbs, for example, or an AR device such as a camera or display, or any object populating the AR scene. In this chapter, we explain general characteristics of tracking and discuss various tracking technologies. We begin with stationary systems, continue with mobile sensors, and discuss optical tracking in detail. Finally, we give a brief introduction to fusion of tracking data from multiple sensors.

Tracking, Calibration, and Registration

In the context of AR, three important terms are associated with the measurement and alignment of objects—tracking, calibration, and registration. These terms overlap in practical use, so we will clarify their meanings as used in this book (Figure 3.1).

To briefly introduce these terms, it is important to recognize their differences. *Registration* refers to the alignment of spatial properties. Objects "registered in AR" are aligned to each other in some coordinate system. Accurate registration of virtual information with physical scene objects in a user's perception is a typical goal of AR systems. *Calibration* is the offline adjustment of measurements [Wloka 1995]. Calibration correlates the readings of a sensor or instrument with those of a standard so as to check and adjust the sensor's accuracy. Calibration is responsible for static registration and is necessary for many nonspatial parameters of tracking systems, while *tracking* is responsible for dynamic registration.

More specifically, **tracking** is a term used to describe dynamic sensing and measuring of AR systems. To display virtual objects registered to real objects in three-dimensional space, we must know at least the relative pose—that is, the position and orientation of the AR display relative to the real objects. Because AR operates in real time, pose measurements must be continuously updated (tracked over time). In the field of AR, "tracking" is generally synonymous

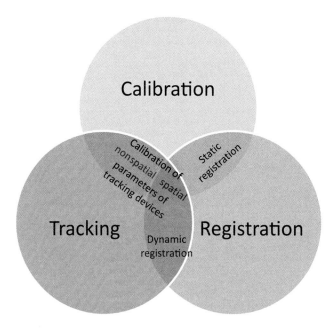

Figure 3.1 An AR system must address three important, overlapping concepts: tracking, registration, and calibration.

with "3D tracking" of the three-dimensional position or the six-dimensional pose (position and orientation) of real entities, as opposed to the idea of tracking two-dimensional objects in image space, which is common in traditional computer vision.

Calibration is the process of comparing measurements made with two different devices, a reference device and a device to be calibrated. The reference device can be replaced with a known reference value or, for geometric measurements, with a known coordinate system. The objective is to determine parameters for using the device to be calibrated to deliver measurements on the known scale. For AR, we need to calibrate the components of the AR system, especially the devices used for tracking.

While tracking means performing measurements continuously, calibration is usually carried out only at discrete times. Depending on the measurement system, calibration may be done just once in a device's lifetime (typically during or after manufacturing), every time before commencing operation, or concurrently with tracking. This last case is not limited to discrete times and, therefore, requires unsupervised execution of the calibration procedure, to avoid disrupting normal use of the tracking. Consequently, it is often called autocalibration. We will discuss calibration procedures for AR in more depth in Chapter 5. In the remainder of this chapter, we operate on the assumption that devices have been properly calibrated.

Registration in AR refers to the alignment of coordinate systems between virtual and real objects [Holloway 1997]. Specifically, see-through displays should show computer graphics elements such that they align with real-world objects. This requires tracking of the user's head or of the camera providing a video background (or both). Obtaining **static registration**, when the user or the camera is *not* moving, requires calibration of the tracking system so as to establish a common coordinate system between virtual and real object. Obtaining **dynamic registration**, when the user or the camera is moving, requires tracking.

Coordinate Systems

In AR, we usually rely on a standard computer graphics pipeline to produce overlays on the real world [Robinett et al. 1995]. Independent of the kind of AR display for which frames are captured, rendered, and composited (see Chapter 2), this pipeline consists of a model transformation, a view transformation, and a projective transformation (Figure 3.2).

Registration implies that the cumulative effect of these transformations must be matched between the real and the virtual. How we deal with the individual transformations depends on the configuration of the AR system and the tracking technology. Certain parameters can be calibrated offline, whereas other parameters change on a frame-by-frame basis and need tracking.

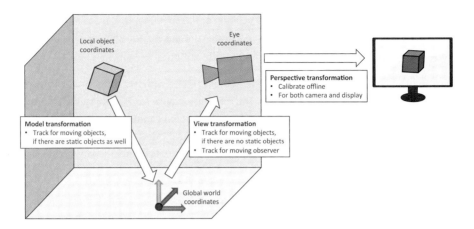

Figure 3.2 AR needs to consider multiple transformation systems. The model transformation describes the pose of moving objects in a static environment. The view transformation describes the pose of a camera, a tracking sensor, or a display in an environment. The perspective transformation describes the mapping from eye coordinates to screen coordinates. Both the model and view transformations can be tracked, enabling registration.

Model Transformation

The model transformation describes the relationship of 3D local object coordinates and 3D global world coordinates. The model transformation determines where objects are placed in the real world. Virtual objects are controlled by the application and do not require tracking, except in very rare situations. For example, object tracking is needed when only an augmented video stream is available from which to derive tracking.

Real objects can be part of a static real scene or can be allowed to move. Static real scenes do not require a model transformation. For every moving real object in the scene with which we want to register virtual information, we must track its model transformation. However, many AR scenarios deal only with moving objects independent of any global coordinate system, in particular when using markers. In this case, we do not need a separate world coordinate system and can use one view transformation per tracked real object instead.

View Transformation

The view transformation describes the relationship of 3D global world coordinates and 3D camera coordinates. Most AR scenarios allow an observer to move in the real world. There-fore, tracking the view transformation is the most important objective. AR typically requires a separate viewing transformation for the camera and the display of the user. If only a single camera needs to be tracked in a video see-through device, no display calibration may be neces-sary. However, other systems—in particular, systems using stereoscopic displays—may require calibration of camera and display.

Projective Transformation

The projective transformation describes the relationship of 3D camera coordinates and 2D device coordinates. Typically, the content of the view frustum (truncated pyramid) is mapped to a unit cube and then projected onto the screen by dropping the Z component and applying a viewport transformation (for obtaining screen units in the correct aspect ratio). The projective transformation is usually calibrated offline. This needs to be done for each camera and each display separately.

Frames of Reference

The previously described transformations define object, world, and eye coordinate systems. Virtual information can be fixed with respect to the global world, a (potentially moving) object, or a person's view (the AR screen). With the user's body as a special case object, we can speak of *world-stabilized*, *object-stabilized* (or in the special case, *body-stabilized*), and *screen-stabilized* information [Feiner et al. 1993b] [Billinghurst et al. 1998a].

We illustrate these concepts with a hypothetical scenario, illustrated in Figure 3.3. Assume that the person in the picture is using a navigational system that he experiences through AR glasses.

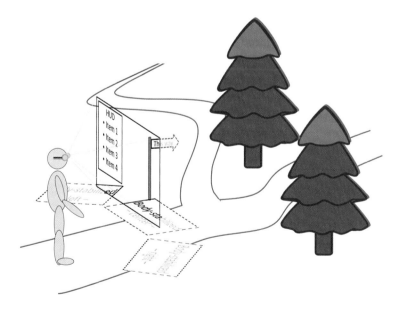

Figure 3.3   Reference frames for mobile AR: Heads-up displays (HUD), which always stay in the user's view, are examples of *screen-stabilized* elements. Annotations that "live" in the 3D world, such as the virtual blue signpost, are *world-stabilized* elements. Annotations that move with the user, but maintain a specific position relative to the body, are *body-stabilized* elements (i.e., the three horizontal windows at the user's knee level, which could show maps, images of destination points, or branch decisions).

The AR interface keeps him informed of his destination, indicates his progress along the chosen route, and helps him make the correct turn decisions. The glasses let him see annotations of the world in front of him, such as the (virtual) blue signpost, which indicates the correct continuation of his path at a branch point. That signpost, which is invisible to anyone not looking through the user's AR glasses, is a world-stabilized AR element, because it behaves just like a physical world object. The user can walk up to (or around) the signpost, which stays stable in the scene.

This AR system also provides a heads-up display (HUD). It appears as a window in the top left corner of the user's AR view. It always stays on the screen as a screen-stabilized AR element. It can, for example, provide menu options that the user might select at any point in time (via any kind of interaction mechanism, such as voice commands, a wearable trackpad, or even eye tracking). Via the menu, the user could, for example, change the preferred route.

Finally, this AR system features body-stabilized AR elements: The three windows at the user's knee level could show, for example, an illustration of the correct continuation for this branch point in the center, a map view with the current trip progress overlaid on the left, and a picture of the final destination on the right. These three panels move with the user when he is walking; in other words, they always stay at the same distance and orientation with respect to the user's body. However, the user can focus on any of the three panels by just looking at them—his head-motion is independent of this body-stabilized information. Usually, to implement this kind of body-stabilized information, the body's orientation needs to be tracked in addition to the head pose.

Characteristics of Tracking Technology

In the previous section, we established *what* to track. In this section, we will examine *how* to track. We begin by discussing the characteristics of tracking technologies. Measurement systems used in tracking can employ a variety of physical phenomena and arrangement options. These choices determine which coordinate systems are being measured, and affect which temporal and spatial properties the tracking has.

Physical Phenomena

Measurements can exploit electromagnetic radiation (including visible light, infrared light, laser light, radio signals, and magnetic flux), sound, physical linkage, gravity, and inertia [Meyer et al. 1992] [Rolland et al. 2001] [Welch and Foxlin 2002]. Specialized sensors are available for each of these physical phenomena.

Measurement Principle

We can measure signal strength, signal direction, and time of flight (both absolute time and phase of a periodic signal). Note that time-of-flight measurements require some form of secondary communication channel to confirm clock synchronization between sender and receiver. Moreover, we can measure electromechanical properties.

Measured Geometric Property

We can measure either distances or angles. This decision influences the mathematical methods we apply to the measurements [Liu et al. 2007]. **Trilateration** is a geometric method for determining locations of points from at least three measured distances, while **triangulation** determines locations of points from two or more measured angles, assuming at least one known distance (Figure 3.4). Knowing the position of three or more points of a rigid object also allows for recovering both the position and the orientation of the object.

Sensor Arrangement

A common approach is to use multiple sensors together in a known rigid geometric configuration, such as a stereo camera rig. Such a configuration can either be sparse, if only a few sensors are used, or in the form of a dense 2D array, such as a digital camera sensor with millions of pixels. Sometimes, it is important to arrange three sensors orthogonally to measure vector-valued quantities, such as acceleration in three fundamental directions. If multiple-sensor configurations are used, then either we need **sensor synchronization** to ensure simultaneous acquisition of measurements, or we need to deal with the fact that measurements from two sensors are taken at slightly different times. The process of combining multiple sensor inputs to obtain a more complete or more accurate measurement is referred to as **sensor fusion** (see the "Sensor Fusion" section at the end of this chapter).

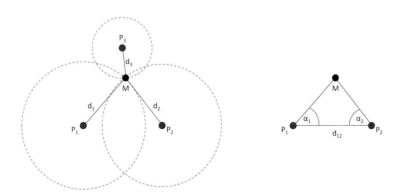

Figure 3.4   (left) Trilateration computes the position of a point M from the known distances d_1, d_2, d_3 to the points P_1, P_2, P_3 by intersection of three spheres. (right) Triangulation determines the position of a point M from two angles α_1 at P_1 and α_2 at P_2 and one known distance d_{12} between P_1 and P_2.

Signal Sources

Sources provide the signal that is picked up by the sensors. Like sensors, sources must be positioned in a known geometric configuration. Sources can be either passive or active.

Passive sources rely on natural signals present in the environment, such as natural light or the Earth's magnetic field. When no external source is apparent, such as in inertial sensing, the signaling method is described as **sourceless sensing** [Bachmann and McGhee 2003].

Active sources rely on some form of electronics to produce a physical signal. Most types of active sources, such as acoustic, optical, and certain radiowave sources, require an open line of sight for the signal to travel to the sensor unperturbed. Active sources can further be categorized into direct active sources, where the source is mounted on the object of interest, and indirect active sources, where the object merely reflects the signal from a source located somewhere else in the environment. In the case of indirect active sources, we must know the geometric properties of the reflecting points on the object of interest, rather than of the sources themselves.

Degrees of Freedom

In measuring systems, a **degree of freedom** (DOF) is an independent dimension of measurement. Registering real and virtual objects in three-dimensional space usually requires determining the pose of objects with six degrees of freedom (6DOF): three degrees of freedom for position and three degrees of freedom for orientation. For most AR applications, one would ideally use tracking systems that deliver full 6DOF. However, certain sensors and technologies deliver only 3DOF orientation (for example, a gyroscope), or only 3DOF position (for example, a single tracked LED), or just one or two specific degrees of freedom (for example, an odometer). These technologies can still be attractive for AR because of specific advantages, such as a high update rate or small form factor. They can be used in combination with other types of sensors to address all input requirements an AR application may have.

Measurement Coordinates

Tracking measures physical quantities relative to a given coordinate system. The choice of coordinate system depends on the tracking technology, but has significant implications for the way the data is used in an AR application.

Global versus Local

We distinguish global from local coordinate systems. *Local* implies a smaller-scale coordinate system established by the user, possibly employing an ad hoc approach. For example, we may measure position relative to a corner of the room we are in. *Global* implies worldwide measurements (or at least very wide area, such as entire-city scale), which is still relative, but with respect to the entire planet. For example, a compass measures heading relative to the Earth's magnetic field.

A global coordinate system allows for a wider range of operation and, therefore, more freedom of movement. Moreover, for the purposes of AR, external geo-registered information, such as data from GIS databases, can be directly used for virtual objects. In contrast, a local coordinate system, with its smaller scale and dedicated short-distance sensor infrastructure, will likely deliver better accuracy and precision of measurements. A user may establish a local coordinate system by placing virtual objects relative to a movable artifact (e.g., a visual tracking marker) in the user's immediate environment without requiring input from a geo-registered database.

Absolute versus Relative

We also distinguish absolute from relative measurements. *Absolute* measurement (e.g., measurement of a moving object's pose) implies that the reference coordinate system is set in advance, while *relative* measurement means that the reference coordinate system is established dynamically (e.g., relative to a previous pose). An example of relative measurement is incremental sensing. A common pattern for incremental sensors, such as a computer mouse, is that they report the difference since the last measurement. Despite the mobility afforded by a self-contained moving sensor, relative measurements are more difficult to exploit in AR, because registration of real and virtual usually is expected to be fixed and not continuously changing. The need to convert relative to absolute measurements typically has a negative effect on precision.

Spatial Sensor Arrangement

Two fundamental types of spatial arrangements for tracking systems exist: outside-in versus inside-out (Figure 3.5) [Allen et al. 2001].

Outside-in tracking means that sensors are mounted stationary in the environment and observe a moving target, such as a head-worn display. Sensors can easily be arranged such that a proper angle for triangulation is guaranteed, which allows for precise position measurement. If orientation measurements are obtained by sensing the position of three or more points on the tracked target, orientation tracking results may not quite be as well conditioned because

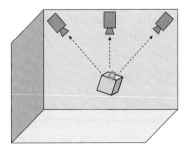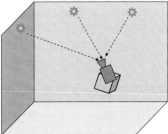

Figure 3.5 The distinction between outside-in and inside-out tracking is made based on where the sources and sensors are placed. In this example, we consider LED beacons as sources and cameras as sensors. (left) Outside-in tracking uses sensors mounted stationary in the environment. (right) Inside-out tracking uses sensors mounted to a mobile or body-worn device.

of the small angular differences from a single sensor in the environment to these points. The outside-in approach has the advantage that users are mostly unaffected by sensor properties, such as weight or power consumption, and that multiple sensors can be used. However, it requires an instrumented environment, and it confines the user to a limited workspace. Both of these limitations are problematic issues for truly mobile AR.

In contrast, inside-out tracking means that sensors move with the tracked object and observe stationary references in the environment. These references can usually be spaced sufficiently far apart to allow for precise measurement of orientation, but position measurements are not quite as well conditioned, especially when tracking across a wide area. Stationary references do not have to be active sources, or even be placed by the user. In fact, computer vision–based tracking is often concerned with pose estimation of a moving camera in a completely unprepared environment (see Chapter 4). Moving sensors support mobile AR well and make the user more independent of any stationary infrastructure. However, the weight, size, and number of sensors are restricted to the capacity afforded by the mobile setup.

Workspace Coverage

Among the tracking technologies that use local measurements, the range (or working volume) of the sensor is an important characteristic. While some sensors can cover a maximum distance of only 1 m (for example, short-range magnetic trackers), others can operate at wide ranges, covering perhaps a hallway (for example, the 3rdTech HiBall), a hangar, or, as in the case of GPS, even the entire Earth's surface. While a larger range is clearly desirable for mobile applications, a tradeoff between range and accuracy is usually required.

Ideally, users would like to freely roam through an arbitrary large environment, both indoors and outdoors, and be free of encumbering artifacts, such as tethers for electronic devices. Tracking systems, however, typically rely on some sort of infrastructure. This infrastructure can either be composed of active devices, such as outside-in tracking systems, or passive targets, such as fiducial targets mounted in the environment or carried by the user. If no physical infrastructure is available, at least a digital model of the relevant real objects or the user is needed, so that a tracking system can detect them. A model of the environment can be constructed in parallel with tracking, as in the case of simultaneous localization and mapping (see the Section "Model-Based versus Model-Free Tracking" and Chapter 4).

Measurement Error

Real-world sensors are subject to both systematic and random measurement errors. Systematic measurement error, such as a static offset, a scale factor error, or a systematic deviation from ideal measurements because of predictable or measurable influences of the environment (e.g., ferromagnetic material in the covered area of a magnetic tracker), can be addressed by improved calibration efforts. Random measurement error, also called noise or jitter, results from uncontrolled influences on the sensing system, and is usually assumed to have a Gaussian distribution. Accuracy, precision, and resolution are important error characteristics of any tracking system.

The **accuracy** of a measurement is determined by how close the measurement is to the true value of the quantity being measured. It is affected by systematic errors and, therefore, can be improved with better calibration techniques, albeit often at a much elevated cost and effort. Such expense is not always justified in a particular situation or use case.

The **precision** of a measurement is defined as how closely a number of measurements of the same quantity agree with each other. Precision varies with the sensor type and with individual degrees of freedom. The precision is impacted by random measurement error. Random error can be limited with filtering techniques, but usually at increased computational cost and higher latency.

The **resolution** of a sensor is the minimum difference that can be discriminated between two measurements. For example, a spatial resolution of 0.01 mm in a position tracker means that the position of a moving probe would be sensed by the tracker in increments of 0.01 mm. (Of course, to actually see an update rate at such a resolution limit, the probe would have to move exceedingly slowly.) Because it assumes the absence of static or dynamic errors, resolution is a theoretical property that is often unachievable in practice. In fact, noise is often much larger than a given resolution limit, especially for cheap sensors.

Temporal Characteristics

There are two important temporal characteristics of tracking systems: update rate and latency. The **update rate** (or temporal resolution) is the number of measurements performed per given time interval. **Latency** is the time it takes from the occurrence of a physical event, such as a motion, to a corresponding data record becoming available to the AR application. Of the two temporal characteristics, latency is arguably the more critical one for real-time applications such as AR, because it determines more directly how much dynamic error is introduced on a system level. The human user expects the system to react immediately and without noticeable delay [Wloka 1995]. Latency will cause virtual objects that should stay registered to physical objects to lag behind when there is object or camera motion, causing unpleasant and disturbing effects. A 60-Hz display requires updates within a time interval of less than 17 ms, which places a tight upper limit on the latency, if target frames must not be missed. Note that *end-to-end* latency encompasses not only the physical measurement of the sensor and the transmission to the host computer, but also all processing required to deliver the AR display to the end user.

Stationary Tracking Systems

In the previous section, we saw that there are many choices in the design of a tracking system. These choices determine the usefulness of a particular tracking system for a given use case. For example, a tradeoff between performance and cost is often required. Another important trade-off concerns the size, weight, and power consumption of the tracking system. It is much easier to build a system that does not have to be portable or mobile. Not surprisingly, then, stationary tracking systems were the first to become popular for virtual reality applications, emerging in the 1990s [Meyer et al. 1992] [Rolland et al. 2001]. Mechanical tracking, electromagnetic track-ing, and ultrasonic tracking systems, because of their stationary nature, are not very popular for AR today. Nevertheless, these systems are useful to understand some basic principles of tracking.

Mechanical Tracking

Mechanical tracking, which is probably the oldest technique, builds on mechanical engineer-ing methods that are very well understood. Usually, the end-effector of an articulated arm with two to four limbs is tracked (Figure 3.6). This requires knowledge of the extent of every limb and measurement of the angles at every joint. Joints can have one, two, or three degrees of freedom in orientation, which are measured using rotary encoders or potentiometers. From the known length of the limbs and the angular measurements of the joints, a mathematical formulation of a kinematic chain can be set up to determine the position and orientation of the end-effector.

This approach delivers high precision and a fast update rate, but the freedom of operation is severely limited by the mechanical structure. Moreover, most mechanical tracking systems can provide measurements only for a single point. The measurements may involve position only or may include both position and orientation. However, movement constraints of the limbs may

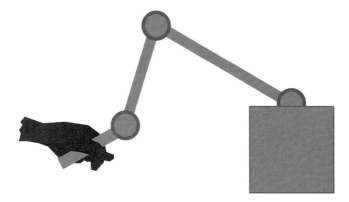

Figure 3.6 Example of a mechanical articulated arm using an arrangement of limbs and joints (here: three each). The angles at the joints are sensed. Such a setup can also provide force feedback.

prevent the arm from reaching the full range of orientations. Thus, mechanical tracking can be seen as an outside-in setup with a severely restricted workspace. For AR, it is undesirable to have the articulated arm in the field of view, where virtual or real objects should be placed.

Mechanical tracking systems are typically found as part of expensive laboratory equipment, and are generally not appropriate for casual users. In turn, mechanical tracking is rarely used for AR today. Nevertheless, due to its high precision, mechanical tracking is sometimes used for calibration or evaluation of other tracking systems.

Electromagnetic Tracking

Electromagnetic tracking uses a stationary source producing three orthogonal magnetic fields (Figure 3.7). Position and orientation are measured simultaneously from magnetic field strength and direction using small tethered sensors equipped with three orthogonal coils. Decreasing field strength with distance and tether length of the sensors typically limit the operating range to a hemisphere of 1–3 m diameter.

In terms of the direction of signal travel, magnetic tracking can be categorized as an inside-out approach. However, the relatively small workspace and tethered sensors do not support as much freedom of operation as other inside-out approaches do. One noteworthy advantage of magnetic tracking is that it does not require an open line of sight; consequently, it can handle occlusions. At the same, it is easily disturbed by ferromagnetic materials and other electromagnetic disturbances in the vicinity. Overall, magnetic tracking approaches are rarely used for AR today.

Figure 3.7   The Razer Hydra is a short-range magnetic tracking device designed for desktop use. The 6DOF pose of two handheld joystick controllers is tracked relative to the spherical base.

Ultrasonic Tracking

Ultrasonic tracking measures the time of flight of a sound pulse traveling from source to sensor. If a separate (wired or infrared) synchronization channel is available, three measurements are sufficient for trilateration. Otherwise, additional measurements are necessary. Multiple ultrasonic sensors can pick up a signal simultaneously, but multiple sources must send their pulses sequentially to avoid interference. This factor, together with the modest speed of sound, limits the update rate to 10–50 measurements per second, which must be shared for all tracked objects. Further limitations include the requirement of an open line of sight for clear reception, susceptibility to disturbances from loud environmental noises, and dependence of the speed of sound on air temperature.

Both outside-in and inside-out configurations exist. Noteworthy early ultrasonic tracking systems included the Intersense IS-600 and IS-900 family of devices [Foxlin et al. 1998], which overcame the relatively slow update rate of ultrasonic transmission through fusion with much faster inertial sensors. Another well-known outside-in configuration is the Bat system (Figure 3.8) developed by AT&T Research Cambridge [Newman et al. 2001]. With this system, wireless emitters, usually worn around the neck, emit a pulse that is picked up by receivers installed in the ceiling tiles throughout an office environment. The signals are coded so that the emitters can uniquely be assigned to a person. Three Bat emitters on a helmet can be combined for full 6DOF head tracking. Bat was the first multiperson wide-area indoor tracking system, but its use requires an elaborate stationary infrastructure.

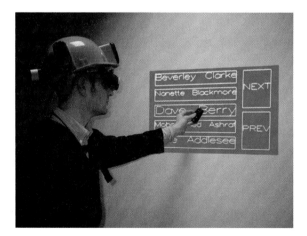

Figure 3.8   The AT&T Bat system was an ultrasonic outside-in tracking system. Three Bat emitters are mounted on a helmet. One emitter in the hand serves as a pointer. Receivers are mounted to the ceiling, and a time-sharing approach allows tracking over wide areas, such as an entire building. Courtesy of Joseph Newman.

Mobile Sensors

While stationary tracking systems are suitable for certain types of VR applications that do not require a user to move much, tracking systems for AR should be mobile. Unfortunately, AR users roaming an unconstrained environment—in particular, outdoors—cannot expect control over the physical infrastructure. Likewise, outdoor users cannot rely on constant quality of wireless services. Consequently, both sensing and computation for tracking must be performed locally on the mobile device, usually without the aid of infrastructure in the environment. This limits the applicable techniques to the ones that can operate with mobile sensors and limited processing power.

Modern mobile devices such as smartphones or tablets are equipped with an array of sensors. While the performance of these sensors is strongly limited by external constraints, the sensors present a significant opportunity, because they are integrated into inexpensive devices and continuously available. We will first consider nonvisual sensors here: Global Positioning System, wireless networking, magnetometers, gyroscopes, linear accelerometers, and odometers. We progress to optical tracking systems in the next section, "Optical Tracking."

Global Positioning System

Global navigation satellite systems—in particular, the Global Positioning System (GPS) developed by the United States [Getting 1993]—measure the time of flight of coded radio signals emitted by satellites in Earth orbit, essentially representing a planet-sized inside-out system (Figure 3.9). If signals from four or more satellites with known current positions in orbit can be

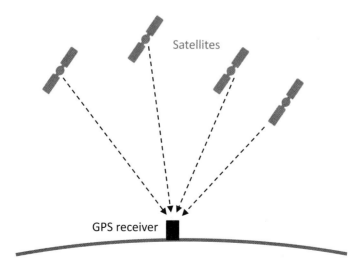

Figure 3.9 Satellite navigation systems such as GPS measure the time of flight of signals received from multiple orbital satellites and determine the position of a mobile receiver through trilateration.

received, it is possible to compute the current position on the Earth's surface. The accuracy of this measurement can vary widely, from 1 to 100 m, depending on the number of visible satellites, the circumstances of signal reception, and the quality of the receiver.

In principle, a 3D position can be estimated, but often only longitude and latitude are used, while height, which is more significantly affected by measurement error, is occasionally considered. Reliable indoor reception is usually not possible, because satellite signals are reflected off walls and lead to multi-path signal propagation, from which position cannot be reliably recovered. Orientation cannot be determined with GPS, but rather must be obtained from other sensors.

Higher accuracy can be obtained with differential GPS (DGPS). DGPS uses a separate correction signal received from ground stations measuring the current atmospheric distortions affecting signal propagation (Figure 3.10). Correction signals are available through commercial services, but require a permanent Internet connection (or an additional radio link) for operating the mobile GPS device.

Real-time kinematics (RTK) GPS further improves the accuracy of DGPS down to an error of just a few centimeters by additionally measuring the phase of the signal. However, RTK has historically required large-sized receivers, typically with diameters of 10 cm or more. Even today, "lightweight" systems are still palm-sized and can weigh as much as 1 kg. Thus, the technology is still too bulky for integration into smartphones and too expensive for consumer products (several thousands of dollars). This is changing, however, as the RTK processing can be shifted

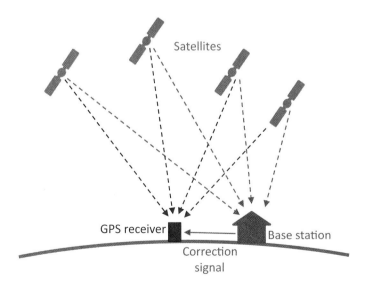

Figure 3.10 Differential GPS improves position accuracy by compensating for measurement errors caused by atmospheric distortions. Correction signals are computed by a network of nearby base stations and transmitted over a wireless network.

to smartphone computations and networked RTK (NRTK) protocols are becoming standardized [Hwang et al. 2012].

GPS measures position only, and update rates are typically 1, 5, or 10 Hz (updates per second). More recent consumer chipsets have achieved an update rate of 50 Hz. GPS is popular in current consumer location-based service applications, but by itself is not fit for high-accuracy tracking, like that required for very precise registration in AR. Recent tests have shown smartphone GPS accuracy to be 5–10 m in urban canyons, and 0.5–5 m in open areas [Dabove and Petovello 2014]. Even so, its global availability makes it attractive as a constraining complement to other positioning techniques, such as computer vision (see Chapter 4). On modern smartphones, GPS is also combined with other sensing techniques, such as inertial sensing and wireless networking signal strength calculations.

Wireless Networks

Existing wireless network infrastructures, such as WiFi, Bluetooth, and mobile phone networks, can be used to determine one's position [Hightower and Borriello 2001]. Every base station offering wireless networking broadcasts a unique identifier (ID), which can be looked up in a database associating this ID with a position on a map. Mobile phones, which are already able to communicate in these networks, are commonly fitted with the ability to infer coarse global position from identified base wireless networks.

The simplest approach to positioning uses only the ID of observed base stations. Improved results can be obtained by measuring the signal strength of base stations to estimate distances and apply geometric reasoning based on trilateration. Unfortunately, dedicated tracking base stations add to the cost of the infrastructure and, consequently, are rarely available. If fewer than three base stations are visible, the position cannot be fully resolved. Usually the accuracy will be within several meters at best, even if enough stations are visible. Moreover, coverage of a certain area may vary due to obstructions by walls and other structural properties.

Better results can be obtained by "fingerprinting" approaches, which require manual mapping of observed signal strength across a workspace. Low-power, low-cost beacons based on Bluetooth are a possible dedicated infrastructure for indoor positioning—for example, in retail applications.

The signal strength of broadcasts from mobile communications cell-towers is an alternative to using WiFi. If a sufficient number of cell-tower signals can be measured, a position can be determined from trilateration or probability maps. Measurements are coarse, however, and cell overlap is limited. Assisted GPS (A-GPS) systems use cell-tower identification as a prerequisite position to accelerate GPS initialization. Given that GPS, WiFi, and cellular radio capabilities are usually simultaneously available in mobile devices, such systems now commonly combine information from all three sources for improved coverage, speed, and accuracy of position measurement [LaMarca et al. 2005] [Sapiezynski et al. 2015]. With several providers (Skyhook,

Google, Apple, Microsoft, Broadcom, and others worldwide) having long competed to map the major urban areas around the globe, and a treasure trove of crowd-sourced signal informa-tion being potentially available from now billions of mobile device users, tracking accuracy for smartphones and tablets in the developed regions of the world is remarkably high. Location measurements, outdoors and indoors, often exceed the average accuracy that GPS receiv-ers can achieve outdoors by themselves (which average 1–10 m, according to Dabove and Petovello [2014]).

Magnetometer

A magnetometer, or electronic compass, measures the direction of the Earth's magnetic field to determine the bearing relative to the magnetic north. It therefore provides global orienta-tion. The measurements are usually made along three axes with 3DOF. Note that the sensor's application interface may still deliver the bearing with only a single degree of freedom. Most miniature magnetometers in mobile devices are based on magnetoresistance, also known as the Hall effect. Unfortunately, in practice, magnetic measurements are often unreliable, since they are subject to distortion from local magnetic fields, such as those created by electric and electronic equipment. Schall et al. [2009] report that distortions of up to 30° can easily be observed (Figure 3.11).

Gyroscope

An electronic gyroscope is a device for measuring rotational velocity. It measures the Coriolis force of a small vibrating object, which preserves the plane of vibration as the device rotates (Figure 3.12). With numerical integration, the orientation can be computed. Three orthogonal gyroscopes are usually combined in a micro-electromechanical system (MEMS) to deliver a full 3DOF orientation measurement. Inertial sensors are sourceless, but provide only relative

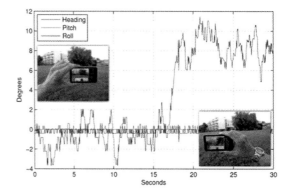

Figure 3.11 Every modern smartphone contains a magnetometer, but precision of that sensor alone is often very poor. The image shows the heading error over time as a metallic watch worn on the user's right hand comes close to the device. Courtesy of Gerhard Schall.

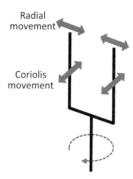

Figure 3.12   MEMS gyroscopes measure the out-of-plane motion of a mass vibrating in a plane orthogonal to the rotation axis.

measurements and so are rarely used alone. They have high update rates, up to 1000 Hz. However, the required integration makes them susceptible to accumulated drift.

Laser gyroscopes or fiber-optic gyroscopes, like those used in aviation, measure angular acceleration based on interference of light (the Sagnac effect) observed at the end of a looped fiber-optic coil (Figure 3.13). Devices based on this principle deliver much better accuracy than mechanical gyroscopes, but laser gyroscopes are still too large and expensive to be used in consumer AR applications. The only documented use to date is the TOWNWEAR system [Satoh et al. 2001], a research prototype funded by the Japanese Mixed Reality Systems Laboratory (see the discussion of this facility in Chapter 1).

Linear Accelerometer

The pendant to gyroscopes for inertial position measurement is the linear accelerometer. Also built using a MEMS approach, this device allows sourceless estimation of accelerations. Acceleration exerts a force on small mass (Figure 3.14), and the resulting displacement is measured along each major axis separately. The MEMS sensor measures the change of electric capacity between a fixed electrode and the moving part, or the piezoresistive effect of bending caused by the moving part. After subtracting the effects of gravity and integrating twice numerically, position can be computed from the acceleration measurements.

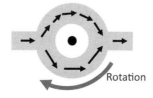

Figure 3.13   Laser gyroscopes based on the Sagnac effect in optical fiber are highly precise.

Figure 3.14 A one-dimensional linear accelerometer measures the displacement of a small mass suspended between springs as the sensor acclerates.

This principle can be used to determine position relative to a starting point. Because the relative measurement is subject to drift, it is either used only for very short durations, or combined with a secondary, absolute position measurement system.

Another common use of accelerometers is to estimate the gravity vector, along which a known constant acceleration of approximately 9.81 m/s^2 occurs, if the device is not moving. Measuring the direction of gravity with a three-axis accelerometer makes it possible to determine inclination with two degrees of freedom. Together with the bearing from a magnetometer, a full 3DOF global orientation can be determined with some tolerance.

Pedometers often use accelerometers to count a user's steps to infer walking distance. This is done by mounting an accelerometer to the body and analyzing maxima of the measured acceleration over time [Foxlin 2005].

Odometer

An odometer is a device frequently used in mobile robotics or vehicles to incrementally measure the distance traveled over ground. A mechanical or opto-electrical wheel encoder determines the number of turns taken by a wheel on the ground. Multiple encoders allow observing turns of the device. For example, inexpensive odometers were used in the traditional computer mouse (Figure 3.15) to observe the rotation of the ball inside the mouse.

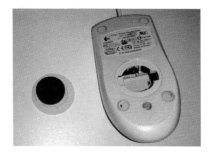

Figure 3.15 A mechanical mouse is a well-known example of 2D odometry, computed from observing the horizontal and vertical motions of a ball on the tracking surface.

Optical Tracking

The sensors discussed in the last section are important because of their mobility. Unfortunately, their accuracy is usually not sufficient to achieve the high-quality registration required in AR. By comparison, digital cameras are small, are cheap, and provide very rich sensory input—literally millions of independent pixels are acquired at once. In a video see-through AR display (discussed in detail in Chapter 2), cameras are already a crucial part of the AR system, but even when other display technologies are employed, optical tracking is easily one of the most important physical tracking principles used today for AR.

Digital cameras are based on either complementary metal oxide semiconductor (CMOS) technology or charge-coupled device (CCD) chips. Both measure light intensity observed in the direction from the camera center to each pixel (Figure 3.16). CMOS sensors are used in most mobile devices, because they are faster, are cheaper, and consume little power. CCD sensors are used if optimal image quality is desired—in particular, in professional photography. In addition to the sensor itself, the lens of the camera plays an important role in determining the characteristics of the camera. Industrial cameras with large lenses provide much better quality than camera phones with tiny lenses of 1–2 mm diameter. Thus, the type of sensor, the lens, and the type of shutter (e.g., global shutter, rolling shutter) determine the physical performance of the camera.

The appeal of optical tracking comes from the fact that even inexpensive cameras provide very rich measurements. The pixels delivered by a camera can be analyzed with sophisticated computer vision techniques. Both cameras and computing power for running computer vision algorithms are important areas of industrial research and product development, leading to continuous improvements. In particular, the results that can be obtained with computer vision technique scales with computational performance, often even without improving the camera system. As a result, Moore's law predicts improved performance of optical tracking.

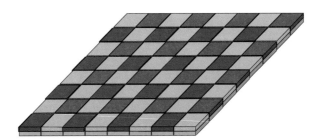

Figure 3.16   Modern digital cameras use CCD sensors to determine the intensity of incoming light. Color is added by using a filter grip with a Bayer pattern.

In the remainder of this section, we investigate the physical and technical principles of optical tracking, and consider varying circumstances, such as

- If a digital reference model is available for comparison with the camera images, or if such a digital reference model must be built on the fly (model-free tracking)
- If the illumination of the environment can be controlled
- If it is acceptible to place artificial fiducials in the environment, or if the environment must be taken "as is"
- How tracked objects can be recognized and discriminated

The actual computer vision techniques used in optical tracking methods are covered in Chapter 4.

Model-Based versus Model-Free Tracking

Using images obtained from a camera requires comparing these images to some reference model. If such a model is obtained prior to starting the tracking system, we refer to the approach as **model-based tracking**. The alternative is called **model-free tracking**—a name that is slightly misleading, because a temporary model is actually acquired on the fly during the tracking. Avoiding the requirement for a premade model increases flexibility. Moreover, on-the-fly techniques such as **simultaneous localization and mapping** (SLAM) can combine 3D tracking with 3D scanning. By comparison, model-free tracking can determine the pose only relative to the starting point, similar to an odometer. With model-free tracking alone, virtual objects in AR must be placed spontaneously and cannot be pre-registered to the real world. Recently, systems that combine the advantages of model-based and model-free tracking have become commercially available—for example, in the Vuforia library.

Illumination

The first aspect of optical tracking to be discussed is the nature of the light. We must distinguish approaches that rely on naturally occurring, passive illumination and those that rely on active illumination.

Passive Illumination

Passive illumination comprises light sources that are not an integral part of the tracking system. Passive illumination comes both from natural light sources, in particular the sun, and artificial light sources, such as ceiling lights. Like humans, conventional cameras see light in the visible spectrum (380–780 nm) reflected off objects in the environment. Using a conventional digital camera with passive illumination is the simplest approach to optical tracking in terms of physical setup.

The challenge of optical tracking with passive illumination is to make sure the objects of interest can be detected quickly and reliably in the images. This requires sufficient image contrast, which, in turn, requires salient visual features in the environment and enough indirect light to make these features stand out in the image. Indoor optical tracking often suffers from insufficient illumination, even if humans are comfortable seeing in such environments. Digital cameras with small lenses may simply not be able to pick up enough light for proper image quality—as anyone who has ever attempted to take a picture of a dim indoor environment with a camera phone without a flash light may confirm.

Active Illumination

Active illumination overcomes the dependence on external light sources in the environment by combining the optical sensor with an active source of illumination. Because active illumination in the visible spectrum changes how the user perceives the environment and is therefore disturbing, a popular approach is to rely on infrared illumination. An infrared light source, often based on LED spotlights (Figure 3.17), illuminates the scene, but goes unnoticed by a human observer. LED beacons can be fixed in the environment, but can also be mounted to target objects, as long as a battery can be included in the device. A camera equipped with an infrared filter picks up only the infrared light, leading to high-contrast images that can easily be processed. This approach is not suited for tracking in the presence of strong sunlight, which contains a significant infrared component.

Structured Light

Structured light goes one step further than active illumination with unstructured light sources by projecting a known pattern onto a scene. The source of the structured light can be a

Figure 3.17   The tracking systems from Advanced Realtime Tracking use active illumination with infrared light. LED spotlights are integrated with an image processor on board of a smart camera with a network interface.

conventional projector or a laser light source. The observed reflections are picked up by a camera and used to detect the geometry of the scene and the contained object. In essence, features in the environment are actively highlighted, if the environment itself is not naturally discriminative enough. Structured light can operate in both the infrared and visual spectra.

Unlike camera sensors, which measure pixelwise light intensities, laser ranging determines the time of flight taken by a laser pulse reflected from a surface. This measurement principle allows for high precision even over large distances, so it is often used in robotics and surveying. In its simplest form, only a single distance is measured. Such single-point laser range finders are handheld devices, which must be manually aimed. These are used, for example, in the construction industry to replace measuring tape.

With the addition of a rotating mirror, the laser can be steered in either one or two dimensions—a configuration sometimes called a laser scanner. One-dimensional laser scanners are frequently mounted on mobile robots as input for autonomous navigation, while stationary two-dimensional laser scanners delivering range images are used for 3D object reconstruction. Longer-range laser sensing, also called LIDAR (blend of "light" and "radar"), is mostly used in surveying applications.

Inexpensive range image sensors have recently become popular for tracking natural human motions in video games. The most prominent example is the Microsoft Kinect (Figure 3.18). The first-generation Kinect used a structured light pattern projected with an infrared laser, while the second-generation Kinect uses a time-of-flight camera. The range image sensors are rigidly

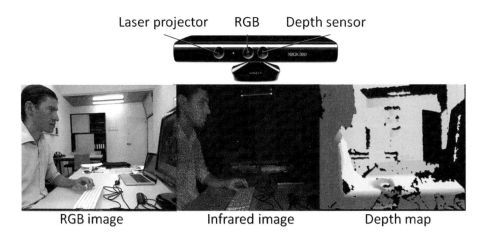

Figure 3.18 (top) The Microsoft Kinect V1 is an RGB-D camera intended for controlling XBox games using gesture recognition. (bottom left) Its RGB camera delivers a conventional color image. (bottom middle) A laser projector casts an invisible infrared dot pattern on the scene. (bottom right) The depth sensor uses an infrared camera to observe the dot pattern and computes a depth map from it. Here the depth map is shown with color coding from red = near to blue = far.

combined with a conventional camera into a single device, called the RGB-D camera (the "D" stands for depth). This class of devices is very appealing for AR, because the devices deliver images and geometric information about the scene, already registered. The RGB-D cameras are now small enough to fit on mobile devices, although power consumption is still a concern for mobile use.

Markers versus Natural Features

Similarly to the distinction between passive and active illumination, we classify tracking targets into those with natural features and those with artificial features. The latter type is often called a **marker** or **fiducial**. Ideally, we would not need to instrument an environment before experiencing AR in it, but instrumentation makes it possible to use simpler and potentially more robust tracking algorithms. If no markers are used, and we track the natural environment, the approach is described as *natural feature tracking*. Both markers and natural features can be used for model-based tracking. With the markers approach, the digital model exists first (generated for ease of distinction and recognition), and a physical object (e.g., a cardboard marker) is manufactured to match it. With the natural features approach, the physical object exists first, and a scanner is used to obtain a digital model to match it. In many cases, the same camera is used first for scanning the environment and later for continuous optical tracking.

Markers

As we have previously noted, optical tracking requires sufficient image contrast to interpret the images. Depending on the circumstances, the surface properties of the target objects may not be sufficient to reliably identify features of the target objects. First, objects may be uniformly colored with little or no texture, such as a white wall, so that images do not contain any identifiable features. Second, objects may have a high specularity, so that their appearance is extremely unstable when moved relative to a camera. Third, objects may have repetitive textures, such as a plaid tablecloth or a facade with identical windows, so that a detail image of the object is ambiguous with respect to where exactly on the object the image was taken.

Such situations, which are difficult to interpret, can be circumvented by using markers (Figure 3.19). Markers are known patterns placed on the surfaces of target objects or known trackable shapes attached to the target objects. The markers are designed to make detecting their appearance in the image as easy and reliable as possible. This goal is addressed by choosing shapes that have optimal contrast and are easily detected.

The most successful marker designs are circular [Hoff et al. 1996] [State et al. 1996] [Foxlin and Naimark 2003] or square shapes [Rekimoto 1998] [Kato and Billinghurst 1999] [Wagner et al. 2008a] [Fiala 2010]. Circular shapes project onto an ellipsoid in the image, while squares project onto a general quadrilateral. Both shapes can easily be detected in the images (Figure 3.20). Circular shapes yield only a single centroid point, while squares yield four corner points. Recovering a full 6DOF pose requires a theoretical minimum of three points. A fourth point is required

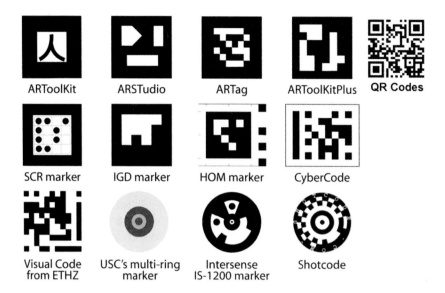

Figure 3.19 Square and circular markers are the most popular marker designs. A large variety of designs have been proposed. Most rely on easily manufactured black-and-white designs and discriminate markers by embedded patterns or barcodes. Courtesy of Daniel Wagner.

Figure 3.20 Markers are easy to detect and were the first optical tracking technology that reached a larger audience. (left) Studierstube tracker running on a Windows CE device, circa 2004. Courtesy of Daniel Wagner. (right) University of North Carolina–Chapel Hill system with colored circular fiducials, circa 1996. Courtesy of Andrei State, University of North Carolina–Chapel Hill.

in practical implementations to obtain a unique solution. This requirement implies that circular shapes must always be used in groups with a known configuration, while a single square suffices for detection. However, all four corners of the square must be properly identified. Identification is facilitated by adding a rotation-invariant pattern inside the circular or square shape to discriminate multiple markers and establish marker orientation.

While printed markers can be glued to flat object surfaces, other marker designs involve spheres attached to target objects in a rigid configuration. Spheres have the advantage that they always project to a disc shape in the image, independent of the vantage point. Consequently, spherical targets are popular for tracking agile objects that will frequently change orientation with respect to the camera—in particular, for tracking humans or human-centric devices, such as wands or shutter glasses. Because a single spherical marker identifies only a single point, at least three such markers are required. Unfortunately, the sphere design does not accommodate the use of a barcode or other stand-alone attribute for identification. Therefore, the distances among a group of three to five spheres are used for unique identification (Figure 3.21). This is a rather weak criterion, and multiple groups must be significantly different in shape to avoid ambiguities.

Markers are often designed as black-and-white shapes, because such a design provides good contrast and is independent of how the camera handles color internally. Moreover, such markers can be easily manufactured with an office printer. Printing on glossy paper should be avoided, however, because it produces disturbing specular reflections at grazing viewing angles. After applying binary thresholding to the image, a search for a black-on-white closed contour shape suffices to identify candidate markers.

Alternatively, retro-reflective foil can be used to manufacture markers. This material, which is well known from its use in safety clothing, casts a large fraction of the light directly back to the incoming direction. When the main source of illumination is a spotlight placed close to the camera, often presented as a ring around the camera, the retro-reflective foil will produce high-contrast images.

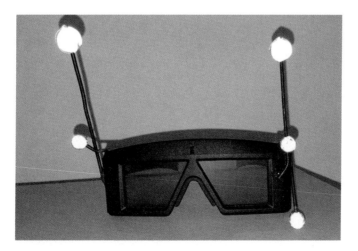

Figure 3.21   Passive infrared targets, such as the "antlers"' attached to the stereoscopic shutter glasses here, consist of four or more (here: five) retroreflective spheres.

A popular approach is to manufacture spherical markers covered with retro-reflective foil and use them with infrared illumination. This results in images with very high-contrast blobs, which are reliably detectable. Flat marker designs using retro-reflective material have also been demonstrated.

Natural Features

If we do not wish or are not able to place markers on target objects, we resort to tracking from naturally occurring features. **Natural feature tracking** typically requires better image quality and more computational resources, and has only recently become popular.

The most frequently used natural features are so-called **interest points** or **keypoints**, which are salient point features on a target object (Figure 3.22). Interest points must be easily found, and their location on the object should remain stable under a changing vantage point. In practice, the use of interest points requires a sufficiently dense and irregular surface texture.

Objects that do not possess much texture, such as non-ornamented facades or some industrial objects, can be tracked using **edge features**, assuming that their outline is easily observable. However, a single edge hardly allows a unique identification without additional knowledge, and multiple edges must be jointly interpreted for reliable target detection (Figure 3.23).

Besides local features, such as interest points and edge features, we can also compare the camera image using whole-image alignment to **keyframes** taken at specific vantage points. Unfortunately, this approach is difficult to scale to larger environments.

Figure 3.22 SIFT interest points detected in an outdoor scene. The size of the circle is an estimate of the interest point's "scale." Courtesy of Martin Hirzer.

Figure 3.23   The Going Out system from Cambridge University tracks samples along strong edges in the image and compares them to a known model of the outdoor scene. Courtesy of Gerhard Reitmayr and Tom Drummond.

The ability to track target objects without preparing them first clearly offers advantages, which will surely cause natural feature tracking to supersede marker tracking in the long run. Nevertheless, one should bear in mind that an intrinsic step of optical tracking is the comparison of image features to a given digital reference model. While the reference model of a marker is given by design, the reference model of a natural target object needs to be obtained from other sources. For human-made objects, computer-aided design (CAD) models may sometimes be available.

If not, it is necessary to obtain a reference model through a separate acquisition step, such as 3D scanning. Such a scanning step is not end-user friendly and represents a major bottleneck in natural feature tracking. Acquisition of small target objects can be hidden from the user to some degree by integrating this operation in the tracking initialization step [Mulloni et al. 2013]. By comparison, acquiring larger models, such as an entire room or even an entire city, will require labor-intensive preprocessing.

Target Identification

If we desire to track multiple objects or track a mobile user in a wide area, identification of targets becomes a major issue of optical tracking. Detecting the right feature or target becomes a second objective, after the accurate measurement of 3D points from images. Clearly, we would like to distinguish as many target objects as possible, but a tradeoff must be made between the number of objects that can be identified and the reliability of the identification. Supporting a larger set of objects necessarily means their appearance will become more similar and can be more easily confused. Higher image resolution can improve this situation, but only if it actually leads to improved image quality. In this section, we consider how this tradeoff affects the design of optical tracking systems.

Marker Target Identification

Barcodes embedded in marker designs have a clear information payload, expressed in the number of bits encoded in the barcode. Typical square markers with a 2D barcode composed of a 6×6 grid, such as ARTag (see Figure 3.19), have a raw information storage capacity of 36 bits. Two bits are required to determine a unique orientation of the pattern. The remaining 34 bits must be split between the actual ID and redundant error correction information. Typical configurations use between 6 and 12 bits for the ID, allowing for a few thousand unique markers. Increasing the grid resolution, and therefore the raw information capacity, negatively affects the chance of successfully extracting a valid barcode from an image. Increasing the number of bits used for the ID reduces the error correction capabilities and increases the chance of confusing barcodes. This puts a practical upper limit on the number of markers.

The number of targets composed of spherical markers that can be reliably distinguished by the sphere distances is much smaller. Typically, assemblies of five spheres are used, which provides some tolerance in case at least one sphere is occluded. However, the distances between spheres must differ by a minimum amount, while the size of the sphere target cannot become too large. In practice, this limits the number of simultaneous targets.

Tracking in wide areas typically means establishing the camera pose of a mobile device relative to a stationary environment. This problem can be interpreted as the tracking of a single, very large target. Because we assume a complete digital model of the large target and all its unique features is available, we need to observe only enough features to determine the pose relative to these features.

This consideration has prompted the design of marker tapestries (Figure 3.24), such as those in the form of large posters with printed markers, or individual fiducials stuck to ceiling tiles [Foxlin and Naimark 2003]. Marker systems that can distinguish only few markers can rely on spatial subdivision to cover larger areas [Kalkusch et al. 2002]. In this scheme, a different model is used in every section—for example, every room—and markers can be reused.

If active illumination is permitted, one can use pulsed LEDs to essentially encode a binary code in the temporal domain. The code can either consist of self-contained pulses for individual LEDs [Matsushita et al. 2003], or multiple LEDs can be pulsed sequentially. With careful time synchronization and high update rates, sequential pulsing allows covering large areas. For example, the HiBall system [Welch et al. 2001] uses a single LED per ceiling tile to cover areas of hundreds of

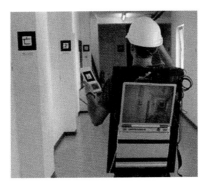

Figure 3.24 Wide-area tracking can be realized by instrumenting an area with fiducials on the wall, if visual pollution is not a concern.

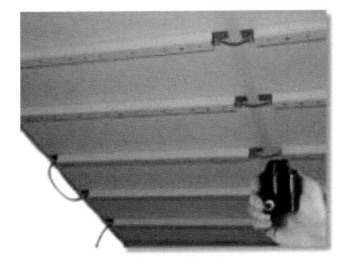

Figure 3.25 The HiBall uses directional optical sensors to detect periodic flashing of LED beacons mounted to the ceiling. Courtesy of Greg Welch, University of North Carolina–Chapel Hill.

square meters (Figure 3.25). Another form of time-varying active illumination can be realized by showing patterns on a conventional screen [Woo et al. 2012].

Natural Feature Target Identification

Natural feature point recognition can scale to hundreds of thousands or even millions of feature points. At this massive scale (e.g., when a feature point database of an entire city is built), an individual feature point recognition in a query image is not discriminative enough for reliable identification of a location. Instead, the co-occurrence of feature points in an image becomes essential.

Figure 3.26   Feature matching allows the system to identify known interest points from a tracking model in a new view of the scene. From a sufficient number of correct point associations, a scene can be identified and the current camera pose can be determined. Courtesy of Martin Hirzer.

We can know with sufficient probability that a feature has been matched only if a certain number of features from points that are known to be close in the real world appear together in an image (Figure 3.26). Tens or hundreds of feature point candidates extracted from a single image are matched with the massive feature point database. Robust statistical techniques are used to exclude spurious matches and determine the most likely matches among the inliers.

Unfortunately, both the success rate and the accuracy of tracking does not hold up when operating in wide areas. First, in a large environment, the number of failed or incorrect identification attempts will be larger. Second, the precision with which the feature points are measured relative to the world coordinates depends on the spatial extent of the environment and other parameters. As a result, successful matching of feature points will not automatically lead to a highly precise pose.

Chapter 4 discusses the fundamental computer vision methods behind marker-based and markerless tracking.

Sensor Fusion

A typical mobile device has multiple sensors: at least one camera plus GPS, inertial sensors, and a compass. Given that individual tracking technologies—optical and non-optical—have distinct advantages and disadvantages, the best results are obtained when tracking makes use of the input provided by all available sensors. An obvious way to improve upon single-sensor tracking is to use multiple types of sensors simultaneously. On the one hand, such a combination of sensors in a hybrid tracking system increases the weight, cost, and power consumption of the resulting system, and requires additional calibration effort for the registration of the sensors with respect to one another. On the other hand, it provides for a superior overall system performance, which overcomes individual limitations.

In signal processing and robotics, the combination of multiple sensors is often called sensor fusion. This approach requires both sensor fusion algorithms and a software architecture to support multiple sensors. A useful categorization of sensor fusion has been proposed by Durrant-Whyte [1988]. Pustka et al. [2011] describe how multiple sensors can be dynamically combined in real-time applications. To date, many successful examples of sensor fusion for AR tracking have been demonstrated [Foxlin 1996] [You and Neumann 2001] [Klein and Drummond 2004] [Bleser and Stricker 2008].

Complementary Sensor Fusion

Complementary sensor fusion occurs when multiple sensors supply different degrees of freedom. No interaction between the sensors is necessary, other than combining the resulting data. Of course, this combination can still be nontrivial, if the sensors are not synchronized and use different individual update rates. Such a situation requires at least some form of temporal interpolation or extrapolation.

The most common use of complementary sensor fusion is to combine a position-only sensor with an orientation-only sensor to yield full 6DOF. For example, in a modern mobile phone, GPS delivers position information, while the compass and accelerometer deliver orientation data.

Several types of sensors, which consist of multiple 1DOF sensor components, can also be seen as instances of complementary sensor fusion. For example, gyroscopes, accelerometers, and magnetic sensors are composed of three orthogonal sensors.

Competitive Sensor Fusion

Competitive sensor fusion combines the data from different sensor types measuring the same degree of freedom independently. The individual measurements are combined into a measurement of superior quality using some form of mathematical fusion.

Redundant sensor fusion is a simple variant of competitive sensor fusion. When the primary sensor is delivering measurements, secondary sensors are ignored. Only when the operation of a primary sensor is not possible does a secondary sensor take over. For example, poor or intermittent GPS reception can be complemented by an odometer in a car and by a pedometer worn by a pedestrian. Hallaway and colleagues [2004] describe a wide-area indoor tracking system switching between a high-quality but limited-range ultrasonic tracker (InterSense IS-600) and a combination of an inertial orientation sensor, a pedometer, and an infrared beacon system.

The main use of competitive sensor fusion derives from the combination of information gained simultaneously from multiple sensors with different characteristics. Because multiple sensors usually have independent update rates and deliver new measurements in an irregular, interleaved fashion, a statistical state model is established and then updated whenever new measurements become available. This statistical fusion approach can also accommodate different sensor characteristics, such as different degrees of freedom and combinations of absolute and relative measurements [Allen et al. 2001]. The most frequently used approaches for statistical sensor fusion are the extended Kalman filter [Welch and Bishop 2001] for cases where a single state model with the right parameters suffices, the unscented Kalman filter [Julier and Uhlman 2004], which can give better results when the state transitions and observation models are highly non-linear, and the particle filter, for cases where multiple "particles" representing possible states of the model must be maintained simultaneously [Doucet et al. 2001].

Statistical sensor fusion is a good approach for combining slow and fast sensors, and absolute and relative sensors. An example of the latter is an **inertial measurement unit** (IMU) for orientation measurement. A full IMU configuration consists of three orthogonal magnetometer, gyroscope, and accelerometer units each (although configurations with fewer sensors are possible). With a Kalman filter, the drift of orientation measurements from the gyroscopes can be stabilized using the other sensors.

An IMU can also be used in combination with slower, more accurate sensors. Such possibilities include combinations of IMU and acoustic tracking [Foxlin et al. 1998] , combinations of IMU and optical tracking [Ribo et al. 2002] [Foxlin et al. 2004] [Bleser and Stricker 2008], and the addition of GPS for outdoor use [Schall et al. 2009] [Oskiper et al. 2012].

Cooperative Sensor Fusion

In **cooperative sensor fusion**, a primary sensor relies on information from a secondary sensor to obtain its measurements. For example, most modern phones contain assisted GPS (A-GPS), which speeds up the initialization of GPS measurements by deriving a position constraint from the ID of the cell-tower to which the phone has established a radio link. Likewise, GPS and compass technologies [Arth et al. 2012] or accelerometers [Kurz and BenHimane 2011] may be used as an index into a database of natural features, so that feature matching has a higher success rate.

In a more general sense, cooperative sensor fusion can be described as any measurement of a property that cannot be derived from either sensor alone. For example, stereo camera rigs

Figure 3.27   The PointGrey Ladybug (here model 3 1394b) is a multi-camera device for omnidirectional imaging. It consists of six cameras, cooperatively imaging a field of view of 360°.

used in optical tracking can be seen as performing cooperative sensor fusion, since their known epipolar geometry allows converting two 2D measurements to a single 3D measurement. Similarly, the joint filtering of the images delivered by the RGB and depth sensor components of an RGB-D sensor [Richardt et al. 2012] allows largely noise-free upsampling of the depth image to a higher resolution.

A similar argument can be used for non-overlapping multi-camera setups. For example, the PointGrey Ladybug camera (Figure 3.27) delivers a panoramic image from six overlapping camera elements, each covering a wide field of view. An object overlapping multiple sectors will likely require detection of features in multiple sub-images, which must be interpreted as a whole.

Another flavor of cooperative sensor fusion is the combination of inside-out and outside-in tracking—that is, a mobile sensor and a stationary sensor. Together, the two sensors allow the recovery of the pose of a target object observed by the mobile sensor in the external coordinate system of the stationary sensor, even though both the target object and the mobile sensor are moving at the same time. The stationary sensor determines the motion of the mobile sensor system and concatenates the result with the motion of the target object as determined by the mobile sensor. This kind of configuration can even allow a tracking system to "look around corners" and track target objects that are occluded from the stationary sensor's location.

For example, Auer and Pinz [1999] discuss a combination of magnetic and infrared sensing. Foxlin et al. [2004] use a combination of stationary and helmet-mounted cameras as well as an IMU. Klein and Drummond [2004] track with a combination of stationary infrared cameras and a normal camera on a tablet computer. This principle can be extended to two or more mobile tracking systems, which mutually track one another (Figure 3.28) for collaborative applications [Ledermann et al. 2002]. Joint tracking from a stationary Kinect and multiple mobile phones was more recently presented by Yii et al. [2012].

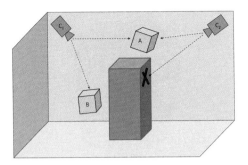

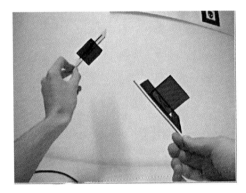

Figure 3.28 (top) Tracking around the corner. Camera C_1 tracks objects A and B, while camera C_2 can see only A. By fusing all available tracking information, the pose of B relative to C_2 can be determined. (bottom) The left marker cannot be tracked using the shown image because its surface is turned away from the camera. However, with the help of a second camera, an augmentation (blue cube) can be successfully placed at the marker's position. Courtesy of Florian Ledermann.

Summary

In this chapter, we surveyed tracking technologies, primarily according to the physical principles of the underlying sensors. We discussed important classification criteria of tracking technologies, such as physical principles, degrees of freedom, and spatial and temporal characteristics. These characteristics impose tradeoffs on the size, mobility, price, and performance of tracking systems. Stationary systems do not have to consider weight or power consumption constraints and can deploy a permanent infrastructure. They do not support a roaming user, however, and are often not desirable for AR. Mobile sensors such as GPS or IMU are ubiquitously available in mobile form factors, but have insufficient performance characteristics to fully support AR. Optical tracking based on digital cameras, therefore, is the most promising technology for AR, if sufficient computational performance for computer vision algorithms is available. In addition, combining optical and non-optical sensors using sensor fusion can greatly enhance the robustness and versatility of mobile tracking. In the next chapter, we review and explore the most relevant computer vision techniques underlying optical tracking approaches in more detail.

COMPUTER VISION FOR AUGMENTED REALITY

This chapter introduces computer vision algorithms for use in AR. It focuses in particular on optical tracking and scene reconstruction, but, as we will see in later chapters, several concepts presented here will also prove important for other AR topics, such as visual coherence, interaction, authoring, navigation, and collaboration. Computer vision for AR is concerned with electronically perceiving and understanding imagery from camera sensors that can inform the AR system about the user and the surrounding environment. AR necessitates real-time approaches—a requirement reflected in the subset of computer vision work reviewed here.

As discussed in Chapter 3, which presented a general overview of tracking technologies, real-time computer vision, aided by other sensors, is a key ingredient to successful augmented-reality tracking and registration. The objective of optical tracking is to determine the pose of an object in the real world relative to a camera. This requires knowledge of cameras and computational algorithms operating on images. It turns out that the most suitable language for concisely modeling, describing, and solving the inherent concepts and challenges involves a reasonably heavy dose of math (impatient readers may skip over the blue boxes).

While we try to introduce all necessary mathematical concepts as soon as they are needed, it is not possible to describe them all in depth. Therefore, we encourage the reader to gain a more in-depth understanding of the material from the literature. The following computer vision textbooks are highly recommended: Hartley and Zisserman [2003], Faugeras [1993], Szeliski [2010], Ma et al. [2003], and a survey on 3D tracking by Lepetit and Fua [2005].

In this chapter, we also aim to describe the necessary components of real-world systems, at least in a simple form. We use a case study approach to introduce computer vision techniques step by step. This case study approach was devised to introduce concepts in a pragmatic and solution-oriented manner. The newly introduced concepts are not limited to the specific case study that introduced them, but are broadly applicable, allowing readers to build up an arsenal of useful AR-relevant computer vision techniques.

- Case study on **marker tracking**: This simple example introduces a basic camera representation, contour-based shape detection, pose estimation from a homography, and nonlinear pose refinement.

- Case study on **multi-camera infrared tracking**: This case study presents a crash course in multi-view geometry. The reader learns about 2D–2D point correspondences in multiple-camera images, epipolar geometry, triangulation, and absolute orientation.

- Case study on **natural feature tracking by detection**: This case study introduces interest point detection in images, creation and matching of descriptors, and robust computation of the camera pose from known 2D–3D correspondences (Perspective-n-Point Pose, RANSAC).

- Case study on **incremental tracking**: This case study explains how to track features across consecutive frames using active search methods (KLT, ZNCC) and how incremental tracking can be combined with tracking by detection.

- Case study on **simultaneous localization and mapping**: This case study explores pose computation from 2D–2D correspondences (five-point pose, bundle adjustment). We also look into modern techniques such as parallel tracking and mapping, and dense tracking and mapping.

- Case study on **outdoor tracking**: This case study presents methods for tracking in wide-area outdoor environments—a capability that requires scalable feature matching and assistance from sensor fusion and geometric priors.

MATHEMATICAL NOTATION

Before we dive into the first case study, we present our mathematical notation:

- Scalar values and functions are written in lowercase italics: a

- Scalar constants are written in capital italics: A

- Vector values and functions are written in lowercase boldface: $\mathbf{a}$
  Vectors are column vectors, and the transpose of a vector is denoted by $\mathbf{a}^T$

- Matrices are written in capital boldface: $\mathbf{A}$; the inverse of a matrix is denoted as as $\mathbf{A}^{-1}$, the transpose of a matrix as $\mathbf{A}^T$, and the inverse transpose as $\mathbf{A}^{-T}$

- Angles are denoted by lowercase Greek letters: α

- Planes in 3D are denoted by uppercase Greek letters: Π

- Indices into vectors and matrices are written as subscripts: a_i, $A_{i,j}$

- For 3D Euclidean space, we use the letters x, y, z as subscripts: $\mathbf{a} = [a_x\, a_y\, a_z]^T$

- For image space, we use the letters u, v as subscripts: $\mathbf{a} = [a_u\, a_v]^T$

- If homogeneous coordinates are required, a subscript w is used: $\mathbf{a} = [a_u\, a_v\, a_w]^T$

- The column vectors of a matrix are denoted by $\mathbf{A}_{C1}$, $\mathbf{A}_{C2}$, ..., and the row vectors of a matrix are denoted by $\mathbf{A}_{R1}$, $\mathbf{A}_{R2}$, ...

- If a name needs further distinction, a prime or superscript is used: a', a^{last}

- Normalization of a vector is denoted as $\underline{N}(\mathbf{x}) = \mathbf{x}/\|\mathbf{x}\|$

Marker Tracking

Tracking square black-and-white fiducial markers has been extremely popular ever since ARToolKit [Kato and Billinghurst 1999] and ARToolKitPlus [Wagner and Schmalstieg 2007] were released as open source software. Marker tracking is computationally inexpensive and can deliver useful results even with rather poor cameras. Its appeal comes from its simplicity: Detecting the four corners of a flat marker in an image from a single calibrated camera delivers just enough information to recover the pose of the camera relative to the marker.

Figure 4.1 provides an overview of the marker tracking pipeline. The pipeline consists of five stages:

1. Capturing an image using a camera with a known mathematical representation

2. Marker detection by searching for quadrilateral shapes

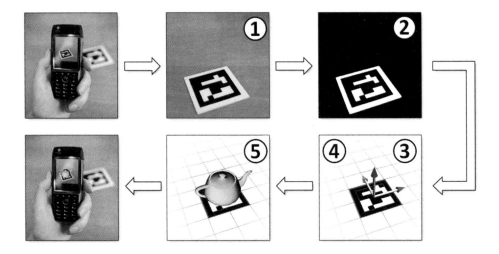

Figure 4.1   The tracking pipeline for square fiducial markers begins with thresholding the image, followed by quadrilateral fitting and pose estimation. With the recovered pose, AR rendering can be performed. Courtesy of Daniel Wagner.

3.   Pose estimation from a *homography*

4.   Pose refinement by nonlinear reprojection error minimization

5.   AR rendering with the recovered camera pose (see Chapter 6)

We discuss each of these stages in the following sections.

Camera Representation

In computer graphics and vision, the standard camera model is the pinhole camera, which is an abstraction of a common physical camera. The pinhole model describes a perspective projection of a 3D point q in object space to a 2D point p in image space (Figure 4.2). It is defined by a center of projection c, through which all observed projections of 3D points must pass, an image plane Π, and a principal point $c'\in\Pi$, which is the normal projection of c to Π. The line through c and c' is called the optical axis, and the distance from c to c' is the focal length f. Using homogeneous coordinates, we can express the perspective projection as a 3×4 matrix **M**:

$$\begin{bmatrix} p_u \\ p_v \\ 1 \end{bmatrix} \propto \mathbf{M} \begin{bmatrix} q_x \\ q_y \\ q_z \\ 1 \end{bmatrix}$$

(4.1)

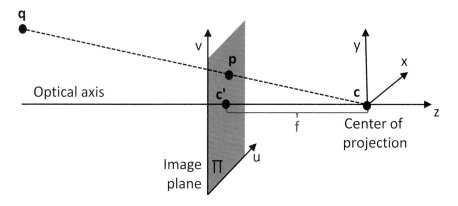

Figure 4.2 The pinhole camera model is widely used in computer graphics and computer vision. In alternative depictions, the center of projection **c** may lie on the same side of the image plane as the 3D point **q**, emphasizing the relationship to an actual hole in one side of a *camera obscura*. Mathematically, there is no difference, but the view direction and camera and image plane coordinate systems will vary. This figure assumes the camera at **c** looking left, down the negative z-axis of the camera coordinate system.

M has 11 degrees of freedom (11DOF), one less than the number of matrix elements, because multiplication by a non-zero scale factor would result in an equivalent camera matrix. The perspective projection depends on **internal and external camera parameters**.

INTERNAL AND EXTERNAL CAMERA PARAMETERS

The internal parameters describe the geometric properties of the camera itself in a 3×3 matrix K, the camera calibration matrix. The external parameters describe the pose of the camera relative to the origin of the world coordinate system in a 3×4 matrix $[R \mid t]$, which is itself composed of a 3×3 rotation matrix R and a translation vector t:

$$M = K \, [R \mid t] \tag{4.2}$$

Camera calibration means determining its internal parameter matrix K. This procedure is done once in an offline step, and afterward K is assumed to be fixed. This assumption implies that no change to the lens—no zooming—is allowed. K is an upper triangular 3×3 matrix with five parameters:

$$K = \begin{bmatrix} f_u & s & c_u \\ 0 & f_v & c_v \\ 0 & 0 & 1 \end{bmatrix} \tag{4.3}$$

(continues)

(continued)

The parameters f_u and f_v describe the focal length of the camera, scaled by the size of a pixel in the directions u and v, respectively. This distinction may be relevant for digital cameras, which often employ a Bayer filter pattern with non-square areas per pixel. However, in most cases, the camera driver resamples the image to square pixels internally. In this case, $f_u = f_v$ can be assumed. The parameters c_u and c_v describe the offset in image coordinates for the principal point **c**, which is often positioned in the center of the image for modern cameras. The skew factor s is needed only if the image directions u and v are not perpendicular, and is often 0 for common cameras.

The 11DOF of the projection matrix **M** can be decomposed into the 5DOF for **K**, 3DOF for **R**, and 3DOF for **t**. The 3×3 matrix **R** is an orthogonal matrix, and its nine elements redundantly encode the 3DOF of orientation. Proper rotation matrices represent a subset of all 3×3 orthogonal matrices (those with determinant 1), so when we try to recover **R** with a tracking algorithm, we prefer a representation with only the minimum of three parameters, such as by using the Lie group **SO**(3) [Grassia 1998].

In this chapter, we assume a calibrated camera with known **K**. All issues and procedures pertaining to calibration and lens distortion are discussed in more detail in Chapter 5.

Marker Detection

We assume a single input marker, which is a black square outline of a given thickness on white background. Here, instead of a more complex 2D barcode, one quarter of the marker interior is covered in black to provide a unique orientation (Figure 4.3).

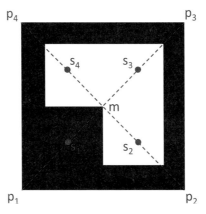

Figure 4.3   A popular marker design consists of a black square surrounding a 2D barcode. In this case, only a single corner is marked in black to determine the marker's orientation.

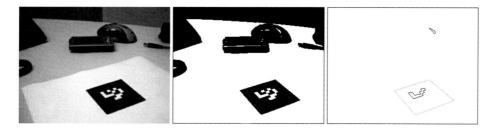

Figure 4.4 (left) Image before thresholding. (middle) Image after thresholding. (right) Detected closed contours considered as marker candidates. Courtesy of Daniel Wagner.

We start by converting a single-channel input image (typically 8-bit grayscale values) into a black-and-white binary image using a threshold operation (Figure 4.4). Variations in lighting conditions make it necessary to select a suitable threshold. This can be done manually or automatically. Automatic threshold selection can be done by analyzing the histogram of the image or, even better, by adapting the threshold based on the gradient of the logarithm of the image intensities [Naimark and Foxlin 2002]. These methods can even deal with strong artifacts such as glossy reflections on the marker. Unfortunately, they are computationally intensive. A cheaper method is to determine the threshold locally (e.g., in a 4×4 sub-area) and interpolate it linearly over the image [Wagner et al. 2008a].

After thresholding, we search for closed contours in the input image (Figure 4.4). Every scan line is examined for edges, indicated by a white pixel followed by a black pixel. If such an edge is found, we follow the edge in the 4-connected neighborhood (up, down, left, right), until we either return to the starting pixel or reach the image border. If a minimum marker height may be assumed, such as 10 pixels, then we need to scan only every 10th line to ensure that we do not miss a marker. The scan line examination is the most expensive aspect, so this approach results in a significantly faster algorithm.

A closed contour is a candidate for a marker if it has sufficient size and we can fit a quadrilateral (Figure 4.5) to the contour [Wagner et al. 2008a]. Contours that are too small are rejected after

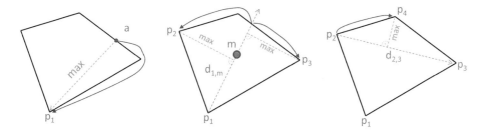

Figure 4.5 Fitting a quadrilateral to a closed contour in three steps.

we inspect the contour's bounding box. For quadrilateral fitting, we start with an arbitrary point a and walk along the contour. The point with the maximum distance to a must be the first corner, which we call p_1. We compute the centroid m of the contour. The corner points p_2, p_3 must lie on either side of the diagonal $d_{1,m}$ through p_1 and m. We find p_4 as the point farthest from p_1 on the left of the diagonal $d_{2,3}$ from p_2 to p_3. The procedure of searching for the farthest point is repeated for every edge to check that the edges between the corners do not contain any additional corners.

Finally, we determine the orientation of the marker by sampling four points $s_i = (p_i + m)/2$ along the diagonals. The black sample reveals the orientation. Multiple samples per corner can be averaged to handle difficult lighting situations.

Pose Estimation from Homography

The four corners of a flat marker are an instance of a frequently encountered geometric situation constraining the known points q_i to lie on a plane. We assume that the marker defines the plane $\Pi':q_z = 0$ in world coordinates, and that marker corners have the coordinates $[0\ 0\ 0]^T$, $[1\ 0\ 0]^T$, $[1\ 1\ 0]^T$, and $[0\ 1\ 0]^T$. We can then express a 3D point $q \in \Pi'$ as a homogeneous 2D point $q' = [q_x\ q_y\ 1]^T$. Mapping from one plane to another can be mathematically modeled as a **homography** defined by a 3×3 matrix H [Hartley and Zisserman 2003].

HOMOGRAPHY ESTIMATION

Homogeneous 2D points $p \in \Pi$ and $q' \in \Pi'$ can be related by a homography H as follows:

$$p = Hq' \qquad (4.4)$$

For tracking applications, one plane is the image plane, and the other plane contains the known points in the world, such as the marker's corners (Figure 4.6). Because the four points are constrained to lie in a plane, they can be expressed with only 2DOF. Consequently, a 3×3 matrix with 8DOF (the ninth element is the scale) is sufficient to relate them to the image plane.

H can be estimated from 2D–2D correspondences using **direct linear transformation** (DLT) [Hartley and Zisserman 2003]. Because we are using homogeneous coordinates, two points are related by a homography only up to scale. When interpreted as vectors, however, they point in the same direction. Thus the cross-product is zero:

$$p \times Hq' = 0 \qquad (4.5)$$

(continues)

(continued)

We write $\mathbf{p}_\times$ for the cross-product of vector $\mathbf{p}$ in matrix form:

$$\mathbf{p}_\times = \begin{bmatrix} p_u \\ p_v \\ p_w \end{bmatrix}_\times = \begin{bmatrix} 0 & -p_w & p_v \\ p_w & 0 & -p_u \\ -p_v & p_u & 0 \end{bmatrix} \tag{4.6}$$

Using this notation, we can write Equation 4.5 as follows:

$$\mathbf{p}_\times \begin{bmatrix} \mathbf{H}_{R1} \\ \mathbf{H}_{R2} \\ \mathbf{H}_{R3} \end{bmatrix} \mathbf{q}' = 0 \tag{4.7}$$

$$\begin{bmatrix} 0 & -p_w & p_v \\ p_w & 0 & -p_u \\ -p_v & p_u & 0 \end{bmatrix} \begin{bmatrix} \mathbf{H}_{R1}\mathbf{q}' \\ \mathbf{H}_{R2}\mathbf{q}' \\ \mathbf{H}_{R2}\mathbf{q}' \end{bmatrix} = 0$$

$$\begin{bmatrix} 0 & -p_w \mathbf{H}_{R2}^\mathsf{T}\mathbf{q}' & p_v \mathbf{H}_{R3}^\mathsf{T}\mathbf{q}' \\ p_w \mathbf{H}_{R1}^\mathsf{T}\mathbf{q}' & 0 & -p_u \mathbf{H}_{R3}^\mathsf{T}\mathbf{q}' \\ -p_v \mathbf{H}_{R1}^\mathsf{T}\mathbf{q}' & p_u \mathbf{H}_{R1}^\mathsf{T}\mathbf{q}' & 0 \end{bmatrix} = 0$$

Since $a^\mathsf{T}b = b^\mathsf{T}a$, we can rewrite this result as follows:

$$\begin{bmatrix} 0 & -p_w \mathbf{q}'^\mathsf{T}\mathbf{H}_{R2} & p_v \mathbf{q}'^\mathsf{T}\mathbf{H}_{R3} \\ p_w \mathbf{q}'^\mathsf{T}\mathbf{H}_{R1} & 0 & -p_u \mathbf{q}'^\mathsf{T}\mathbf{H}_{R3} \\ -p_v \mathbf{q}'^\mathsf{T}\mathbf{H}_{R1} & p_u \mathbf{q}'^\mathsf{T}\mathbf{H}_{R2} & 0 \end{bmatrix} = 0 \tag{4.8}$$

From this 9×3 matrix, we can pull out a 9×1 vector $\mathbf{h}$ made from the elements of $\mathbf{H}$:

$$\begin{bmatrix} 0 & -p_w \mathbf{q}'^\mathsf{T} & p_v \mathbf{q}'^\mathsf{T} \\ p_w \mathbf{q}'^\mathsf{T} & 0 & -p_u \mathbf{q}'^\mathsf{T} \\ -p_v \mathbf{q}'^\mathsf{T} & p_u \mathbf{q}'^\mathsf{T} & 0 \end{bmatrix} \begin{bmatrix} \mathbf{H}_{R1}^\mathsf{T} \\ \mathbf{H}_{R2}^\mathsf{T} \\ \mathbf{H}_{R3}^\mathsf{T} \end{bmatrix} = 0 \tag{4.9}$$

From one 2D–2D correspondence, we have now obtained three equations in the unknown coefficients of $\mathbf{h}$. These equations are linearly dependent, so we retain only the first two. We require a minimum of four input points to determine eight unknowns. From N pairs $\mathbf{p}_i = [p_{i,u}\, p_{i,v}\, p_{i,w}]^\mathsf{T}$ and $\mathbf{q}'_i = [q'_{i,u}\, q'_{i,v}\, q'_{i,w}]^\mathsf{T}$, we set up a $2N \times 9$ matrix:

$$\mathbf{A} = \tag{4.10}$$

$$\begin{bmatrix} 0 & 0 & 0 & -p_{1,w}q'^\mathsf{T}_{1,u} & -p_{1,w}q'^\mathsf{T}_{1,v} & -p_{1,w}q'^\mathsf{T}_{1,w} & p_{1,v}q'^\mathsf{T}_{1,u} & p_{1,v}q'^\mathsf{T}_{1,v} & p_{1,v}q'^\mathsf{T}_{1,w} \\ p_{1,w}q'^\mathsf{T}_{1,u} & p_{1,w}q'^\mathsf{T}_{1,v} & p_{1,w}q'^\mathsf{T}_{1,w} & 0 & 0 & 0 & -p_{u,i}q'^\mathsf{T}_{1,u} & -p_{u,i}q'^\mathsf{T}_{1,v} & -p_{u,i}q'^\mathsf{T}_{1,w} \\ \cdots & \cdots & \cdots & \cdots & \cdots & \cdots & \cdots & \cdots & \cdots \\ 0 & 0 & 0 & -p_{N,w}q'^\mathsf{T}_{N,u} & -p_{N,w}q'^\mathsf{T}_{N,v} & -p_{N,w}q'^\mathsf{T}_{N,w} & p_{N,v}q'^\mathsf{T}_{N,u} & p_{N,v}q'^\mathsf{T}_{N,v} & p_{N,v}q'^\mathsf{T}_{N,w} \\ p_{N,w}q'^\mathsf{T}_{N,u} & p_{N,w}q'^\mathsf{T}_{N,v} & p_{N,w}q'^\mathsf{T}_{N,w} & 0 & 0 & 0 & -p_{N,u}q'^\mathsf{T}_{N,u} & -p_{N,v}q'^\mathsf{T}_{N,v} & -p_{N,u}q'^\mathsf{T}_{N,w} \end{bmatrix}$$

(continues)

(continued)

The homogeneous equation system $\mathbf{A}\,\mathbf{h} = 0$, which is overdetermined for $N > 4$, can be solved using singular value decomposition (SVD). The goal of the SVD is to determine the non-zero values of $\mathbf{h}$ solving the equation system. $\mathbf{A} = \mathbf{U}\mathbf{D}\mathbf{V}^{\mathrm{T}}$ is decomposed into an upper triangular $2N \times 9$ matrix $\mathbf{U}$, a diagonal 9×9 matrix $\mathbf{D}$, and an upper triangular 9×9 matrix $\mathbf{V}$. If the elements of $\mathbf{D}$ are sorted in descending order, then $\mathbf{h}$ is the smallest singular vector—that is, the last column of $\mathbf{V}$. We reassemble $\mathbf{h}$ into the original homography matrix $\mathbf{H}$.

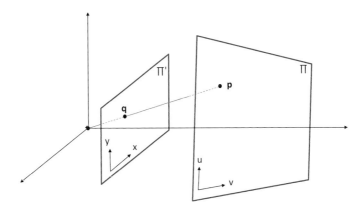

Figure 4.6   A homography relates points in two planes in 3D.

From $\mathbf{H}$, we must recover the camera pose $[\mathbf{R} \mid \mathbf{t}]$ for use in the AR rendering, as explained next.

POSE ESTIMATION FROM HOMOGRAPHY

Recall that our points lie in the z-plane, so the third column $\mathbf{R}_{C3}$ of the rotation matrix $\mathbf{R}$ has no effect. Thus, we can use $\mathbf{H}$ and the camera calibration matrix $\mathbf{K}$ to expand the projection to the image plane as follows:

$$\mathbf{p} \propto \mathbf{M}\mathbf{q} \tag{4.11}$$

$$\propto \mathbf{K}[\mathbf{R} \mid \mathbf{t}][q_x \, q_y \, q_z \, 1]^{\mathrm{T}}$$

$$\propto \mathbf{K}[\mathbf{R}_{C1} \mid \mathbf{R}_{C2} \mid \mathbf{R}_{C3} \mid \mathbf{t}][q_x \, q_y \, 0 \, 1]^{\mathrm{T}}$$

$$\propto \mathbf{K}[\mathbf{R}_{C1} \mid \mathbf{R}_{C2} \mid \mathbf{t}][q_x \, q_y \, 1]^{\mathrm{T}}$$

$$\propto \mathbf{H}\mathbf{q}'$$

We see that $\mathbf{H} = \mathbf{K}[\mathbf{R}_{C1} \mid \mathbf{R}_{C2} \mid \mathbf{t}]$. Therefore, the camera pose can be computed from

$$\mathbf{H}^{\mathrm{K}} = \mathbf{K}^{-1}\mathbf{H} \tag{4.12}$$

(continues)

(continued)

by recovering the third row of the rotation matrix (up to scale) as the cross-product of the first two columns: $\mathbf{R}_{C_1} \times \mathbf{R}_{C_2}$. However, the first two columns of $\mathbf{H}^K$ will usually not be truly orthonormal because of noise in the point correspondences. Therefore, a proper rotation needs to be enforced. First, we scale the columns of $\mathbf{H}^K$ with the geometric mean of the rotation components. The scaled third column directly yields $\mathbf{t}$:

$$d = 1/\sqrt{|\mathbf{H}^K_{C_1}| \cdot |\mathbf{H}^K_{C_2}|} \tag{4.13}$$

$$\mathbf{h}_1 = d\,\mathbf{H}^K_{C_3}$$

$$\mathbf{h}_2 = d\,\mathbf{H}^K_{C_2}$$

$$\mathbf{t} = d\,\mathbf{H}^K_{C_3}$$

We establish orthonormal auxiliary coordinates $\mathbf{h}_{1,2}\ \mathbf{h}_{2,1}$ (Figure 4.7):

$$\mathbf{h}_{1,2} = \underline{\mathbf{N}}(\mathbf{h}_1 + \mathbf{h}_2) \tag{4.14}$$

$$\mathbf{h}_{2,1} = \underline{\mathbf{N}}(\mathbf{h}_{1,2} \times (\mathbf{h}_1 \times \mathbf{h}_2))$$

Finally, we recover the columns of $\mathbf{R}$:

$$\mathbf{R}_{C_1} = (\mathbf{h}_{1,2} + \mathbf{h}_{2,1})/\sqrt{2} \tag{4.15}$$

$$\mathbf{R}_{C_2} = (\mathbf{h}_{1,2} - \mathbf{h}_{2,1})/\sqrt{2}$$

$$\mathbf{R}_{C_3} = \mathbf{R}_{C_1} \times \mathbf{R}_{C_2}$$

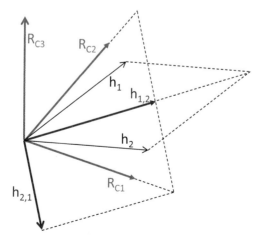

Figure 4.7 To compute a pose from a homography, the rotation components of the homography need to be ortho-normalized first.

Pose Refinement

Pose estimation cannot always be computed directly from imperfect point correspondences with the desired accuracy. Therefore, the pose estimation is refined by iteratively minimizing the **reprojection error**. When a first estimate of the camera pose is known, we minimize the displacement of the known points q_i in 3D, projected using $[R|t]$, from its known image location p_i. Using homogeneous coordinate representations (turning p into a 3D vector by adding a zero as the third element), we can minimize the errors as follows:

$$\underset{R,t}{\mathrm{argmin}} \sum_i (K[R \mid t]q_i - p_i)^2 \qquad (4.16)$$

This kind of quadratic minimization problem must usually be solved iteratively [Boyd and Vandenberghe 2004]. In more abstract form, we can think of the projection as a function $f(x) = b$, mapping model parameters x (the camera pose) to data points b (measurements):

$$\underset{x}{\mathrm{argmin}} \| f(x) - b \|^2 \qquad (4.17)$$

NONLINEAR OPTIMIZATION

If f is linear, $f(x) = Ax = b$ can be solved in the least squares sense using the pseudo-inverse $A^+ = (A^T A)^{-1} A^T$. However, a perspective projection function f is usually nonlinear, and the minimization can be computed with the Gauss-Newton method. In every iteration, x is computed by updating its previous value so as to minimize the residual $f(x) - b$.

$$x^{new} = x - J^+(f(x) - b) \qquad (4.18)$$

In Equation 4.18, J^+ is the pseudo-inverse of the Jacobian matrix J of the partial derivatives of f at x. The Levenberg-Marquardt method improves upon the Gauss-Newton method by interpolating between a Gauss-Newton step and a steepest gradient descent. The latter converges more slowly, but more reliably, ensuring that each iteration makes a step forward toward the minimum.

Multiple-Camera Infrared Tracking

In general, the known points in the world will not be constrained to a plane, as assumed in the previous section on tracking of flat markers. For tracking arbitrary objects, we require general pose estimation, which addresses the problem of determining the camera pose from 2D–3D correspondences between known points q_i in world coordinates and their projections p_i in image coordinates.

In this section, we describe a simple infrared tracking system designed to track rigid body markers composed of four or more retro-reflective spheres (an approach introduced in Chapter 3). It uses an outside-in setup with multiple infrared cameras [Dorfmüller 1999]. A minimum of two cameras in a known configuration—a calibrated stereo camera rig—is required. With this strategy, the additional input and wider coverage of the scene from multiple viewing angles will improve the tracking quality and the working volume. In practice, four cameras set up in the corners of a laboratory space are a popular configuration. Use of more than two cameras will improve the performance of the system, but is not fundamentally different from the stereo case.

The stereo camera tracking pipeline consists of the following steps:

1. Blob detection in all images to locate the spheres of the rigid body markers
2. Establishment of point correspondences between blobs using epipolar geometry between the cameras
3. Triangulation to obtain 3D candidate points from the multiple 2D points
4. Matching of 3D candidate points to 3D target points
5. Determination of the target's pose using absolute orientation (as described, for example, by Horn [1987] and Umeyama [1991])

Blob Detection

We discussed the principles of targets made from spherical markers in the "Markers versus Natural Features" section in Chapter 3. The targets are composed of four or five spheres covered with retro-reflective foil in a known rigid structure. The cameras capture images of infrared light reflected off the spheres, resulting in images that include high-intensity blobs for each sphere.

The blob detection, which is sometimes done directly on the camera hardware, is very simple: The binary input picture is scanned for connected regions consisting of white pixels. Regions that are too small or too elongated are rejected. For the remaining regions, the centroid is computed and returned as a candidate point. Because all spheres have similar appearance, the data association required for target identification must be resolved in a subsequent step.

Establishing Point Correspondences

The candidate 2D points in the two images Π_1 and Π_2 can be related using epipolar lines. Figure 4.8 shows the epipolar geometry of two cameras with centers c_1, c_2 and image planes Π_1, Π_2. A 3D point q projects to $p_1 \in \Pi_1$ and $p_2 \in \Pi_2$. The **baseline** (e) from c_1 to c_2 intersects Π_1 at the epipole e_1 and Π_2 at the epipole e_2.

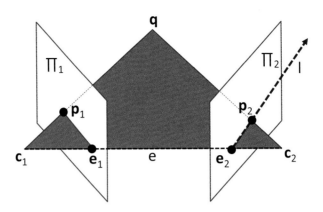

Figure 4.8   The epipolar plane is defined by two camera centers and a point in 3D.

Tracking with stereo cameras usually involves establishing correspondences for a given point q in the two images. This means we know that there is a 2D point $p_1 \in \Pi_1$, which is the projection of q, but we do not not know where q is. We would like to find p_2 in Π_2 to triangulate q. We know that p_2 must lie on the **epipolar line** l passing through e_2.

EPIPOLAR LINE

The epipolar line is defined as $l = F \cdot p_1$, where F is the **fundamental matrix** relating the cameras, and H is the homography mapping from Π_1 to Π_2. F can be computed as the product of the skew-symmetric matrix $()_x$ of e_2 and H:

$$F = (e_2)_x \cdot H \tag{4.19}$$

We are considering a stereo camera system, which has already been calibrated (for details on calibration, see Chapter 5). The world coordinate system is chosen so that it coincides with the camera coordinate system of Π_1. Therefore, we know both the internal parameters K_1, K_2 of the cameras and the external parameters $[R \mid t]$ relating the second to the first camera. In this case, we can rewrite F using the **essential matrix** E [Hartley and Zisserman 2003]:

$$F = K_2^{-T} E K_1^{-1} \tag{4.20}$$

$$= K_2^{-T} t_x R K_1^{-1}$$

We can then determine the epipolar line l, on which p_2 must lie:

$$l = K_2^{-T} t_x R K_1^{-1} p_1 \tag{4.21}$$

To find the projection of q in Π_2, p_2, we search along the epipolar line l for interest points that correspond to the scene observed at p_1. Any candidate point in Π_2 closer than a threshold to l is considered for triangulation. Ideally, only a single candidate point in Π_2 will meet this requirement. A useful verification step for the matching is to compute epipolar lines from the first camera to the second, and vice versa, and retain only associations that are consistent in both directions. If no unique match can be found, the right data association must be determined from the structure of the target. First, however, we need to compute the 3D point corresponding to the associated 2D points—a technique called triangulation. We begin by investigating the simple case of triangulation from just two cameras, and then proceed to the general solution that works for three or more cameras.

Triangulation from Two Cameras

Assuming that we have found p_1 and p_2, we can compute q by identifying intersecting rays originating at c_1 and c_2. Due to various calibration errors, the rays will not meet exactly (Figure 4.9). For two cameras, we can find the two closest distance points along the rays, d_1 and d_2, and compute their midpoint q [Schneider and Eberly 2003].

CLOSEST POINT TO TWO RAYS

We start with two rays that come closest to each other at points d_1 and d_2 (Figure 4.9):

$$d_1 = c_1 + t_1(p_1 - c_1) = c_1 + t_1v_1 \tag{4.22}$$

$$d_2 = c_2 + t_2(p_2 - c_2) = c_2 + t_2v_2$$

Because the connecting line from d_1 to d_2 is perpendicular to both rays, the dot product of the connecting line and each ray must be zero:

$$v_1 \cdot (d_2 - d_1) = 0 \tag{4.23}$$

$$v_2 \cdot (d_2 - d_1) = 0$$

After solving this linear system of equations for t_1 and t_2, the point q is finally obtained:

$$q = (c_1 + t_1v_1 + c_2 + t_2v_2)/2 \tag{4.24}$$

This triangulation for two cameras can be useful as an initialization step, if it is followed by nonlinear reprojection error minimization. The midpoint computation by itself is a simple geometric error minimization that depends on the scene setup and is not related to tracking quality. Minimization of the reprojection error requires more expensive methods (see "Robust Pose Estimation").

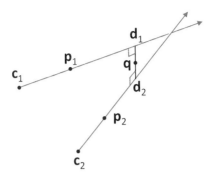

Figure 4.9   The rays through camera centers c_i and image plane coordinates p_i may not properly intersect in space. We can identify the midpoint at their closest distance.

3D POINT FROM MULTIPLE 2D OBSERVATIONS

From the previous discussion of pose estimation from homography, recall that, if $\mathbf{p} = \mathbf{Mq}$, then we can eliminate the homogeneous scale factor using a cross-product:

$$\mathbf{p}_\times \mathbf{Mq} = 0 \tag{4.25}$$

$$\begin{bmatrix} 0 & -1 & p_v \\ 1 & 0 & -p_u \\ -p_v & p_u & 0 \end{bmatrix} \begin{bmatrix} \mathbf{M}_{R1} \cdot \mathbf{q}^\mathsf{T} \\ \mathbf{M}_{R2} \cdot \mathbf{q}^\mathsf{T} \\ \mathbf{M}_{R2} \cdot \mathbf{q}^\mathsf{T} \end{bmatrix} = 0$$

$$\begin{bmatrix} p_v \mathbf{M}_{R3}^\mathsf{T} \cdot \mathbf{q} & - & \mathbf{M}_{R2}^\mathsf{T} \cdot \mathbf{q} \\ \mathbf{M}_{R1}^\mathsf{T} \cdot \mathbf{q} & - & p_u \mathbf{M}_{R3}^\mathsf{T} \cdot \mathbf{q} \\ p_u \mathbf{M}_{R2}^\mathsf{T} \cdot \mathbf{q} & - & p_v \mathbf{M}_{R1}^\mathsf{T} \cdot \mathbf{q} \end{bmatrix} = 0$$

We stack the first two equations for each point $\mathbf{p}_i = [p_{i,u}\ p_{i,v}]^\mathsf{T}$ from the N cameras into an equation system $\mathbf{AX} = 0$ with a $3 \times 2N$ matrix $\mathbf{A}$:

$$\mathbf{A} = \begin{bmatrix} p_{1,v} \mathbf{M}_{1,R3}^\mathsf{T} \cdot \mathbf{q} - \mathbf{M}_{1,R2}^\mathsf{T} \cdot \mathbf{q} \\ \mathbf{M}_{1,R1}^\mathsf{T} \cdot \mathbf{q} - p_{1,u} \mathbf{M}_{1,R3}^\mathsf{T} \cdot \mathbf{q} \\ \cdots \\ p_{N,v} \mathbf{M}_{N,R3}^\mathsf{T} \cdot \mathbf{q} - \mathbf{M}_{N,R2}^\mathsf{T} \cdot \mathbf{q} \\ \mathbf{M}_{N,R1}^\mathsf{T} \cdot \mathbf{q} - p_{N,u} \mathbf{M}_{1,R3}^\mathsf{T} \cdot \mathbf{q} \end{bmatrix} \tag{4.26}$$

Triangulation from More Than Two Cameras

We now consider triangulation for more than two cameras, which cannot rely on a midpoint computation. However, a solution for N cameras can be computed with the DLT method, which minimizes an algebraic error. Because we have a calibrated multi-camera setup, we have, for each camera, the internal calibration matrix and the external parameters relating it to the world coordinate system defined by the first camera. Therefore, we can compute the projection matrix $\mathbf{M}$ for each camera.

Like the DLT in pose estimation from homography, this equation system can be solved by SVD [Szeliski 2010]. The result is the singular vector corresponding to the smallest singular value. After computing three or more points on a rigid object in this way, the object's pose can be computed using a variant of absolute orientation (see the "Absolute Orientation" section).

Matching Targets Consisting of Spherical Markers

The candidate points $\mathbf{q}_i$ obtained from the triangulation step must be matched to the target points $\mathbf{r}_j$. Even with epipolar constraints, it will often happen that $j \leq i$; that is, there may be more candidate points than target points because of ambiguous observations. Even more spurious candidate points may result from spheres that are occluded in certain images.

The association from candidate points to target points is resolved using the known geometric structure of the target. The distance between any two points and the angles of the triangle formed by any three points should yield a unique signature. An optimal approach for designing such markers is given by Pintaric and Kaufmann [2008].

We select all permutations of j points out of the i candidate points and compute the signature of this permutation. The signatures are then compared to the target signature, and permutations with an error exceeding a threshold are rejected. Among the remaining permutations, the one with the lowest error is elected.

Absolute Orientation

After candidate point association, we are left with two sets of corresponding points—the observed points $\mathbf{q}_i$ and the target points $\mathbf{r}_i$. The latter are specified in a reference coordinate system, and we would like to compute the pose $[\mathbf{R} \mid \mathbf{t}]$ of the observed target relative to the reference coordinate system.

We compute the **absolute orientation** using the method described by Horn [1987]. It requires at least three points. The centroid of the three points can be used to determine the translation from the reference coordinate system to the measurement coordinate system. The rotation is computed from two parts. First, we define a rotation from the measurement coordinate system into an intermediate coordinate system defined by the q_i. Second, we do the same for r_i. Finally, we concatenate the two rotations to obtain R.

HORN ALGORITHM

The translation t is determined from the difference of the centroids:

$$q^c = (q_1 + q_2 + q_3)/3 \tag{4.27}$$

$$r^c = (r_1 + r_2 + r_3)/3$$

$$t = q^c - r^c$$

To compute the rotation R, we assume the origin at q_1 and the x-axis x aligned with the vector from q_1 to q_2. The y-axis y is orthogonal to x and lies in the plane given by q_1, q_2 and q_3. The z-axis z is the cross-product of x and y.

$$x = \underline{N}(q_2 - q_1) \tag{4.28}$$

$$y = N((q_3 - q_1) - (((q_3 - q_1) \cdot x)x))$$

$$x = y \times z$$

The 3×3 matrix $[x \mid y \mid z]$ defines a rotation from the measurement coordinate system to the intermediate coordinate system. We compute an equivalent rotation $[x_r \mid y_r \mid z_r]$ from the reference coordinate system to the intermediate coordinate system. The desired rotation matrix is simply the product of the second rotation with the inverse of the first:

$$R = [x_r \mid y_r \mid z_r][x \mid y \mid z]^T \tag{4.29}$$

Because we cannot assume perfectly accurate measurements in practice, this approach must be refined by minimizing the least squares error, while considering all measurements.

We have now recovered the pose $[R \mid t]$ of a single target and can use it for AR rendering. Several targets can be handled at the same time, as long as their signatures are sufficiently different to discriminate them.

Natural Feature Tracking by Detection

In the previous two case studies, we have considered artificial markers. These approaches work well with minimal computational demands, but, for most applications, we would like to avoid the visual clutter introduced by markers. We can use natural feature tracking to determine the camera pose from observations in the image without instrumenting the environment with markers. Rather than first creating a digital tracking model and then populating the physical environment with physical markers to match that tracking model, natural feature tracking takes the opposite approach: First a suitable digital model is reconstructed by scanning the physical environment, and then the tracking model is matched at runtime to observations from the camera.

In this section, we consider monocular tracking with a single camera. The wide availability of mobile devices with built-in cameras makes this the preferred tracking hardware for mobile AR. Of course, stereo cameras or multi-camera setups can also be used for natural feature tracking. Using more than one camera increases the hardware cost and computational demands, however, and few mobile devices are equipped with more than one camera.

The restriction to a single camera implies that the objective of tracking is to determine correspondences between 2D points in the camera image and known 3D points in the world. We can try to determine such 2D–3D correspondences either densely or sparsely. **Dense matching** means that we try to find a correspondence for every pixel in an image. **Sparse matching** means that we try to find a correspondence for a small but sufficient number of salient interest points selected from the image.

Until a few years ago, methods relying on matching sparse interest points had received more research attention, for a number of reasons. First, tracking models consisting of sparse interest points are easier to produce, as only digital representations of some points of interest must be created, while the rest of the physical objects can be neglected. The resulting tracking models are rather compact and can be efficiently stored and processed for matching. Second, sparse interest points are handled independently. If a particular interest point cannot be found due to occlusion or changes in illumination, the tracking algorithm itself is not seriously disturbed. Third, the discrete nature of interest points provides resilience against background clutter. Incorrect matches can be classified as outliers and removed without affecting the pose estimation, as long as a sufficient number of correct matches remain.

Dense matching has one important advantage over sparse matching: It can better deal with harsh environments. For example, objects with poor texture, repetitive structures, and reflective surfaces, such as metal, can be handled by dense matching in a much more robust way than is possible with sparse matching. Matching many redundant image points can also better accommodate image noise resulting from poor lighting conditions, although this comes at the price of increased computational cost for handling dense image points rather than sparse ones. Recent developments have rekindled the interest in semi-dense and dense matching. We therefore return to this topic when discussing SLAM approaches later in this chapter. For now, however, we consider only sparse matching.

Specifically, we first describe **tracking by detection**. The camera pose is determined from matching interest points *in every frame anew*, without relying on **prior** information gleaned from previous frames. The interest points are represented by **descriptors**, which are data structures designed for quick and reliable matching. Descriptors are created for the interest points found in the new camera image and matched with the ones in the tracking model.

This approach is simple and does not make any assumptions about the kind of camera movement. If the camera pose cannot be determined in one frame—for example, if the user is inadvertently covering the camera—this omission will not affect the tracking in the next frame. Tracking by detection is also simpler to implement than tracking relying on prior information, because no history must be maintained. Tracking with prior information is covered in the "Incremental Tracking" section.

A typical pipeline for tracking by detection of sparse interest point consists of five stages:

1. Interest point detection

2. Descriptor creation

3. Descriptor matching

4. Perspective-n-Point camera pose determination

5. Robust pose estimation

We discuss each of these stages in the remainder of this section. Note that the last two stages, Perspective-n-Point camera pose and robust pose estimation, are usually carried out together. We discuss them separately here for ease of understanding.

The execution of the pipeline starts with the capture of a new frame from the camera. An interest point detector is applied to detect candidate points for matching. For each of the candidates, a feature descriptor is created and matched with the descriptor database from the tracking model. Every match yields a 2D–3D correspondence, which is then forwarded to a pose estimator using the Perspective-n-Point algorithm. With a sufficient number of matches, the pose estimation problem is over-determined. Sometimes, however, there may be a substantial number of outliers resulting from incorrect matches. In such a case, a robust pose estimation technique must be employed to suppress the influence of outliers.

Interest Point Detection

The research community has devoted considerable efforts to the question of what a good "interest point" or "feature" should be. Shi and Tomasi [1994] state pragmatically that the right features are exactly those that can be matched reliably. In practice, that means the area around the interest point should be visually distinct. It should be sufficiently textured, with high-contrast intensity changes occurring within a small local neighborhood and forming reliably identifiable structures, such as corners or T-junctions, or circular blobs.

Some additional desirable properties take more global image information into account and, therefore, are rarely addressed by interest point detectors. For example, ideally an interest point should not be part of a repetitive structure, so that it will not be easily confused with other interest points in the scene. Moreover, interest points should be relatively uniformly distributed in the image.

The interest point selection should be *repeatable*, meaning that the detection algorithm should select the same interest points independent of observation parameters such as viewpoint and illumination condition. In addition, point detection should be robust to rotation, scale, and perspective transformation, as well as to lighting changes. It should be not too sparse (so that a reliable result can be computed) or too dense (so that the system can handle the computations in real time).

Various approaches exist that fulfill some or many of these requirements. For in-depth evaluations of different interest point detectors, see, for example, the work by Mikolajczyk and Schmid [2004] or Gauglitz et al. [2011]. We will first look at the classic Harris corners, followed by interest points based on differences of Gaussian and FAST.

Harris Corners

Given that an image has two dimensions, detecting a point means that there must be a strong gradient both in the horizontal and vertical directions. Thus, suitable interest points will generally be shaped like either circular blobs or corners. The Harris detector [Harris and Stephens 1988] uses image auto-correlation to determine corners.

CORNER DETECTORS BASED ON AUTO-CORRELATION

The most popular formulation of a corner detector is based on the auto-correlation matrix $\mathbf{A}(x,y)$ describing how similar an image $I(x,y)$ is to a shifted version of itself considering an image patch $I(x \pm W_x/2, y \pm W_y/2)$ of dimension $W_x \times W_y$:

$$\mathbf{A}(x,y) = \begin{bmatrix} \sum_{i,j} I_x(x+i,y+j)^2 & \sum_{i,j} I_x(x+i,y+j)I_y(x+i,y+j) \\ \sum_{i,j} I_x(x+i,y+j)I_y(x+i,y+j) & \sum_{i,j} I_y(x+i,y+j)^2 \end{bmatrix} \quad (4.30)$$

I_x and I_y denote the partial derivatives of I in x and y direction. The principal curvature—the strength of the image gradients—is expressed in the eigenvalues λ_1, λ_2 of $\mathbf{A}$. If both eigenvalues are small, there is no significant curvature, and the region is uniform. If one eigenvalue is large, then we are examining an edge region. If both eigenvalues are large, we have found a corner region. The computation of the eigenvalues is costly, so the Harris corner detector uses a scoring function ρ that can be expressed with the trace of $\mathbf{A}$ rather than the eigenvalues themselves:

$$\rho(x,y) = \lambda_1 \lambda_2 - k(\lambda_1 + \lambda_2)^2 \quad (4.31)$$

$$= \det(\mathbf{A}(x,y)) - k \cdot \text{trace}(\mathbf{A}(x,y))^2$$

(continues)

(continued)

Subsequently, non-maximum suppression is performed in an 8-connected neighborhood. Candidates with a response lower than a predefined percentage of the maximum response are removed.

The "good features to track" proposed by Shi and Tomasi [1994] are similar to Harris corners, but rely on a score that is more costly to compute, because it requires access to the eigenvalues. This score requires that both eigenvalues be larger than a percentage τ of the maximum response:

$$\rho(x,y) = \min(\lambda_1, \lambda_2) \tag{4.32}$$

$$\rho(x,y) > \tau \cdot \max_{x,y} \rho(x,y)$$

Difference of Gaussian

Harris corners are not invariant against changes in scale, so they do not perform well when the camera is translated along the viewing direction. As part of the work on SIFT, Lowe [2004] addresses this problem by detecting local extrema of the image filtered with differences of Gaussian (DOG), a method that operates in the scale space obtained from an image pyramid.

SCALE SPACE SEARCH

First, an image pyramid I_d, $d \in [0..N]$ is built from the convolution of I with differences of Gaussian filters G at different scales given by σ and k (with $k > 1$). This image pyramid is computed as a sequence of image convolutions and differencing:

$$G_\sigma(x,y) = \frac{e^{\frac{-x^2+y^2}{2\sigma^2}}}{2\pi\sigma^2} \tag{4.33}$$

$$I_d = I * G_{k^{d+1}\sigma} - I * G_{k^d\sigma}$$

The image differencing computes the contrast on different scales. Local extrema in the scale space are found by inspecting each pixel's 26-connected neighborhood in the pyramid. If an extremal point is found, its exact location is determined by quadratic minimization. Candidates with weak contrast (small absolute values) and candidates on edges (only one large eigenvalue in the auto-correlation matrix) are suppressed. DOG is arguably a superior detector because of its notion of scale, but the Gaussian convolution makes its computation expensive.

FAST

Rosten and Drummond [2006] have proposed a detector optimized for speed. Their **features from accelerated segment test** (FAST) detector is highly suitable for real-time video processing applications, and particularly those with constrained computational resources such as mobile AR, because of its high-speed performance. FAST uses a discretized circle centered on the candidate point (Figure 4.10). A point is classified as a corner, if there exists a contiguous arc of pixels with sufficient contrast to the center pixel, which covers up to three quarters of a circle. There exist multiple variations of FAST, named after the arc length in pixels: FAST9, FAST10, FAST11, and FAST12. A tradeoff must be made when choosing N, the number of contiguous pixels, and the contrast threshold value d. The goal is to avoid increasing the number of detected corner points such that features are produced with potentially bad repeatability, while still keeping the computations as simple and efficient as possible. General shortcomings of this feature detector include limited robustness to noise and motion blur, which can wipe out features fairly quickly. The high-speed testing method illustrated in the right image in Figure 4.10 can lead to multiple features detected adjacent to one another.

As an improvement to the simple high-speed test, Rosten and Drummond [2006] propose a machine learning approach that creates a decision tree for determining the order of the arc pixels to be tested, with the goal being to exit the test as early as possible. This machine learning version of the algorithm is the one most commonly used, especially for arc lengths smaller than 12. When the machine learning version is not used, an arc length of 12 pixels (FAST12) is commonly employed.

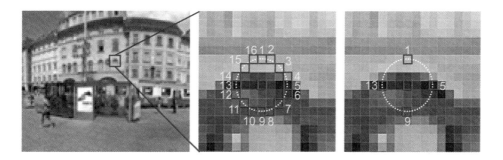

Figure 4.10 FAST searches for a contiguous sequence of pixels on a circle, which are consistently lighter or darker than the center. Early exit can be found by first testing the pixels at the top, bottom, left, and right (right image). Often, an improved detection method based on machine learning and a precompiled decision tree algorithm is used, allowing better generalization for arc lengths smaller than 12 pixels. Courtesy of Gerhard Reitmayr.

FAST12 CORNERS

FAST12 uses a circle consisting of 16 pixels s_i, $i \in [1..16]$. A corner is found, if 12 contiguous pixels are all lighter or darker than the center by a threshold d. Rapid rejection can be determined by first testing s_1 (top), s_9 (bottom), s_{13} (left), and s_5 (right). Because FAST detection itself does not determine the strength of the interest point, the score ρ is used, which considers the pixels darker than the center, S^D, and the pixels lighter than the center, S^L:

$$S^D = \{s_i(x,y) | s_i(x,y) \leq I(x,y) - d\} \qquad (4.34)$$

$$S^L = \{s_i(x,y) | s_i(x,y) \geq I(x,y) + d\}$$

$$\rho(x,y) = \max(\sum_{s_i \in S^D} |s_i - I(x,y)| - d, \sum_{s_i \in S^L} |s_i - I(x,y)| - d)$$

Descriptor Creation

After an interest point has been selected, a descriptor must be computed—a data structure suitable for matching the interest point to the tracking model or other images. Ideally, the descriptor should be unique for every point on the tracking model, but identical for arbitrary viewpoints and lighting conditions. A good descriptor captures the texture of the local neighborhood, while being largely invariant to changes in illumination, scale, rotation, and affine transformations. The simplest descriptor is the image patch around the interest point. Because these image patches are not invariant to rotation and scale, they are mostly used for incremental tracking approaches (see the "Incremental Tracking" section later in this chapter).

Here, we concentrate on the most popular descriptor for sparse interest points, the scale invariant feature transform (SIFT) proposed by Lowe [Lowe 1999, 2004] [Skrypnyk and Lowe 2004]. We suggest that readers also look at related work for more information on other popular approaches, such as SURF [Bay et al. 2006], BRIEF [Calonder et al. 2010], and Ferns [Ozuysal et al. 2007]. Several survey and descriptor comparison papers provide a good overview [Mikolajczyk and Schmid 2005] [Moreels and Perona 2007] [Gauglitz et al. 2011].

For a point $\mathbf{p} = [x \; y]^T$, SIFT obtains a scale σ_p from a DOG detector. For every pixel in the patch centered on $\mathbf{p}$, the orientation θ and magnitude g of the gradient are computed. The orientations are inserted into a histogram, weighted by g and the Gaussian of the distance of the pixel to $\mathbf{p}$. The peak of the histogram is chosen as the descriptor orientation θ_p (Figure 4.11). The following operations are relative to the frame of reference given by x, y, σ_p and θ_p.

The image patch is subdivided into a $K_x \times K_y$ grid, and a separate weighted orientation histogram with K_b bins is computed. The descriptor is taken to be the feature vector resulting from the concatenation of the $K_x \times K_y \times K_b$ bins. The vector is normalized to minimize the influence of illumination variation. The standard SIFT descriptor has $4 \times 4 \times 8 = 128$ dimensions.

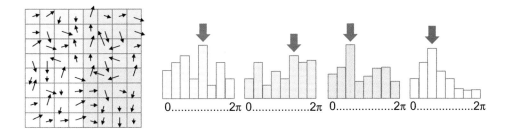

Figure 4.11 SIFT determines gradient vectors for every pixel of the (here: 8×8) image patch (left). A (here: 2×2) descriptor array with (here: 8-bin) histograms relating cumulative gradient vector magnitude to gradient orientation is built (right). In this example, the descriptor has $2 \times 2 \times 8 = 32$ dimensions.

Wagner et al. [2008b] present a variant of SIFT optimized for embedded devices, such as mobile phones, called PhonySIFT. It uses only $3 \times 3 \times 4 = 36$ dimensions and FAST (rather than DOG) for detection. Because FAST does not provide a scale estimate, the input image is downsampled into a pyramid by averaging rather than convolution, and FAST is applied on every level separately. This approach determines interest points at a fraction of the computational cost, but with a larger number of outliers. These outliers can be managed with careful geometric verification, so that the accuracy of the final pose result is not affected.

Descriptor Matching

Given the descriptors of interest points detected in the image, we must try to find the best match from interest points in the tracking model. The simplest matching score of two descriptors represented as feature vectors is their Euclidean distance. For a given descriptor from the image, the descriptor in the tracking model with the smallest distance represents the best match. This match should be unique; thus, if the ratio of the smallest distance and the second smallest distance is larger than some threshold (typically set at 80%), the interest point is discarded.

If the number of descriptors in the tracking model becomes so large that an exhaustive search for the best match cannot be performed in the available time, heuristic search structures must be used. A typical approach is to rely on hierarchical search structures such as **k-d trees**. Searching in logarithmic time can then be performed, albeit at the expense of a small number of missed matches. If a k-d tree is not efficient enough, a **spill forest** [Wagner et al. 2008b] can be used. With this approach, multiple spill trees (i.e., k-d trees with a certain overlap, with randomized dimensions for pivoting) are searched and the results combined.

Any approximate search structure can lead to incorrect matching results, producing outliers that affect the pose computation. Therefore, robust and efficient outlier removal is very important. It is useful to apply a cascade of removal techniques, starting with cheapest method and finishing with most expensive technique.

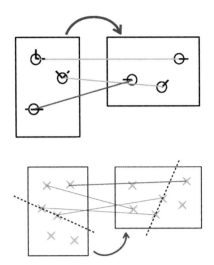

Figure 4.12   (top) A simple rotation check can be derived from the dominant orientation provided by the SIFT descriptor. All keypoints must have the same relative rotation. (bottom) A line check tests whether corresponding features consistently lie on either side of a line connecting two randomly selected features. Courtesy of Daniel Wagner.

An inexpensive first test relies on an overall orientation check. Descriptors relying on orientation histograms, such as SIFT, already provide the rotation of an interest point. It is easy to check that all matched interest points in the image have a consistent orientation with respect to the target model (Figure 4.12, top). As a second test, a line check can be constructed by randomly selecting two pairs of corresponding features. All additional feature pairs must consistently lie on either side of the line connecting the selected features (Figure 4.12, bottom).

Perspective-n-Point Pose

The problem of recovering the 6DOF pose of a calibrated camera from N 2D–3D point correspondences is known as the Perspective-n-Point (PnP) problem, where "n" denotes the number of correspondences. Given that every correspondence provides two constraints, a minimum of three 2D–3D correspondences is necessary for six constraints matching the 6DOF. With only three points, this P3P algorithm delivers up to four ambiguous solutions. A fourth point correspondence is required to determine the unique solution.

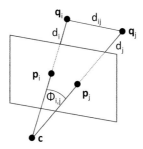

Figure 4.13   The P3P algorithm relies on computing the distance d_i from the camera center $\mathbf{c}$ to a 3D point $\mathbf{q}_i$.

P3P ALGORITHM

Several versions of the P3P algorithm have been developed [Quan and Lan 1999]. Here, we describe the simplest one (Figure 4.13):

1. Select any two points $\mathbf{q}_i$, $\mathbf{q}_j$ from the given three points.

2. Create a triangle $\mathbf{cq}_i\mathbf{q}_j$ from the two selected points and the (unknown) camera center $\mathbf{c}$.

3. Determine $\mathbf{d}_{ij} = |\mathbf{q}_j - \mathbf{q}_i|$ and $\cos\theta_{i,j}$:

$$\cos\theta_{i,j} = \underline{\mathbf{N}}(\mathbf{q}_i - \mathbf{c})\cdot\underline{\mathbf{N}}(\mathbf{p}_i - \mathbf{c}) \tag{4.35}$$

4. Set up Equation 4.36 with two unknowns $d_i = |\mathbf{q}_i - \mathbf{c}|$ and $d_j = |\mathbf{q}_j - \mathbf{c}|$:

$$d_{ij}^2 = d_i^2 + d_j^2 - 2d_id_j\cos\theta_{ij} \tag{4.36}$$

5. Consider the other two pairs of input points. Every pair yields one polynomial equation of degree 4, and together they form a set of three equations in d_1, d_2, d_3. This set can be solved in closed form with at most four solutions. In practice, a unique solution can be easily obtained with four points: The P3P problem is solved for each subset consisting of three points out of the four points, and the common solution is retained.

6. Compute the position of $\mathbf{q}_i$ in camera coordinates, $\mathbf{q}_i^C$:

$$\mathbf{q}_i^C = \mathbf{c} + d_i \cdot \underline{\mathbf{N}}(\mathbf{p}_i - \mathbf{c}) \tag{4.37}$$

7. Compute the pose $[\mathbf{R} \mid \mathbf{t}]$ by aligning $\mathbf{q}_i$ and $\mathbf{q}_i^C$, using absolute orientation (see the "Absolute Orientation" section).

8. Perform nonlinear refinement of the pose (see the "Pose Refinement" section).

Robust Pose Estimation

A larger number of data points is generally desirable, as it improves the numerical optimization. Of course, the larger the input data set, the higher the probability that outliers are present, which will contaminate the result. We would prefer to find a good initialization from a data set, even if it contains strong outliers, and then converge the results to obtain an accurate solution. The goal is to select an all-inlier subset from a contaminated set of data points.

RANSAC

Such a robust initialization can be arrived at using **random sampling consensus** (RANSAC) [Fischler and Bolles 1981]. The main idea of RANSAC is to estimate the model parameters $\mathbf{x}$ from a randomly chosen subset of the data points. For camera poses, P3P is often used, since it requires only three 2D–3D point correspondences. For every one of the remaining—potentially many—point correspondences, we compute the residual error, assuming the camera pose computed from the three chosen points. A data point with a residual smaller than a threshold counts as an inlier. If the ratio of inliers to outliers is not sufficient, the procedure is repeated. RANSAC terminates if either enough inliers are found or a maximum number of iterations is reached. Finally, $\mathbf{x}$ is re-estimated using all inliers from the iteration with the largest number of inliers.

M-Estimator

For improved accuracy, the result of the initial pose estimation (in our case, that obtained with RANSAC) is forwarded to robust iterative pose refinement, very similar to the procedure described in the "Pose Refinement" section. For this purpose, we can use an **M-estimator** ("M" stands for "maximum likelihood") [Triggs et al. 2000]. The underlying idea is to down-weight the influence of data points producing large residuals in the minimization by replacing the L2 norm on the residual, $|f(x) - b|^2$, with another function, $\rho(f(x) - b)$. One popular M-estimator is the Tukey estimator (Equation 4.38), which is essentially a blend of a parabolic function and a constant function (Figure 4.14).

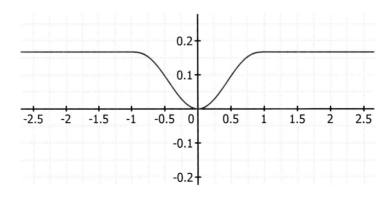

Figure 4.14   Tukey estimator with $K = 1$.

$$\rho(x) = \begin{cases} K^2/6(1 - (1 - (x/K)^2)^3), & \text{if } |x| \leq K \\ K^2/6, & \text{if } |x| > K \end{cases} \qquad (4.38)$$

The Tukey estimator must be used with caution: It is not convex, which means that optimization can get stuck in a local minimum. Moreover, the function is flat when the solution is too far from the optimum, which defeats the purpose of gradient computation. Thus, the Tukey estimator must be used only with solutions that are sufficiently close to the global minimum or a reasonable local minimum.

Incremental Tracking

Many AR tracking systems use tracking by detection because of its simplicity and because it is convenient to handle outlier identification and pose estimation simultaneously—most outliers among the candidate features are rejected during robust pose estimation. However, the difficulties of this approach should not be underestimated. Tracking by detection is most successful for really simple tracking models, such as those involving a handful of square markers, where matching is trivial. Scaling the matching to large natural feature models is much more difficult, as will become evident in the section "Outdoor Tracking."

Since AR requires real-time update rates, neither the camera pose nor the projection of feature points to the image will change drastically from one frame to the next. Tracking by detection ignores this coherence, so that the tracking problem becomes harder to solve than necessary: Not only is ignoring frame-to-frame coherence wasteful in terms of precious computational resources, but the tracking system may also encounter situations that are difficult to interpret by examining a single image in isolation. Such cases could often be interpreted much more easily with information from the previous frame.

A tracking system that uses information from a previous step is said to use **incremental tracking** or recursive tracking. If the last tracking iteration was successful, there is good reason to believe that we can be successful again by searching for the inliers from the last frame and searching close to their last known positions. Such an approach can significantly facilitate both components of detection:

- **Local search.** Interest point extraction benefits from limiting the search to a small window around the prior position.

- **Direct matching.** The matching can be done by simply comparing the image patch around an interest point to the image patch in the image being searched. This avoids the costly creation and comparison of descriptors, though it works only for simple tracking models and small camera motions. In practice, incremental tracking typically relies on good prior information of the camera pose.

Incremental tracking requires two components: an incremental search component and an interest point matching component. Incremental (active) search is performed near the location of the interest point in the last frame. For such near distances, suitable matching is often based on the Kanade-Lucas-Tomasi technique or zero-normalized cross-correlation.

Active Search

When an initial estimate of the camera pose is extrapolated from the last known pose using a motion model, the technique is described as **active search.** Rather than assuming a zero-order motion model, which predicts that the camera will remain still, a first-order motion model provides a simple but effective prediction: The camera is assumed to continue moving with constant spatial and angular velocity, which is approximated from the difference to the last frame or frames. A second-order motion model may yield even better results, if additional acceleration information is available, such as from a gyroscope sensor. We can also use assumptions about acceleration characteristics—for example, for a camera mounted to a large vehicle.

In the simplest case, if no 3D tracking model is available, a motion model can be obtained purely from the 2D positions of interest points (Figure 4.15, left). In this case, the motion is estimated directly from the image-space translation of the feature points.

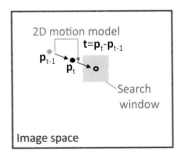
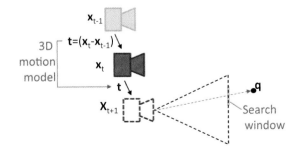

Figure 4.15   Active search in 2D (left). Active search in 3D (right).

However, if a 3D tracking model can be obtained, a corresponding 3D motion model will usually give a better result (Figure 4.15, right). The predicted new position of the camera is used to reproject those feature points of the tracking model that corresponded to inliers in the last frame to new 2D positions in the current frame. If the motion model is accurate, the interest points we would like to find will likely appear very close to these 2D positions. It is therefore sufficient to limit the interest point search to a small window around the 2D position.

If the tracking model consists of a geometric description of the scene, the template image can also be prepared by synthesizing a new image of the scene from the predicted camera pose. Such a **tracking by synthesis** approach can rely on simple geometric features, such as edges [Drummond and Cipolla 2002]; alternatively, if a textured model is available, a synthetic image can be efficiently generated on the GPU [Reitmayr and Drummond 2006].

Kanade-Lucas-Tomasi Tracking

The classic approach to incremental tracking is the Kanade-Lucas-Tomasi (KLT) tracker [Lucas and Kanade 1981] [Tomasi and Kanade 1991] [Shi and Tomasi 1994] [Baker and Matthews 2004], which extracts points from an initial image and then tracks them using optical flow.

Tracking with KLT aims to find the parameters $\mathbf{x}$ of a warp $\mathbf{w}$ that transforms a template image T into the input image I. The warp $\mathbf{w}$ will often be restricted to an affine transformation, which is sufficient to model the deformation of an image patch observed after a small camera motion. For such small, incremental motions, affine transformations are very similar to perspective distortion effects, which would be much more expensive to compute.

LUKAS-KANADE ALGORITHM

The tracking parameters $\mathbf{x}$ are computed by minimizing the intensity differences error after warping interest points $\mathbf{p}_i$ with $\mathbf{w}$:

$$\sum_i (I(\mathbf{w}(\mathbf{p}_i, \mathbf{x})) - T(\mathbf{p}_i))^2 \tag{4.39}$$

Incremental Lucas-Kanade tracking assumes that a previous estimate is known: $\mathbf{x}^{\text{new}} = \mathbf{x} + \Delta\mathbf{x}$. With a first-order Taylor expansion, we can write

$$\sum_i (I(\mathbf{w}(\mathbf{p}_i, \mathbf{x} + \Delta\mathbf{x})) - T(\mathbf{p}_i))^2 \tag{4.40}$$

$$\approx \sum_i \left(I(\mathbf{w}(\mathbf{p}_i, \mathbf{x})) + \left(\frac{\delta I}{\delta \mathbf{w}} \frac{\delta \mathbf{w}}{\delta \mathbf{x}} \right) \Delta\mathbf{x} - T(\mathbf{p}_i) \right)^2$$

$$= \sum_i (\mathbf{J}\Delta\mathbf{x} + \mathbf{r}(\mathbf{p}_i, \mathbf{x}))^2 \tag{4.41}$$

In Equation 4.41, $\mathbf{r}$ is the residual between the warped input image and the template, $\mathbf{r}(\mathbf{p}_i, \mathbf{x}) = T(\mathbf{p}) - I(\mathbf{w}(\mathbf{p}, \mathbf{x}))$, and $\mathbf{J}$ is the so-called steepest descent image, the gradient

(continues)

(continued)

image $\delta I / \delta \mathbf{w}$ warped with the Jacobian of the warping function, $\delta \mathbf{w} / \delta \mathbf{x}$. With the pseudo-inverse $\mathbf{J}^+$ of the steepest descent image, this equation can be solved in closed form for $\Delta \mathbf{x}$:

$$\Delta \mathbf{x} = \mathbf{J}^+ \mathbf{r}(\mathbf{p}_i, \mathbf{x}) \tag{4.42}$$

Equation 4.42 is used to update the estimate of x until the error $\|\Delta \mathbf{x}\|$ is deemed small enough. In its most general form, J depends on both the image gradient and the current parameters x. However, if we restrict **w** to an affine warp $\mathbf{w}^{\text{affine}}$, the Jacobian is constant and can be precomputed:

$$\mathbf{w}^{\text{affine}}(\mathbf{p}, \mathbf{x}) = \begin{bmatrix} x_1 + 1 & x_3 & x_5 \\ x_2 & x_4 + 1 & x_6 \end{bmatrix} \begin{bmatrix} p_x \\ p_y \\ 1 \end{bmatrix} \tag{4.43}$$

An important recent development that can replace KLT focuses on descriptor fields [Crivellaro and Lepetit 2014]. With this new approach, a novel local descriptor describing image locations replaces the image intensities used in matching. Descriptor fields provide significantly improved matching performance in difficult conditions such as environments with many specular reflections, while being very computationally efficient.

Zero-Normalized Cross-Correlation

Searching for the optimal position of a feature point using optical flow requires solving an optimization. It may be simpler—and therefore faster—to just scan the entire search window for the best position. Such a scan can be done using a robust image comparison metric, which gives a score indicating how well two images are aligned. Ideally, such a metric should be invariant to local changes in intensity resulting from illumination differences between template and input image.

The zero-normalized cross-correlation (ZNCC) for an image patch of size $V_x \times V_y$ around the position (x, y) has these desired properties. Typical patch sizes are 5×5 or 7×7.

ACTIVE SEARCH WITH ZNCC

For an input image I and a template image T, we denote the average values as $\bar{I}$ and $\bar{T}$ and the standard deviations as σ^I and σ^T. The ZNCC score ρ^{ZNCC} is computed as follows:

$$\rho^{\text{ZNCC}}(x, y) = \frac{\dfrac{1}{V_x V_y} \sum_{x,y} I(x,y) T(x,y) - \overline{IT}}{\sigma^I \sigma^T} \tag{4.44}$$

(continues)

(continued)

We use ZNCC to search for the best match in an active search window
$(x \pm W_x/2 \times y \pm W_y/2)$ around the predicted position (x,y):

$$\underset{i \in \pm W_x/2, j \in \pm W_y/2}{\operatorname{argmin}} \quad \rho^{\text{ZNCC}}(x + i, y + j) \tag{4.45}$$

One disadvantage of active search using ZNCC over KLT is that only translation in the image plane is considered. If the motion incorporates a strong rotation or zoom, pure ZNCC may not be ideal. However, the motion model used in the active search can also be used to warp the image patch. We compute a warped version of the template image and compare it to the input image. The warped template image will likely be similar enough to the input image that ZNCC is sufficient. The difference in the warp computed in KLT is that it is predetermined by the motion model, rather than subject to an optimization. Because the warp represents only an intermediate step to get us closer to the goal, an affine warp is usually sufficient (Figure 4.16). Such an affine warp can be rapidly computed by resampling the template image with bilinear interpolation.

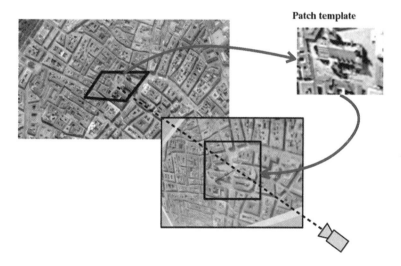

Figure 4.16   A patch taken from the template image (top left) is affinely warped using the estimated camera pose from a motion model (top right). The warped patch is compared to the current camera image (bottom). Courtesy of Daniel Wagner.

Hierarchical Search

Even a medium-quality video stream of 640×480 pixel resolution at 30 Hz from a handheld camera often contains hundreds of features, which can move 50 pixels or more from frame to frame. Naive tracking would require very large search windows, making the tracking computationally expensive. It is therefore advisable to adopt a hierarchical approach, which determines the final camera pose in steps of decreasing magnitude.

It is usually sufficient to employ a simple two-level image pyramid (Figure 4.17), downsampling the input image to a quarter of its original resolution first [Klein and Murray 2007]. Only a small number of strong features (e.g., 20–30 features) is tracked at this resolution using the predicted camera pose from the motion model. In contrast, the search window is large—for example, 5×5 pixels (corresponding to 20×20 pixels at the original resolution). The camera pose resulting from this coarse tracking step is improved relative to the pose from the motion model, but is not yet accurate enough. Even so, it is adequate for initialization of tracking at the full

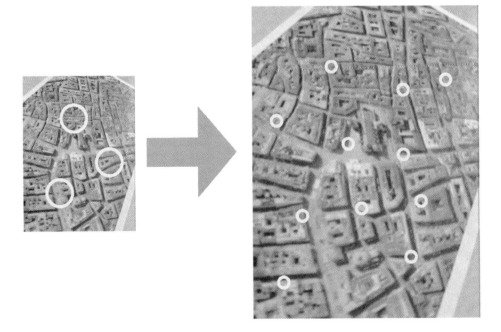

Figure 4.17 A two-level hierarchical search starts on a 2×2 subsampled image, with only a small number of interest points used to obtain a first estimate of the camera pose. In a second step, the full set of interest points is considered at full resolution, but with a much smaller search window. Courtesy of Daniel Wagner.

resolution. The tracking at full resolution employs all features (e.g., the 200 strongest features), but uses a much smaller search window (e.g., 2×2 pixels). After removing outliers, a nonlinear refinement can be used to obtain the final camera pose.

Combined Detection and Tracking

Pure incremental tracking cannot be initialized unless we start with a known camera pose. Early approaches used manual initialization, but modern tracking systems [Wagner et al. 2009] combine the detection and incremental tracking approaches (Figure 4.18).

The detection approach does not require a prior pose and may require a fair amount of computational cycles, since it does not have to meet a strict frame rate. Detection can also be extended with target recognition, such that the right tracking model is retrieved from a potentially very large database.

Incremental tracking requires information on the prior pose, but can rely on temporal coherence. Upon initialization, this method can be used to extract the template image from the video stream rather than relying on the stored tracking model. The fresh template image reflects current environmental conditions such as illumination, which makes the tracking resilient to harsh conditions such as blur, glossy reflections, or strong tilt (Figure 4.19).

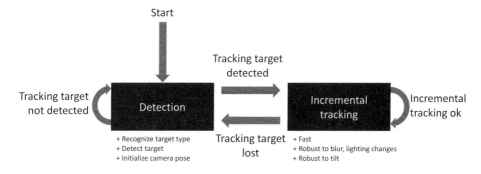

Figure 4.18   Tracking and detection are complementary approaches. After successful detection, the target is tracked incrementally. If the target is lost, the detection is activated again.

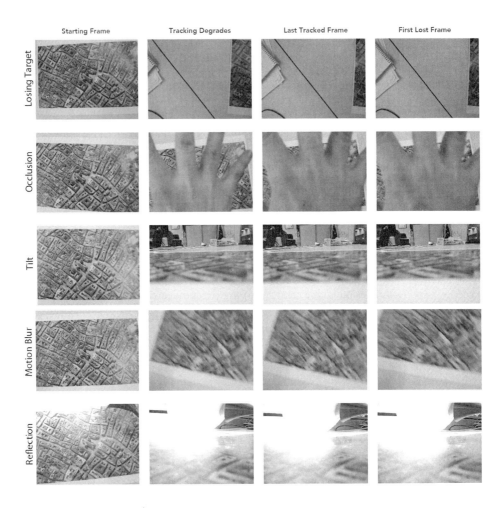

Figure 4.19 These images show several tracked sequences until incremental tracking using patch warping finally breaks in the rightmost column. The tracking is robust against losing the target, occlusion, tilt, motion blur, and reflections. Courtesy of Daniel Wagner.

Simultaneous Localization and Mapping

To this point, we have assumed that a tracking model for reference is available before tracking starts. In the case of model-free tracking, we do not have such a tracking model at hand. The simplest form of model-free tracking, which can be seen as a precursor to simultaneous localization and mapping (SLAM), is sometimes called **visual odometry** [Nistér et al. 2004]. In a nutshell, visual odometry means continuous 6DOF tracking of a camera pose relative to an abitrary starting point. This approach originally comes from the field of mobile robotics. Visual odometry computes a 3D reconstruction of the environment, but uses it just to support the incremental tracking. A basic visual odometry pipeline encompasses the following steps:

1. Detect interest points in the first frame—for example, using Harris or FAST corners (see "Interest Point Detection").

2. Track the interest point in 2D from the previous frame—for example, using KLT (see "Kanade-Lucas-Tomasi Tracking").

3. Determine the essential matrix between the current and previous frames from the feature correspondences with a five-point algorithm (see "Five-Point Algorithm for Essential Matrix") inside a RANSAC loop (see "Robust Pose Estimation").

4. Recover the incremental camera pose from the essential matrix.

5. Since the essential matrix determines the translation part of the pose only up to scale, this scale must be estimated separately, so that it is consistent throughout the tracked image sequence. To achieve this aim, 3D point locations are triangulated from multiple 3D observations of the same image feature over time (see "Triangulation from More Than Two Cameras"). This approach is called **structure from motion** (SFM).

6. Proceed to the next frame.

All algorithms in this outline have already been introduced, with the exception of the five-point algorithm, which we will discuss next.

Five-Point Algorithm for Essential Matrix

To determine the relative camera motion from 2D point correspondences, Nistér's [2004] algorithm computes E from five point correspondences. Since $E = t_\times R$, we can compute the relative pose $[R \mid t]$ between the cameras by decomposing E into R and t using SVD. The optical centers of the two camera viewpoints must be different (i.e., $\|t\| > 0$). Otherwise, the implicit triangulation—and thus E—is ill-defined. To achieve these aims, SLAM systems have to be initialized with a distinct (sideways or forward) "traveling" motion, and fail if the camera is rotated only.

NISTÉR'S ALGORITHM

Recall that corresponding observations p_1, p_2 in two cameras with known internal calibration K_1, K_2 can be related by the essential matrix E:

$$p_2^T K_2^{-T} E K_1^{-1} p_1 = 0 \tag{4.46}$$

Inserting five point correspondences into Equation 4.46 yields a 5×9 matrix, since E has nine elements. Using SVD or QR factorization, a nullspace of this matrix can be computed, which can be written in terms of four 3×3 matrices X, Y, Z, W and four scalars x, y, z, w:

$$E = xX + yY + zZ + wW \tag{4.47}$$

(continues)

(continued)

Since $\mathbf{E}$ is homogeneous, we set $w = 1$. We now combine Equation 4.47 with a constraint based on the fact that the determinant of every fundamental or essential matrix is zero:

$$det(\mathbf{E}) = 0 \tag{4.48}$$

We obtain nine more constraints by combining Equation 4.47 with the following equation, which expresses the special structure of $\mathbf{E}$:

$$2\mathbf{E}\mathbf{E}^{\mathsf{T}}\mathbf{E} - tr(\mathbf{E}\mathbf{E}^{\mathsf{T}})\mathbf{E} = 0 \tag{4.49}$$

This yields a 10×20 matrix consisting of monomials $x^i y^j z^k$ with $i + j + k \leq 3$. This matrix is reduced with Gauss-Jordan elimination (see Nistér's paper for details). We obtain an polynomial of degree 10 with 10 solutions for z. The real roots of this polynomial are back-substituted to finally recover $\mathbf{E}$. We decompose $\mathbf{E}$ into $\mathbf{R}$ and $\mathbf{t}$ using SVD:

$$\mathbf{E} = \mathbf{U}\mathbf{D}\mathbf{V}^{\mathsf{T}} \tag{4.50}$$

$$\mathbf{W} = \begin{bmatrix} 0 & -1 & 0 \\ 1 & 0 & 0 \\ 0 & 0 & 1 \end{bmatrix}$$

$$\mathbf{R} = \mathbf{U}\mathbf{W}^{-1}\mathbf{V}^{\mathsf{T}}$$

$$\mathbf{t}_{\times} = \mathbf{V}\mathbf{W}\mathbf{D}\mathbf{V}^{\mathsf{T}}$$

If Nistér's algorithm appears daunting to implement, there are alternative approaches, such as those proposed by Li and Hartley [2006] or Stewénius et al. [2006].

Bundle Adjustment

A naive visual odometry approach, such as that previously described, will likely accumulate drift over time. This problem can be attacked by minimizing reprojection error through **bundle adjustment** [Triggs et al. 2000]. For a camera with calibration $\mathbf{K}$, let $\mathbf{p}_{k,i}$ denote the projection of 3D point $\mathbf{q}_i$ to the frame obtained with camera pose $\mathbf{X}_k$. We want to minimize the reprojection error of a metric ρ as follows:

$$\underset{\mathbf{x}_k, \mathbf{q}_i}{\mathrm{argmin}} \sum_k \sum_i \rho(\mathbf{K}\mathbf{X}_k\mathbf{q}_i - \mathbf{p}_{k,i}) \tag{4.51}$$

The function ρ is a robust estimator (such as the Tukey estimator), and $\mathbf{p}_{ki}$ is a homogeneous vector with three elements.

Like the pose refinement described earlier in this chapter, this problem is usually solved with a Gauss-Newton or Levenberg-Marquardt method. However, the problem space can quickly

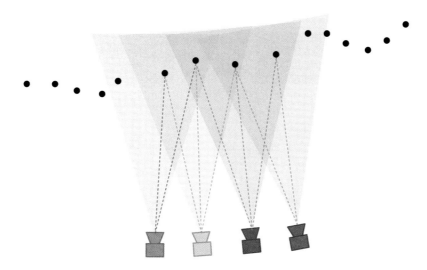

Figure 4.20   A windowed bundle adjustment limits the computational effort by only optimizing over neighboring camera poses.

become very large. The problem can still be solved efficiently by partitioning the parameters into camera poses and 3D points. Moreover, the computation is limited to a certain spatial region. A **windowed bundle adjustment** is optimized only over a fixed number of adjacent frames (Figure 4.20).

For very large scenes, **pose graph optimization** [Kummerle et al. 2011] goes one step further: Only the camera poses of selected keyframes are considered for optimization. The keyframes form nodes in a graph, where an edge between two keyframes indicates that both observe a common part of the scene. Rather than optimizing for global pose, only relative pose changes along edges are considered with this technique.

Parallel Tracking and Mapping

The naive visual odometry described previously considers points only as long as they are tracked. If a point moves out of sight and is later reacquired, naive visual odometry is not able to relate the second sighting to the first one. In contrast, SLAM aims to create a map using consistent data association of observations to points in the scene [Davison et al. 2007]. Unfortunately, such a map can grow quickly in terms of the number of points as the camera is exploring the scene, and computing global bundle adjustment may quickly become infeasible.

Parallel tracking and mapping (PTAM) [Klein and Murray 2007] is a modern approach, which decouples the tracking from the mapping (Figure 4.21). PTAM lets both tracking and mapping execute in parallel threads, but permits them to have different update frequencies.

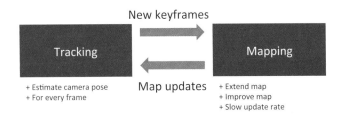

Figure 4.21   Parallel tracking and mapping uses two concurrent threads, one for tracking and one for mapping, which run at different speeds.

The tracking thread operates at full frame rate (e.g., 30 Hz). It projects the points stored in the map into the current frame using a motion model, and searches for correspondences. It then computes the camera pose from these correspondences.

The mapping thread runs at a much slower rate, taking as long as a few seconds per iteration. It is coupled to the tracking thread via keyframes—that is, frames from the video stream that represent a diverse set of camera poses. New keyframes are added if a minimum baseline to all other keyframes exists and the tracking quality is good enough to make the camera pose trustworthy.

When a new keyframe is acquired, the mapping thread extends the map in two ways. First, for all points from the existing map that are found in the new keyframe, the new observation is used to improve the triangulation. Second, new map points are found in the keyframe and added to the map. These points are projected into neighboring keyframes to obtain a triangulation. The extended map is then optimized in the background using bundle adjustment. When the camera is not exploring new areas and delivering new keyframes, the mapping thread uses the idle time to refine the map by progressively checking all points in all keyframes, thereby improving their position estimates and identifying spurious data associations and outliers.

Relocalization and Loop Closure

Consistent data association in SLAM is required for two distinct problems. The first problem is relocalization, referring to the need to restart tracking after it is lost—for example, after temporary occlusion or rapid motion. Tracking needs to be restarted in the same map coordinate system as before, so that the map data remains meaningful.

The second problem is loop closure, referring to the problem of recognizing that the camera is revisiting a part of the scene that has already been mapped, so that points in the map are not mapped twice. Mathematically, this problem is similar to relocalization. In practice, however, the problems can pose very different challenges. While the tracking is working, loop closure can start with good information on the prior camera pose and avoid incorrect data associations. In contrast, relocalization is invoked when tracking is lost, so it must be able to reliably search through the entire model, as the user may have moved an arbitrary distance since the tracking failure.

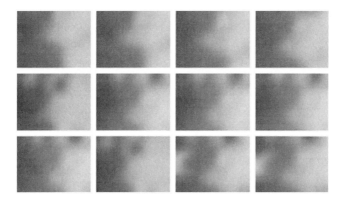

Figure 4.22   Small blurry images computed by resampling 640×480 source images to 40×30 pixels, blurred with a Gaussian kernel of size 5 pixels. Courtesy of Daniel Wagner.

Keyframe-based SLAM handles loop closure implicitly by reprojecting features to nearby keyframes. This reprojection does not scale indefinitely in the number of keyframes, so this form of loop closure remains applicable only to small scenes.

Relocalization could be performed by extracting interest points from the current frame and comparing them to all points. However, keyframe-based SLAM typically uses template matching of patches taken from the keyframes and avoids computing costly descriptors such as SIFT. This does not scale well with increasing map size.

Instead, a popular technique for relocalization in keyframe-based SLAM is to generate an inexpensive descriptor out of the whole keyframe. The keyframe is downsampled to a small blurry image (SBI) [Klein and Murray 2008], which is tiny (e.g., 40×30 pixels) and heavily blurred to suppress high frequencies (Figure 4.22). With dense-enough spacing of the keyframes, a simple ZNCC comparison to the current camera image will yield good re-localization performance. Once a sufficiently similar keyframe has been identified, its camera pose can be adopted to search for known map points in the current image and restart tracking.

In large workspaces, a more scalable approach for detection is required. The standard approach here is to compute descriptors for the map points and use a hierarchical search structure, such as a k-d tree [Lowe 2004] or vocabulary tree [Nistér and Stewenius 2006] for efficiently searching a very large map.

Dense Mapping

Interest point–based approaches such as PTAM rely on a sparse point cloud and do not work well in areas with poor texture. Dense tracking of all points in an image is much more resilient against such poor image conditions, because more information is incorporated. On the down side, dense tracking is computationally intensive.

Two recent advances in hardware have made real-time dense tracking both possible and highly attractive. First, inexpensive RGB-D sensors, such as the Microsoft Kinect, deliver depth measurements directly, without any need to compute point triangulations via software. Second, the GPU can be used for massively parallel numeric computation. This has brought about a revival of dense and semi-dense mapping algorithms, and the ongoing significant increase in computation power, even on mobile computing platforms, further supports this trend. Semi-dense SLAM techniques have already been shown to be feasible in real time without sophisticated hardware support [Engel et al. 2014].

The first approach to successfully leverage the new hardware possibilities for dense SLAM was KinectFusion [Newcombe et al. 2011]. An overview of this technique is shown in Figure 4.23. The tracking part of KinectFusion interprets the depth image from an RGB-D sensor as a point cloud. The camera pose is determined by aligning the current depth image to the previous one with an **iterative closest point** (ICP) algorithm [Arun et al. 1987]:

1. For each point in the current depth image, the closest point in the previous depth image is determined. Per-point normals are computed using finite differences on the input data, and then used to compute a point-to-plane distance metric to determine the data associations.

2. Using these point associations, the rigid transformation that minimizes the residual error is computed.

3. This transformation is applied to all points.

4. The procedure is repeated until the error is deemed small enough.

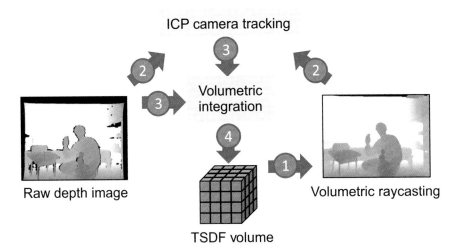

Figure 4.23 KinectFusion obtains a live geometry estimate of the scene from a depth sensor. The depth map is converted into a point cloud and tracked with ICP. Reconstruction is performed by fusing new depth observations into a volume.

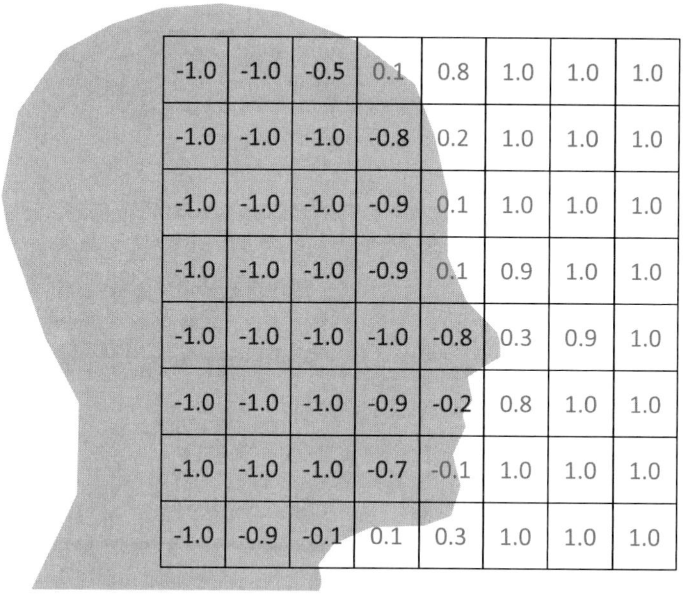

-1.0	-1.0	-0.5	0.1	0.8	1.0	1.0	1.0
-1.0	-1.0	-1.0	-0.8	0.2	1.0	1.0	1.0
-1.0	-1.0	-1.0	-0.9	0.1	1.0	1.0	1.0
-1.0	-1.0	-1.0	-0.9	0.1	0.9	1.0	1.0
-1.0	-1.0	-1.0	-1.0	-0.8	0.3	0.9	1.0
-1.0	-1.0	-1.0	-0.9	-0.2	0.8	1.0	1.0
-1.0	-1.0	-1.0	-0.7	-0.1	1.0	1.0	1.0
-1.0	-0.9	-0.1	0.1	0.3	1.0	1.0	1.0

Figure 4.24   The truncated signed distance function defines for every point in space the distance to the closest isosurface.

The mapping part of KinectFusion represents the scene as a volume storing a **truncated signed distance function** $t(\mathbf{q})$ (Figure 4.24). After transforming new depth data into the global coordinate system using the result of the tracking, t is integrated into v using a running average (Figure 4.25) computed with the aid of an auxiliary volume w [Curless and Levoy 1996].

DEPTH IMAGE INTEGRATION

The truncated signed distance function $t(\mathbf{q})$ describes the distance from $\mathbf{q}$ to the closest surface point s with normal **n**. The distance is considered only in an interval of $\pm\delta$ around s:

$$t(\mathbf{q}) = \min(1, \delta \, \| \, q - s \, \|) \cdot \mathrm{sgn}(\underline{N}(q - s) \cdot \mathbf{n}) \qquad (4.52)$$

Because not every voxel is updated in every frame, a per-voxel counter is stored in a second volume $w(\mathbf{q})$:

$$w^{\mathrm{new}}(\mathbf{q}) = \min(W^{\mathrm{max}}, w(\mathbf{q}) + 1) \qquad (4.53)$$

$$v^{\mathrm{new}}(\mathbf{q}) = \frac{v(\mathbf{q}) \cdot w(\mathbf{q}) + t(\mathbf{q})}{w(\mathbf{q}) + 1}$$

For visualization or AR, a depth map of the reconstructed scene can be extracted from v using GPU raycasting. Because of the integration over time, this depth map does not suffer from sensor artifacts; thus, it is used for determining the ICP in the following frame.

Recent work has explored other forms of **dense** SLAM. DTAM [Newcombe et al. 2011b] computes dense mapping from RGB images alone without the help of a depth sensor. RGB-D SLAM [Kerl et al. 2013] is a keyframe-based SLAM approach that uses RGB-D images rather than just RGB images, and can run with less computational effort on a CPU. LSD-SLAM [Engel et al. 2014] explores a **semi-dense** mapping—an efficient compromise between sparse and dense mapping. With LSD-SLAM, depth estimates are obtained from small-baseline stereo matching on subsequent frames from an RGB camera. All pixels with a suitable depth estimate are then used for depth matching to keyframes.

Outdoor Tracking

The tracking methods we have described so far are primarily intended for indoor use. Of course, AR has many outdoor use cases, such as tourist navigation or engineering inspection, that require tracking to work outdoors. Outdoor tracking is generally more difficult than indoor tracking for the following reasons:

- **Mobility**. The user is free to go anywhere. Tracking needs to cover a very wide area and needs to run on mobile devices such as smartphones, which are comparatively slow and have little storage. Miniature sensors such as GPS and compasses on smartphones have poor accuracy, and most cameras have a narrow field of view. Wireless network connectivity is unpredictable.

- **Environment**. An outdoor environment will likely include many areas with poor or unusable textures (street, grass) and repetitive structures (windows, fences), which cannot be discriminated visually. Moreover, temporal variations can quickly make any tracking model outdated—just consider moving cars, changing weather conditions, or seasonal foliage.

- **Localization database**. The tracking model—for wide area coverage, we call it a localization database—can grow very large. Searching such a database takes a long time and does not scale easily. Creating a localization database from systematic outdoor image acquisition is a very labor-intensive process, and incremental updating of such a database is usually not supported.

- **The user**. In general, we cannot expect a naive user of an AR system to understand the system's operation in depth. When indoors, the user deals with only a small workspace, and it is usually clear that the AR device must be pointed toward the workspace. When outdoors, it may not be clear where in the surroundings the user can expect AR coverage. Not being able to start tracking or see AR overlays may be frustrating for the user.

Figure 4.25   The main square of Graz, Austria, represented as a 3D point cloud computed using SFM from a large set of panoramic images. Courtesy of Clemens Arth.

Collectively, these issues raise the bar for an acceptable outdoor AR tracking solution. The most successful solutions employ some form of model-based natural feature tracking relying on a localization database, usually in the form of a large point cloud annotated with descriptors and other information (Figure 4.25).

Tracking—or localization—is based on the natural feature matching techniques we discussed earlier, but must be enhanced with additional measures to make the solution scalable. These enhancements fall into one of four areas: (1) scalable visual matching strategies, (2) use of prior information from sensors to prune the search space for visual matching, (3) use of prior information from geometry, and (4) simultaneous tracking, mapping, and localization.

Scalable Visual Matching

When tracking models grow to a very large size, such as an entire city, naive matching of features via descriptors computed from interest points becomes infeasible. A naive approach is inefficient, because matching features one by one with the entire database takes too long. A naive approach is also ineffective, because even sophisticated descriptors such as SIFT are not discriminative enough.

To improve the efficiency (i.e., the search speed), the database is organized into a tree, usually through k-means clustering of the features. The number of steps required for searching for a particular feature in such a tree is logarithmic in the number of features. To achieve a large enough increase in efficiency over linear search, the branching width of the tree is often very wide, such as 10–50 branches.

The features extracted from the query image are affected by noisy measurements, so they may not exactly match the features in the database. The matching must therefore tolerate small differences between input feature and database feature. These tolerances become more difficult to maintain as the number of features grows and the average difference between features becomes smaller. As a result, the matching may not return a unique result, but rather a list of putative matches, ranked by similarity to the input features. Recall that usually a best match is accepted only if the ratio to the second best match is less than 0.8. Depending on how the pivoting elements in the tree are chosen, sometimes input features may not even return the closest match, because a wrong path in the tree is searched. This can lead to incorrect or missing data associations.

To improve the effectiveness of the matching, we must find an approach that can tolerate a certain amount of bad data associations. The most popular algorithm for this purpose is the **bag-of-words** model. It builds on the co-occurrence of image features, which are often called "visual words" in this context to emphasize the relationship to text retrieval. While detecting individual image features may not suffice to ensure reliable localization from millions of features, the co-occurrence of features in an image can deliver the necessary discriminative power.

A **vocabulary tree** [Nistér and Stewenius 2006] is a search tree in which the original leaves corresponding 1:1 to features are omitted. The intermediate nodes directly above the original leaves, each associated with a visual word (a quantized descriptor), become the new leaves. Each visual word has an **inverted file structure** as its payload, rather than a list of features. Recall that the tree was created from the features associated with a 3D point cloud, which in turn was created with SFM by extracting interest points from a collection of source images. The inverted file for a visual word points to the indices of all those images from which the descriptor was extracted. The source images refer to the 3D points extracted from them.

Visual words that contain features extracted from the same image will, in turn, vote for this image. Thus, by running all features extracted from a query image through the vocabulary tree, we obtain a histogram of votes for certain images. We select the source image with the highest rank in the histogram, since it is most likely to show the same scene as the query image. The features from the query image are now matched against the features associated with the 3D points of the selected source image. This process can be made more robust against outliers by considering multiple top-ranked source images. We retain only those associations from interest points in the query image to 3D points that actually appear together in one of the source images. The 2D–3D associations resulting from this procedure are then forwarded to the usual RANSAC P3P with additional geometric verification (see the "Perspective-n-Point Pose" section earlier in this chapter).

The original vocabulary approach was enhanced by Irschara et al. [2009] with so-called **virtual views**. That is, in the preprocessing, the 3D points obtained from SFM are re-projected into "virtual views" created by setting up a regular grid of virtual cameras. These virtual views act only as containers for co-occurrence of features having geometric proximity in the space of possible viewpoints. Because the number of virtual views can become very large, a compressed version of the virtual view set is obtained by greedily merging virtual views with similar feature sets. The net result of this enhancement is a better representation of the spatial coherence of features in the vocabulary tree.

Sattler et al. [2011] propose to speed up data association by replacing the indirect matching via source images with direct matching. Visual words directly store a list of associated features. Among the visual words found in a query image, the ones with only a few descriptors are inspected first. Successful matches initiate a 3D active search, where nearby 3D points are back-projected into the query image to find additional matches [Sattler et al. 2012].

For even larger-scale pose estimation, Li et al. [2012] have introduced a world-scale pose localization pipeline. Their technique addresses the problem of determining where an uncalibrated-camera photograph was taken by estimating a 6DOF camera pose with respect to a large geo-registered 3D point cloud.

Prior Information from Sensors

Modern mobile devices are usually equipped with multiple sensors: GPS, magnetometers, and linear accelerometers. Although the performance of these sensors can vary significantly depending on environmental conditions, they are generally suitable for obtaining prior information in outdoor localization. This prior information is then refined by image-based localization. The pruning of the localization database using the sensor's prior information leads to a significantly smaller database, thereby increasing both the runtime efficiency and the success rate of the localization. Moreover, the size of the database after pruning is largely independent of the overall database size. Consequently, such a pruning technique can be used to download relevant features over the air to a mobile client on demand.

GPS is the most obvious source of prior information. Given a geo-aligned SFM reconstruction, we can determine globally registered coordinates for both the 3D points and the camera poses. This information can be used to organize the database into a regular or irregular geographic grid (Figure 4.26), using an idea similar to the virtual views discussed in the "Scalable Visual Matching" section. Only feature points from virtual views sufficiently close to the GPS prior are considered for matching. If we assume that most features will be observed at a limited distance, we can even organize the database simply by quantizing the geo-coordinates of the 3D points [Takacs et al. 2008].

Figure 4.26 After reconstruction, the relevant parts of an urban area can be subdivided into cells. By preselecting cells based on a GPS measurement as a source, one can substantially prune the relevant portions of the reconstruction database. Courtesy of Clemens Arth.

A horizontal orientation estimate provided by a magnetometer is also suitable for database pruning. The features can be presorted according to the heading resulting from projecting the normals at feature points to the ground plane. Arth et al. [2012] use eight overlapping bins spaced 45° apart, each covering a 60° field of view (Figure 4.27).

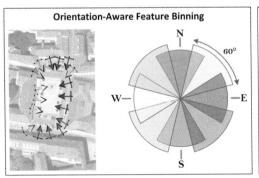
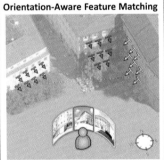

Figure 4.27 A magnetometer (compass) can be used as a source of prior information to narrow the search for point correspondences to those with a normal facing approximately toward the user. Courtesy of Clemens Arth.

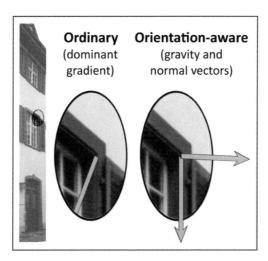

Figure 4.28 Features with an orientation aligned to gravity rather than to a visual attribute such as the gradient can be matched more reliably. Courtesy of Clemens Arth.

A vertical orientation estimate is provided by measuring gravity using linear accelerometers. Gravity has two uses in AR. First, it can replace dominant gradient orientation in SIFT-like features [Kurz and BenHimane 2011]. In urban environments, where most features are found on building facades and consequently have a vertical orientation, using gravity-aligned features improves matching performance (Figure 4.28). Second, gravity can be used to estimate the inclination of the view. This provides an opportunity for vertical binning of features, similar to the horizontal binning performed by the magnetometer. However, the gain of vertical binning is smaller due to the fact that the streets below the buildings and the sky above the buildings do not contain reliable interest points.

Taken together, the use of sensors as sources of prior information can improve the success rate of localization by as much as 15% [Arth et al. 2012]. However, the main improvement from using this technique is greater speed of searching resulting from the database pruning. On mobile devices, which typically have very limited memory bandwidth, this may be the main reason to adopt such a technique.

Prior Information from Geometry

The widespread availability of online geographic information systems (GIS) such as Google Maps and OpenStreetMap offers another source for prior localization data. GIS provides

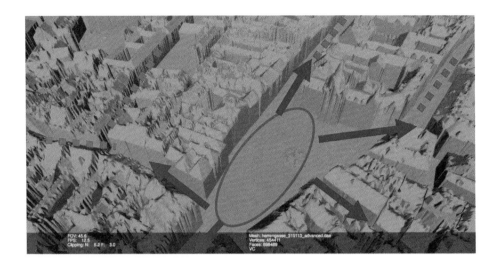

Figure 4.29   The potentially visible set for the central square contains the street segments immediately connected to the square (blue arrows), but not the street segments after one or more turns (dashed red lines).

building outlines and sometimes digital elevation models (DEM). By extrapolating the building outlines and integrating them with DEM, a coarse 3D model of an urban environment can be computed.

When this information is combined with prior-pose data from GPS and a magnetometer, the resulting model can be used to prune a localization database. Potentially visible sets [Airey et al. 1990] can be computed by first determining which portion of the model (such as facades or walls, in case of an indoor model) may be visible from the camera pose indicated by the prior information, and then pruning the search space correspondingly. Such a computation provides a stronger reduction than just information on the prior position [Arth et al. 2009] (Figure 4.29). Moreover, 3D points that are found to be sufficiently close to a facade obtained from GIS are marked as belonging to that facade. This imposes an additional semantic structure on the point cloud, which can be used to improve inlier verification during matching. Alternatively, facades can be matched directly to GIS data [Arth et al. 2015].

Simultaneous Tracking, Mapping, and Localization

In the section "Simultaneous Localization and Mapping," we discussed SLAM, which can provide model-free tracking, but only relative to an local starting point. For outdoor AR display of globally registered information (such as street names), SLAM alone is not a suitable approach.

Of course, if we had a way to connect the relative coordinate system from SLAM to the globally registered information at least once, SLAM would offer several useful opportunities for outdoor tracking. For instance, it does not require a premade tracking model. Instead, SLAM relies on current visual information from the environment, which can incorporate many phenomena, such as weather-related effects, that are valid for only a short period of time. Moreover, SLAM can run entirely self-contained on a mobile device without any need for additional infrastructure. Finally, the map created by SLAM integrates information from many spatially adjacent viewpoints into a single data structure. If a single camera image with a narrow field of view is insufficient for a localization procedure operating on a large database, the aggregate information collected in the map may be enough to succeed.

These opportunities can be harvested by adopting simultaneous tracking, mapping, and localization (Figure 4.30). With this approach, a client-side SLAM system is combined with server-side localization. Client and server are loosely coupled through a wireless network, and each host operates asynchronously at its own speed. The server-side localization can take full advantage of the scalable server technology without affecting the mobility of the client.

The client continuously updates the server as soon as the map is extended. These map updates can simply consist of a message containing a keyframe and the associated local pose. The server collects this information and repeatedly attempts to obtain a global pose from it. If the server is successful, it notifies the client. The client can then upgrade its local pose to a global pose, and start displaying globally registered information. The client can continue to operate in global coordinates, even if the server does not provide any additional pose updates. The client can even perform relocalization with global coordinates using only its local map information.

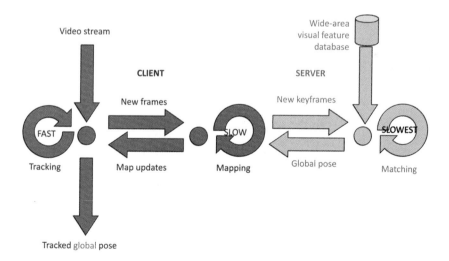

Figure 4.30 Conventional SLAM (blue) performs tracking and mapping simultaneously on a mobile client device. By adding a localization server (orange), a third concurrent activity is added: matching to a global database of visual features for wide-area localization. Client and server operate independently, so the client can always run at the highest frame rate.

Figure 4.31   A panorama obtained with real-time panoramic SLAM. Courtesy of Clemens Arth.

The simplest approach for client-side SLAM is panoramic localization and mapping [DiVerdi et al. 2008] [Wagner et al. 2010], which creates panoramas like the one shown in Figure 4.31 in real time. Rather than obtaining the local structure from motion with 6DOF, the user is constrained to stand still and perform only rotational motion with the camera (Figure 4.32). Such an exploratory mode of using AR is very common for outdoor users.

Constraining the motion to just rotation narrows the SLAM problem to image alignment with 3DOF, which requires only computing a homography and can be easily handled in real time even on slow devices. Panoramic SLAM also does not require a baseline to be established before initializing the SLAM map, which is known to be difficult for untrained users [Mulloni et al. 2013]. Not surprisingly, the number of features that can be matched to an outdoor localization database grows roughly linearly with the field of view of the camera [Arth et al. 2011]. Mapping larger panoramas improves the chances of eventually performing successful localization (Figure 4.33). Consequently, it is preferable to repeated attempts to compute localization from single narrow-field-view images.

Figure 4.32   With panoramic SLAM, the user may perform only rotational motion, such as when exploring the immediate environment. Courtesy of Daniel Wagner.

Figure 4.33 The yellow lines show the feature matches obtained from a panoramic image. Note how certain directions, where facades are directly observed, perform very well, while directions facing down a street perform poorly. This illustrates why a wide field of view is needed for reliable outdoor localization. Courtesy of Clemens Arth.

If a full 6DOF SLAM system is available, the user is not constrained to stay in a particular location. Therefore, a wider variety of viewpoints can be obtained, while the user can also freely explore the environs. Figure 4.34 illustrates a user visiting multiple viewpoints. Computing global pose from a 6DOF SLAM map is algorithmically equivalent to loop closure [Ventura et al. 2014a], as discussed in the "Simultaneous Localization and Mapping" section. SLAM map and global reconstruction are related by a a 7DOF similarity transform (3DOF position + 3DOF orientation + 1DOF scale). This transform can be determined by point cloud alignment [Umeyama 1991], but it may be difficult to obtain the required matches from a small SLAM map. Ventura et al. [2014b] present an efficient solution for four 2D–3D correspondences using optimal Gröbner bases, and Sweeney et al. [2014] provide a high-accuracy solution to the more general problem with $n \geq 4$ correspondences, formulated as a minimization of a least-squares cost function.

If the server successfully performs localization, the loop closure information computed as a by-product can be used by the client in local bundle adjustment to limit the drift of the local map. The map is essentially anchored to the 3D points matched by the server, resulting in a much more stable and scalable mapping. Simultaneously, the map incorporates recent observations, which cannot be stored in the global database (Figure 4.35).

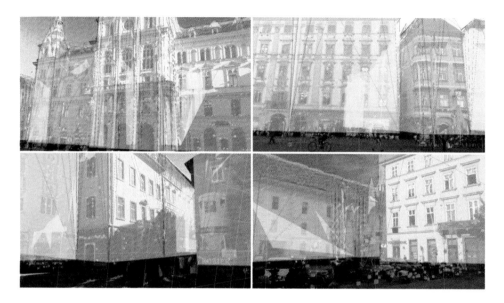

Figure 4.34 Multiple images from a sequence tracked with 6DOF SLAM on a client, while a localization server provides the global pose used to overlay the building outlines with transparent yellow structures. Courtesy of Jonathan Ventura and Clemens Arth.

Figure 4.35 This SLAM sequence starts with tracking a facade (overlaid in yellow), for which a global pose has been determined by a server. The images in the bottom row cannot continue tracking with information known to the server; the poster in the foreground, which has been incorporated into the SLAM map, is used for tracking instead. Courtesy of Jonathan Ventura and Clemens Arth.

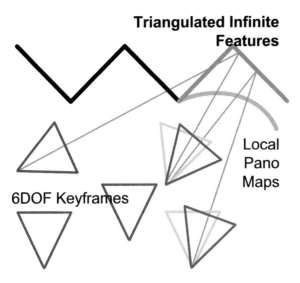

Figure 4.36   A SLAM system that can handle both general 6DOF motion and pure rotation has the advantage that the user is not constrained to a certain type of motion. It also presents the opportunity to recover 3D features (magenta) from panoramic features (cyan) when additional views become available. Courtesy of Christian Pirchheim.

Recall that a limitation of SLAM systems is the fundamental need for a camera baseline of significant size relative to the distance of the objects to be modeled. In the outdoors, such objects may be easily tens or hundreds of meters away. SLAM systems rely on moving viewpoints and fail if the camera is rotated only.

Given that it is often difficult to establish a sufficient baseline outdoors, and that users may prefer rotational motions to explore their surroundings, it would be helpful to combine panoramic and 6DOF SLAM into a single system. A system that can dynamically switch between panoramic and 6DOF mode will avoid tracking failures if the user inadvertently makes the "wrong" kind of motion (Figure 4.36). Such a combined SLAM can be built by analyzing the motion according to a GRIC score [Gauglitz et al. 2014c].

With appropriate organization of the map, it is also possible to opportunistically recover 3D information from panoramic map parts, which helps to further densify and expand the maps [Pirchheim et al. 2013]. As a result, tracking robustness is increased significantly (Figure 4.37).

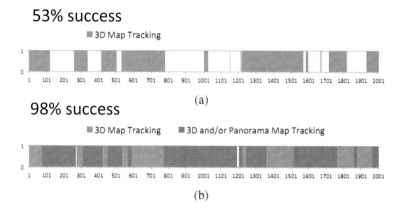

Figure 4.37   The combination of 6DOF and panoramic SLAM delivers much more robust tracking performance during arbitrary user motion. (a) Conventional 6DOF SLAM can track the pose for only 53% of the frames. (b) Combined SLAM can track the pose in 98% of the frames. Courtesy of Christian Pirchheim.

Summary

In this chapter, we discussed computer vision algorithms for 3D tracking. We investigated seminal use cases and discussed the associated mathematical techniques.

Square marker tracking relies on extracting a quadrilateral shape from an image with simple thresholding and computing a pose from the homography estimated from the four corners of the marker. It is also possible to refine the camera pose from an initial estimate.

Multi-camera infrared tracking uses two or more cameras to triangulate targets reflecting infrared light. Assuming the geometric configuration of the cameras is known, a 3D point may be triangulated from two or more observations using epipolar geometry. The local coordinate system of a target may also be related to a global coordinate system using absolute orientation.

Natural feature tracking by detection goes beyond artificially prepared scenes by matching camera images to a tracking model built from a real environment. Interest points (e.g., Harris, DOG, or FAST) are extracted from the image, and descriptors such as SIFT are created from the interest points. These descriptors provide an efficient means for searching for matches with the tracking model. Successfully matched points can be used to compute the camera pose using the Perspective-n-Point algorithm, usually embedded in a RANSAC loop with robust estimation.

Incremental tracking uses active search methods to follow interest points from one frame to the next, often using KLT or NCC for matching. Prior information for the camera that supports this kind of incremental search is obtained from a motion model or from a hierarchical search.

While incremental tracking cannot work without initialization, it is usually combined with tracking by detection.

SLAM does not rely on a premade model, but instead builds the tracking model using structure from motion while the camera is exploring the environment. This requires first estimating a relative camera pose from 2D–2D interest point correspondences—for example, using a five-point algorithm, then triangulating 3D points, and finally limiting map drift using bundle adjustment. Modern SLAM is usually decoupled into parallel tracking and mapping threads and incorporates relocalization and potentially loop closure capabilities. In contrast to keyframe-based SLAM, which operates with sparse 3D points, dense mapping takes all pixels from the input image into consideration. This provides enhanced robustness in difficult environments, but usually requires additional hardware or very efficient alignment techniques.

Outdoor tracking must address the additional challenge of searching a very large localization database. The most popular approach for scalable visual search relies on the use of a vocabulary tree. The database can further be pruned using prior information derived from mobile sensors, such as GPS or a magnetometer, or data obtained from a geographic information system. Mobile devices can deliver scalable outdoor tracking by performing small-scale SLAM locally and cooperating with a localization server for obtaining global pose. The local SLAM should support both panoramic and full 6DOF motion, leaving the user free to explore the environment at will. We can assume that outdoor tracking systems will rapidly improve in the near future, as systematic mapping and reconstruction efforts from leading online map providers are already progressing.

CHAPTER 5

CALIBRATION AND REGISTRATION

Using a tracking system creates the need to handle multiple coordinate systems. These coordinate systems need to be reconciled with each other, so that a correct overlay of virtual objects on tracked physical objects is ensured. This process, which is called registration, is required to convert the poses from tracking into the coordinate system of the rendering application. Registration is also necessary to align the rendering camera with respect to a tracked display. We have already seen how a tracking coordinate system can be registered to an object coordinate system using the absolute orientation algorithm in Chapter 4.

Registration in AR means that several components need calibration. In this chapter, we begin by examining the calibration of the camera's internal parameters and lens distortion, then turn our attention to displays, discussing the calibration of optical see-through head-mounted displays without and with the help of an additional pointing device. We also discuss hand–eye calibration, which is useful if outside-in and inside-out tracking systems are used simultaneously. Finally, we discuss issues and error sources in AR registration. As mentioned in Chapter 3, impatient readers may skip over the blue boxes.

Camera Calibration

We begin our discussion with the inner workings of a camera. Calibrating a camera encompasses measuring the internal camera parameters and the nonlinearities resulting from lens distortion.

Internal Camera Parameters

For the tracking techniques described in Chapter 4, we have assumed that the internal camera calibration matrix K (see the "Camera Representation" section in Chapter 4) is known. Recall that the projection matrix is composed of internal and external parameters: $M = K[R \mid t]$. Without any prior information, K can be obtained by first determining M and then decomposing M into K, R, and t.

The most widely used algorithms for camera calibration were proposed by Tsai [1986] and later by Zhang [2000]. We assume a set of 2D–3D point correspondences of a known reference object, a **calibration target**. The most popular type of calibration target is a checkerboard or a rectangular grid of dots, from which regularly spaced points can easily be extracted. Unlike in the case of homography estimation, the 3D points must not lie in a single plane. This can be achieved by arranging two calibration targets in an orthogonal configuration or by taking multiple pictures of a single calibration target from different angles (Figure 5.1).

Figure 5.1 Two or more images of a calibration pattern consisting of a regular grid of dots with known dimensions are sufficient to perform calibration of internal camera parameters.

TSAI ALGORITHM

Recall the relationship $\mathbf{p}_\times\mathbf{M}\mathbf{q} = 0$ between a 3D point $\mathbf{q}$ and its 2D image $\mathbf{p}$ from Chapter 4:

$$\mathbf{p}_\times\mathbf{M}\mathbf{q} = 0 \tag{5.1}$$

$$\begin{bmatrix} p_v\mathbf{M}_{R3}^T \cdot \mathbf{q} & - & \mathbf{M}_{R2}^T \cdot \mathbf{q} \\ \mathbf{M}_{R1}^T \cdot \mathbf{q} & - & p_u\mathbf{M}_{R3}^T \cdot \mathbf{q} \\ p_u\mathbf{M}_{R2}^T \cdot \mathbf{q} & - & p_v\mathbf{M}_{R1}^T \cdot \mathbf{q} \end{bmatrix} = 0$$

We can compute $\mathbf{M}$ from these relationships using a DLT method similar to the one for homographies. We rearrange the coefficients of $\mathbf{M}$ into a 12×1 vector $[\mathbf{M}_{R1}, \mathbf{M}_{R2}, \mathbf{M}_{R3}]^T$:

$$\begin{bmatrix} 0 & -p_w\mathbf{q}^T & p_v\mathbf{q}^T \\ p_w\mathbf{q}^T & 0 & -p_u\mathbf{q}^T \\ -p_v\mathbf{q}^T & p_u\mathbf{q}^T & 0 \end{bmatrix}\begin{bmatrix} \mathbf{M}_{R1}^T \\ \mathbf{M}_{R2}^T \\ \mathbf{M}_{R3}^T \end{bmatrix} = 0 \tag{5.2}$$

Equation 5.2 has only two degrees of freedom, so six or more point correspondences must be stacked into an equation system to determine the 11DOF of $\mathbf{M}$. This system is solved with SVD, and the solution is iteratively refined with Levenberg-Marquardt minimization.

The left 3×3 submatrix of $\mathbf{M}$ is composed of the orthonormal rotation matrix $\mathbf{R}$ and the upper triangular calibration matrix $\mathbf{K}$, that is, $[\mathbf{M}_{C1} \mid \mathbf{M}_{C2} \mid \mathbf{M}_{C3}] = \mathbf{KR}$. It can be decomposed using **RQ factorization**. To achieve this aim, we express the inverse rotation $\mathbf{R}^{-1}$ as the product of three orthogonal rotation matrices:

$$\mathbf{R}^{-1} = \mathbf{R}_x\mathbf{R}_y\mathbf{R}_z =$$

$$\begin{bmatrix} 1 & 0 & 0 \\ 0 & \cos(\theta_x) & -\sin(\theta_x) \\ 0 & \sin(\theta_x) & \cos(\theta_x) \end{bmatrix}\begin{bmatrix} \cos(\theta_y) & 0 & \sin(\theta_y) \\ 0 & 1 & 0 \\ -\sin(\theta_y) & 0 & \cos(\theta_y) \end{bmatrix}\begin{bmatrix} \cos(\theta_z) & -\sin(\theta_z) & 0 \\ \sin(\theta_z) & \cos(\theta_z) & 0 \\ 0 & 0 & 1 \end{bmatrix} \tag{5.3}$$

Each of the three orthogonal matrices is chosen such that when it is multiplied with $\mathbf{M}$, one of the three values below the diagonal becomes zero. The result of the multiplications is the upper triangular matrix $\mathbf{K} = \mathbf{MR}^{-1} = \mathbf{MR}_x\mathbf{R}_y\mathbf{R}_z$. We first select θ_x such that element $(3,2)$ becomes zero:

$$\cos(\theta_x) = -\frac{m_{3,3}}{\sqrt{m_{3,2}^2 + m_{3,3}^2}}, \quad \sin(\theta_x) = \frac{m_{3,2}}{\sqrt{m_{3,2}^2 + m_{3,3}^2}} \tag{5.4}$$

Similarly, we select θ_y such that element $(3,1)$ becomes zero and θ_z such that element $(2,1)$ becomes zero.

Correcting Lens Distortion

The lenses of real cameras are imperfect and do not follow the pinhole model with sufficient accuracy. If this is not already done in the firmware of a digital camera during factory-time calibration, it may be necessary to correct for lens distortions. When considering lens distortion, we must distinguish between radial and tangential forms of distortion. Radial distortion expands or compresses the image as a function of distance from the lens center, which leads to either pincushion or barrel distortion effects (Figure 5.2). Tangential distortion moves image points along a tangent to a circle around the lens center. Note that these effects are not necessarily symmetric in the image, as the center of the sensor and the center of the lens may not be aligned. It is usually necessary to compensate for radial distortion, while the effects of tangential distortion are much smaller and can usually be neglected.

To address radial distortion, we can compute undistorted image points $\mathbf{p}$ from distorted image points $\mathbf{d}$ and the center of projection $\mathbf{c}$. The most popular method uses the following polynomial approximation:

$$
\begin{aligned}
r &= \sqrt{(d_u - c_u)^2 + (d_v - c_v)^2} \\
p_u &= d_u + (d_u - c_u)(K_1 r^2 + K_2 r^4 + \cdots) \\
p_v &= d_v + (d_v - c_v)(K_1 r^2 + K_2 r^4 + \cdots)
\end{aligned}
\tag{5.5}
$$

The distorted points are obtained from a calibration pattern, as mentioned earlier. For conventional cameras, considering a single coefficient K_1 is usually satisfactory. In contrast, for wide-angle lenses, it may be necessary to consider two coefficents K_1 and K_2. Considering more than two coefficients typically does not improve the result and makes the calibration process much more fragile. Figure 5.3 shows a video image that has been undistorted by texture mapping onto a regular 10×10 grid, with texture coordinates derived from Equation 5.5.

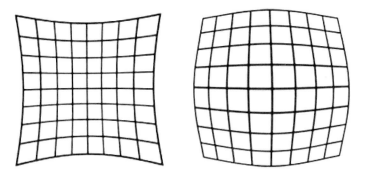

Figure 5.2   Radial distortions: (left) pincushion distortion and (right) barrel distortion. Courtesy of Gerhard Reitmayr.

Figure 5.3   (left) Video image with lens distortions clearly visible on the curved door and frame. (right) The same image, rectified using texture mapping parameters derived from lens distortion calibration. Courtesy of Anton Fuhrmann.

Display Calibration

A fully calibrated AR system requires calibration not only of the input side, but also of the output side—namely, the display. With known internal and external camera parameters, we have enough information for presenting registered AR overlays on a video see-through display.

For an optical see-through display, head tracking must be used instead of camera tracking to inform the registration of the AR overlay. The head tracking can be done in an outside-in fashion—for example, with a camera attached to a head-mounted display. Nevertheless, head tracking alone does not identify the pose of each eye relative to the display. Since an HMD places the display relatively close to the eye, a precise calibration of the eye-display transformation is required. Luckily, we may assume that this transformation is static and can be calibrated once the HMD is donned. This assumption will remain valid, unless major adjustments to the fitting of the HMD on the head are made during the session.

Because the user sees the composite image only in the optical see-through display, we must turn the usual image-based calibration approach around, putting the human in the loop. The system displays calibration patterns, and the user is asked to align a structure in the physical environment with the pattern. This procedure can take various forms, which differ in the freedom afforded to the user.

In the work of Oishi and Tachi [1995], the user's head is fixed at a given position, and a "shooting gallery" presents calibration patterns at varying distances (Figure 5.4) to the user. Azuma and Bishop [1994] use a "bore-sight" approach, where a crosshair pattern must be aligned with a physical line of sight (Figure 5.5).

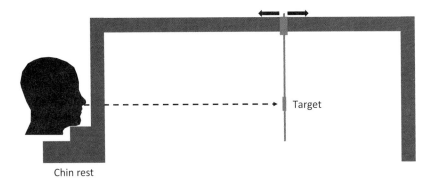

Figure 5.4   Calibrating an HMD using a shooting-gallery approach. The user's head is fixed on a chin rest, and the user must aim at targets shown at varying distances.

Figure 5.5   Bore-sight approach for HMD calibration. The user must align the HMD view with an edge of a box.

In this section, we discuss two approaches that allow the user to move freely, while providing constraints for calibration one by one, rather than jointly. The single point active alignment method proposed by Tuceryan et al. [2002] asks the user to align a crosshair with a known point in the real world, while the method suggested by Fuhrmann et al. [2000] uses an additional tracked pointing device. Both methods provide significantly improved convenience over methods requiring the user to hold still during calibration, which has made this type of approach very popular among practitioners. These methods can further be enhanced by storing previous calibration results, and then propagating them from one session to the next or even from one eye to the other (for stereoscopic displays.) Such reuse can further reduce the calibration effort for the user [Fuhrmann et al. 2000] [Genc et al. 2002].

Recently, tracking systems for real-time tracking of the user relative to the display have become popular. User-tracking systems can be used for stationary optical see-through displays such as a virtual showcase [Bimber et al. 2005] as well as for handheld or head-mounted displays. Baričević et al. [2012] describe a handheld display with head tracking for user-perspective rendering. A similar approach is taken by the commercial Amazon Fire Phone, which uses four front-facing cameras simultaneously. Itoh and Klinker [2014] use a pupil tracker mounted inside

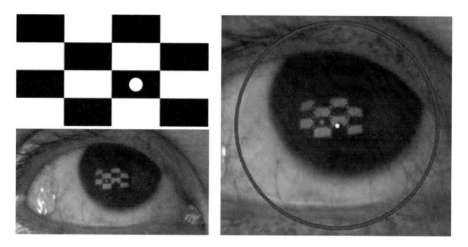

Figure 5.6 An inward-facing camera mounted in an HMD can be used to detect a projected checkerboard pattern and derive the eye's position and orientation relative to the display. Courtesy of Alexander Plopski.

an HMD for adjusting registration in real time. Plopski et al. [2015] describe an eye-tracking system with a camera inside an HMD, which detects the reflection of a calibration pattern from the display in the user's eye (Figure 5.6).

Single Point Active Alignment Method

The single point active alignment method (SPAAM) [Tuceryan et al. 2002] is one of the most popular methods for HMD calibration. It assumes that an optical see-through HMD is tracked relative to the world W. The tracked point on the HMD is labeled H, and the tracking transformation is denoted as $\mathbf{M}^{W \to H}$. The eye E of the user observes a point $\mathbf{q}$ given in world coordinates at the 2D location $\mathbf{p}$ (Figure 5.7).

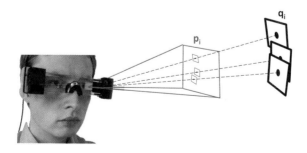

Figure 5.7 The single point active alignment method works by presenting a sequence of crosshair targets in the display, which the user must align with a known real-world point. Courtesy of Jens Grubert.

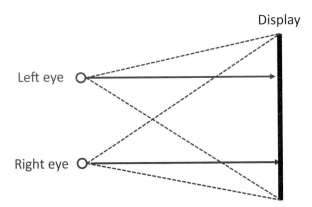

Figure 5.8   In the general case, the user will see the display inside an HMD under an off-axis projection. The viewing direction, which is normal to the image plane, is not centered inside the viewport. Consequently, a skewed viewing frustum must be used.

The goal of the calibration is to determine the projection matrix from head-to-eye coordinates, $\mathbf{M}^{H \to E}$:

$$\mathbf{p} = \mathbf{M}^{H \to E} \, \mathbf{M}^{W \to H} \mathbf{q} \qquad\qquad (5.6)$$

As discussed in the "Camera Representation" section in Chapter 4, a general projection matrix has 11DOF, combining internal and external parameters. In general, the display will not be exactly centered in front of the eye, which leads to an off-axis projection (i.e., the internal camera parameters c_u and c_v of Equation 4.3 will not correspond to the screen center). The resulting viewing frustum will be asymmetric (Figure 5.8).

The goal of SPAAM is to compute $\mathbf{M}^{H \to E}$ from at least six 2D–3D correspondences (or, better yet, 12–20 correspondences) obtained with user interaction. A series of crosshair markers displayed at locations $\mathbf{p}_i$ on the screen are presented for the user. The user must visually align the crosshair with a known point $\mathbf{q}$. When the user confirms the alignment by pressing a trigger button, the system records the 2D–3D correspondence $(\mathbf{p}_i, \mathbf{q}_i)$ with $\mathbf{q}_i = \mathbf{M}^{W \to H} \mathbf{q}$ and advances to the next calibration point.

The desired projection matrix can be computed from these correspondences using the DLT technique described in the previous section "Internal Camera Parameters."

Head-Mounted Display Calibration Using a Pointing Device

The calibration method proposed by Fuhrmann et al. [2000] requires an additional tracked pointing device, which must be aligned with the on-display crosshair instead of the static

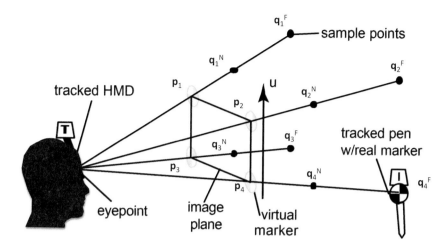

Figure 5.9 If a pointing device is available, it can replace the fixed known point in the world used in SPAAM with direct user input. The user can manually select the distance of the 3D points by stretching out the arm. Courtesy of Anton Fuhrmann.

calibration point used by SPAAM. Such a pointing device will often be part of the AR setup, including a trigger to confirm the alignment. The advantage of the pointing device is that instead of having to move the head to achieve the alignment, the user can move the arm, which is typically both more precise and more convenient (Figure 5.9). Moreover, this approach can be used for video see-through calibration of "magic mirror" setups, which require the user to look toward a stationary display while performing the calibration input.

This method requires the user to define lines rather than individual points, by specifying two points for the same crosshair location: one near location q^N, with the arm held close to the head, and one far location q^F, with the arm fully stretched out. The size of the crosshair indicates if a near or far point is requested. The procedure is repeated four times, giving one line (q_i^N, q_i^F) per crosshair point p_i near a corner of the screen, thereby approximating the viewing frustum.

If the transformation of the pointing device D is tracked as $\mathbf{M}^{W \to D}$, we store $\mathbf{M}^{W \to H}(\mathbf{M}^{W \to D})^{-1}$ for each of the eight input points.

Recovery of the transformation from H to E can be based on geometric considerations, or it could use a DLT method equivalent to the one in SPAAM. The geometric method may be faster to compute. First, the four lines should intersect in the eyepoint, which is computed in the least squares sense. Averaging the direction of the lines yields a reasonable approximation of the viewing direction, which is initially assumed to be orthogonal to the image plane Π. The vertical and horizontal directions of the image plane are estimated from the intersections of Π with the lines. From this information, the camera up-vector can be estimated. These estimates are often sufficient, if followed by nonlinear refinement.

Hand–Eye Calibration

In the "Absolution Orientation" section of Chapter 4, we saw that the coordinate systems of two tracking systems can be aligned using the absolute orientation method if a set of points can be measured by both tracking systems. This technique is commonly used in AR when we want to align tracking coordinates with the modeled real environment. In other cases, two tracking systems may be deployed that are rigidly linked, but cannot observe common reference points. For example, a camera may be mounted to a display. In this scenario, the camera performs inside-out tracking of objects in the world, and the display is externally tracked from an outside-in tracker. We would like to know the transformation from display to camera.

In robotics, a similar situation is encountered when a camera (eye) E is mounted on the end-effector (hand) H of the robot R. The robot unit mechanically tracks $R - H$, and the camera visually tracks $E - T$ of a calibration target T. Since the static transformations $R - T$ and $H - E$ are unknown, we would like to calibrate $H - E$ from the measurements of the two tracking systems without a common reference object.

We can achieve this hand–eye calibration by obtaining several measurements $\mathbf{M}_k^{R \to H}$ and $\mathbf{M}_k^{E \to T}$. We concatenate pairs of measurements (k, k') into relative transformations:

$$\begin{aligned} \mathbf{A} &= (\mathbf{M}_k^{R \to H})^{-1} \mathbf{M}_{k'}^{R \to H} \\ \mathbf{B} &= (\mathbf{M}_k^{E \to T})^{-1} \mathbf{M}_{k'}^{E \to T} \end{aligned} \qquad (5.7)$$

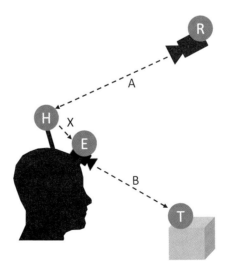

Figure 5.10   Hand–eye calibration must be used if two tracking systems are used simultaneously, but no common reference point is available. Here we are interested in the unknown static transformation X from the user's head H to a head-mounted camera E. An external tracking system R measures the transformation A to the user's head H, and the camera E measures the transformation B to target object T. From A and B, X can be computed.

From these relative transformations, we can compute a least squares solution of the hand–eye calibration $X = M^{H \rightarrow E}$ using the following equation:

$$A_i X = X B_i \tag{5.8}$$

The classic algorithm by Tsai and Lenz [1989] solves this problem by determining first the rotation and then the translation part of X.

TSAI-LENZ ALGORITHM

We first separate the measurements into rotation and translation: $A = [R^A \mid t^A]$, $B = [R^B \mid t^B]$. Rotations are represented as quaternions. A rotation of an angle θ around an axis given as a unit vector $[w_x \ w_y \ w_z]^T$ is expressed in quaternion form q as follows:

$$q = [q_w \ q_x \ q_y \ q_z]^T = \left[\cos\frac{\theta}{2} \ \sin\frac{\theta}{2} w_x \ \sin\frac{\theta}{2} w_y \ \sin\frac{\theta}{2} w_z \right]^T \tag{5.9}$$

It can be obtained from a rotation matrix R:

$$q_w = \frac{\sqrt{1 + R_{0,0} + R_{1,1} + R_{2,2}}}{2} \tag{5.10}$$

$$q_x = \frac{R_{2,1} - R_{1,2}}{4 q_w}$$

$$q_y = \frac{R_{0,2} - R_{2,0}}{4 q_w}$$

$$q_z = \frac{R_{1,0} - R_{0,1}}{4 q_w}$$

Since a unit quaternion has only 3DOF, we can work with only three components, q_x, q_y, q_z, to compute an auxiliary 3-vector, q'. Let q^A and q^B be such three-component representations of R^A and R^B, respectively. We compute q' as follows:

$$(q_i^A + q_i^B)_\times q' = q_i^B - q_i^A \tag{5.11}$$

At least two pairs of measurements (A_i, B_i) are required to solve this problem in the least squares sense, since $()_\times$ is singular. We recover the fourth component of q' from the other three by applying the fact that the 4-vector must have unit length. The desired rotation q^X is related to q' as follows:

$$q^X = \frac{2q'}{\sqrt{1 + |q'|^2}} \tag{5.12}$$

(continues)

(continued)

The resulting quaternion can be transformed back to a rotation matrix:

$$\mathbf{Rot}(\mathbf{q}) = \begin{bmatrix} 1 - 2(q_y^2 + q_z^2) & 2(q_x q_y - q_w q_z) & 2(q_w q_y + q_x q_z) \\ 2(q_x q_y + q_w q_z) & 1 - 2(q_x^2 + q_z^2) & 2(q_y q_z - q_w q_x) \\ 2(q_w q_y - q_x q_z) & 2(q_y q_z + q_w q_x) & 1 - 2(q_x^2 + q_y^2) \end{bmatrix} \qquad (5.13)$$

The desired translation $\mathbf{t}^X$ can be obtained with another least squares solution:

$$(\mathbf{Rot}\,(\mathbf{q}_i^A) - \mathbf{I})\mathbf{t}^X = \mathbf{Rot}\,(\mathbf{q}^X)\mathbf{t}_i^B - \mathbf{t}_i^A \qquad (5.14)$$

Registration

Now that we have a working knowledge of the calibration procedures that must be carried out offline, before an AR application can be used, we can consider techniques that preserve proper registration at runtime.

The complex interplay of system components implies that many potential sources of error can affect registration. As mentioned in the "Temporal Characteristics" section in Chapter 3. we can distinguish between *static error*, which affects accuracy, and *dynamic error*, which affects precision. Correction of static error mainly requires improved calibration, which accounts for all misalignments between the measurement and the reference coordinate system. A major source of static error that has not been addressed yet are systematic nonlinearities in the measurements provided by the tracking system. Obviously, dynamic errors are most severe, as they cannot be addressed with static calibration. In this category, we mainly have to combat error propagation and latency.

Geometric Measurement Distortions

Sensor systems can suffer from a variety of challenging conditions. For example, magnetic tracking system can be affected by metal and magnetic fields in the environment, and depth sensors such as the Kinect have a noticeable bias toward distances at the far end of the workspace.

These geometric distortions will usually be nonlinear, but monotonic. This implies that they can be corrected in a way that is conceptually similar to distortion correction for optical lenses. First, a calibration step is performed to obtain a mathematical function describing the distortion. Second, at runtime, every measurement is transformed with the inverse of the function to recover the true value.

The calibration step consists of taking samples of the distorted measurements such that the entire working range of the tracking system is covered. The measurements must be associated with a ground truth obtained from a second, independent measurement system. This second system can be either a trustworthy measurement system, such as a mechanical system (e.g., a robotic arm), or a manual setup, such as a regular grid created with a measurement tape.

The resulting array of calibration measurements can be either used directly as a lookup table or converted into an interpolation function. The lookup table approach requires searching for the closest neighbors of a measurement value, and inverting the distortion by interpolation from these neighbors. Alternatively, a low-order polynomial can be fitted to the measurements, usually separately in each dimension. Bryson [1992] has reported that a polynomial of order 3–4 delivers the best results for magnetic tracking, and Kainz et al. [2012] have reported a similar finding for depth data from a Kinect V1.

Error Propagation

A problem that plagues many practical AR systems is error propagation, which can amplify small errors resulting from jittery tracking or insufficient calibration by orders of magnitude. While the original error might be small enough to pass unnoticed, the amplified, dependent error may no longer be tolerable.

Various interactions between system components can lead to error amplification, but the most common problem is that small rotational errors will lead to large translational errors. Consider outside-in tracking of an HMD in the situation where the user is facing the stationary tracking system, but is relatively far away from it. Because of the limited camera resolution, the user's viewing direction as reported by the tracking system contains a small rotational error. A virtual object located near the stationary tracking system will be placed incorrectly with respect to the real world by an amount proportional to the distance from the user to the tracking system, which is large (Figure 5.11).

The effects of error propagation can be minimized by avoiding the dynamic concatenation of coordinate systems in favor of directly expressing the relationship of one coordinate system in

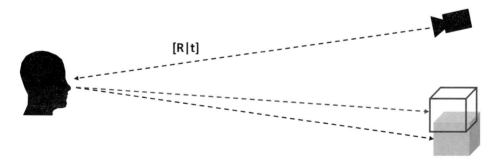

Figure 5.11   Error propagation can significantly disturb registration quality, because small angular errors can create large errors in position. Here the error in the rotation introduced by the external tracking system leads to a strong misregistration of the red virtual cube to its real-world counterpart.

terms of the other. For example, real-world objects can be stored and manipulated directly in tracker coordinates without going through an intermediate world coordinate system. If local object coordinates are used, the average coordinate magnitude should be minimal. This effect can be achieved by choosing the origin of the local coordinate system as the center of gravity for the object.

Latency

If user motion is observed by a tracking system, a corresponding image cannot be presented immediately. There will necessarily be a certain amount of latency until the system is able to present an AR image, which reflects the observed motion. The end-to-end-delay [Jacobs et al. 1997] consists of several components:

- The physical measurement process performed by the sensor and the time to transmit the result to the host computer
- The processing of the measurement by the host computer
- The image generation performed by the host computer
- Video synchronization between the image generator and the display, which can introduce an additional delay of one frame (e.g., up to 16.7 ms for a 60-Hz update rate)
- An internal delay in the display until the image is finally shown

For a moving user, the temporal error resulting from latency directly translates into spatial error, because the augmented images are presented at a wrong (outdated) position or have a wrong (outdated) camera pose.

In particular, for human head motion, such as when turning the head while wearing an HMD, latency can easily be the strongest source of spatial errors. The speed of head motion at a peak of 500 mm or 50° per second can lead to a registration error of up to 20–60 mm. Holloway [1997] quotes an error of 1 mm per 1 ms of delay as a rule of thumb. By comparison, most other sources of error, such as error resulting from incorrect calibration or tracking jitter, remain less than 10 mm.

The effects of latency are related to the speed of motion, so they change dynamically with the activities of the user. The perceived effect is "image swimming," in which the image presented to the user lags behind the actual motion and catches up when the motion stops. This kind of system behavior leads to overshooting during three-dimensional interaction and, in severe cases, can even lead to motion sickness.

Filtering and Prediction

If measurements suffer from jitter, the sensor data must be filtered to become smoother. Similarly, if multiple tracking systems are used together, we require a filter that compensates for noise in the measurements of the individual tracking systems, which is not correlated among the systems. In this way, we obtain smoothed tracking data, which is more suitable for a high-quality AR experience. More importantly, with filter-induced noise reduction, we can use a suitable motion model (see the "Incremental Tracking" section in Chapter 4) to predict and, therefore, compensate for a certain amount of latency.

Widely used approaches for statistical filtering of sensor data include the Kalman filter and the particle filter. Both can be formulated as "recursive" filters, which rely on the most recently computed state, thereby running in a tracking loop with a constant memory requirement.

The **Kalman filter** [Kalman 1960] assumes that the error can be described by a normal distribution and that a linear combination of the system state and the measurement can be used to identify and remove the error. This filter operates in two steps: a predictor step and a corrector step. The predictor step forecasts the future system state based on previous values, weighted by age. The corrector step uses the information from a new incoming measurement to update the state and prevent drift. Most practical sensor systems have nonlinear behavior, which can be addressed with more advanced models such as the **extended Kalman filter** [Welch and Bishop 1995] and the **unscented transform** [Julier and Uhlmann 2004].

A **particle filter** can be used if the error cannot be approximated with a normal distribution [Isard and Blake 1998]. It is a sequential Monte Carlo technique [Doucet et al. 2001] which models the system state as a collection of discrete particles. Each particle is iteratively reweighted depending on how well the extrapolation of its dynamic behavior can predict the system state observed in the measurements.

The result of the filtering is a motion that allows for extrapolation to predict motion [Azuma and Bishop 1994] and to compensate for latency. After obtaining a measurement, a prediction of the system state corresponding to the camera pose is made that reflects the estimated latency. The result is the most likely camera pose *at the moment when the image is presented*.

To allow for fine-grained prediction, the pipeline can be decomposed into finer steps, with data streams synchronized by extrapolation and interpolation [Jacobs et al. 1997]. First, the tracking system must be configured to deliver higher frequency than the the display rate requires [Wloka 1995]. In particular, IMU devices used as secondary tracking sources can deliver very high update rates [Azuma and Bishop 1994]. Second, the image generation must be set up to render a larger viewport than will finally be used by the display. The final image generation presents a modified image, based on an updated prediction of the camera pose using the most recent tracking data (Figure 5.12). The image modification can be done by cropping from a wide field-of-view image [Mazuryk et al. 1996], by using a cube map [Regan and Pose 1994], or by using per-pixel image warping [Mark et al. 1997]. It is also possible to delay the display of the video stream in video see-through AR [Bajura and Neumann 1995].

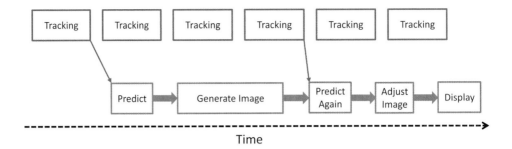

Figure 5.12 Given a high-enough update rate from the tracking system, prediction can be used to compensate for registration errors resulting from latency. First, an image is generated based on a predicted camera pose. After the image is completed, another round of prediction from updated tracking information is used to adjust the image so that it matches the user's viewpoint when the image is finally presented.

If fusion of multiple sensors is used, temporal registration must also be enforced among the sensors. This is usually based on timestamps associated with the individual measurements during acquisition. Ideally, the update rate of the sensors will be high enough so that the sensor fusion can simply combine measurements that were taken at the same time, or at least at closely matching times. If a statistical filter is used, the filter can be set up so that measurements from separate sensors can be incorporated into the filter at different times, whenever new data becomes available [Welch and Bishop 1997].

Summary

To obtain proper calibration for AR, all components of the system need to be carefully calibrated. Offline calibration must cover the tracking system (internal camera parameters, lens distortion, other systematic distortion of the tracking system), the display (calibration of see-through HMDs, hand–eye calibration), and the objects in the real world relative to the tracking system (absolute orientation). Configurations that produce substantial error propagation should be avoided, if possible.

At runtime, careful synchronization of all system components is necessary to ensure correct temporal and spatial registration. This will likely require motion prediction (often based on Kalman or particle filters) to compensate for the effects of unavoidable latency.

CHAPTER 6

VISUAL COHERENCE

In this chapter, we examine how to obtain *visually coherent* output from an AR system. Specifically, this chapter investigates how real and virtual objects can be combined so that the virtual objects blend seamlessly into the real environment to the point where they are indistinguishable from the real world. While not all types of AR applications have seamlessness as their ultimate goal, visual coherence is important for areas such as entertainment, education, and commerce. We have already discussed one important component of visual coherence, spatial registration, in Chapter 5. In this chapter, we concentrate on appearance-related issues, mainly relying on techniques from real-time photorealistic computer graphics.

Registration

One of the key requirements for AR is that the real and virtual scenes must be registered. Recall that the need for spatial registration in every frame of the AR display is the reason why real-time pose tracking is necessary. Given the relative pose of the observer (or camera) to the scene, virtual objects can be positioned and oriented correctly in the output image (Figure 6.1). In the general case of a three-dimensional object to be embedded into an image of the real scene, the virtual object must be rendered from a virtual camera with internal and external camera parameters corresponding to the real camera.

With such a calibrated camera, essential depth cues can be generated. Depth cues are stimuli that allow a human to interpret the thee-dimensional structure of an observed scene [Goldstein 2009]. There are approximately 15–20 different depth cues, which can be broadly categorized as monocular or binocular cues. Monocular cues can be observed from a single image (Figure 6.2),

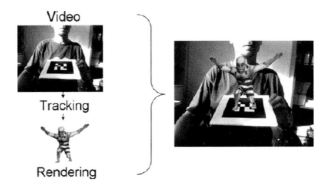

Figure 6.1   A simple AR rendering pipeline. A video of the real world is acquired and combined with separately rendered computer graphics elements—in this case, the green monster. Courtesy of István Barakonyi.

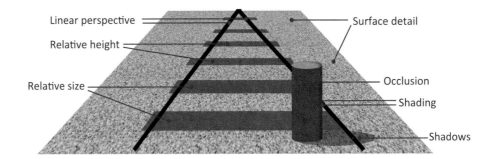

Figure 6.2   Monocular depth cues allow the interpretation of a scene structure from a single image.

while binocular cues are observed in pairs of images. These cues can be invoked only by special display systems. For example, binocular parallax (differences seen by two eyes) can be produced only by a stereoscopic display device.

 Given that many of today's AR displays use a monocular video see-through mode, monocular depth cues are more important for AR in general. They can be produced purely by means of computer graphics software. Among the most important cues are the following:

- *Relative size*: The farther away an object is from the observer, the smaller it becomes.
- *Relative height*: More-distant objects have their base higher in the image.
- *Perspective*: Parallel lines converge as they extend farther away from the observer.
- *Surface detail*: Closer objects reveal more fine-grained surface detail or texture gradient.
- *Atmospheric attenuation*: More-distant objects appear more blurred and bluish due to atmospheric effects.
- *Occlusion*: Objects closer to the observer obscure objects farther away in the screen space.
- *Shading*: Objects are illuminated according to the position and orientation of light sources.
- *Shadows*: Objects cast shadows on other objects.

Three-dimensional computer graphics are well equipped to deliver all of these cues. Several cues, such as size, perspective, height, and surface detail, are straightforward to produce with a virtual camera that is geometrically registered to the real one. Atmospheric attenuation is mostly relevant for far-field outdoor AR and is not discussed here. However, the remaining depth cues—in particular, occlusion, shading, and shadows—require special treatment in AR rendering.

To bring together virtual and real, AR rendering must extend a conventional computer graphics pipeline (Table 6.1). A video see-through pipeline is better suited for this objective than an optical see-through pipeline, because it allows full control over the appearance of the final image. We therefore assume a pipeline for video see-through AR in this chapter, which consists of the following stages:

1. *Acquisition*: Acquire a model of the real scene (geometry, materials, illumination).
2. *Registration*: Establish common geometric and photometric properties between the real scene and the virtual scene.
3. *Compositing*: Merge the real scene and the virtual scene into a single image.
4. *Display*: Present the composite image to the user.

Table 6.1   A Pipeline for Visual Coherence Must Perform Acquisition, Registration, and Compositing of Multiple Data Sources

Data Source	Acquisition	Registration	Compositing
Geometry	Geometric reconstruction, SLAM	Geometric registration	Occlusion, diminished reality
Light sources, materials	Light probes	Photometric registration	Common illumination
Images	Video capture	Camera calibration	Camera simulation, stylization

Obviously, this pipeline is more complicated than the standard rendering pipeline of computer graphics, which has to deal with just a virtual scene. An AR rendering pipeline must deal with both a real scene and a virtual scene, and must provide registration for both the *geometric* registration and the *photometric* aspects of both scenes.

The foundations for geometric registration (often just called "registration") were laid in the previous chapters. That is, we have seen how to obtain geometric pose updates (Chapter 3), how to provide real-time acquisition of geometry (Chapter 4), and how to align the real scene with the virtual scene (Chapter 5). With the knowledge of the geometry of the real scene and its alignment to the virtual scene, we can directly proceed to geometric compositing. First we will discuss the topic of resolving **occlusion** between virtual and real objects—the main application of geometric compositing in AR.

Photometric registration is more complicated. It describes the alignment of the perceived brightness and color between the virtual scene and the real scene and, therefore, is an essential component of visual coherence. Convincing simulation of how light travels between virtual and real objects and finally arrives at the observer requires acquisition of not only the geometry of the real scene, but also of its surface materials and of the real light sources.

With both photometric and geometric registration, we are equipped with a complete description of virtual and real scenes. *Compositing*—that is, rendering the virtual and real objects together—still requires solving a **common illumination** problem of light traveling between virtual and real objects. For a survey of photorealism in AR, see the work of Jacobs and Loscos [2004] and Kronander et al. [2015].

An aspect of compositing that is not handled by common illumination is the removal of real objects from the scene, also called **diminished reality**. The background covered by the unwanted object can often not be observed, but must be recovered by other (e.g., probabilistic) means.

Because approximations and errors in the acquisition and registration are usually unavoidable, the compositing stage must also take care that the resulting discrepancies are, at least, perceptually minimal. One measure to handle this issue is **camera simulation**, which takes physical camera behavior into account during the rendering of the virtual scene, so that the results match the images of the real scene. Another measure is to apply **stylization** filters to the entire composite image.

Occlusion

Simply drawing computer graphics objects on top of a video background with a registered camera is not sufficient to create the impression of a scene in which the virtual and the real coexist. Consider the image in Figure 6.3. The virtual Lego man is rendered correctly in terms of screen position and perspective. The failure to consider occlusion with the real-world Lego woman on the left, however, leads to a composition that is irritating and not effective in conveying the 3D position of the virtual object. This problem originates from the lack of appropriate depth cues that humans expect from their real-world experience.

Occlusion is one of the strongest depth cues and must be resolved to create a plausible AR scene. We can distinguish two cases: A virtual object may be either in front of or behind a real object. The case where the virtual object is in front is easier to handle. In the simplest implementation, we just have to draw the virtual object on top of the video background, and it will occlude any real object contained in the video. In the case where a virtual object is behind a real object, proper handling of occlusions is more difficult, as we will need a strategy to distinguish visible from occluded virtual objects during rendering.

The basic algorithm to achieve this effect uses **phantoms** [Breen et al. 1996]. Phantom rendering makes use of the standard *z-buffer* (depth buffer) capability of a modern graphics

Figure 6.3 (a) The virtual character is placed at the correct position, but occlusion by the physical character is not considered. (b) Correct occlusion rendering creates a much more realistic impression without conflicting cues. Courtesy of Denis Kalkofen.

processing unit (GPU). A phantom is a virtual representation of a real object, which is rendered invisibly; that is, only the z-buffer is modified. This establishes correct depth values for the real object visible in the video, so that the virtual object can be rendered to appear occluded or partially occluded. If the phantom objects are correctly registered, then hidden fragments from the virtual objects can be rejected by the standard z-buffer algorithm. The following pseudo-code explains the details:

1. Draw the video image to the color buffer.

2. Disable writing to the color buffer.

3. Render phantoms of the real scene, only to the z-buffer.

4. Enable writing to the color buffer.

5. Draw virtual objects.

Phantoms are most often defined using conventional polygonal models, which can be readily rendered using standard graphics hardware (Figure 6.4). However, other representations of phantom models are possible, as long as a depth buffer can be established. For example, Fischer et al. [2004] use first-hit isosurface raycasting on a model volumetric model. Alternatively, the depth can be derived dynamically without explicit models. An overview of such approaches is given in the "Model-Free Occlusion" section. First, however, we investigate how problems with basic occlusion can be overcome with occlusion refinement and probabilistic occlusion.

Figure 6.4   Phantom rendering fills the z-buffer with the depth values of a virtual model of a real object. Courtesy of Denis Kalkofen.

Occlusion Refinement

The quality of occlusion achieved using the phantom rendering approach depends on the quality of the input data. The main sources of inaccuracy are the models themselves, errors in the static registration, and errors in the dynamic registration (i.e., tracking errors):

- Virtual models that do not faithfully represent their real-world counterparts cannot produce correct occlusion masks.

- Incorrect static registration between the virtual and real-world coordinate systems means that phantom objects will be rendered at a wrong location or with a wrong orientation.

- Incorrect dynamic registration resulting from tracking errors can deteriorate an otherwise correct static registration, as the camera pose is estimated incorrectly.

These errors lead to occlusion masks that do not correspond to the extent of the real object in screen space. Unfortunately, humans are quite good at detecting such inconsistencies, which is why it is desirable to provide some sort of error correction for these inconsistencies. We call such a correction *occlusion refinement*. Refinement methods are based on heuristics, but produce good results in many practical situations.

The main idea of occlusion refinement is that, in general, only the silhouettes of a phantom object must be accurate to yield correct occlusion between nonpenetrating virtual and real objects. Consequently, only the edges of a polygonal model that form the silhouette, must be corrected. This correction can be estimated in image space. Conceptually, for every outer edge of an occluding polygon that is part of an occlusion boundary, the video image is searched for a corresponding nearby edge representing the true occlusion boundary. The polygon is then adjusted to match the edge found in the image. Moreover, a transparency gradient can be applied to the alpha buffer near the occluding edges during rendering of the occluding polygons. This results in blurred edges that make any remaining inaccuracies less obvious.

Klein and Drummond [2004] use edge tracking to identify those edges in the video that must correspond to the phantom, and then modify the phantom geometry to match the observation. In contrast, DiVerdi and Höllerer [2006] work purely in image space. They use a pixel shader to compute an edge correction for every pixel along an edge separately (Figure 6.5).

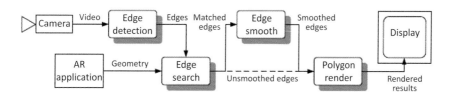

Figure 6.5   A possible approach for occlusion refinement can be performed purely on the GPU. First, edges are detected in the video image and matched with edges of the virtual models. The corrected edges are then superimposed with alpha blending on top of the polygon from which they were derived.

Figure 6.6   By searching near the projected edge of a phantom object for the true edge of the corresponding real objects (left), occlusion boundaries can be corrected (right). Courtesy of Stephen DiVerdi.

The shader searches along the normal direction of the edge for a gradient maximum, storing the result of that search in an auxiliary texture. Occluding polygons are rendered with per edge-pixel occlusion correction (Figure 6.6). If the detected edges are too noisy, an optional edge smoothing step can be introduced. Zheng et al. [2014] go one step further by computing optical flow between the camera image and a rendering of a textured model, to obtain dense correspondences for occlusion refinement.

Probabilistic Occlusion

Fuhrmann et al. [1999] describe a probabilistic approach to phantom rendering. They deal with articulated models such as a moving human, equipped with a motion capturing system for real-time acquisition of the pose of dynamically moving limbs. For areas where no precise tracking can be established, such as human hands, a probabilistic model is used (Figure 6.7). This model consists of multiple nested surfaces, which become more transparent from innermost to outermost shell. In this way, the transparency observed in the final image roughly corresponds to the probability that the hand is in a particular region. An implementation using modern graphics hardware would probably use a volumetric texture or a 3D distance field computation in a shader for the same purpose. This method could easily enhance AR applications with hand tracking or where tracking uncertainty of some sort is available.

Model-Free Occlusion

AR should operate in dynamic real-world environments, and it is not always possible to obtain phantom objects beforehand. Therefore, several techniques have been developed to facilitate obtaining a depth map of the scene dynamically, either through special hardware measures or by making certain assumptions.

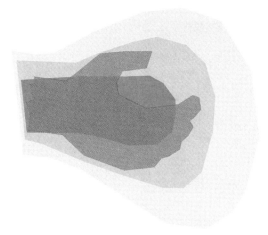

Figure 6.7   A probabilistic approach to phantom rendering. For areas without precise tracking, such as the hands, a probabilistic phantom model consisting of increasingly transparent shell surfaces can be used.

On one end of the spectrum of techniques, object segmentation may rely on user input to select a foreground object. Lepetit and Berger [2000] present such an approach, which lets the user manually segment the foreground object in at least two keyframe images. The system tracks the contour of this object in successive frames and uses this information to compute correct occlusions with this object. The advantage of this technique is that no explicit three-dimensional model is necessary. Several recent works deal with semi-manual reconstruction of objects in the scene [van den Hengel et al. 2009] [Bastian et al. 2010], which can be used to determine occlusion in a similar fashion.

On the other end of the spectrum, the most obvious approach to fully automatically obtaining depth maps in real time is the use of a dedicated depth sensor—for example, a stereo camera rig [Wloka and Anderson 1995] or a time-of-flight camera [Gordon et al. 2002] [Fischer et al. 2007]. An example is given in Figure 6.8. If no rigid assembly of depth sensor and video camera for video see-through augmentation is available, the registration between the depth image and the video image must be computed dynamically from tracking information, and the depth image must be reprojected into the view space of the video camera. The reprojected depth image must be transmitted to the GPU to be used in per-pixel depth computations. Recent RGB-D sensors are already calibrated in the factory.

Some applications use a segmentation of foreground and background as a binary z-buffer. Such a foreground mask can then be used for computing occlusion effects. Because the depth information is very coarse, this approach is primarily useful for static camera setups, where the roles of foreground and background objects do not change over time.

 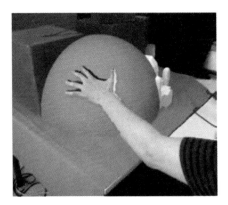

Figure 6.8   (left) The hand is incorrectly occluded by the virtual object. (right) A depth sensor provides a simple way to resolve depth with real-world objects for every pixel at frame rate. Courtesy of Lukas Gruber.

One application area that meets this requirement is a virtual studio, which uses a digital background for broadcast television production. Grundhöfer et al. [2007] describe a virtual studio setup that uses imperceptible flash keying for determining the outline of a speaker in front of the background (Figure 6.9). The foreground is illuminated by a flashlight in alternating frames at 60 Hz and synchronized with a camera. The system can therefore segment the background as the difference of image pairs with and without flash.

Segmentation can also be based on detecting certain objects or object types in the scene. For example, a large body of work focuses on hand detection in the field of computer vision. Since pointing with the hand or finger is a very appealing direct form of interaction, hand detection is also popular in AR. For example, the system presented by Weir et al. [2013] uses hand

 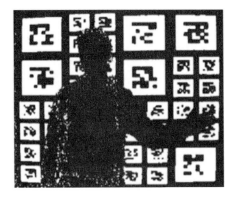

Figure 6.9   (left) A speaker in a virtual studio in front of a live background. (right) Using structured light, the speaker in the foreground can be segmented in real time. Courtesy of Oliver Bimber.

Figure 6.10 In this demo called "BurnAR," which was presented at IEEE ISMAR 2011, a user's hands are segmented based on skin color. The detected hands are virtually ignited. Courtesy of Peter Weir, Christian Sandor, Matt Swoboda, Thanh Nguyen, Ulrich Eck, Gerhard Reitmayr, and Arindam Day.

segmentation based on skin color (Figure 6.10). Hand detection can be employed to determine correct occlusion. Usually, the heuristic assumption is that the hand is the foreground object and, therefore, occludes any virtual object. While color-based segmentation works directly with the video camera without a need for additional hardware, a disadvantage of this technique is that it is usually not very robust and can easily fail in challenging lighting conditions.

Photometric Registration

Just computing occlusion between virtual and real objects is not sufficient for producing realistic images for AR application. We also have to compute *photometric* registration, which lets us resolve how virtual objects can be consistently illuminated with virtual objects. To achieve this aim, we need to know not only the geometry of virtual and real objects, but also the incident illumination of the real scene—that is, the light sources. Their number and characteristics have a strong influence on the computational complexity of the resulting light simulation.

We can limit this complexity by assuming that for typical small AR workspaces all light sources are distant and can be treated as external to the scene (Figure 6.11). This assumption is reasonable if we allow only the sun or ceiling lights as light sources, but not desk lamps or candles. The restriction to distant lights simplifies the illumination computation significantly.

To understand why this is important, we must first discuss **local illumination** and **global illumination**. Local illumination means that only the light transport from the source to a surface point in the scene is considered. In contrast, global illumination also considers complex light

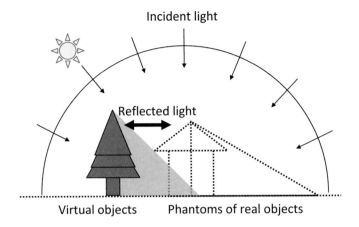

Figure 6.11   Mutual light interaction between virtual and real objects is considered only for the local real scene. The distant scene just sends light.

interactions with other objects in the scene. Therefore, global illumination naturally produces reflection, refraction, and shadowing effects. Soft shadows, for example, are simply the result of light coming from many directions, with some light being blocked and other light not being blocked. Global illumination can also produce reflections by considering the material of the reflecting object: Shiny objects produce **specular reflections**, whereas matte objects produce **diffuse reflections**. Purely diffuse (so-called Lambertian) reflections are easier to compute, because the direction of the reflection and the viewing direction can be neglected.

A distant light source assumption restricts the need for illumination computation, since the local scene does not contain any light sources. First, all incoming light can be modeled as directional light and stored in a two-dimensional table—an **environment map** [Blinn and Newell 1976]—indexed purely by direction, but not by position in the scene (Figure 6.12). In other

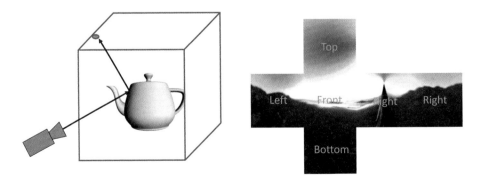

Figure 6.12   An environment map is an efficient representation of the illumination an object receives from its surroundings.

words, the light received by a surface point in the scene is assumed to be independent of the position of this point. Second, light transport leaving the scene need not be computed. It would be relevant only if light leaving the scene were reflected back into it, which is ruled out by the light source definition. Instead, reflections from distant objects outside the scene are jointly encoded with light sources in the environment map. Third, distant light sources can usually be limited to low frequencies, given that scenes in which hard shadows are produced by distant area light sources are rare.

Image-Based Lighting

To use environment maps for **image-based lighting**, it is usually necessary to use **high dynamic range** (HDR), which implies representing the illumination in environment maps in meaningful physical units with floating-point precision, rather than as arbitrary fixed-precision quantities. If the environment map represents incoming light (**radiance**) from the point of view of an observer, it is called a *radiance map*. A map that has been pre-convolved with a suitable kernel to directly represent outgoing light (**irradiance**) after reflection is called an *irradiance map*.

We can use a radiance map to apply image-based lighting to virtual objects in the scene. In its simplest form, image-based lighting is used only as local illumination; that is, only the light transport from the source to a surface point in the scene is considered. No effects of global illumination, such as indirect light reflection or shadowing by other objects in the scene, are considered in this case. The combined effects of emissive light sources and reflections from surfaces in the distant environment, which appear combined in a radiance map, can still produce compelling results (Figure 6.13).

The first work generally credited with integrating correctly illuminated virtual objects into digital images was presented by Nakamae et al. [1986]. This early work concentrated on the

Figure 6.13 Two examples of image-based lighting of a plate of fruits with radiance maps representing two different illumination conditions. Courtesy of Thomas Richter-Trummer.

addition of buildings to outdoor scenes in still images. The radiance was explicitly computed from the known position of the sun rather than stored in an environment map.

Genuine image-based lighting approaches appeared in the 1990s. For example, State et al. [1996a] demonstrated real-time illumination using reflections from a chrome sphere applied via spherical texture mapping capabilities. Debevec [1998] introduced image-based lighting with HDR and differential rendering (discussed in more detail later). Sato et al. [1999] acquired a combined geometric and radiance map of the environment using stereoscopic reconstruction from omnidirectional stereo cameras as well as a sequence of omnidirectional images taken with different shutter speeds, then computed realistic illumination using raycasting.

In the 2000s, programmable texture mapping on the GPU has allowed interactive use of image-based lighting. Agusanto et al. [2003] have used radiance maps to produce specular reflections on virtual objects. Pessoa et al. [2010] have dynamically rendered separate environment maps for selected objects. These synthetic environment maps incorporate not only environment light, but also reflections from other virtual objects. A similar idea has been pursued by Meilland et al. [2013], who synthesize per-object environment maps from a light field representation of the real scene.

Light Probes

The acquisition of a radiance map is effectively achieved with a **light probe**. This tool can take the form of either a *passive light probe* (a reflective "gaze object" placed in the scene and observed by a camera) or an *active light probe* (a camera placed in or near the scene). The objective is to acquire an omnidirectional representation of radiance, so a light probe that can deliver a wide field of view is preferable.

Passive light probes often employ mirrored spheres (Figure 6.14) as gaze objects. Spheres can deliver a horizontal field of view of approximately 300° and can be observed by a camera with a conventional lens. A camera placed directly in the scene would require a special fish-eye lens.

 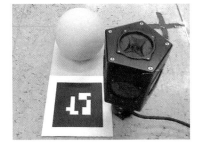

Figure 6.14 (left) A light probe in the form of a diffuse sphere and mirror sphere captures the real-world illumination. (right) An omnidirectional camera, such as the Point Grey Ladybug, can serve as an active light probe. Courtesy of Lukas Gruber.

The goal of the light probe is typically to obtain HDR images. Debevec and Malik [1997] describe how HDR images can be rapidly computed from a series of still images taken with increasing exposure times after calibrating the nonlinear exposure response function of the camera. Today, the availability of cameras that are able to compute HDR images in hardware has significantly eased the challenges of this application.

On hardware supporting spherical environment maps, the image of a spherical gaze object can be used directly for environment mapping [State et al. 1996a]. Today, cubic environment maps are more common, because they are view independent. Such cube maps require resampling the source images taken from a light probe, though.

The material of a gaze object depends on the application. Most commonly used are mirror-like materials—for example, metal with chrome coating—for recording specular reflections [Debevec 1998] [Agusanto et al. 2003]. The specular material is necessary to allow the recording of HDR images. Kanbara and Yokoya [2004] use a blackened mirror sphere to record only intensive light sources and filter out low-frequency lighting. Their sphere is attached to a fiducial marker to identify the gaze object in the image in real time. In contrast, Aittala [2010] employs a diffuse sphere (a ping-pong ball) to acquire only diffuse illumination, and extracts the image of the sphere using simple circle detection.

Some researchers also use flat objects as diffusely reflecting light probes. For example, Aittala [2010] mentions gaze objects doubling as fiducial markers, which are easily detected using available marker tracking techniques. Pilet et al. [2006] use a planar object with known texture, which can easily be tracked (Figure 6.15). They sample irradiance guided by the normal of the tracking target, while the user moves the object. Given that the tracked object can be used for interaction with the scene at runtime and need not be removed, it can be used for incrementally updating the radiance map, if the illumination changes.

Figure 6.15   A planar tracking target, such as a textured rectangle, can be used as simple light probe to estimate the dominant lighting direction. A virtual object can have realistic shading and cast a shadow. Courtesy of Julien Pilet, Andreas Geiger, Pascal Lagger, Vincent Lepetit and Pascal Fua.

Pilet et al. [2006] and Aittala [2010] compute the illumination directly from the observations of the gaze object. Both compute a set of point light sources to obtain effects such as specular highlights and cast shadows. Aittala additionally projects the residual energy that is not captured by the explicit light sources into an environment map representation that can be used for ambient illumination.

In contrast to passive light probes, active light probes obtain the environment map directly. A camera with a fish-eye lens or an omnidirectional mirror placed directly in the scene acquires images of all directions in one step [Sato et al. 1999]. Some applications allow the omnidirectional camera to be placed so that it can remain in the scene at runtime—possibly close to the scene, but just outside the field of view of the camera providing the AR video feed [Supan et al. 2006] [Grosch et al. 2007] [Knecht et al. 2010] [Kán and Kaufmann 2012a]. Using a special HDR camera, HDR environment illumination can be provided dynamically to the application.

Offline Light Capturing

If preprocessing is acceptable, the environment map can be captured with conventional stitching of multiple images [Szeliski 2006]. Stitching can also be performed in real time [DiVerdi et al. 2008] [Wagner et al. 2010], but there is no guarantee that the user will cover the space of all possible directions.

An environment map is an instance of a 2D **light field**: It describes the intensity, or color, of the light rays arriving at a single point from arbitrary directions. This point is approximately valid for the entire scene, if distant light sources can be assumed. In larger scenes, however, the position cannot be neglected. In this case, a 5D light field can be used; it stores a separate environment map for many 3D positions in space [Löw et al. 2009]. Notably, this approach is very memory intensive.

A 4D light field, which provides 2D environment maps only for positions on a given 2D surface, is good compromise between coverage and storage requirements. Meilland et al. [2013] capture such a light field with an RGB-D SLAM system. They use the depth data to align overlapping keyframes and use the redundant observations per surface point to compute exposure and HDR values for all keyframes. The result is interpreted as an unstructured lumigraph [Buehler et al. 2001], from which environment maps are synthesized.

Photometric Registration from Static Images

For many practical AR applications, using light probes or offline capturing is too complicated. Ideally, we would like to recover the incident illumination just from a single photograph or video frame. This problem has a long tradition in computer vision, going back to the seminal work of Land et al. [1971] on the Retinex algorithm. The Retinex algorithm is based on the assumption that illumination has a lower frequency in image space than does surface texture. Obviously, the Retinex idea suffers from the fact that a single image will not contain enough information to automatically recover illumination in arbitrary scenes. Therefore, various forms of additional information are employed to derive geometric prior data that helps with the image decomposition into illumination and surface texture [Barron and Malik 2015].

Some approaches rely on input from the user. For example, the user can interactively identify surfaces and light sources to let the system recover illumination and place convincing virtual objects in an image [Karsch et al. 2011]. Crowdsourced user annotations can be collected in image databases [Bell et al. 2014] to guide image decomposition.

Images with depth also provide geometric prior information with which to reason about observed image properties [Chen and Koltun 2013] [Lee et al. 2012]. If no depth channel is available, geometric prior information can be obtained by fitting 3D models from a database to objects in the image so as to obtain geometric information from which diffuse reflections can be inferred [Kholgade et al. 2014]. Depth and illumination can also be estimated by matching them with databases of RGB-D images and environment maps, respectively [Karsch et al. 2014].

Another way of obtaining previously obtained geometric prior information is by detecting object contours [Lopez-Moreno et al. 2013]. Contours provide a good cue for estimating the surface normal vector on the contour, which can then be used to trace back the position of the light source.

These methods provide impressive results, but they are intended for recovering illumination for each image individually and require additional measures to do so. In AR, we usually do not operate on a single image, but rather on a video sequence. Thus, we require real-time methods ensuring temporal coherence, such as the ones discussed in the next section.

Photometric Registration from Specular Reflections

Recall that specular reflections observed on a known object allow direct estimation of the incident light from the reflected direction. This principle can be applied not only to a light probe, but also to any specular object with known shape in the scene.

For example, Tsumura et al. [2003] and Nishino and Nayar [2004] use the reflection in the human eye as a natural light probe. Lagger and Fua [2006] detect specular highlights on small moving objects. Hara et al. [2003, 2008] estimate the light source position and the reflectance parameters from a single image without a distant light source assumption. Mashita et al. [2013] infer the real-world lighting by detecting specular highlights on planar objects.

Jachnik et al. [2012] capture a 4D light field over a small planar surface (a glossy book cover). These researchers heuristically separate the observations into diffuse and specular reflections by assuming that the diffuse reflection varies only with position, but not with the viewing direction, while the specular reflection varies only with viewing direction, but not with position. The specular reflection is used to reconstruct an environment map, while the diffuse part can be used for color bleeding effects.

Photometric Registration from Diffuse Reflections

If no specular reflections can be identified in the scene, we can attempt to compute photometric registration from diffuse reflection instead. Diffuse surfaces are more common—in particular, for indoor scenes. Recovering incident light from such surfaces is a more difficult type of inverse rendering problem, because we have to separate the contributions of light from many directions. Often only a single dominant light direction is estimated.

One of the first systems capable of autonomously estimating such a single distant point light and ambient light from estimated scene geometry was Stauder's [1999] video conferencing system. By estimating ellipsoid geometric models from a background segmentation, this system obtained a directional light estimate.

A more mathematically consistent approach to store directional illumination is provided by **spherical harmonics** (SH), which represents a 2D function over all possible directions on a sphere as a linear combination of a set of basis functions [Ramamoorthi and Hanrahan 2001]. It is often sufficient to store only a low-frequency representation, which can be compressed in SH form with only a few (e.g., 9, 16, or 25) numerical coefficients for per cache entry (Figure 6.16). Moreover, diffuse light transport can be computed very inexpensively in SH form [Sloan et al. 2002] and stored in a surface texture map (e.g., per vertex in a triangle mesh).

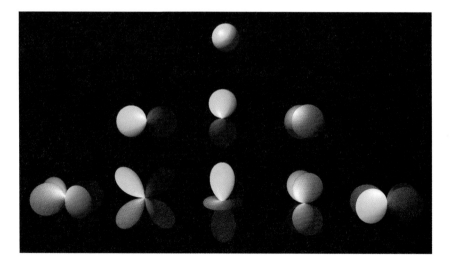

Figure 6.16 Spherical harmonics are basis functions defined over a spherical domain. The three rows show the spherical harmonics for bands 0, 1, and 2.

Gruber et al. [2012] have demonstrated that an SH framework is able to recover real-world lighting in real time with just an RGB-D camera (Figure 6.17). These researchers reconstruct the scene from depth images. Assuming only diffuse reflection, they solve for incident directional light in SH form from selected sample points on the reconstructed surfaces. The sample points must have a good distribution of surface normals. Since diffuse reflection aggregates light from all directions, shadows from other objects in the scene must be computed for every sample point. With image-space optimizations [Gruber et al. 2015], such a system can estimate both dynamic incident light and shadows cast from dynamic real objects at 20 frames per second on a desktop GPU.

Figure 6.17   Directional light can be estimated from diffuse objects, such as the church model, and applied to a virtual object, such as the white ball. The right column shows the estimated incident light as a cube map. Note how the change of the strongest lighting direction, indicated by the red dot in the environment map, corresponds to the movement of the white highlight on the dome. Courtesy of Lukas Gruber.

Boom et al. [2013] have presented a system that estimates a single point light source from arbitrary scene geometry. They assume diffuse reflection for the entire scene. Their approach is based on segmenting the image by color into superpixels for which constant **albedo** (i.e., diffuse reflectance) is assumed. Knowing the albedo allows for recovering the light source with reasonable accuracy.

Knorr and Kurz [2014] estimate incident light from human faces. Their method uses offline machine learning from a variety of faces under different illumination conditions. The online method applies a face tracker and matches distinctive observation points of the detected face to the training database to estimate the real-world light in SH.

Photometric Registration from Shadows

Another method for estimating light sources is to observe the shadows in an image. The principal method is based on full or partial knowledge of the shadow caster's geometry and the correct classification and measurement of the shadow appearance in the image. In practice, this means detecting the shadow and its contour in the image. Surface points on the contour are traced back to the object geometry boundary of the shadow caster, which also has to be visible. From there, the direction of one or multiple light sources can be estimated (Figure 6.18). For example, Hartmann et al. [2003] utilize a light probe with special geometry characteristics, known as the "shadow catcher," which reliably captures shadows from any direction. Detecting shadows in natural images is usually more challenging [Wang and Samaras 2006] [Ikeda et al. 2012] [Arief et al. 2012] [Okabe et al. 2004] [Mei et al. 2009].

Outdoor Photometric Registration

When AR is operating outdoors, a full geometric model of the scene is usually not available, which makes photometric registration more difficult. However, a simple illumination model

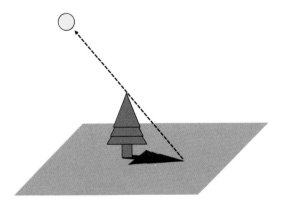

Figure 6.18   The direction of a light source may be estimated by forming a ray from a unique point in a shadow's contour to the corresponding surface point on the shadow caster.

can be derived from the fact that, during daytime, direct illumination from the sun is, by far, the strongest light source. Knowing the time of the day and the geographic position, an analytical model of the sun can be used as a first estimate [Nakamae et al. 1986] [Madsen and Nielsen 2008] [Liu and Granier 2012]. The sky can be approximated as a secondary, large area light source. For improved results, shadow cues in the image can be used [Cao and Shah 2005] [Cao and Foroosh 2007].

Reconstructing Explicit Light Sources

Global illumination effects that go beyond environment mapping usually require *explicit position of light sources* instead of directional radiance (Figure 6.19). We can convert every pixel (direction) in a radiance map into an explicit light source by assuming that the light source is at a fixed large distance from the scene center. For a high-resolution radiance map, however, the number of light sources may be excessive.

One method to limit the number of light sources is regular subsampling of the radiance map [Supan et al. 2006]. With this technique, the pixels contained in a region of the map after applying the subdivision are averaged and replaced by a light source located at the midpoint of the region, using an intensity proportional to the average pixel value. This approach yields a fixed number of light sources, but does not take into consideration the inhomogeneous distribution of light in the environment.

A more sophisticated approach relies on adaptive subdivision [Debevec 2005]. With this technique, the environment map is recursively subdivided along the longest axis in such a way

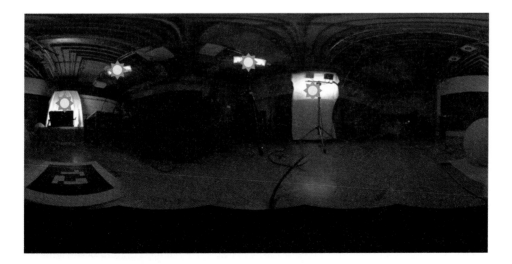

Figure 6.19 Explicit light sources can be estimated by subdividing an environment map into regions of equal radiance and determining a representative point in each region. Courtesy of Lukas Gruber.

that the resulting regions have approximately equal radiance. This process is repeated until the desired number of regions has been determined, and finally the light sources are estimated from each region as described previously.

Common Illumination

With a model of the real scene, the virtual scene, and the incident light, we can compute **common illumination** between the virtual and real objects according to a real-world lighting situation. We begin by discussing the kind of light transport involved.

Direct illumination describes light traveling from the source directly to an object, where it is reflected toward an observer. *Indirect illumination* describes light traveling from the source to a first object, where it is reflected toward a second object. The light bounces around and, eventually, reaches the observer. If light does not reach a first object because it is reflected by a second object closer to the light source, the second object casts a *shadow*. A full global illumination simulation can involve many bounces of light between objects. While indirect illumination is usually much weaker than direct illumination, indirect illumination substantially contributes to visual realism—in particular, for indoor environments, which are not directly illuminated by the sun.

Both the first and second objects mentioned previously can be either real or virtual. This implies that there are four possible combinations: *real-to-real*, *real-to-virtual*, *virtual-to-real*, and *virtual-to-virtual*. Among these combinations, only real-to-real is implicitly given in the video image; the three combinations involving a virtual object must be computed with illumination simulation. This includes the virtual-to-real combination, which may result in only subtle changes of the real objects.

The compositing of real and virtual is based on differential rendering, which is described next, followed by global illumination principles and methods.

Differential Rendering

Even with a careful photometric registration, common illumination will likely never be perfect, because it is almost impossible to fully account for all interactions of light in a scene. Nevertheless, we would like to preserve at least the subtle illumination effects already naturally present in the camera image of the real scene, even if these subtleties do not fully carry over to the virtual parts of the scene. The process that allows for real-world illumination effects to be preserved is called **differential rendering**. It was first introduced by Fournier et al. [1993]. Here, we use the differential rendering formulation of Debevec [1998].

Given the geometry and materials of the scene as well as the parameters of camera and light sources, it is possible to compute a light simulation L_R corresponding to the original scene (i.e., without any virtual objects). After inserting the virtual objects into the scene description, a second light simulation L_{R+V} can be computed, which represents the scene containing both virtual and real objects. All pixels showing virtual objects can be replaced by L_{R+V}. For all pixels showing real objects, the difference $L_{R+V} - L_R$ represents how the illumination of the real part of the scene is changed by adding the virtual objects. This difference is added as a correction term to the camera image L_C (Figure 6.20):

- For pixels showing virtual objects: $L_{final} = L_{R+V}$
- For pixels showing real objects: $L_{final} = L_C + L_{R+V} - L_R$

The second expression, for pixels showing real objects, can be interpreted as an error term $L_C - L_R$ that is added to the simulation result L_{R+V} to correct any inaccuracies in the modeling L_R of the original scene L_C. Pixels that are indirectly illuminated by virtual objects will be brightened ($L_{R+V} - L_R$ positive), while pixels on which virtual objects cast a shadow will be darkened ($L_{R+V} - L_R$ negative).

Differential rendering is more difficult if the scene modifications also permit **relighting**—that is, changes to the light sources and not just to the scene objects. In particular, the removal of light sources, which leads to the disappearance of shadows, is difficult to achieve without artifacts. In contrast, the addition of new virtual light sources works very well in practice owing to the fact that light can be linearly added. Therefore, the methods described in the following sections will usually leave the real illumination unchanged or restrict themselves to adding a few secondary light sources.

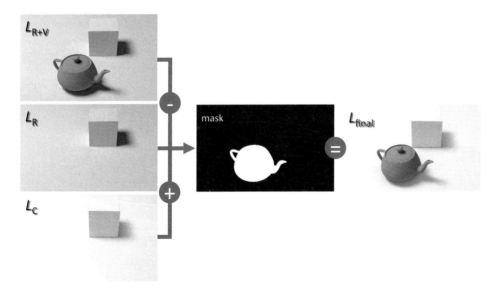

Figure 6.20 Differential rendering combines the light contributions of newly added virtual objects, as calculated against a virtual representation of the physical scene L_R and the live video input. Courtesy of Peter Kán.

Real-Time Global Illumination

The two light simulations required for differential rendering are typically computed with a global illumination method (Figure 6.21). Real-time global illumination faces two main dimensions of complexity:

- *Light transport.* The first dimension is concerned with the type of light transport that is being simulated. Shadow algorithms are the simplest class, as they allow only the removal of light. Diffuse global illumination allows soft shadows and color bleeding, in which light is reflected off strongly colored surfaces to nearby objects. A common extension is to add specular effects (reflection, refraction, and caustics) only for selected objects. Allowing arbitrary diffuse and specular light transport for the entire scene has the highest complexity.

- *Scene.* For a static scene with static lighting, where only the camera is allowed to move, all light transport can be precomputed. Precomputation can overcome all online performance problems, but may require excessive computational resources and storage, especially, if specular effects must be supported. Dynamic objects in the scene make it necessary to compute at least the effects of these objects on the light transport for every frame. A scene with both dynamic objects and dynamic light sources has the highest computational cost.

These two dimensions, together with the size of the scene, determine the computational cost of global illumination. Real-time updates for large dynamic scenes with complex light transport characteristics are still elusive on high-performance workstations, let alone mobile computers. To make global illumination more tractable, most contemporary global illumination methods introduce a factorization into two rendering passes. The first pass computes the light transport

Figure 6.21   Real-time path tracing enables realistic global illumination effects, as demonstrated in this comparison of local (left) and global (right) illumination rendering for augmented reality. Courtesy of Peter Kán.

in the scene, while the second pass collects the information on the distributed light to form the final image. This separation into two passes has several advantages.

First, we can choose the *type of light transfer* for either pass independently. For example, the first pass can simulate only diffuse light transfer from the light sources, while the second pass can incorporate specular effects to improve the subjective visual realism (even though not all possible kinds of light transport are simulated by the overall system). This arrangement is convenient, as it makes the first pass view independent and, therefore, potentially more efficient.

Second, we can choose the *rendering method* for either pass independently. For example, the first pass may use expensive ray-tracing, but only for a limited number of rays, while the second pass uses rasterization with more efficient GPU shaders.

Third, we can choose the *update rate* for either pass independently. While the second pass must always run at the frame rate, the first pass can update at a lower rate. At the extreme, the first pass for a completely static scene can be entirely precomputed. Even if dynamic objects must be accommodated, the first pass can run at a lower rate than the second pass, or the first pass can use a lazy update strategy, delivering updates only if and where the scene changes.

The data structure connecting the two passes largely determines the methods available to the second pass and the effects that the second pass can achieve. If the results from the first pass are amortized over multiple frames, the resulting data structure is sometimes called **radiance cache** or **irradiance cache** [Ward et al. 1988], depending on whether outgoing or incoming illumination is stored, respectively. The cache must be able to answer queries about the illumination at a particular 3D point in the scene and a particular 2D direction. As this technique is very memory intensive, similar to light fields, various subsampled cache representations are popular.

When the cache is indexed *only by position*, the resulting organization is suitable for representing diffuse transfer, because the reflection direction is irrelevant. Many approaches use such purely spatial organization schemes. For example, **photon maps** [Jensen 1995] are commonly organized in sparse kd-trees. *Shadow volumes* allow looking up if a 3D point is in shadow. Classic **Radiosity** methods [Cohen et al. 1993] store radiance on surface points or small surface patches.

When the cache is indexed *only by orientation*, the resulting organization is known as an environment map. It is usually takes the form of a cube map, which is supported directly by the GPU. A cube map consists of six square textures, each with a subtended angle of 90° in either direction. *Radiance maps* for image-based lighting are one important use case for an orientation-only cache.

When the cache is indexed *in projective space*, it consists of the 3D positions associated with the entries of a 2D depth map, as seen from a given point of view. This organization combines properties of position and orientation. The depth map represents only a subset of the surface points in the scene, so it cannot serve as a general-purpose cache. However, depth maps on the GPU can be generated from arbitrary scenes using the z-buffer and efficiently transformed using shadow mapping hardware. **Instant Radiosity** [Keller 1997] takes this approach.

If we desire a cache with *both position and orientation*, position is usually the main index. The information for all orientations is stored compactly in the cache entry. **Irradiance volumes** [Greger et al. 1998] and **light propagation** volumes [Kaplanyan and Dachsbacher 2010] belong to this category. These representations often use an SH representation to reduce memory requirements.

Now that we have introduced the important concepts of real-time global illumination, we are ready to apply these concepts to common illumination problems. We will organize the discussion in the following sections by increasing complexity of the light transport. We begin with the addition of cast shadows onto a scene, continue with diffuse global illumination, and conclude with specular global illumination.

Shadows

Shadows are prominent depth cues that help a human observer mentally determine the three-dimensional structure of a scene. Sugano et al. [2003] affirm through a user study that shadows do, indeed, increase the perceived realism of the AR scene. If computing both reflections and shadows is too costly, computation of just of the shadows is an attractive alternative. The first pass computes a shadow representation, and the second pass consults this representation in the shading of the surface points in the final image. Many shadowing techniques exist [Eisemann et al. 2011], with the seminal techniques being shadow volumes [Crow 1977] and shadow mapping [Williams 1978].

A *shadow volume* is a frustum that encloses objects that lie in shadow with respect to a given shadow-casting polygon and a light source. The sides of the frustum are called shadow volume polygons. The shadow volume technique of Everitt and Kilgard [2002] is based on the *stencil buffer*, a standard feature of a modern GPU. The shadow volumes technique works in four passes:

1. The scene is drawn without illumination (i.e., as if in shadow).
2. Rasterization of the front-facing shadow volume polygons increments the stencil buffer.
3. Rasterization of the back facing shadow volume polygons decrements the stencil buffer.
4. The scene is drawn again, and all its fragments with a stencil buffer value of zero are not in shadow and are, therefore, rendered illuminated.

In common illumination, we must consider not only shadows among real objects and shadows among virtual objects, but also shadows cast from real to virtual, and vice versa. While shadows caused by real lights among real objects are naturally visible in the video image, and shadows among virtual objects are easily created using one of the standard shadowing approaches mentioned earlier, mixed shadow interaction between virtual and real requires special consideration.

Haller et al. [2003] proposed a modification of the method developed by Everitt and Kilgard, which is applicable to common illumination. In the first pass, the shadows cast from virtual objects to real objects are rendered. In the second pass, all virtual objects including any received shadows from virtual or real objects are rendered.

After initializing the frame buffer with the video, the first pass renders the phantoms into the z-buffer. The shadow volumes of the virtual objects are drawn into the stencil buffer. Using the stencil buffer mask, the shadows cast from virtual to real objects are created. This is done by blending all pixels from the video, which are marked as being in shadow by the stencil mask, with a dark transparent color, so as to create the impression of a shadowed region.

The second pass is comparable to the conventional stencil-based shadow volume rendering. The whole scene, including virtual objects and phantom objects, is rendered into the color buffer. The shadow volumes for both virtual and phantom objects are drawn into the stencil buffer. Using the resulting stencil buffer as a mask, the whole scene is drawn again with only ambient and emissive components, so that the regions of virtual objects that are in shadow appear unlit by the light sources in the scene (Figure 6.22).

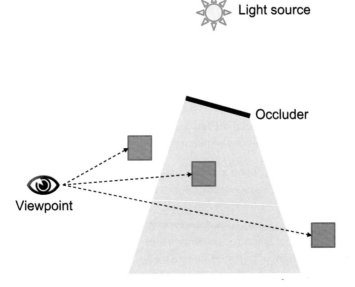

Figure 6.22   The shadow volume algorithm determines an object to be in shadow by calculating, via stencil buffer operations, that a view ray entered a shadow volume but did not exit it.

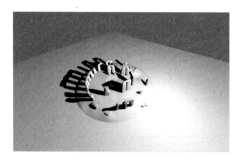

Figure 6.23   (left) A virtual scene with shadow mapping effects. (right) View of the shadow map as seen from the light source, with distance encoded as gray values. Courtesy of Michael Kenzel.

Most modern rendering systems build on the alternative technique of *shadow mapping*, because the underlying projective texture mapping is fully accelerated on the GPU. Shadow mapping is a two-pass technique. It works by first rendering a depth buffer of the scene from the perspective of a light source, and then using this shadow map in a second pass, where the scene is rendered from the observer's point of view, to determine whether a fragment is occluded from the point of view of the light source (Figure 6.23). If the depth of the fragment in the light source coordinates is larger than the entry in the shadow map, the fragment is in shadow.

State et al. [1996a] use shadow maps to cast shadows from virtual to real objects. Gibson et al. [2003] and Supan et al. [2006] create *soft shadows* by superimposing shadow maps from a large number of light sources estimated by a light probe. Such a blending approach for creating soft shadows can be precomputed even for dynamic illumination changes, if the scene is static and shadow receivers can be determined in advance [Kakuta et al. 2005].

The approach of darkening pixels depicting shadows cast from virtual to real objects through blending does not work correctly if a virtual-to-real shadow overlaps with a real-to-real shadow. Pixels that are already naturally dark would be made even darker with this technique, resulting in an inconsistent shadow impression. This problem, called **double shadowing** (Figure 6.24), is a result of the omissions of a semi-global illumination approach, where certain light–object interactions—in this case, occlusions—are not taken into account.

Some authors aim to suppress double shadowing by extending the shadow mapping approach. Jacobs et al. [2005] propose to protect a real shadow from further darkening with a stencil mask. This mask is geometrically estimated from the occluding phantom and the light source, and refined using a Canny edge detector on the input image. Another approach to avoid double shadowing is presented by Madsen and Laursen [2007]. They estimate the surface albedo using a limited form of inverse rendering based on shadow mapping from the real light sources. With the estimated albedo, the effects of shadows from both real and virtual objects can be taken into account.

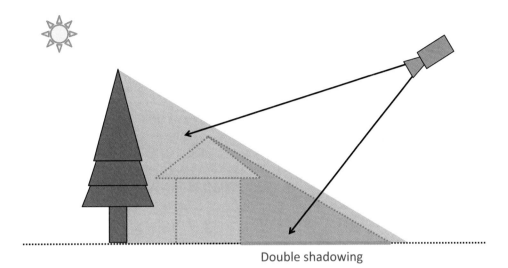

Double shadowing

Figure 6.24 Simply adding the virtual shadow of the virtual tree to an area that is already in shadow from a real object (here: a house) leads to incorrect double shadowing.

Diffuse Global Illumination

If we want not only shadows, but also reflections, a full global illumination simulation is required. Taking this approach will eliminate problematic issues such as double shadowing as well. In this section, we concentrate on global illumination algorithms for diffuse light transport.

The classic *Radiosity* method turns the surfaces in a scene into discrete, small polygonal patches and solves the light transport among the patches. While the second pass can simply render the illuminated patches, the first pass requires computing the global visibility among a large number of patches, which is inherently expensive. Consequently, patch-based Radiosity is rarely used in today's real-time systems that have to deal with dynamic scenes.

Fournier et al. [1993] described the first application of the Radiosity method to simulate common global illumination. This early work was not aimed at real-time performance and used some simplifying assumptions. The scene geometry was roughly approximated by object bounding boxes, and various parameters, such as the camera position, reflectance, and light source intensities, were manually estimated from the image. Later extensions allowed for dynamic objects [Drettakis et al. 1997] and more accurate light transport [Loscos et al. 1999].

More recent approaches aim at real-time performance at least for the second pass. A popular approach takes advantage of the fact that direct illumination can be efficiently computed on the GPU using shadow mapping, while indirect illumination can be simulated with limited accuracy. For example, Grosch et al. [2007] propose to store indirect illumination in an *irradiance volume.* In the first pass, the radiance transfer from all possible directions onto a static scene is precomputed and combined into a set of basis irradiance volumes in SH form. In the second pass, the direct illumination is computed using shadow maps, while the indirect illumination is obtained as a sum of the basis irradiance volumes, weighted by the actual light intensity. The contributions from the irradiance volume are collected with per-sample shadow mapping.

Nowrouzezahrai et al. [2011] propose a light factorization algorithm for scenes with simple real geometry. The key contribution of their work is the separation of real-world lighting into direct light and indirect light. Direct light is handled by extracting point light sources from image-based lighting and applying them with shadow mapping. Radiance transfer of individual objects is precomputed and represented in SH form [Sloan et al. 2002], which allows for its efficient combination with indirect light, also represented in SH form. Animated objects are approximated by a collection of spheres, which enables their cumulative radiance to be approximated quickly.

Knecht et al. [2010] combine Instant Radiosity with differential rendering. Instant Radiosity computes an approximation to diffuse global illumination by repeated hardware shadow mapping. In the first step, virtual photons are shot from the primary light sources and bounce in the scene. Where a photon hits a surface point, a **virtual points light** (VPL) is created. In the second step, surface points are shaded by gathering illumination from the VPL set. The gathering is accelerated by computing one shadow map per VPL. Knecht et al. also proposed a modification called *Differential Instant Radiosity*, in which every photon's path is evaluated twice, with and without virtual objects. This approach leads to an efficient way of computing the illumination after virtual objects are added to the scene. The primary light sources are attached either to an explicitly known light source (e.g., a flashlight) or to the brightest spots in a radiance map obtained with an active light probe.

Lensing and Broll [2012] also use a VPL approach, but, unlike Knecht et al. [2010], they apply the light from a VPL using splatting and not shadow mapping. Their main contribution is to support moving real objects by using an RGB-D camera to obtain the geometry of dynamically moving and even deformable real objects. Because the depth images would be too noisy for computing illumination, they smooth the depth image with a guided edge-preserving filter, which results in a better surface normal estimation. No real-world geometry exists beyond the current field of view, and all light sources are virtual. Consequently, only effects adding virtual light to the scene can be achieved.

Franke [2013] has proposed a global illumination method using volumetric, rather than surface-oriented, light transfer. Unlike Grosch et al. [2007], who use *irradiance* geometric volumes, Franke uses light propagation volumes [Kaplanyan and Dachsbacher 2010], which are volumes representing radiance. A VPL set is computed, and each VPL contribution is injected into a small volume, with directional radiance modeled by SH. To enable differential rendering, the difference in light propagation before and after adding virtual objects is computed.

Figure 6.25 (left) Soft shadows cast from the bed to the dragon underneath. (right) Diffuse color bleeding from the ping-pong paddle to the cartoon character's face. In both examples, real geometry and illumination are reconstructed in real time. Courtesy of Lukas Gruber.

Gruber et al. [2015] describe an approach for real-time common illumination of scenes with deformable real objects and dynamic lighting from an RGB-D camera (Figure 6.25). Their pipeline consists of three steps: geometric reconstruction, photometric registration, and global illumination. Both large scenes and moving objects are supported without precomputation by combining volumetric reconstruction with image-space depth filtering. Global illumination is computed in screen space using a differential rendering variant of directional occlusion [Ritschel et al. 2009]. The global illumination is also used for photometric registration via inverse rendering in SH form [Gruber et al. 2012].

Specular Global Illumination

The main restriction of the view-independent methods described in the previous section is that they do not allow for specular effects from shiny surfaces, such as metal, and translucent materials, such as glass. These effects can be computed in real time, as demonstrated by Knecht et al. [2013] with their specular extension to Differential Instant Radiosity. Unfortunately, a rasterization approach such as the one described by Knecht et al. cannot support arbitrary combinations of diffuse and specular light transport. Doing so usually requires an approach based on ray-tracing, which is more expensive.

One of the first, albeit not real-time capable, methods for specular global illumination was introduced by Grosch [2005]. The first pass uses ray-tracing for a differential version of photon mapping. Surfaces are classified as diffuse or specular. Photons are reflected or refracted by specular surfaces, but stored on diffuse surfaces. If a photon hits a virtual object, a negative amount of light (**antiradiance**) is stored in the place where the photon would hit the real object. The second pass uses ray-tracing from the eye to produce a final image with reflections, refractions, and caustics from virtual objects affecting real imagery.

Kán and Kaufmann [2012a] use a similar approach based on the real-time ray-tracer OptiX [Parker et al. 2010]. Like Grosch, they use ray-tracing in both passes and combine it with photon mapping (Figures 6.26 and 6.27). However, they evaluate the differential rendering in the second pass with separate shadow rays for virtual and real images, rather than using antiradiance. These authors later extended their approach with differential irradiance caching [Kán and

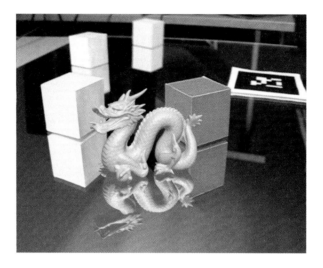

Figure 6.26 Specular reflections of virtual and real objects in a real mirror table surface, produced with real-time ray-tracing. Courtesy of Peter Kán.

Figure 6.27 Refractions computed with real-time ray-tracing let the user's hand appear realistically through the virtual glass. Courtesy of Peter Kán.

Kaufmann 2013]. With this technique, the second pass harvests direct lighting by ray-tracing, but indirect lighting is collected via an irradiance cache. The irradiance is computed on strategically selected locations and efficiently splatted into the screen space using rasterization, rather than ray-tracing.

Franke's [2014] work on delta voxel cone tracing improves upon his previous work on delta light propagation, supporting all combinations of light transport between surfaces of arbitrary glossy or diffuse characteristics. This work combines a light propagation volume with cone tracing. In cone tracing, filtering over a solid angle subtended by a pixel in screen space is not performed by averaging multiple rays. Instead, a single ray is cast through a multi-resolution radiance volume. Filtering is implicitly performed by sampling coarser levels of the hierarchy, as the ray moves farther away from the eye. This work can deal with glossy real objects and rendering realistic images in real time, but the light propagation is still precomputed.

Diminished Reality

While most applications of AR are concerned with the addition of virtual objects to a real scene, **diminished reality** describes the conceptual opposite—namely, the seamless removal of real objects from a real scene. This term was coined by Fung and Mann [2004] to describe the deliberate modification of a visual scene to exclude undesirable objects. These researchers presented a method to remove planar objects from a video sequence and replace them with another texture.

Oftentimes, the undesirable property of the objects in question is that they are aesthetically displeasing. For example, black-and-white fiducial markers, which have high contrast and therefore stand out unnaturally in an everyday environment, can be removed [Siltanen 2006]. In collaborative AR, head-mounted displays prevent users from establishing face and eye contact, which has prompted attempts to remove the head-mounted displays and replace them with synthesized facial expressions [Takemura and Ohta 2002].

The concept of diminished reality is technically related to image completion. For example, in media production, it is frequently necessary to remove certain undesirable artifacts such as scratches on analog film or certain objects, such as safety wires, from the images. Unlike image completion, which is mostly performed offline in post-production, diminished reality is concerned with performing such removal in real time and with only minimal input from the user. Consequently, diminished reality must address three problem areas:

- Determination of the *region of interest* (ROI), which should be removed
- Observation or modeling of the area hidden by the ROI, to provide the input data for the following synthesis step
- Synthesis of a new image with substituted content for the removed ROI

In the following sections, we discuss these tasks in more detail.

Determination of the Region of Interest

The ROI is a continuous set of pixels on the screen that contains the object to be removed by the diminished reality system. The ROI can be exact (i.e., consist exactly of the pixels occluded by the object) or conservative (i.e., cover a superset of the pixels occluded by the object). Moreover, if the object or the camera is moving, the ROI will change over time. In this case, a mechanism is required for tracking the ROI over time, which further complicates matters.

The ROI may be specified in several ways. One approach is to let the user point out the region in the image manually. The user may outline the object contour directly, or may give an indirect specification, such as a bounding rectangle or a set of strokes on the object. A bounding rectangle can be used as a conservative ROI [Zokai et al. 2003] or may be used to initialize active determination of the object contour [Herling and Broll 2010]. Strokes may be used for initial-izing object segmentations [Lepetit et al. 2001]. Once a contour is determined, it can be tracked through a sequence of frames [Lepetit et al. 2001] [van den Hengel et al. 2009].

Alternatively, the ROI can be determined from a model of the object to be removed. This strat-egy assumes that a geometric or appearance-based model of the ROI is already available. For a static object, its model is projected into the current view like a phantom object, but its footprint in the image is used to describe the ROI. A moving object must be tracked to be identified for removal on a frame-by-frame basis. The advantage of model-based ROI tracking is that it is frequently available as a by-product of the determination of the camera pose.

Finally, if the ROI is an articulated object such as a force-feedback arm, the ROI can be deter-mined by simulating the joint angles of the articulated device [Cosco et al. 2009].

Observation and Modeling of the Hidden Area

To diminish a scene and remove a particular object, that scene must be replaced with a view of the background. Since the background cannot be observed directly from the live video feed of a camera used in an AR setup, the necessary information about the background must be obtained from other sources.

The simplest approach is to make no direct observation of the background, but instead to syn-thesize the hidden area from observations in the vicinity of the ROI. This approach is based on the assumption that there is a sufficient degree of spatial coherence in the image. It is often realized using a form of **inpainting**—that is, copying of suitable pixels from other parts of the image.

For a static scene, a simple alternative is to acquire a reconstruction beforehand, typically through an offline procedure. For example, Cosco et al. [2009] seek to establish simple proxy geometry together with a collection of images used as projective textures. Similarly, Zokai et al. [2003] use multiple reference photographs and a simple geometric model. Often, the geometry is just given as a background plane [Enomoto and Saito 2007].

A more complex offline approach is described by Lepetit et al. [2001]. They work with image sequences from a single camera that moves around the scene, thereby revealing different portions of the background over time. By reconstructing the camera path and triangulating background features, they obtain a textured geometry of the background. However, the use of a single camera makes it difficult to ensure that sufficient coverage of the background is available along the camera path.

For direct observation of the background at runtime, multiple cameras are necessary. Static cameras have the advantages that their external calibration can be performed offline and that they do not need attention at runtime. However, moving cameras can give better coverage of dynamic scenes. For example, Enomoto and Saito [2007] use marker tracking and multiple handheld cameras related by homographies to transfer image information from one view to the other. A number of systems [Kameda et al. 2004] [Avery et al. 2007] [Barnum et al. 2009] use information from multiple cameras for making objects visually transparent rather than completely removing them (see the discussion in Chapter 8).

Removal of the Region of Interest

If the ROI is to be replaced with a valid background and not simply painted over, two main approaches may be used: inpainting and image-based rendering.

Inpainting does not require obtaining a model of the background, but instead relies on samples from the vicinity of the ROI to fill in the blank areas. A very simple approach uses linear interpolation of pixels from either side of the ROI border. This can, for example, be executed with a scanline-oriented algorithm. Despite its simplicity, linear interpolation can often produce reasonable results for very small or thin regions. Unfortunately, for larger regions, the lack of detail becomes rapidly apparent.

Siltanen [2006] proposes a method in which a rectangular ROI is covered by mirroring an area around the border to the inside of the region to be hidden. This mirroring is done for each of the four edges of which the region border consists. The four flipped areas are interpolated to produce the final value for a pixel inside the hidden region. Korkalo et al. [2010] extend this work to deal with dynamic lighting. A low-frequency texture over the hidden area is estimated by linear interpolation. A detail texture is produced using the flipping technique, but scaled by dividing by the low-resolution texture. At runtime, the low-frequency texture is computed for every frame, accommodating dynamic changes to the lighting, and then modulated with the detail texture to simulate consistent surface detail.

The PixMix method introduced by Herling and Broll [2012] formulates inpainting as a real-time optimization problem (Figure 6.28). These researchers search for a mapping of pixels from the source (the vicinity of the ROI) to the target (the ROI), which optimizes two constraints: (1) Neighboring pixels of the target should come from neighboring pixels of the source and (2) the neighborhood appearance of the target pixels should be similar to the neighborhood

Figure 6.28   PixMix produces diminished reality effects from a real-time camera stream by copying suitable pixels from the removed object's surroundings. Courtesy of Jan Herling and Wolfgang Broll.

appearance of their corresponding source pixels. From an initial coarse guess, random changes to the source position are iteratively tested. If an improvement is found, it is propagated to the neighboring target pixels. Only local modifications are made, and no global optimal search is attempted. Nonetheless, a coarse-to-fine approach using an image pyramid lets this algorithm converge to a plausible result in real time. Herling and Broll further describe how a locally planar ROI can be tracked through subsequent frames of the video sequence using homography tracking to ensure temporal coherence.

Image-based rendering relies on images acquired from a different camera or camera position to fill the hole. The images are warped to match the current camera position. The reprojection requires some form of geometric approximation of the background scene. The core idea of such image-based algorithms is that images from the auxiliary camera are applied to proxy geometry using projective texture mapping or a similar form of mapping, and then a new image is synthesized by depicting the textured proxy from the current point of view. Various forms of image-based techniques can be applied here, including application of meshes [Cosco et al. 2009], para-perspective projection together with a hierarchical subdivision of the background [Zokai et al. 2003], and a plane sweep algorithm [Jarusirisawad et al. 2010].

Projector-Based Diminished Reality

Diminished reality is also possible in projection-based AR. The challenge here is to determine the right image content to project onto the objects to be "removed" from the scene. In the correct configuration, the user observes the projected images and has the impression that the real surface, which receives the projection, vanishes or at least appears mostly transparent.

One such configuration uses a head-mounted projector together with objects coated with retro-reflective material. This approach has been called "optical camouflage" [Inami et al. 2003]. Due to the reflection properties of the retro-reflective coating, the images from the head-mounted projector are largely thrown back to the viewer. The advantage of this setup is that it allows for a limited range of movement of the observer without head tracking and without dynamic adjustment of the projected imagery. For example, this setup has been used to disguise a haptic input device [Inami et al. 2000] and to make a part of a car cockpit disappear [Yoshida et al. 2008].

An alternative configuration uses diffuse surfaces for projection. The use of projectors with strong light makes it possible to radiometrically compensate for existing surface texture [Bimber et al. 2005]. This approach can be used to make objects visually disappear [Seo et al. 2008]. Such an effect is limited to objects lying flat on the physical surface, or else is view dependent and requires head tracking for a moving user.

Camera Simulation

Even if we fully address the common illumination problem using the most advanced rendering techniques, a significant source of photometric inconsistency remains in video see-through AR, resulting from the limited image quality of the physical camera. The pixel appearances in the video-camera backdrop and in the augmentations rendered with computer graphics should match. Any difference in image quality between virtual and real objects will reveal a seam between the virtual world and the real world. Such seams may be intentional in certain AR applications, but are undesirable in many other applications.

By "image quality," we specifically mean the artifacts of the imaging process based on a real camera as opposed to the ideal virtual camera used to generate the virtual objects. For example, computer graphics assumes a perfect pinhole camera, while in reality a physical camera lens may introduce significant distortions. Many other sources of imperfections are also found in typical consumer-grade video cameras. Among the most noticeable artifacts are lens distortion, blur, noise, vignetting, chromatic aberrations, Bayer mask artifacts, and tone mapping artifacts; these issues are discussed in the following subsections.

Lens Distortion

Most of today's digital video cameras used in AR applications are relatively low-cost consumer products such as webcams or the built-in cameras found in smartphones. These cameras have very small lenses and short focal length and usually introduce significant barrel distortion. A similar problem exists with distortions resulting from the optical system of a head-mounted display.

For AR, there are two alternatives for distortion compensation:

- In video see-through AR, the video image exhibiting radial distortion can be rectified by inverting the distortion, as shown in Figure 6.29.
- If the video image should not be modified, or if an optical see-through display is used, the computer-generated image can be modified to match the distortion present in the perceived real scene.

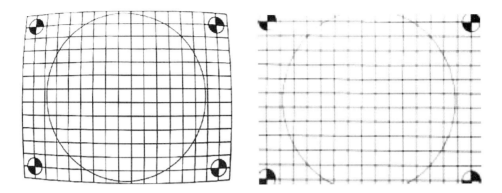

Figure 6.29   (left) Distorted video image of calibration pattern. (right) Rectified image. Courtesy of Anton Fuhrmann.

The classic camera calibration technique described by Tsai [1986] determines radial distortion using an analytical model. This model allows distortion correction (rectification) for every point of an image directly. Unfortunately, computing individual corrections for every point of an image is not a very economical solution. Instead, we prefer to make efficient use of the graphics hardware to distort the imagery for AR overlays in the same way the camera does.

To implement a general image distortion mechanism using graphics hardware, one can take advantage of the texture mapping mechanism [Watson and Hodges 1995] [Fuhrmann et al. 2000]. The source image is used as a texture, which is mapped onto a screen-aligned quad mesh (Figure 6.29). By determining the inverse of the distortion function for every vertex of the mesh, the image can be rectified. Note that an unavoidable side effect of this type of rectification is the loss of a small amount of image information near the corners due to the zooming effect.

If a closed form description of the distortion is not available, the distortion can be acquired manually by measuring the on-screen positions of a calibration pattern consisting of a square grid shown to the camera. After measuring the positions of the grid corners, these positions can be directly mapped as texture coordinates onto the undistorted quad mesh. The texture hardware rectifies the distorted images, using linear interpolations inside the quads.

Blur

Blur effects caused by the camera stem from two major sources: defocusing and motion blurring. The blur caused by defocusing depends on the distance from the focal plane of the camera to the object. Motion blur results from the temporal integration of color intensities in the image sensor. Both sources of blur lead to characteristic, less than fully sharp portions of the image, which stand in clear contrast to the crisp and sharp appearance of the computer-generated parts of an AR scene. The easiest solution for natural integration of real and virtual images is to blur computer-generated objects so as to match their real-world appearance, after the necessary amount of blur has been measured.

If the focal length of a camera is known, it is easy to determine how out-of-focus virtual objects should be represented, given their depth in the scene. Unfortunately, auto-focus cameras usually do not report their current focus. Alternatively, defocus and motion blur can be measured from observing a known object in the scene. Okumura et al. [2006] describe the design of a special fiducial marker with a circular black-on-white boundary, which can be used to estimate blur in the image by determining the intensity gradient observed along the boundary.

Fischer et al. [2006] estimate motion blur from tracking information. Assuming a tracked camera and a static scene, they determine the screen-space motion of the object center for each object. They apply blur to an object proportional to its motion, if the object's velocity exceeds a threshold of 5–10 pixels per frame. Klein and Murray [2010] also work with tracking information, but consider only rotational motion and apply motion blur to the whole image. They determine the screen-space motion of sample points from a low-resolution (24 × 18) grid and apply a blur filter oriented along the tangent of the local blur direction. Motion blur resulting from moving objects in front of a static background has not been considered in any of the aforementioned approaches, although it should be straightforward to incorporate this factor.

Blur can be rendered in several different ways. One approach is to draw an object multiple times, each time with a slight offset in the direction of the blur and with increasing transparency (alpha value). The drawing can be done in object space, or it can be performed in screen space by rendering to a texture first, and then displaying the result multiple times as a **billboard** (i.e., a texture-mapped, view-plane–aligned quad). Alternatively, the blur can be applied in postprocessing, via a pixel shader on an already-rendered image. To increase the speed of the process, a separable Gaussian filter is usually applied.

Both of these approaches consider blur only in image space. If a correct 3D motion blur is desired, the method described by Park et al. [2009] can be applied: It works by overlaying multiple billboards with alpha blending. Given two billboards B_0 and B_1 created at times t_0 and t_1, the true shape of a blurred *in-between* object at time t ($t_0 < t < t_1$) is estimated by warping B_0 and B_1 before rendering, and cross-dissolving the results. This can easily be done using texture hardware. An affine warping based on projecting the corners of the object's bounding box to the desired location is used to approximate a correct, but more expensive perspective warping.

Kán and Kaufmann [2012b] use real-time ray-tracing to implement a physically based depth-of-field effect in AR, which applies correct blur effects to all components of the image. They simulate an aperture by stratified jittered sampling of rays and distinguish different ray types (real/virtual) to compute the L_{R+V} and L_R components required for differential rendering.

Noise

Digital video cameras with small sensors can also be subject to considerable amounts of noise. This noise has certain characteristics, which vary with the camera model, the intensity, and the color channel [Irie et al. 2008]. To reproduce the kind of noise from a particular camera, it must be calibrated first. This can be done by observing a suitable static scene for a number of frames N without moving the camera [Fischer et al. 2006]. For each pixel $\mathbf{p}_i$, the N observations $o_{i,j}$ are averaged to determine the mean μ_i. The pixels $\mathbf{p}_i$ are then quantized into M bins B_k according to their mean μ_i, and for each B_k, the mean μ_k and standard variation δ_k are computed. These computations are done separately for each color channel (red, green, and blue). The statistical values μ_k, δ_k are used to determine the settings for the noise intensity and variation.

At runtime, appropriately scaled Gaussian noise is applied to each pixel in the computer-generated image belonging to a virtual object (*not* to background pixels). As a source of the noise, a texture containing Gaussian noise is precomputed. To ensure that every pixel $\mathbf{p}_i$ is affected by noise, a pixel shader is executed. It chooses a random offset into the noise texture, so that no repetitive pattern can be perceived. The noise value from the texture is scaled according to the statistics μ_k, δ_k from the bin B_k to which $\mathbf{p}_i$ belongs, and added to $\mathbf{p}_i$. This is done separately for each color channel.

To best match the noise empirically observed by a particular camera, some variations can be introduced. The first variation concerns the size of the disturbance. The observed noise is often larger than a single pixel; consequently, the noise modification could also be splatted over multiple pixels. The second variation concerns the duration of the disturbance. It may be appropriate to avoid high-frequency flickering by displaying a particular noise disturbance for several successive frames. The amount of these variations can again be governed by a random number distribution.

Vignetting

The term *vignetting* describes the effect of lens geometry in darkening image corners and edges. The amount of vignetting caused by a certain camera lens can be observed by acquiring the image of a homogeneously illuminated plane and averaging intensities over multiple frames. Vignetting can be simulated for virtual objects by blending with a precomputed vignetting mask or by darkening pixels proportionally to the radial distance from the image center in a shader.

Chromatic Aberrations

Differences in refraction for light of different colors (wavelengths) through the physical lens cause slight color anomalies, which become visible especially at object boundaries. They can be measured in a calibration step by observing a pattern kept in neutral gray tones through the camera, and aligning the slightly shifted patterns that show up in the individual color channels.

Assuming that the green color channel has no aberration, the calibration enables determining an offset for the red and blue channels for every position in the image. From this calibration data, the color aberration can be simulated by blurring or offsetting the rendering accordingly.

Bayer Pattern Artifacts

A **Bayer mask** is an array of color filters placed in front of certain camera sensors to capture individual contributions for the red, green, and blue channels. These contributions are mixed to obtain the final color for a pixel. A Bayer mask usually produces a certain amount of cross-talk between the color channels and some blurring. If the Bayer pattern is known, the image can be subsampled into the individual Bayer channels, and the behavior of the camera chip can be simulated in this representation. Two steps should be considered in this process.

First, the camera chip performs various video processing operations, typically involving sharpening and quantization. Usually, this behavior is not exactly specified and needs to be reverse-engineered from observation.

Second, most cameras deliver their data in YUV format (luminance Y and chrominance U, V). Data is converted from RGB to YUV by the camera chip, and usually back to RGB on the host computer. The YUV format represents the Y component at a much higher spatial resolution than the U and V components, usually according to the ratio 4:1:1. The Bayer image obtained by the previous step is therefore converted to YUV and then to RGB for final compositing.

Tone Mapping Artifacts

Apart from these imperfections, inconsistencies in a composited AR image may arise from the arbitrary tone mapping converting physical radiance values to RGB values delivered by the camera. In most cases, it is not feasible to perform any accurate color calibration of a consumer camera. This leads to noticeable inconsistencies between the colors of virtual and real objects. Such inconsistencies will degrade the perceived realism, especially, if the rendering of virtual objects is based on physical simulation (such as a global illumination technique).

To address this issue, Knecht et al. [2011] propose a color auto-calibration technique for virtual objects that approximates the tone mapping observed in the camera image. They assume that a differential rendering approach, such as that described by Debevec [1998], is used. Recall that in this approach a global illumination simulation L_R of the scene containing only real objects is available and can be compared to the camera image L_C. By sampling corresponding pixels from L_R and L_C, a description of the mapping function from simulated radiance values to observed color values is obtained. Radiance values that are not present in L_R are synthesized by a simple heuristic based on the swapping of color channels. Finally, a tone mapping function is generated by applying polynomial regression on the samples.

Stylized Augmented Reality

While most computer graphics techniques are aimed at photorealistic rendering, the field of non-photorealistic rendering (NPR) is concerned with the generation of stylized images. For example, NPR techniques can simulate pencil drawings, oil paintings, or cartoons. Such an NPR style can be applied to virtual objects in AR [Haller and Sperl 2004]. If the styling is applied to both the virtual components and the real components of an AR scene, the approach is called **stylized augmented reality** [Fischer et al. 2008].

Differences in representation or appearance between virtual and real objects can be disguised by applying such uniform stylization, so as to improve immersion or satisfy an artistic desire. Technically speaking, two approaches to create stylized AR are possible. One approach is to apply separate stylization techniques to the real and virtual parts of an image. This has the advantage that special knowledge about the content can be used. For example, the rendering algorithm for the virtual objects may generate a normal buffer in addition to the color buffer; the normal buffer can then be used for NPR shading. Alternatively, the whole image may be subjected to an NPR algorithm operating in image space after compositing the virtual and real parts (Figure 6.30). This approach has the advantages of being simpler and eliminating the need for separate tuning of two rendering techniques.

A number of examples of stylized AR have been published over the years. For example, Haller et al. [2005] present a loose and sketchy rendering based on brush strokes that coarsely follow object contours. Fischer et al. [2005] use many small brush strokes to create a pointillist impression. Animated cartoons in AR, as discussed by Fischer et al. [2008], can use motion squash and stretch, motion blur, and motion lines to convey movement of virtual objects. Chen et al. [2008] present an approach for simulating watercolor effects in AR. They create the impression of fluid colors by subdividing the image into irregular tiles and average the colors in each tile. Edges are extracted from the original image and used for enforcing temporally coherent behavior of the tiles.

 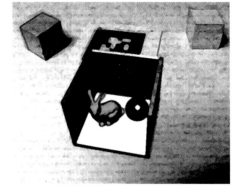

Figure 6.30   Stylized AR can be used for artistic impression, where the real and virtual parts of the scene assume the same style. Original scene image courtesy of Peter Kán.

Summary

This chapter has discussed the concept of visual coherence in AR scenes. The AR rendering pipeline brings together virtual and real portions of an image. To obtain visual coherence, we must obtain geometric and photometric registration. Geometric registration is feasible, if highly accurate tracking and a reasonably precise model of the real scene are used. Photometric registration is more involved, as the transport of light between real and virtual objects must be simulated. The simplest set of techniques deals with only shadows between virtual and real objects. Such shadows can be obtained by adapting standard shadow simulation techniques from computer graphics. If advanced common illumination effects beyond shadows are desired, it becomes necessary to model the environment illumination and then apply this illumination to virtual objects. Diminished reality is also possible with techniques for seamlessly removing real objects from the combined AR scene.

Beyond considering the scene space shared by virtual and real objects, it may be worthwhile for coherence techniques to simulate the properties of the camera used to obtain the real images and apply such simulation—for example, geometric distortions, blur, or noise—to the virtual objects. Stylized augmented reality aims to unify the appearance of the real and virtual images by using artistic approaches.

CHAPTER 7

SITUATED VISUALIZATION

In Chapter 6, we examined *how* computer graphics can be seamlessly embedded in a real scene, while we silently assumed that it is well known *what* information should be presented in AR. In truth, this is an important problem. The power of AR as a novel user interface paradigm derives in large part from its ability to display information that is relevant to a situation, task, or user. To successfully communicate the desired information, it must be put in an appropriate visual form. This is done through the application of suitable visualization techniques.

Visualization for AR differs from conventional visualization primarily by its interaction with the real scene, which becomes an intrinsic part of the visualization [Kalkofen et al. 2011]. In this chapter, we investigate **situated visualization** techniques that somehow take the real world into account.

The term *situated visualization* was coined by White and Feiner [2009] to describe a form of context-aware computing, where the context is defined as part of the physical scene. Such a context does not necessarily have to be a single object. It can be anything from an isolated point in space (Figure 7.1) to a large area such as a particular city district, as long as the artifact has some semantic meaning in the real world.

What does not count as situated are visualizations that are merely registered in three-dimensional space, usually as a result of deploying a particular tracking technology. For example, many AR applications that use fiducial markers as a tracking aid register their virtual content relative to a particular marker (Figure 7.2). The marker is obviously a physical object but does not have any significance in the real world other than to facilitate tracking. The AR application can be transported to an arbitrary alternate location without affecting its semantics, which is why it cannot be called situated. This type of visualization is not significantly different from visualization in VR and is not discussed further in this chapter.

Figure 7.1 Textual annotations describing points of interest for tourists are a good example of situated visualization. Courtesy of Raphael Grasset.

Figure 7.2   Inspecting an AR visualization of a three-dimensional mathematical model is a compelling application, but not a situated visualization, because no semantically significant real-world object is referred to. Courtesy of Anton Fuhrmann.

We start our investigation of situated visualization by considering the challenges that this type of visualization must meet. This examination provides us with an understanding of the design problem we face. The remaining sections deal with one important design idea each. We first discuss how to address fundamental registration issues. This is followed by an exploration of approaches for labeling and laying out information in AR. We then consider the use of X-ray visualization to convey hidden information. The following section outlines an alternative, spatial manipulation of the scene, which can be used to uncover information, if X-ray visualization is not desired. Finally, we discuss various forms of information filtering that make it possible to handle scenes that are densely populated with information.

Challenges

Situated visualization faces the same challenges as traditional visualization, including the same primary challenge—*data overload*. When too much data is presented, it leads to a cluttered presentation and impairs understanding. To build the necessary understanding, users also must be able to explore the data *interactively*.

In addition, the embedding of situated visualizations into the real world requires addressing several other issues. *Registration errors* affecting the placement of the visualization may lead to the communication of false information. Even if registration is perfect, a viewer's ability to easily discern important from irrelevant information can be reduced by *visual interference* between

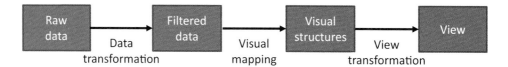

Figure 7.3   The visualization pipeline includes three stages: data transformation, visual mapping, and view transformation.

real and virtual objects. Moreover, the real world (including the user's viewpoint) is constantly changing and requires adjustments to the visualization. To avoid distractions, the adjustments must be performed in a way that ensures *temporal coherence*. In the following subsections, we discuss each of these challenges in more detail.

Data Overload

Presenting a large amount of data in AR quickly leads to a cluttered presentation, which makes it difficult for a viewer to gain insight into the data. This problem is aggravated in AR, which often has a limited presentation space, such as a smartphone display. Azuma et al. [2001] identified this situation as the problem of increasing data density. They refer to two complementary solutions to manage the data. The first solution is to reduce the amount of data by **filtering** [Feiner et al. 1993a] [Julier et al. 2002]. The second solution is to create a visualization **layout** that avoids interference with other important information. Spence [2007] refers to the issue of data density in information visualization as data overload.

Early on, visualization research developed architectural models to cope with this problem [Haber and McNabb 1990] [Card et al. 1999]. These models generally incorporate three steps: *data transformation*, *visual mapping*, and *view transformation* (Figure 7.3).

- Data transformation reduces the amount of data by filtering or aggregating data points.
- Visual mapping creates visual structures of the data such as color and shape.
- View transformation determines properties such as the position and scale of the visual structures, addressing the layout problem.

User Interaction

In contrast to hand-drawn illustrations, a core aspect of computer-supported visualization is the ability to interactively explore the data. In the area of information visualization, the design of user interfaces was heavily influenced by the "information seeking mantra" of Shneiderman [1996]:

- Overview: Gain an overview of the entire collection
- Zoom: Zoom in on items of interest

- Filter: Filter out uninteresting items
- Details-on-demand: Select an item or group and get details when needed

While Shneiderman did not intend these steps to be prescriptive [Craft and Cairns 2005], many successful visualizations have been designed by following this mantra. Therefore, designers of situated visualizations should also consider these recommendations, as they will likely support users getting valuable insights into the data.

Registration Errors

Situated visualizations have an additional requirement relative to conventional visualizations— namely, registration to an artefact that is present in the real world. Tracking errors can lead to inaccurate registration, causing misalignments between the augmentations and the real-world objects they refer to. To cope with this problem, visualizations should take the precision of the registration into account. For instance, the error can be communicated to the viewer by integrating a virtual copy of the real-world context into the visualization (Figure 7.4).

Visual Interference

Visualizations generally emphasize the relevant parts of data in a way that guides the viewer's attention to this information. Without this emphasis, such information might be overlooked, because it does not stand out from the rest of the data. In situated visualization, the viewer's attention is guided toward the important parts of the scene, while irrelevant aspects of the real world are not distracting. Achieving this outcome requires avoiding visual interferences between the visualization and the real world. Kalkofen et al. [2007] identified this challenge as a

 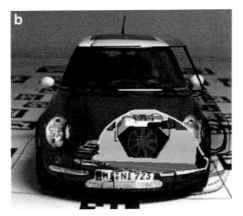

Figure 7.4   (left) The registration error causes a misalignment of virtual content and the real-world context—in this case, the engine compartment. (right) The registration error can be resolved by integrating a copy of the context—in this case, the outlines of the car—into the visualization. Courtesy of Denis Kalkofen.

Figure 7.5   The focus of a visualization can be emphasized to avoid visual interferences with the background and to guide the viewer's attention. Courtesy of Denis Kalkofen.

focus and context visualization problem in AR: The relevant part of the scene is the focus, while the rest of the scene provides context. Figure 7.5 shows that the focus is emphasized to guide the viewer's attention and the rest of the scene is deemphasized to avoid distractions.

Visual interferences between the visualization and the real world can also be caused by the placement of the augmentations, which can cause occlusions of the augmented real-world object and other important landmarks. View management techniques have been developed that prevent such occlusions by rearranging the virtual content [Bell et al. 2001] [Grasset et al. 2012].

Temporal Coherence

A major difference of AR visualization over conventional visualization is that the real-world context is not static, but rather changes over time. For instance, people or cars may pass through the video image, or the lighting conditions may change. Consider the visualization of the internals of a car in Figure 7.6. While the internals are clearly visible in the yellow car, the same visualization is obscured when the car is red.

Hence, static augmentations may be effective for a certain amount of time, but then cease to be effective at a later time. If we want to ensure consistent effectiveness, situated visualizations must be able to *adapt* to changing environmental conditions. However, frequent and strong adaptations are also undesirable, because they can distract the viewer. Therefore, visualizations must behave in a *temporally coherent* way. This aspect is especially important for constrained layouts, where simple viewpoint changes can readily introduce significant changes.

Figure 7.6   (top) The visualization clearly shows the internals of the car in the rear. (bottom) A poor choice of color severely impacts the perception of the occluded visualization. Courtesy of Denis Kalkofen.

Visualization Registration

We start the discussion of methods leading to situated visualization with the issue of registration. Recall that situated visualization must refer to a real-world artefact, which may or may not be a moveable object. We can distinguish two situations on this basis:

- The visualization is given in local coordinates of a potentially moveable object.
- The visualization is given in global coordinates relative to a stationary object or physical location.

These two options lead to different types of visualization design.

Locally Registered Situated Visualization

In the local case, to apply the situated visualization, we must first detect the presence of the object referred to or otherwise establish the local coordinate system. When this detection step relies on dynamic object recognition—for example, using image search—the artifact referred to might potentially not be unique. This ambiguity can be intentional. For example, advertising can be expressed relative to a particular brand logo. Whenever that logo occurs, the situated visualization would be displayed. Another example of visualization relative to a dynamically detected object is documented by White et al. [2006], who describe virtual vouchers to support botanists in their fieldwork. This system is able to identify various types of leaves by image recognition when the leaf is placed on an instrument clipboard.

Globally Registered Situated Visualization

If the visualization refers to a stationary artifact or a particular location, it can be expressed in absolute global coordinates. In this case, it is not strictly necessary to detect the referred object, as long as a global localization system is available. If no object detection is performed, however, there is a certain danger that the environment may have changed since the database was created, such that the relevant object is no longer there. A possible alternative to global localization, then, is to first establish a coarse global location (e.g., using GPS) and then search for objects known to be in the vicinity.

One advantage of global references is that the situated visualization can easily be put in geometric relation to other globally registered visualizations. This relationship can become relevant for certain algorithms such as dynamic layout generation (see the section "Annotations and Labeling").

As an example for globally referenced visualization, consider the case of AR for subsurface infrastructure visualization [Schall et al. 2008]. Infrastructure providers such as utility companies maintain geospatial databases for their buried assets, such as power lines or gas pipes. For maintenance procedures, it is necessary to locate these assets in the field. Maintenance workers can navigate to a given location and observe a situated visualization of the relevant infrastructure. In this case, the visualized data is precisely referenced to global geographic coordinates, but not necessarily related to any (visible) object.

Another example where AR can visualize globally referenced information that is not tied to a particular physical object is sensor data visualization. Suppose environmentalists, urban planners, and other professionals regularly visit a site to collect impressions relevant for their professional activities. Sensors deployed throughout this environment, either by the professionals as part of their site visits or as part of a permanent monitoring infrastructure, might deliver important information on the environment—for example, air pollution or moisture levels. Rather than having to relate such sensor information to observations made on the site after returning to the planning office, it would be useful to be able to observe sensor data in situ—that is, directly in the environment where the data is collected.

This approach was explored by White and Feiner [2009] with SiteLens, a system that is designed to display carbon monoxide levels in New York City, with the data being obtained from both mobile and stationary sensors. Veas et al. [2012a] discuss Hydrosys, a system that displays

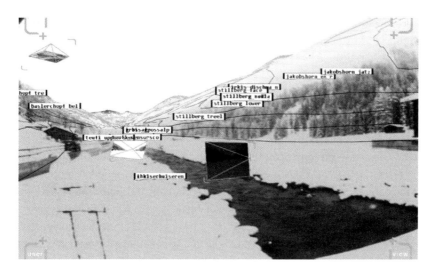

Figure 7.7   Hydrosys displays locations of stations in a global sensor network as well as interpolated temperature plotted as geodesic contours. Courtesy of Eduardo Veas and Ernst Kruijff.

hydrological information in the Swiss Alps, based on a widely deployed global sensor network. This network collects information on issues such as water levels or temperature, which is relevant for glacier monitoring (Figure 7.7).

Registration Uncertainty

Situated visualization requires precise registration of virtual and real scene elements. Two major sources of error can affect this registration. First, the position and orientation of virtual objects may not exactly match those of their real counterparts. Second, the position and orientation of the virtual camera may not exactly match those of the real camera. Both types of errors degrade the quality of the resulting visualization, because the overlaid graphics will not properly align with objects in the physical world. As a result, augmentations can be ambiguous or even misleading, if they point to the wrong object.

This problem can be partially addressed by making situated visualizations adaptive to registration uncertainty. Many tracking techniques enable estimation of the amount of tracking error. Using geometric relationships, as, for example, encoded in a scene graph, the error estimate can be transformed into screen-space error. Such a screen-space error can be used to parameterize visualizations so that they become more error tolerant.

MacIntyre et al. [2002] propose several types of error-tolerant visualizations. One such approach enlarges the silhouette of a phantom object such that the resulting screen-aligned shape is certain to cover the corresponding real object even in the presence of registration errors. Another idea is to dynamically switch textual labels placed on top of a real object to a representation that uses a leader line between label and object. The latter representation is more robust against registration errors and, therefore, is used when the registration error exceeds a certain threshold.

Annotations and Labeling

One of the major advantages of situated visualization is its ability to present information close to real-world objects in the form of **annotations**. According to the definition given by Wither et al. [2009], an annotation must always be composed of a spatially dependent component, which anchors the object in the real world, and a spatially independent component, which introduces additional information not otherwise contained in the real world. This definition is very broad and encompasses many possible applications from the domain of interactive guidance systems, such as for navigation, tourism, or maintenance instructions. Perhaps the most important class of annotations comprises textual labels, which provide explanations or hints concerning real-world artifacts.

Labeling Fundamentals

Placement of textual labels has been widely studied in conventional 2D maps, but the 3D case turns out to be very different and more complicated. In this section, we will explain some fundamental considerations in these applications. First, we must first distinguish internal from external labels. Second, we require objectives for proper placement of labels. Third, we need to choose an appropriate representation of the screen space where labels are to be placed. Fourth, we must choose anchor points for any leader lines that are required.

Internal and External Labels

Two principal approaches to placing a label are possible: internal and external. Internal labels are placed directly over the object—that is, within its silhouette. If the object is partially occluded, the label should be placed over the visible portion to avoid any ambiguities. In contrast to internal labels, external labels are placed outside the object's silhouette but should be in the object's vicinity to avoid any ambiguities. External labels use a leader line to link the label to an anchor point inside the silhouette of the object to which that label refers.

Placement Objectives

The placement of labels over a view of a three-dimensional scene should follow a number of widely accepted criteria:

- Labels should be placed close to the referred objects.
- Labels should not overlap.
- External labels should not be placed over other important objects.
- The length of each leader line should be minimal.

- Crossings of leader lines with each other and with labels are undesirable.

- Temporal coherence should be maintained—label positions should not abruptly change from one frame to the next.

Formulating these criteria mathematically leads to a constrained optimization problem, which is known to be NP-hard. However, solutions can be computed using heuristic optimization strategies. Several published approaches derive useful solutions using relatively simple greedy algorithms that find suitable placements for one label after the other, given some ordering of the labels [Azuma and Furmanski, 2003].

Area Representation

For solving the optimization problem, it is necessary to have a representation of the screen area that enables determination of whether a point is occupied by the object to be labeled, by another important object that should not be disturbed, or by a background (such as grass or sky) where labels and leader lines can freely be placed. Such an area representation can either be discrete, based on the screen-aligned bounding boxes of objects [Bell et al. 2001], or sampled, being given as a two-dimensional array of arbitrary spacing (not necessarily identical to screen resolution). In both cases, hidden surface removal must be performed to correctly identify occlusions among objects.

A sampled representation can easily be produced on the GPU by rasterizing the scene objects into an id-buffer. Unfortunately, reading back the id-buffer can introduce significant latency. Therefore, Hartmann et al. [2004] perform the rasterization on the CPU, while Stein and Décoret [2008] execute the whole algorithm on the GPU.

Choosing the Anchor Point

If the anchor point to which a leader line should be attached is not given by the application, it should be determined in a suitable way. In general, the anchor point should be chosen at a surface position of the object that is visible in the current frame. For convex objects (or if only a bounding box of the object is available), the centroid is a reasonable choice. In contrast, for arbitrarily shaped objects, a more robust procedure is to iteratively apply morphological thinning and assign the anchor point to the last remaining position before the object completely disappears.

Optimization Techniques

With an appropriate understanding of the objectives for label placement, we can formulate placement as an optimization problem. Because the problem needs to be solved for every frame, it must be handled efficiently. Suitable optimization methods use either (1) a sparse formulation with forces or bounding boxes or (2) a dense formulation that is amenable for parallel evaluation on the GPU.

Optimization Using Forces

Hartmann et al. [2004] formulate label placement as an optimization problem carried out on force fields set up in image space. The force fields model the following forces applied to a label:

- An attractive force from an object's 2D projection to the screen space
- A repulsive force from the object boundary (so that a label is placed either fully internally or fully externally)
- A repulsive force from the projection of other objects
- A repulsive force from the screen boundary
- A repulsive force from other labels

All the force fields are combined using a weighted average. First, a heuristic is applied to initialize the label position. Second, labels follow the gradient of the combined force field, until a minimum is found. Interfering labels that overlap in the screen space are adjusted dynamically using a simple greedy heuristic that favors larger labels.

Optimization Using Bounding Boxes

Bell et al. [2001] approximate the 2D projection using screen-aligned 2D bounding boxes. The empty space remaining after subtracting the space occupied by the bounding boxes is considered as a site for placing the labels. The algorithm of Bell et al. begins by determining the size of the visible portion of the object to which the label will be attached. If it is large enough, an internal label can be placed; if not, the algorithm searches for a suitable site for placing an external label. External labels are placed by a greedy algorithm that prioritizes labels in front-to-back order but could also use other kinds of priorities. After placing a label, the occupied area is forbidden for other labels.

Optimization on the GPU

Stein and Décoret [2008] use the power of modern GPUs to implement a greedy real-time optimization that considers all possible placements for a label. The order in which labels are considered is based on the use of a Voronoi diagram to approximately sort the anchor points from inward (i.e., from the center of the scene) to outward (i.e., toward the screen boundary). This algorithm renders a texture representation of forbidden regions for the label, which considers important objects, other labels, and leader lines. Finally, a GPU program systematically tests all remaining locations and determines the optimum.

Temporal Coherence

If the optimization problem is solved for every frame independently, the placement of labels can vary significantly from frame to frame, resulting in occlusions (Figure 7.8) or a jumpy appearance (Figure 7.9). As a countermeasure, an additional hysteresis constraint can be introduced, which penalizes large label displacements. Moreover, if a label must be displaced over a larger distance, this transition can be animated over several consecutive frames for a smoother transition.

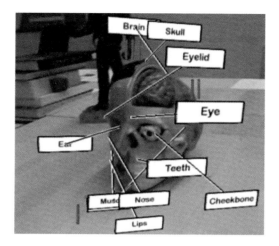

Figure 7.8 Even if a proper layout is found for one viewpoint, it can lead to various types of occlusions for another viewpoint, such as (I) annotations occluding each other, (II) annotations occluding the object of interest, or (III) leader lines crossing each other. Courtesy of Markus Tatzgern and Denis Kalkofen.

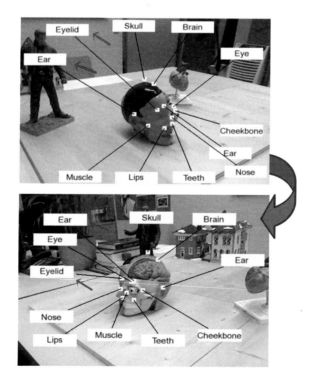

Figure 7.9 Without temporal coherence, rotating the camera may cause two labels (marked with red and blue arrows) to change order unexpectedly. Courtesy of Markus Tatzgern and Denis Kalkofen.

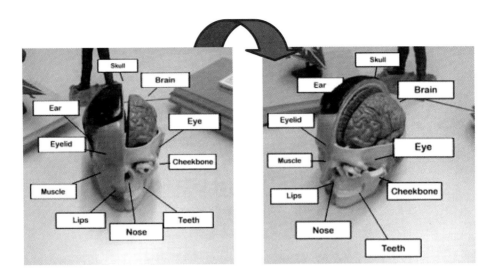

Figure 7.10   Hedgehog labeling enforces temporal coherence in label placement. Courtesy of Markus Tatzgern and Denis Kalkofen.

Label layout in 2D image space cannot address temporal coherence of objects are moving in a 3D scene. A 3D layout can address this issue more adeptly, because labels can follow object motion in world space [Pick et al. 2010]. A temporally coherent view management approach can use this idea to compute a constrained layout for a label with 3D geometry. A 3D label consists of a 3D annotation billboard, a 3D pole (the equivalent of a 2D leader line), and an anchor point on a real-world object. Only adjustments to the length of the pole and a small displacement of the annotation billboard in image space are allowed, while the orientation of the pole is fixed in object space. Figure 7.10 illustrates this strategy, which resembles a "hedgehog" [Tatzgern et al. 2014b]. Label placement has enough freedom to produce high-quality layouts without suffering from temporal coherence problems.

Image-Guided Placement

In AR, it will frequently be the case that only a subset of the objects in the environment is known to the application. In this case, the video image itself should be analyzed for areas of less visual interest, where labels can be placed without occluding salient content unknown to the application. To that end, Leykin and Tuceryan [2004] use a machine learning approach to automatically determine the readability of text over textured backgrounds. A similar goal is pursued by Rosten et al. [2005] with a technique that searches the image for features according to an interest point operator and tracks regions where such features are absent. Tanaka et al. [2008] subdivide the screen according to a rectangular grid and compute viewability as a weighted combination of RGB values, variance of saturation in HSV color space, and variance of luminance in YCbCr color space for every grid cell. An annotation is then placed in a grid with a low

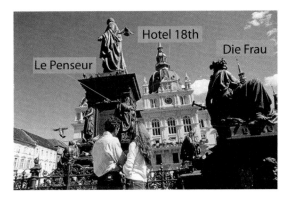

Figure 7.11   (top) Naïve placement of labels occludes the objects of interest. (bottom) Saliency-guided placement avoids occlusions and prefers empty areas, such as the sky. Courtesy of Raphael Grasset.

viewability value. Grasset et al. [2012] analyze the salience of the video input and place labels in areas of low saliency, where they are unlikely to cover up important real-world information. For example, labels may be placed in the sky (Figure 7.11).

Legibility

Overlaid information should be easily understandable on a cognitive level. However, we need to ensure not only the availability of cognitive support, but also **legibility**. By legibility, we mean low-level perceptual factors, such as sufficient size and contrast of the overlaid information.

First and foremost, legibility is a concern with textual labels, which must be read by the user. It is also relevant for all kinds of graphical information. Placing computer-generated information over a live video background can be problematic, if the background is very salient, uses strong colors, or includes textures containing high frequencies. This undesirable situation is further exacerbated in optical see-through systems, where a fully opaque overlay cannot be obtained, such that the maximum color fidelity is limited.

If the full extent of real-world objects and their visual properties appearing in the scene is known in advance, view management can determine the optimal placement of certain elements such as labels and largely avoid situations of poor legibility.

The legibility of text over various backgrounds in an optical see-through display was investigated by Gabbard et al. [2007]. They conducted a series of user studies and found that—as might be expected—user performance in search tasks is significantly affected by background texture and text drawing style. Gabbard et al. considered text placed on a uniformly colored billboard, which occludes the background, as well as text emphasized with outlines and drop shadows. The contrast achieved between the background and the emphasis color (i.e., the color of the billboard, outline, or shadow) as well as the contrast between the emphasis color and the text color significantly determine legibility. Note that the use of billboarded text may not be possible in scenarios that do not allow larger areas of the background to be occluded.

While an earlier study by the same group [Gabbard et al. 2006] showed good outcomes when saturated green was used as an emphasis color, the best results in dynamic environments would be achieved by adapting the emphasis color to the background. For example, Mendez et al. [2010] ensure that a minimum difference in visual saliency between foreground objects (such as labels) and background objects is achieved.

X-Ray Visualization

An important application of AR is to reveal hidden artifacts by artificially removing occlusions from real-world objects. This so-called **X-ray visualization** resembles the superhuman ability to look through solid matter—a favorite superpower in science fiction. A synthetic view of hidden artifacts is shown in the context of a real scene, so that an observer can infer spatial and semantic relationships between visible and hidden objects. Naïvely superimposing a virtual object on top of a real scene (Figure 7.12, top) does not lead to satisfactory results, as fundamental rules of depth perception are lost. Likewise, uniformly applying transparency to the virtual object (Figure 7.12, bottom) does not resolve this problem—Buchmann et al. [2005] showed that uniform transparency destroys spatial relationships. Moreover, it can lead to display clutter.

A better way to produce X-ray visualizations is to render the object causing the occlusion with adaptive transparency, with the goal of revealing enough of the occluded object underneath so that it is easily comprehensible, while the major structural properties of the occluder are mostly preserved. Such a representation is often called **ghosting** [Feiner and Seligmann 1992] in computer-based illustration.

Figure 7.12 (top) Naïve overlay of a hidden synthetic object on top of a real scene. (bottom) Overlay of a synthetic object with uniform transparency. Courtesy of Denis Kalkofen.

Ghostings from Object Space

Ghostings in AR can be produced by extending the phantom rendering approach presented in Chapter 5. Standard phantom rendering merely discriminates fully visible from fully occluded pixels through the use of a z-buffer. In contrast, a ghosting can be produced by determining for every occluded pixel of a virtual object the degree of occlusion (or transparency) of the occluder, which is then used for alpha-blending the occludee and the occluder.

For example, a ghosting can be generated by setting the transparency of the fragment based on a linear function of the object's principal curvature. For a given phantom, curvature can be precomputed and stored per vertex or as a texture. The curvature is then looked up or interpolated per fragment and converted into transparency after applying some scale and bias. The rationale of this approach is that strongly curved portions of the phantom's surface define its shape and should be more opaque, while flat areas can be made more transparent.

Another attribute that can be used to steer transparency is the dot product of the surface normal and the viewing direction. When the surface normal is perpendicular to the viewing direction at the silhouette of a phantom object, the dot product is 0. In contrast, for surfaces viewed in the direction of the normal vector, the dot product is 1. This property can easily be converted into a transparency value. Silhouette and principal curvature are complementary in terms of the aspects of an object's shape that they convey and can be used together.

Ghostings from Image Space

All attributes computed in object space, such as silhouette or curvature, generally suffer from imperfections of registration. Any mismatch in the pose of a real object and its phantom will lead to a displacement of the local effects derived from the phantom geometry, and these displacements will be disturbing to the viewer. Moreover, in AR, several (or all) of the real objects in a scene are often unknown and, consequently, cannot be used as phantoms. The only available information concerning these real objects may be their representation in the video image. However, we can make use of the assumption that we would like to show hidden virtual objects and treat everything that is visible in the video frame as an occluder.

To do so, we can try to identify the **shape hints** in the video image that convey the shape of the visible objects and set per-pixel transparency corresponding to the pixel's importance as a shape hint. One simple way of finding shape hints is to use an edge detector. After identifying which pixels of an image contribute to edges (e.g., using Canny edge detection), the edges can be emphasized. For example, after rendering a basic image with the video image as the background and virtual objects superimposed on top of it, the edges can be rendered in an opaque color on top of the basic image, resulting in a stylization similar to hidden-line graphics. In this way, a coarse ghosting is produced, which preserves some important depth relationships between real and virtual objects.

Artificially colored edges are a strong visual distraction, however, and extracting all edges from the entire video frame may lead to excessive clutter. Suppressing clutter is a general requirement for all techniques that rely on emphasizing shape hints. A reasonable approach to prevent excessive use of shape hints is to limit them to the areas of the image surrounding the virtual objects. These areas can be determined either manually—for example, by letting the user place a magic lens [Mendez et al. 2006]—or by computing an area from the screen projection of the virtual object. Rendering the virtual objects to a stencil or id-buffer and applying a distance transform to this buffer yields such a region with a chamfered boundary, which can be used to determine transparency of the shape hints—in our case, the edge pixels (Figure 7.13). Computing the distance transform can be done on the GPU [Rong and Tan 2006].

Figure 7.13 In this example, the body of a real car is the occluder for a virtual engine. After extracting contours as important shape hints, a 2D distance transform is applied to make the occluder seem more solid. Courtesy of Denis Kalkofen.

Edges extracted from the image are effective in conveying shape but have a tendency to lead to clutter and cannot convey the impression of a dense occluder. If such a dense occluder is acceptable or even desirable, a distance transform can be applied to the edge image and used to determine transparency. This operation will lead to larger areas of occlusion around the edges, with transparency gradually increasing in the direction away from the edge. The resulting visualization resembles an image produced by deriving transparency from curvature, as suggested earlier.

Edges are important shape cues but do not represent the only valuable information for supporting spatial perception. In general, we want to preserve visually **salient** image features, which are often defined as the joint effect of contrast measures found in attributes such as hue, luminosity, orientation, or motion. Salient features have been found to attract a viewer's gaze [Treisman and Gelade 1980].

Saliency can be computed from an image by analyzing its contrast on the levels of an image pyramid and adding up the effects across the levels of the pyramid [Itti et al. 1998]. To do so, the image is concerted to a color space such as $L^*a^*b^*$, which directly encodes luminosity and red–green and blue–yellow color opponency. In this representation, an image pyramid is computed. Central differences are determined for every pyramid level and every channel of the $L^*a^*b^*$ image, and all differences are combined. Motion can be considered by computing the changes in luminosity over time. All of these computations can be efficiently performed in a fragment shader.

Figure 7.14 X-ray visualization technique with areas of homogeneous texture assigned to a particular level of transparency to achieve a consistent appearance. Courtesy of Stefanie Zollmann.

Sandor et al. [2010b] use this saliency computation to determine transparency of a ghosting. The transparency level for a fragment is computed from the difference between the saliency of the occluding image and the saliency of the occluded image.

In contrast to the approch of determining saliency per pixel proposed by Sandor et al. [2010b], Zollmann et al. [2010] determine saliency per area, based on a superpixel segmentation of the image. This strategy has the advantage that properties of consistent regions in the image can be exploited for the ghosting. Texturedness is one such property of a region that provides an important additional measure of saliency. Moreover, transparency can be determined per region (Figure 7.14). Because the regions are determined by segmenting natural boundaries in the video image, no additional spatial frequencies are introduced by the transparency modulation, leading to a less cluttered result.

Implementation with G-Buffers

The implementation of ghostings is based on geometric buffers (G-Buffers) known from non-photorealistic rendering [Saito and Takahashi 1990]. In a three-pass rendering approach, the first pass renders the individual objects of the scene into a set of buffers, the second pass applies image processing techniques to the buffers, and the third pass composes the final result from the individual buffers by sweeping over the buffers in depth order.

Buffer Rendering

The rendering uses multiple G-Buffers, each containing an approximation of scene objects belonging to a particular group. Using this technique, we can isolate the styling applied to

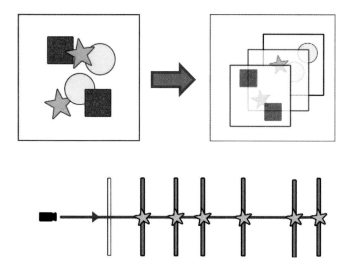

Figure 7.15 (top left) An illustration of a scene. (top right) One possible G-Buffer volume. Notice that the G-Buffer does not represent a depth layer. (bottom) Composition by front-to-back traversal of the G-Buffer volume. Courtesy of Erick Mendez and Denis Kalkofen.

different groups, while the collection of all G-Buffers approximates the whole scene. During buffer rendering, we use the regular rendering pipeline to extract all the necessary information that will be used during the processing of the buffers. The scene is traversed in a single pass with multiple render targets—namely, multiple G-Buffers. Every object is rendered to exactly one of the G-Buffers, which is determined by its group membership (Figure 7.15).

Buffer Processing

For every buffer, image processing techniques can be applied to compute additional information— for example, to detect edges or regions with high curvature, to extract regions with particular color or depth values, or to mark a particular region supplied interactively by the user. Some techniques consider more than just the fragment's value, such as its neighborhood, fragment values of other buffers in the same G-Buffer, or fragment values from different G-Buffers. In this way, multiple additional image components containing auxiliary information can be added to the G-Buffer.

Scene Compositing

In the final compositing step, the information from the set of G-Buffers is merged into a final image using a front-to-back traversal of the G-Buffers (Figure 7.15, right). Note that simple blending of the G-Buffers is not enough: Per-pixel occlusions are essential for the desired effects. Since the G-Buffers are already available in view coordinates and in screen resolution, the problem is reduced to sorting the depth components of the G-Buffers. Once this sorting has taken place, we proceed to combine all of the fragments into a single output. The compositing rules used during this process can arbitrarily alter the contribution of a particular pixel from one of the G-Buffers. For example, color or transparency of a particular pixel may be modified based on the importance of the pixel that was visited along the ray before the current one.

Spatial Manipulation

If a scene is densely populated with objects, and several visible and hidden objects that are in close proximity must be shown simultaneously, a ghosting may not be sufficient to uncover all relevant information. Instead, it may be more instrumental to trade unoccupied screen space for an increased visibility of relevant objects. Spatial manipulation of the objects in the scene achieves precisely that end—in AR, we can rearrange the scene. We can create the illusion that either some objects have moved or otherwise changed to make room for hidden objects. Both the moved object and the revealed object could be either real or virtual. In this section, we take a closer look at two types of spatial manipulations: explosion diagrams and space distortions.

Explosion Diagrams

Explosion diagrams originate in hand-drawn technical illustrations as a technique to present object assemblies. The key idea of explosion diagrams is that the parts of a complex object are arranged in such a way that it becomes possible to mentally reassemble the object. In that way, usage of the available screen space for showing visual information on the parts is maximized, while the perception of the object's spatial structure is still well supported. Finding a suitable layout of the exploded parts relative to each other is therefore essential in the generation of successful explosion diagrams.

When using explosion diagrams as a visualization technique in AR, finding the right arrangement of parts is not the only challenge that must be addressed: AR also requires that parts from the real world be convincingly relocated. To achieve this goal, visual information must be transferred from the original location to the destination location (Figure 7.16). After this transfer of visual information, the original location must be filled with new imagery. Finally, correct mutual occlusion between virtual and real must be resolved.

For the displacement of real world parts, a **video-textured phantom** can be used [Kalkofen et al. 2009] [Tatzgern et al. 2010]. This is a virtual representation of a real-world object, which is texture mapped with the live video image. Projective texture coordinates are computed for each surface point of the video-textured phantom from a viewpoint corresponding to the current camera image; that is, each vertex of the phantom is transformed to the original vertex position which it occupied before displacement.

This computation can easily be performed in a vertex shader and applied to the geometry of the phantom object after it has been displaced to a new location. Video-textured phantoms are rendered with texture mapping, but without any shading, since we can assume that illumination effects are already present in the video texture of the real object, and only a single

Figure 7.16   (top) Exploded phantom rendered using basic shading. (bottom) With video-textured dual phantom rendering, visible pixels are exploded and uncovered background pixels are colored black. Courtesy of Markus Tatzgern and Denis Kalkofen.

rendering pass is required. Therefore, the rendering of video-textured phantoms is computationally very inexpensive. Moreover, this technique works for zero displacement and results in the same effect as when using a conventional phantom rendering approach. This property makes it straightforward to produce animated explosion diagrams, which start from an unmodified real object.

Video-textured phantoms enable us to move real-world parts to new locations on the screen and reveal hidden objects at the original screen location. However, the uncovered area will usually not be fully occupied by virtual objects. The pixels that are not occupied by the virtual object should not show the original video image, but rather should show a background color.

To this end, a second rendering pass is executed, which initializes unoccupied pixels from the uncovered area with the background color. This **dual phantom rendering** algorithm may be expressed as the following:

1. Switch to render target T_1.
2. Clear render target T_1.
3. Render video-textured (displaced) phantoms to T_1.
4. Render virtual objects to T_1.
5. Switch to render target T_2.
6. Fill T_2 with the current video image.
7. Render phantoms at their original location in background color.
8. Superimpose T_1 on top of T_2.

If multiple phantoms overlap in screen space, dual phantom rendering may not yield correct results, as shown in Figure 7.12, top. In such a case, video information from one undisplaced phantom is transferred to another displaced phantom, so it appears twice in the frame. To suppress this artifact, it is necessary to only copy those pixels from the video that are visible in the original video frame. This goal can be achieved by first rendering phantoms to an id-buffer. For every fragment of a video-textured phantom, the modified algorithm first determines whether the corresponding fragment at the original location is visible, before writing the information from the video frame to the new location. If the fragment is not visible at the original position, a replacement color, synthetic shading, or inpainting must be used (Figure 7.17). This algorithm is called **synchronized dual phantom rendering**:

1. Switch to render target T_1 (id-buffer).
2. Clear render target T_1.
3. Render all phantoms to T_1.
4. Switch to render target T_2.
5. Fill T_2 with the current video image.
6. Fill those pixels in T_2 that correspond to the phantom to be displaced with the background color.
7. Render video-textured (displaced) phantoms to T_2, relying on T_1 to control usage of the video image.
8. Render virtual objects to T_2.

Space Distortion

Sometimes hidden information should be revealed, but there is no unoccupied space, so an explosion diagram cannot be applied. However, a video-textured phantom might be able to be scaled down to occupy less screen space, thereby making room to display a hidden object.

Figure 7.17   (top) Incorrectly textured exploded phantom. (bottom) Synchronized dual phantom rendering can identify pixels that cannot be video-textured and apply a different rendering style to these pixels. Courtesy of Markus Tatzgern and Denis Kalkofen.

This idea is applied in the **melt** visualization technique proposed by Sandor et al. [2010a]. In their example, occluding buildings in an outdoor environment are scaled down in vertical directions to unveil hidden objects. The scaling generates the impression that these buildings are "melted." Sandor et al. point out that this technique is particularly effective when there are multiple layers of occluders, because it avoids the clutter of conventional X-ray visualization.

Variable perspective view [Veas et al. 2012b] is an AR visualization technique developed to combine views from different perspectives in a single image. It combines two virtual cameras, the main camera (mc) and the secondary camera (sc; also known as the far camera). This method applies a skinning algorithm for skeleton animation, as shown in Figure 7.18. It uses a single joint with two bones with the following parameters: d is the distance to the rotation axis (the distance from the main camera to the joint), α is the angle of rotation, and φ is the area of effect (where the rotation will be interpolated).

All vertices in the virtual scene are weighted according to their distance from the main camera to the rotation axis. The weight of vertices defines whether they fall in the view of the main camera, in the view of the secondary camera, or in the transition zone, where they are

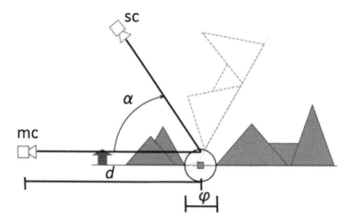

Figure 7.18   (top) The variable perspective view integrates a first-person perspective of the foreground and a virtual top-down view of the distant scene in one image. Courtesy of Eduardo Veas. (bottom) The variable perspective view is achieved by applying principles from skeleton animation to the tilted part of the scene geometry.

interpolated. To further extend the overview, the secondary camera is placed at a distance from the AR view, enabling it to capture more information from the digital data, while correctly registering the video for real-world context.

Information Filtering

A notorious problem of information display in AR is that too much information leads to display clutter, thereby hindering—rather than assisting—a user in understanding the environment. Techniques intended to reduce the amount of augmented information presented to a reasonable volume are generally called **information filtering**. Information filtering can be achieved by either of the following two strategies: The filtering can be based on knowledge about the importance of the information to the application or user (*knowledge-based* filter), or it can be based on *spatial* considerations, supplied either in screen space or in object space. In this section, we investigate these two possibilities and give examples of their application.

Knowledge-Based Filter

A knowledge-based filter for AR was described by Feiner et al. [1993]. KARMA (Knowledge-based Augmented Reality for Maintenance Assistance) automatically creates technical illustrations suitable for AR based on a set of communicative goals provided to an illustration generator, the intent-based illustration system. This generator uses a rule-based approach to synthesize illustrations. Internally, it tries to satisfy a set of constraints resulting from the communicative goals (such as the goal to show a particular object) and the current real-world situation (such as which objects are visible from the current viewing position of the user). KARMA represents knowledge in the form of rules that specify which kind of illustration (or illustration style) can satisfy a particular constraint. The process of synthesizing a particular illustration, therefore, becomes a procedure of searching for and backtracking to the right application of rules from the available set.

KARMA's illustration engine was originally conceived to deliver illustrations for VR, but it was extended to cover AR specifics by supplying certain constraints that the system cannot alter, such as the position of physical objects. Figure 1.4 shows an example of superimposed maintenance instructions for a laser printer viewed through an optical see-through HMD.

Spatial Filter

Spatial filtering uses geometric or geographic information, which is directly derived from the AR scene representation, to reduce the amount of information. A simple example would be a labeling algorithm (refer to the section "Annotations and Labeling") that labels objects in order of increasing distance from the observer and terminates the process when it runs out of available screen space.

Oftentimes the spatial filtering is combined with a degree of interactive control. A classic example is a **magic lens** technique. Originally introduced by Bier et al. [1993] as a 2D user interface widget, a magic lens is a region of a 2D or 3D environment that is rendered in a different style than its surrounding. Typical uses of magic lenses include enhancing data of interest, revealing hidden information, and suppressing distracting information.

In 3D, magic lenses can be defined as a region either in screen space or in object space [Viega et al. 1996]. Magic lenses in screen space—called flat magic lenses—affect every object that has a projection falling into the area covered by the magic lens. Magic lenses in object space—called volumetric magic lenses—affect every object inside the lens region. Both types of lenses can be used in AR to limit certain types of augmentations or annotations to an area of interest.

For example, Looser et al. [2007] discuss the use of a handheld magic lens for object magnification, object selection, and discovery of hidden information. In their approach, a user wearing an HMD holds a tracked wand in the hand. The tip of the wand is coupled to the magic lens, so it can be conveniently placed in the environment.

Bane and Höllerer [2004] present another type of spatial filter, the X-ray tunnel (Figure 7.19). The tunnel defines a bounded region in screen space, extending it from the user's position in the direction of view. It is essentially a special type of magic lens, which is suitable for uncovering hidden structures at a distance. This kind of visualization resembles looking down a tunnel into an inner portion of the scene. Inside the tunnel, the region closest to the observer is empty,

Figure 7.19 The X-ray tunnel enables a user to look inside a building and gives hints about the distance of the uncovered geometry.

while a middle region displays objects in wireframe to establish some context. Finally, in the region of interest at the far end, the virtual object is rendered and a uniformly colored background is displayed to ensure sufficient contrast. Depth perception is supported by displaying "rails" that give a perspective foreshortening cue and by numerical display of the distance to the hidden object. Users can opt to display semantic entities, such as interior rooms, in their entirety rather than depicting arbitrarily sliced geometry. This can aid hidden scene understanding significantly.

Mendez et al. [2006] describe the use of magic lenses for context-driven visualization in AR (Figure 7.20). The multipass rendering technique they discuss can render arbitrary sets of concave lenses. Moreover, these lenses can be associated with special effects (e.g., ghosting effects) that are dynamically applied based on properties of an object. The properties are supplied by the application as markup information attached to scene objects. This approach makes it very easy to combine certain types of magic lens effects and apply effects selectively. For example, an effect could remove certain unimportant objects from the scene, while important, but occluding, objects are rendered using a transparency effect.

Combined Knowledge-Based and Spatial Filter

The focus–nimbus technique proposed by Julier et al. [2002] represents a hybrid knowledge-based and spatial filtering strategy. These researchers argue that the level of detail of information

Figure 7.20   A magic lens reveals the vessels inside a liver model. Courtesy of Erick Mendez and Denis Kalkofen.

Figure 7.21   (left) Unfiltered overlay of the available information produces a cluttered display. (right) By applying the focus–nimbus filter, the overlays are limited to information of high-enough relevance—in this case, the building outline and entrance. Courtesy of Simon Julier.

provided for a specific object in the scene should consider both the importance of an object for the user's current task and the proximity to the user. Annotations for an object that is too unimportant or too far away are faded out. To compute this combined measure, the user's current task and position are used to define a focus region, and the attributes of every object define a nimbus region. Annotations for the objects are displayed to a degree that is determined by how much focus and nimbus intersect. Task-specific attributes influence the extent of focus and nimbus, such that an object that is highly relevant for the user will have a larger nimbus. Julier et al. describe the application of their technique in an urban warfare scenario (Figure 7.21).

Any form of filtering, including the hybrid focus–nimbus approach, leads to the suppression of potentially relevant information. Ideally, less relevant information should be redacted rather than suppressed. In keeping with this aim, Tatzgern et al. [2016] proposes to aggregate related data points by clustering, rather than removing data with a filter. Clustering has the advantage over filtering that the complete information space is preserved. Some commercial AR browsers cluster data uniformly to control clutter, although this does not necessarily lead to a better overview and does not scale to large data sets. Tatzgern, however, proposes creating an information hierarchy by recursive clustering of annotations. This representation is conceptually similar to semantic level of detail. The clustering combines user-controlled spatial attributes (e.g., distance) with nonspatial attributes (e.g., semantic tags). The weighted sum of these attributes provides a ranking of the data's relevance for the user.

To avoid visual clutter, a display algorithm shows data that is relevant for the user in more detail, while adapting the overall amount of information shown to the available screen space. It does so by solving an incremental optimization problem, deciding which nodes in the hierarchy are selected for display. Users can interactively adjust priorities to drill down on data deemed relevant, and reveal all available details on demand (Figure 7.22).

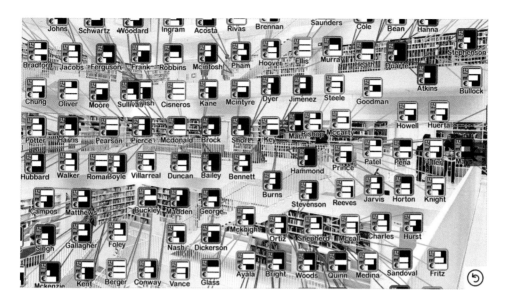

Figure 7.22 Icons representing the location of books selected in a library. (top) Showing all books matching to a query at once leads to clutter. (bottom) Clustering the books by similarity and displaying only clusters for groups of books produces an easily comprehensible view. The user can click on the clusters to further unfold them. Courtesy of Markus Tatzgern and Denis Kalkofen.

Summary

Visualization determines how information should be shown. In AR, this primarily means determining which additional information should be shown, since the user is already perceiving all information present in the real world. Situated visualization is a principle of visualization for AR where information is attached to real-world objects. Annotation and labeling techniques are necessary for this kind of visualization, to avoid illegible layouts and cluttered displays. Another important principle for AR is the use of X-ray visualization to uncover hidden or otherwise imperceptible structures—for example, through the use of ghostings or explosion diagrams. Finally, information filtering techniques such as magic lenses are useful in delivering the right amount of task-dependent information to the user.

CHAPTER 8

INTERACTION

After understanding AR input, which is dominated by computer vision techniques, and AR output, which is dominated by computer graphics techniques, we turn our attention to human–computer interaction, the link between input and output. We first revisit input and output modalities, albeit now from a designer's perspective rather than from an engineer's perspective. We then discuss tangible user interfaces and several other user interface concepts relevant to AR, such as interfaces involving paper, haptics, and agents.

The chapters immediately following this one build on the foundations laid here and dive deeper into specific topics. Chapter 9 discusses *modeling* and *annotation*, Chapter 10 explores *authoring*, Chapter 11 examines *navigation*, and Chapter 12 focuses on *collaboration*.

Output Modalities

Since the effect of an interaction in AR is evident only from the resulting augmentation, the placement of the augmentation is essential. As we saw in Chapter 2, AR offers a large variety of approaches for presenting augmentations to the user, which have distinct implications for the interaction style. Here, we begin by considering where augmentations can be placed.

Augmentation Placement

A real object serving as a registration target provides a frame of reference for an augmentation (Figure 8.1). To make this frame of reference intuitively understandable to the user, the augmentation is most commonly placed on or next to a real object. Of course, it is possible to place augmentations in free space, but, in most cases, virtual objects supported by real objects are easier to interpret.

Possibly the simplest case involves flat horizontal surfaces, such as desktops. Flat surfaces can be augmented with flat 2D content or can be used as supporting surfaces for virtual 3D objects. Likewise, placing virtual objects on vertical surfaces simulates pictures or wall-mounted objects.

If a detailed geometric model of the real environment is available, objects can be placed anywhere on the surface. This idea has been combined with simulated physical behavior to let

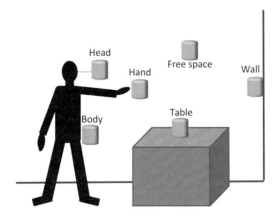

Figure 8.1 Augmentations can be placed relative to the user's head or body, or relative to the environment.

virtual miniature cars race across the room [Wilson et al. 2012] and to turn furniture items into mini-golf obstacles [Jones et al. 2010]. Even the entire set of surfaces surrounding the user can be augmented—for example, for interactive dramatic experiences [Jones et al. 2014].

Augmented moving objects must be tracked or reconstructed before augmentations can be placed. This step is often an essential prerequisite, because moving objects add dynamic aspects to the experience. Moreover, users can manipulate physical objects to control application behavior, a concept known as **tangible user interface** [Ishii and Ullmer 1997]. Augmenting directly on top of tangible objects leads to **tangible AR** [Kato and Billinghurst 1999], which we will discuss in more detail later in this chapter.

One important place for augmentations is the human body. When a body part serving as a reference for the augmentation is moved, the augmentation moves along and, consequently, stays put in the same relative pose. While information can be placed on other humans in a way that is conceptually similar to augmentation of inanimate objects (consider virtual name tags), augmenting one's own body is particularly appealing for several reasons. First, one's own body is always available. Second, relying on body parts avoids any instrumentation of the user. Third, humans have intimate knowledge and precise control over their body—a phenomenon known as **proprioception**, or the sense of the relative position of body parts [Mine et al. 1997]. The choice of body part allows the design of several augmentation layouts. Common choices include the head, torso, arm, and hand.

A **head-referenced display** always remains stationary in the user's field of view. This is convenient for placement of information that should always be visible, such as status messages. However, the user cannot see her own head and does not perceive any registration between real and virtual. Consequently, this type of display, although it is very useful and frequently employed, is often not perceived as "genuine" augmented reality.

A **torso-referenced display** can take the form of virtual objects being displayed as directly attached to the torso—for example, in the form of a virtual toolbelt. Alternatively, it can extend the body shape into space—for example, in the form of a vendor's tray. The latter shares some similarity with a head-referenced display in that it seemingly lacks a referenced real object. The difference becomes evident when the user moves her head relative to the torso to adjust the field of view onto the virtual display.

A **hand-referenced display** places information in the palm of the user's hand, potentially resembling a real object held in the hand. It can be moved with high agility and manipulated with the user's other hand. An **arm-referenced display** has similar properties, but is not as natural. This option is primarily attractive if the hands are used with manipulation of real objects, but the augmentations should stay in the user's field of view for rapid context switches between real and virtual.

Other body parts can be used as reference as well, but their ergonomic properties make them less attractive for self-augmentation. Nevertheless, medical and health applications might

Figure 8.2   Skeleton tracking provides whole-body input. The user's body motions have been transformed into motion arrows. Courtesy of Denis Kalkofen.

greatly benefit from directly displaying information on a particular body part. This can even involve full-body augmentation, which is attractive for dance or sports instructions (Figure 8.2).

Agile Displays

While discussing the placement of the augmentations, we have assumed that we have the technical capability of displaying augmentations anywhere. In reality, an AR experience designer must consider which part of the environment can actually be covered by a given display. The highest amount of flexibility is afforded by a mobile display, which is carried or worn by the user. Alternatively, a stationary display with wide coverage may be built from a wide-angle projector or an array of projectors covering every surface of interest.

Arrays of stationary projectors have the advantage that the augmentation is visible in plain sight, for any number of users and without any encumbrances to those users. Moreover, such arrays can be extended into **projector-camera systems** (Figure 8.3), which use a camera and a projector with overlapping fields of view. A projector–camera system combines dense output with dense input, with both components using millions of pixels. The camera either interprets the image illuminated by the structured light from the projector or is combined with a depth sensor. In both cases, the result is an adaptive projection system that can react to a moving user and a changing environment. In contrast, projected augmentations are restricted to physical surfaces and cannot invoke personalized experiences for multiple users. Projection also requires careful instrumentation of the environment and does not work well outdoors in daylight conditions.

Compared to projectors, **mobile displays** such as head-mounted or handheld displays are more economical and have the additional advantage that they allow personalized experiences for multiple users. While a see-through HMD usually presents only a single (augmented) view of the environment (Figure 8.4, top), a handheld display presents an augmented **copy** of the environment (Figure 8.4, middle). This situation has both advantages and disadvantages. Handheld

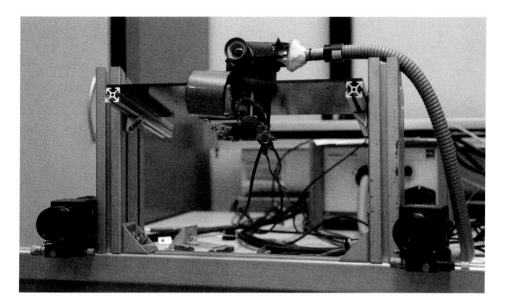

Figure 8.3   A projector–camera system consisting of a compact projector (middle) and a set of stereo cameras (left and right). Courtesy of Christian Reinbacher.

displays may be cumbersome to hold up, yet may cover only a small portion of the user's field of view because of the small display size. The user has to divide attention between the real world and the augmented image. These disadvantages are partly offset by the additional input channels provided by a handheld device. The user can move the device independently of the gaze direction with one hand and operate the device's touchscreen with the other hand. These input capabilities partly compensate for the limitation that the user's hands are not free for other activities.

A third category, which combines aspects of the first two, is formed by **agile projectors**, which can change the location of projection over time. Steerable projectors, for example, can be placed on motorized pan-tilt platforms to reach all surfaces in an environment visible from the mounting points. As long as the object of interest does not move or change too fast, the steerable projector can continuously augment it. Miniature projectors are handheld devices that can be wielded like a flashlight (Figure 8.4, bottom). Shoulder-mounted projectors keep the users, hands free, while objects in front of the user are augmented. Head-mounted projectors fulfill a similar role, with the additional advantage that the direction of projection always remains aligned with the main viewing direction. This principle has primarily been used in combination with retro-reflective surfaces in the environment to obtain better contrast. Unfortunately, the battery-powered projectors of today can only produce low-contrast images, while tethered projectors are obviously not suitable for serious mobile operation.

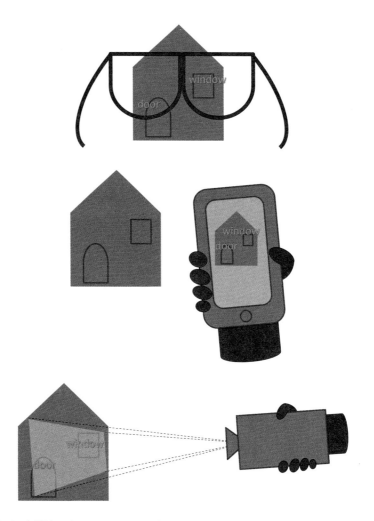

Figure 8.4   (top) AR head-mounted display. (middle) Handheld AR. (bottom) Projector AR.

Magic Lenses

AR can be used as an ambient display for continuously providing a stream of additional information registered to the user's surroundings. The input from the user is limited to look-ing at a particular object or pointing the camera at it. We call this interaction style **augmented browsing**. While browsing interaction is minimal, it is potentially very powerful, because it supports human thinking without monopolizing attention. Many important use cases of AR are essentially based on browsing—for example, medical diagnosis [State et al. 1996b], navigation [Mulloni et al. 2012], tourism [Feiner et al. 1997] (Figure 8.5), and underground infrastructure inspection [Schall et al. 2008]. The information for augmented browsing is often taken from existing databases containing geo-registered information or information on people and

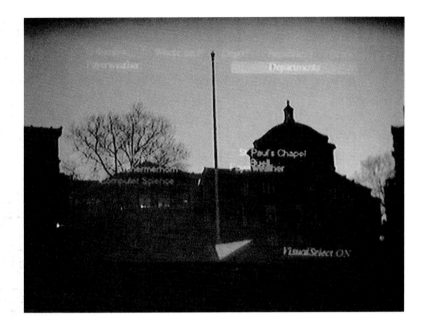

Figure 8.5 The Columbia Touring Machine was the first AR browser. Courtesy of Columbia University.

objects. "Windows on the world" [Feiner et al. 1993b] even goes so far as displaying the output of legacy 2D desktop applications as augmentations in a three-dimensional environment.

Browsing with an HMD has the advantage that the user's hands remain free, while tracking the user's gaze direction naturally determines the focus of attention. Unfortunately, a naïve implementation of such an "always-on" augmentation can be disturbing in cluttered environments. The user should at least have an easy way of switching the augmentation on and off.

Browsing with a handheld display results in a slightly different usage pattern: The handheld display becomes a physical **magic lens** through which the user may look into an altered (augmented) version of the real environment (Figure 8.6). One can interpret a magic lens as an instance of a **Focus+Context** display [Kosara et al. 2003], which presents two information displays side-by-side. By alternating between looking at the real world directly and looking at the screen, the user can implicitly select whether the augmentation is needed—a choice that must be explicitly controlled with an HMD.

Of course, a magic lens can be realized with an HMD as well. A popular approach is to represent the lens by a tracked, but otherwise passive, prop, such as a physical clipboard or a physical lens. In this case, the user cannot look around the magic lens to see the non-augmented focus area.

Similar restrictions apply to magic lenses in projector-based AR. By wielding a handheld projector (a **flashlight**), the user can select a focus area for augmentation, but cannot look around the

Figure 8.6   A magic lens lets the user perceive the skeleton structure of a person. Courtesy of Anton Fuhrmann.

augmentation. Even so, simply pointing the flashlight temporarily away to reveal the unmodified real world may be more intuitive than turning off the augmentation on an HMD.

Placement of the focus area of a magic lens is conceptually very similar to selection of an object in a three-dimensional environment with raycasting [Bowman et al. 2005]. A ray is implicitly defined by the gaze direction on an HMD, the image center (or any other point) on a handheld display, or the orientation of a handheld prop or flashlight. Raycasting is typically used to select the first object encountered along the ray. Optionally, the selection may be extended to all objects contained in the view frustum or flashlight cone. The main difference between 3D selection and magic lens manipulation is that the effects of applying the magic lens are immediately evident in the browsing experience. In contrast, selection of an object is usually a preparatory step for invoking a command (e.g., to move or delete an object). However, magic lens manipulation and selection can be combined into a single interaction, if the user is equipped with an explicit trigger (e.g., a button) for selecting a particular object in focus during augmented browsing.

A few examples do not use a magic lens with raycasting, but rather use its position in the environment directly. One example of such direct spatial interaction with a handheld device is the AR Tennis application developed by Henrysson et al. [2005]. In this application, a virtual table tennis ball traveling through the air is visible only on the magic lens. At the same time, the magic lens serves as the paddle to hit the ball.

Figure 8.7 (left) Selection by touching. (right) Selection by raycasting.

In general, a user's ability to interact in three dimensions in this way may be limited by the small field of view of a handheld device. Some variations of raycasting, however, use a ray of finite length for selection, comparable to someone pointing with a cane (Figure 8.7). Leigh et al. [2014] argue that the distance from the manipulator to the manipulated object is actually a continuum. At one extreme, the range is zero, if the manipulator is touching the manipulated object, leading to tangible interaction. At the other extreme, the manipulated object is beyond the manipulator's reach and must be approached with a magic lens or by raycasting. As an example of a tangible magic lens, Leigh et al. show how a smartphone can be used for interacting at a distance of just a few centimeters in front of a screen by detecting small color patterns displayed on the screen.

Input Modalities

During the discussion of output modalities, we mentioned that the user continuously controls the viewpoint or focus of augmentation—for example, by moving the head while wearing an HMD. This form of interaction is an integral part of most AR experiences. If we want to go beyond augmented browsing, which casts the user in the role of a passive observer, we must add a consideration of suitable input devices and methods. AR can draw from the rich variety of techniques that have been developed for both VR and for **natural user interfaces**. The latter is an umbrella term for user interfaces that progress beyond the classical desktop and, in particular, involve gestures and touch.

Tracking and Manipulation of Rigid Objects

In Chapter 3, we extensively discussed how to obtain 6DOF pose measurements of a rigid object. These sparse tracking methods deliver high update rates and high precision, but only for a few points or objects.

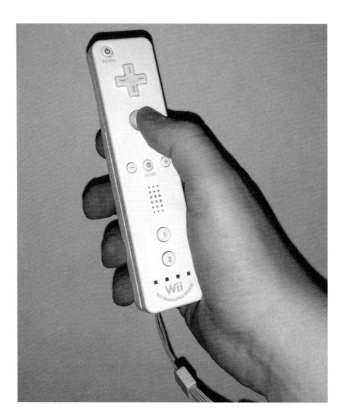

Figure 8.8   The Nintendo Wiimote is a 3D input device for consumer video games.

The most important use case for sparse tracking probably concerns the user's head or a camera to control the viewpoint. In addition, the interaction often relies on tracking a handheld device for three-dimensional pointing and movement. Alternatively, the hand itself can be used—for example, by attaching a tracking target to the back of the hand, which is relatively rigid. To achieve this aim, the pose tracking is often complemented by conventional controls, such as button or switches. For example, the Nintendo Wiimote is a handheld device resembling a remote control with 6DOF tracking and several buttons (Figure 8.8).

Pinch gloves achieve a similar capability with electrical contacts on the fingertips, so that a user can trigger an action by pressing two fingers together. For example, the gloves used by Tinmith Hand [Piekarski and Thomas 2002] detect pinch gestures to operate head-registered menus (Figure 8.9). The thumb of each glove is instrumented with a fiducial marker for image-plane manipulation [Pierce et al. 1997] of virtual objects.

Tracked objects need not be held in the hand permanently. If multiple tracked objects are available, the user can communicate intentions by moving and arranging the objects. This leads to the aforementioned **tangible interaction**.

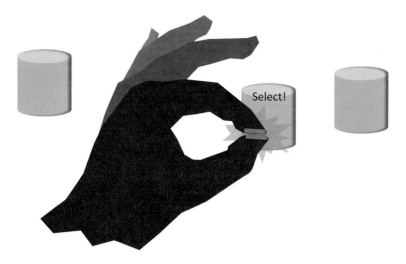

Figure 8.9   Pinch Gloves detect when the user presses fingertips together and interpret this gesture as a selection.

Body Tracking

Obviously, sparse tracking restricts the interaction to one or a few discrete points, comparable to a three-dimensional version of a mouse cursor. Such minimal input capabilities cannot capture the true richness of human interaction with the real world. Consequently, recent developments try to incorporate dense tracking methods, which rely on the rich sensory input from cameras or depth sensors to deal with the full range of human motions and, potentially, with arbitrary changes in the environment.

Human motion capture is usually processed into **skeleton tracking**, because knowing the pose of each bone in the human skeleton is sufficient for most kinds of interactions. Tracking just the skeleton is also easier than tracking the entire human shape, given that possible skeleton configurations are greatly restricted by anatomic constraints.

For some applications, it may be sufficient to track only the relevant parts of the body, such as the head, arm, or hand. Hand tracking is of particular importance, since we primarily rely on our hands for manipulation of our environment. Hand tracking can be seen as a special case of skeleton tracking. Collectively, though, the hand and fingers have more than 20 degrees of freedom and allow for very precise and fine-grained manipulation. Consequently, the problem of reliably tracking the entire hand (Figure 8.10) has received a lot of attention in research [Oberweger et al. 2015].

Song et al. [2014] discuss a system for recognizing in-air gestures made with the unoccupied hand in front of a handheld device. Their approach can be used for various interactions such as menu selection or panning. One advantage of this approach for mobile AR is that the gestures

Figure 8.10   Hand and finger tracking. Courtesy of Markus Oberweger.

are considered only if the hand moves into the field of view of the mobile device. This makes it easy to avoid inadvertent recognitions.

Gestures

An important use case for body or hand tracking is gestural interaction. Early work concentrated on postures, which are static body or hand configurations—for example, a flag alphabet. Such postures are rarely part of our natural everyday interaction. Today, sufficient computational power is available for detecting dynamic gestures of moving body parts. Dynamic gestures have the advantage that they can simultaneously provide qualitative and quantitative input. For example, a user making a "framing" motion (Figure 8.11) simultaneously indicates the

Figure 8.11   The viewfinder gesture requires both hands.

intention to perform a viewfinder operation and the magnitude of the desired zoom by the distance of the hands to each other. Tracking and recognition of such hand gestures with wearable cameras and computer vision has been demonstrated, for example, by Kölsch et al. [2004].

Gesture languages are very expressive, but require more learning than conventional menu-based interfaces. White et al. [2009b] suggest that semi-transparent animations of likely gestures can ease the learning. In general, though, gestures have poor affordances and can be difficult to remember. Moreover, self-occlusion from the user's body can lead to situations where reliable recognition of gestures is problematic.

As an example of a gestural interaction language for AR, consider HandyAR [Lee and Höllerer 2007], which tracks the user's outstretched hand and establishes a coordinate system fitted to the palm of the hand (Figure 8.12). Virtual objects can be attached to the open hand for inspection and manipulation. Actions can be triggered by making a fist gesture. The hand tracking system also allows resting the open hand, palm down, on a surface. This prompts the system to acquire a map around the hand using a SLAM method [Lee and Höllerer 2008]. After map initialization, further tracking is self-contained and does not require the presence of the hand. In this way, virtual objects can be placed at arbitrary locations in the environment.

Touch

The precision of free-space gestures often suffers from a lack of physical support, which affects delicate operations. Given that humans have an excellent sense of touch, it would be desirable to build touch interfaces—that is, surfaces that sense touch, while providing passive haptic feedback. Early touch solutions could recognize just a single point on the surface, but today's surface interactions rely on **multi-touch** detection. Small touch surfaces use capacitive sensing, while larger displays often use optical methods, such as total internal reflection.

Figure 8.12 HandyAR uses the hand as a reference coordinate system for interaction with objects. Courtesy of Taehee Lee.

A touch surface is often combined with a display to create a **touchscreen**, which unifies input and output into one natural space. Since the screen can show arbitrary interactive information registered to the touching fingers, a touch screen almost fulfills our requirements for AR, with the exception that the registration is only 2D and not 3D.

Multi-touch surfaces, which combine conventional graphical user interfaces with 2D gestures, have become the de facto interface standard for mobile computing. Given that many of today's AR systems use handheld computers with touchscreens, touch input is the natural choice for controlling the on-screen experience: The user operates the magic lens with both hands. The nondominant hand moves the magic lens coarsely with full 6DOF to observe the desired focus area. The dominant hand operates the touchscreen to provide a 2DOF offset relative to the nondominant hand. As a result, the ray-based selection of objects underneath the finger is perceived as "touching" the objects in the image plane [Pierce et al. 1997]. In addition, conventional controls such as buttons can be placed in a designated area of the screen or appear on demand near objects.

A known problem of touch screens is the "fat finger problem": Fingers occlude the object of interaction and the surroundings, making it difficult to aim precisely. LucidTouch [Wigdor et al. 2007] overcomes this problem by adding a touch surface on the **back** of a flat handheld device (Figure 8.13).

A popular means of combining spatial AR and touch interfaces is to turn ordinary, uninstrumented surfaces into virtual touchscreens by means of a projector–camera system [Pinhanez 2001]. For example, the system can project a menu item on a surface near the user's outstretched hand (Figure 8.14).

LightSpace [Wilson and Benko 2010] uses multiple depth sensors to let a user pick up a digital item from one interaction surface and drop it on another surface by simply touching

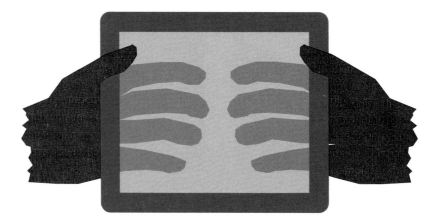

Figure 8.13 LucidTouch simulates a semi-transparent screen with a touch interface on the back.

Figure 8.14   Turning an ordinary surface into a touchscreen with a projector–camera system. Courtesy of Claudio Pinhanez (copyright IBM 2001).

that surface. If a certain number of depth samples immediately over an interactive surface is observed, a touch event is created. The system does not attempt to discriminate humans from other objects, but rather uses simplified physics to manipulate virtual objects. For example, a user can pick up a virtual item from the table by sweeping it over the table boundary into her open hand. LightSpace also allows for determining a user's motion in the free space between interaction surfaces.

Touch of the entire body can be sensed by pressure-sensitive surfaces. For example, Gravity-Space [Bränzel et al. 2013] is an environment with instrumented surfaces (floor, furniture), which senses the weight distribution and additional physical attributes to infer a user's body pose. Registered output is provided by projecting information on the surfaces.

GravitySpace illustrates how the rules of physics governing the real world can be used to design natural user interfaces. With this type of application, our lifelong experience with the physical behavior of real objects can be used for intuitive handling of virtual objects.

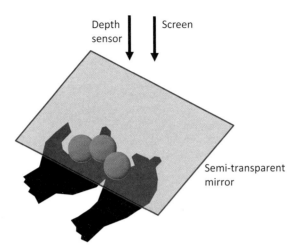

Figure 8.15   The HoloDesk uses a combination of a stationary optical see-through display with a depth sensor to simulate physical interaction of the user's hands with virtual objects.

Physically Based Interfaces

Physically based interfaces use off-the-shelf simulation software intended for computer games to make virtual objects interact with real objects. The simulation can be kept computationally lightweight, since it need not be very exact. However, just as for visual coherence, **phantom geometry** representing the real world is required for **physical coherence**.

The phantom geometry can be reconstructed in advance. Jones et al. [2010] let the user place virtual objects on surfaces in such a system. The objects remain bound to the surface, but otherwise can exhibit any desired physical behavior. For example, the user can flick around photos in a collection or play a game of augmented miniature golf.

If phantom geometry is sensed online with a depth sensor, the physical coherence simulation can also handle moving and deformable objects, such as the human user. To avoid complex deformable models, nonrigid entities can be represented by simple geometric approximations, such as collections of rigid spheres. In most cases, a user will not be able to notice the approximations. This interaction design has been used in Beamatron [Wilson et al. 2012], a room-sized setup with a steerable projector, and desk-sized setups such as HoloDesk [Hilliges et al. 2012] (Figure 8.15) and MirageTable [Benko et al. 2012].

Tangible Interfaces

One important difference between AR and VR is that AR users can naturally interact with physical objects in the environment. Such real interaction is direct and convenient, and can easily be used to influence the AR experience. Thus, the interaction with the virtual world becomes tangible. **Tangible user interfaces** were originally proposed by Fitzmaurice et al. [1995] and Ishii and Ullmer [1997] as a form of ubiquitous computing. By instrumenting or sensing everyday objects in the user's surroundings, these objects are transformed into input or output devices for the computer. AR is related to tangible user interfaces, since it also incorporates the physical reality surrounding a user into the interaction. If we manipulate tracked physical objects, which are also augmented, the result is **tangible AR**.

Tangibles on Surfaces

Before the advent of large-format touchscreens, using tangible objects with table-format displays was a popular approach. Such tables are often instrumented with a projector–camera system for object detection, tracking, and even reconstruction [Leibe et al. 2000]. Placing the projector–camera system underneath the table hides the technology and avoids occlusion problems caused by users standing between the projector–camera unit and the table surface. As long as a tracking system is available, a large-format screen or an HMD can be used as well.

After a tangible object is placed on the table surface, it can be left there. The placement establishes input, yet leaves the user unencumbered, with hands free. The Tangible Media Group at MIT developed a series of tangible interfaces in table format. The metaDESK [Ullmer and Ishii 1997] showed a campus map, with position, orientation, and scale determined by the placement of scale models of two famous campus buildings. An equivalent method for map manipulation is universally known today in the form of the two-finger gesture for multi-touch displays. Urp [Underkoffler and Ishii 1999] is an architectural planning application that allows users to place tangible objects as stand-ins for buildings and inspect the effects of variations of traffic, sunlight, and wind. Illuminating Light [Underkoffler and Ishii 1998] simulates an optical workbench with tangible devices such as laser sources, prisms, and mirrors. All of these scenarios share a specific characteristic: They operate only on the 2D space of the table surface. In contrast, tangible AR can extend the scope of the interaction in the third dimension.

Tangibles with Generic Shape

Early work on tangible AR used multiple square fiducial markers as tangible objects. The markers can be arranged on a table, resulting in a configuration similar to the tangibles on surfaces just discussed (Figure 8.16). The markers can also be picked up and tracked with 6DOF. If just a single camera is used, only markers fitting into the field of view can be tracked. Some designs also use a tapestry or tablecloth covered with markers as a global reference frame. Because the location of the markers on the tapestry is known, the observation of a single marker allows the determination of a global pose.

Square markers are generic shapes with no particular affordances that must be decorated with informative graphics to convey a meaning to the user. Nonetheless, they have many degrees of

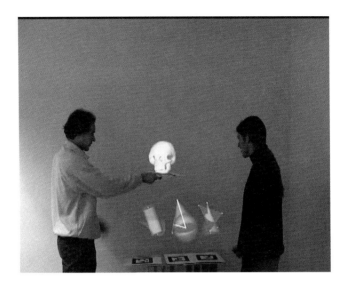

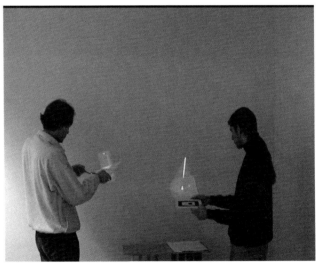

Figure 8.16 Generic tangibles, such as markers, can be used to collaboratively manipulate virtual objects. Courtesy of Gerhard Reitmayr and Hannes Kaufmann.

freedom suitable for direct manipulation. Consequently, one can find a wide array of creative uses for this kind of setup (Figure 8.17):

- A single tangible can be translated and rotated to manipulate objects or to modify a parameter. This is most often done on a horizontal surface. However, by picking up the tangible, the tangible's height over the surface can be used as an additional parameter [Spindler et al. 2012].

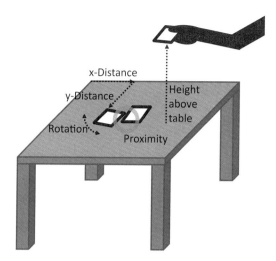

Figure 8.17　Tangible operations and their associated parameters.

- Multiple markers can be arranged to express the spatial relationship of associated objects—for example, to arrange instruments on a dashboard.

- The distance between two markers can be used to express a scalar value. Two markers moved very closely together can trigger an "association" command. For example, a "red paint" marker placed next to a virtual object can be used to change the object's color to red.

- Removing a marker quickly from the field of view or covering it with the hand can be interpreted as triggering a command. The system may also memorize the last known location and place a virtual object there.

- Markers held in the hand can be used to express gestural input. Motions such as shaking, turning, circular motion, tilting, or pushing can easily be determined by analyzing the motion trajectory and comparing it to a template. For example, shaking can be identified by searching for a motion with large velocity, but very small changes in object position.

Tangibles with Distinct Shapes

While generic tangibles may encourage creative interpretation, tangible interfaces can possess additional expressive power when the tangible objects have meaningful shapes that can be immediately recognized and suggest a certain use. Tangibles may resemble tools such as a paddle or flashlight, or they may be containers such as tablets, books, or boxes.

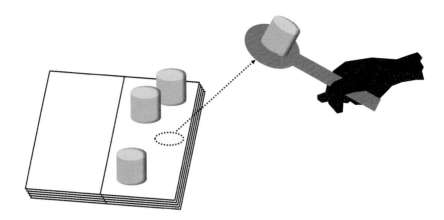

Figure 8.18   Magic book and paddle.

A **magic book** is a physical book with tracked pages (Figure 8.18). Augmentations can be registered to the book pages, either as flat computer-generated content on the page (e.g., an animated drawing) or as 3D objects that are attached to and pop out from a page, when opened, similar to the cardboard pop-outs of kids' books.

A **paddle**—a marker attached to a grip—provides a rich gestural vocabulary for object manipulation. VOMAR [Kato et al. 2000] employs a paddle to scoop furniture items from a magic book and drop them into a dollhouse, where they can be pushed around until the user is satisfied. Fjeld and Voegtli [2002] discuss an educational application for chemistry that uses a paddle for 3D object assembly: The user composes molecules from individual atoms by placing them at the desired location in space, with chemical laws constraining the placement to plausible locations.

The **personal interaction panel** (Figure 8.19) combines a stylus with a tablet [Szalavári and Gervautz 1997]. This approach leverages two-handed interaction in a familiar form factor. The tablet serves as a mobile frame of reference for the stylus and can be augmented with various objects, ranging from 2D controls, such as buttons and sliders, to 3D objects, such as volumetric data sets.

A rotary plate (Figure 8.20) is used in the MagicMeeting environment [Regenbrecht et al. 2002]. It allows multiple users seated around a table to adjust the orientation of a virtual object placed on the platter for design inspection.

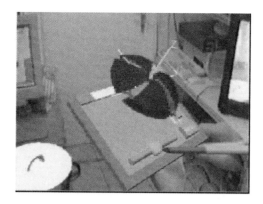

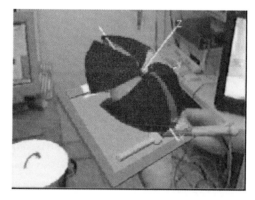

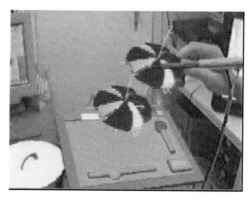

Figure 8.19 Personal interaction panel. Courtesy of Zsolt Szalavári and Michael Gervautz.

Figure 8.20 An interaction similar to the rotary plate of MagicMeeting.

The CoCube [Brown et al. 2003] is a essentially just a handheld box (Figure 8.21). Three-dimensional virtual objects can be placed inside the box, with the walls of the box rendered as transparent material. Two-dimensional content, such as text, can be rendered on the surfaces of the box. Rotating the box leads to scrolling of the text, as if the box was a scroll of scriptures.

The two-handed magic lens of Looser et al. [2007] uses two physical handles representing the left and right edges of the lens. By moving the handles, the user can scale and deform a lens surface, which behaves like a rubber sheet connected to the handles.

Figure 8.21 The CoCube is a versatile tangible object, which can show either virtual 3D objects inside the cube or 2D information, such as text, on its surfaces.

Transparent Tangibles

Tangibles and the surface underneath often form a Focus+Context relationship, which is important for the interface design. To take advantage of this relationship, we would like to display augmentations simultaneously on both a tangible object and the surface. If we want to steer clear of head-worn and handheld displays to keep the user unencumbered, the augmentations can be generated by projectors. Unfortunately, an approach using just a single projector is not sufficient. Projection from above generates occlusions from the tangible to the surface, and a surface with a built-in display cannot augment the tangible object.

If we want to use only a single display, transparent tangibles on a display table provide a convenient way to address this problem: Augmentations shown on the display directly under the tangibles are perceived by the user as belonging to the tangible object. For example, the metaDESK [Ullmer and Ishii 1997] places a transparent magic lens on the display to show a focus view of the map (e.g., a magnification).

DataTiles [Rekimoto et al. 2001] places transparent tiles on an interactive display. This system is able to sense the placement of the tiles, and also accepts input with a stylus. This combination turns the tiles into interactive widgets. Each tile displays user interface elements that can be manipulated with the stylus. By arranging multiple tiles, the user selects and connects application components. CapStones [Chan et al. 2012] includes similar transparent tangibles that can be both arranged and stacked.

The stylus-and-tablet interface of Schmalstieg et al. [1999] is a transparent variant of the personal interaction panel. The user works in a volume above a stereoscopic back-projection table with a tablet and a stylus made from transparent material (Figure 8.22). In ergonomic terms,

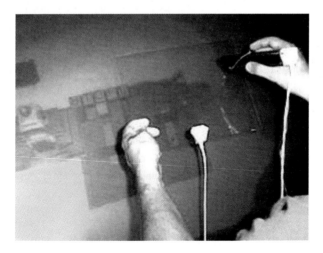

Figure 8.22   With a transparent tablet and stylus interface, a stereoscopic projection can be turned into a tangible 3D interface.

this configuration resembles a painter's workspace with brush, palette, and canvas. The stylus, which serves as the primary interaction tool, alternates between the tablet and the table, for example, to drag and drop objects. The tablet can also be used directly as a magic lens.

Virtual User Interfaces on Real Surfaces

Placing virtual touch widgets on physical surfaces such as a tablet or a table is a convenient way to add complex interfaces to an AR experience. Solutions known from desktop or mobile user interfaces can be reused, and most users will be familiar with the operation of those interfaces.

The virtual user interfaces can be placed on a generic tangible object. In the simplest case, this is just a flat surface, such as a tablet [Szalavári and Gervautz 1997] or a blank wall [Newman et al. 2001]. Penlight [Song et al. 2009] places context-sensitive virtual user interfaces next to a stylus used on a drafting table. The augmented stylus can invoke virtual drawing layers, which serve as dynamic cues, while hovering above a surface location, or it can be used as measuring tool.

Marner et al. [2009] explore the use of tangible tools with more distinct shapes, such as a virtual airbrush. They call this tangible a **virtual-physical tool**, in recognition that it combines a physical shape with virtual user interface elements.

The idea of placing virtual user interfaces on real surfaces can be used for interface design and virtual prototyping of cockpits. Users can experiment with different interface layouts by placing generic tangibles [Poupyrev et al. 2002] and can reprogram the interface functions on the fly [Rekimoto et al. 2001] [Walsh et al. 2013]. Instead of tangibles, gestures on surfaces can be used to specify new widgets as well [Xiao et al. 2013]. By projecting virtual user interfaces onto cockpit mockups, the ergonomic properties of a virtual prototype can be investigated.

The experience of virtual user interfaces can be enhanced by leveraging the passive haptics of the physical surface. For example, generic tangible objects can be enhanced for use as special-purpose tangibles by embossing structures for user interface elements, such as a straight track for a slider or a circular track for a rotary dial. Henderson and Feiner [2010] propose to opportunistically repurpose existing physical structures on real surfaces for placing widgets. For example, a crease between two panels could be interpreted as a slider, while a screwhead or knob could be interpreted as a button object. Controls that are graphically superimposed on these physical structures can be operated significantly faster and more reliably than their purely virtual counterparts.

If no suitable surface is available, for instance, in mobile applications, the user's hand or arm can serve as a substitute. SixthSense [Mistry and Maes 2009] and OmniTouch [Harrison et al. 2011]

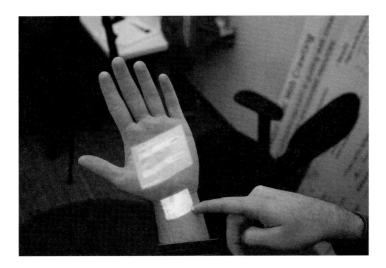

Figure 8.23 OmniTouch uses a projector and depth camera to turn the user's own hand into a touchscreen. Courtesy of Microsoft Research.

explore the projection of interfaces on the user's hand or lower arm (Figure 8.23). With depth sensing, the user's own body can be turned into a touchscreen. For example, the user might dial a phone number using the palm of the hand as a keypad.

Augmented Paper

Paper is an important artifact of our everyday world. While the desktop computing paradigm simulates the work with paper documents to some degree, the handling of physical paper and digital documents is usually separated. Wellner [1993] has argued for the integration of physical and virtual document management, introducing the DigitalDesk as a system to support this aim. The DigitalDesk consists of a table instrumented with a projector–camera system. Physical paper documents can be arranged on the table and are picked up by the camera, while the projector augments the table with additional virtual documents. Using a pen or fingers, both of which are tracked by the overhead camera, the user can control the operation of the Digital-Desk. The system can be instructed to read text or numbers using character recognition or to capture an image from a physical document. For example, a user can point out a handwritten number and forward it to a digital calculator for further processing.

Mackay and Fayard [1999] describe the application of the DigitalDesk concept to a variety of domains that heavily rely on the use of paper in organizing their daily work. For example, such a system might be applied to construction drawings used by civil engineers, paper-based story-boards used by film producers, and flight strips used by air traffic controllers.

Figure 8.24 Augmented maps consists of a conventional paper map and projected interactive content. Courtesy of Gerhard Reitmayr, Ethan Eade, and Tom Drummond.

Another common paper-based artifact used in everyday work life is a map. Reitmayr et al. [2005] describe augmented maps, an approach related to the digital desk that tracks and augments large-scale maps (Figure 8.24). Such a system might be used, for example, in a command-and-control scenario. Dynamic information can be superimposed directly on the map, allowing the presentation of geographically embedded information and interface controls. Augmented maps can handle multiple simultaneous maps and offer additional tools for interacting with the map content. A tracked blank paper card can be positioned so that it points to a particular location on the map. The system can use the blank area on the card to project related information, such as a photo taken at the location that the user points to. A more versatile tool is based on a small handheld computer, which is also tracked by the overhead camera. The handheld computer is operated through its touchscreen and presents arbitrary user interfaces to interact symbolically with an object on the map that the handheld computer points to. To make the creation of the user interface fully dynamic, the code for the user interfaces is shipped through the wireless network to the handheld computer, where it is interpreted on the fly.

PaperWindows are individual tracked pieces of paper, which allow the user to leave the surface of the desktop and interact with paper in a more natural way [Holman et al. 2005]. An infrared tracking system in combination with an overhead projector determines what the user is doing with the PaperWindows and presents arbitrary content on each of them. Users can physically manipulate PaperWindows and employ a variety of gestures, including holding, co-locating, collating, and flipping pieces of paper as well as performing gestures with the fingers on the paper, such as rubbing or pointing. This vocabulary of gestures allows a wide variety of typical office document tasks to be carried out without any need for a symbolic interface, such as activation of a PaperWindow, selection of content, copy and paste, load and save, scrolling, or annotation.

The interface proposed by Petersen and Stricker [2009] also combines gesture recognition with augmented paper. Users can point to a physical object to retrieve contextual information in the form of a virtual sheet of paper, which is shown on a wall-mounted display. Their gestures are observed using an overhead camera, which can also digitize other paper documents. Users can print a physical copy of this sheet, which is able to detect physical handwritten annotations using an imperceptible dot pattern to transfer information back to the virtual space.

Multi-view Interfaces

At the beginning of this chapter, we discussed various options for placing augmentations in the environment. With a suitable setup, multiple locations can be augmented simultaneously, rather than sequentially. Such an approach can heighten the impression that the user is part of a responsive environment, or it can simply be used to show an increased amount of information at once.

Elmqvist [2011] defines a **distributed user interface** as "a user interface whose components are distributed across one or more of the dimensions input, output, platform, space, and time." Among these five dimensions, space (multiple locations) and output (multiple displays) are relevant here. We describe an interface involving either multiple locations or multiple displays, or both, as a **multi-view interface.**

Multi-display Focus+Context

Multiple displays are particularly relevant to AR applications when they are complementary. For example, a 2D display can be combined with a 3D display, or a small high-resolution display can be combined with a large lower-resolution display, or a mobile display can be combined with a stationary display. Such complementary displays are often paired in the same location to provide **Focus+Context**. We begin by discussing multi-display interaction with two-dimensional content.

THAW [Leigh et al. 2014] uses the camera of a smartphone to track the mobile device location relative to a vertical stationary display. Because the smartphone is held very close to the display surface, the image directly under the smartphone is not visible. The smartphone can be turned into a magic lens that modifies the view of the underlying display, and the smartphone's touchscreen can be used to provide additional input.

In contrast, Spindler et al. [2012] use a handheld tablet held over a large horizontal display so that users can see both the tablet and the display. The tablet displays a magic lens, aligned with the image plane of the display. However, the user can freely modify the height of the tablet over the display to select a "layer" of information.

Rekimoto et al. [2001] propose **augmented surfaces**, which combine surfaces instrumented by projector–camera systems with mobile devices, such as notebook computers. When the user places a notebook on the augmented surface, the notebook's position is detected, and the augmented surface area around the notebook extends the displays area of the notebook. This design allows concurrent use of tangible interaction and conventional desktop interfaces.

Shared Space

In the field of visualization, **coordinated multiple views** is an approach with multiple views, which are not only arranged in an adjacent or overlapping manner, but also show a synchronized visual representation. For example, if a user selects a city from an alphabetical list view, the corresponding geographic location may be highlighted in a map view, and vice versa.

In a three-dimensional environment populated by multiple displays, coordinated multiple views are often employed in the form of a **shared space** (Figure 8.25): A common global coordinate system is shared across all displays, but every display has an individual tracked viewpoint. Consequently, augmentations appear in the same 3D location everywhere. The idea of a shared space was first explored for collaboration, using multiple head-mounted [Schmalstieg et al. 1996] [Billinghurst et al. 1998b] or handheld [Rekimoto 1996] displays.

The **virtual ether** (Figure 8.26) proposed by Butz et al. [1999] replaces the one-to-one relationship between users and displays of the **shared space** with a one-to-many relationship. The

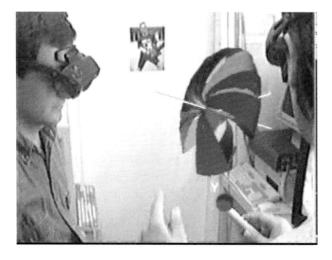

Figure 8.25 A shared space for collaborative viewing of virtual objects can be built with individual head-mounted displays. Courtesy of Anton Fuhrmann.

Figure 8.26   The virtual ether is a three-dimensional model of the space surrounding the users, which can be populated by virtual objects and observed with a variety of displays, such as notebooks, wall-projection, and HMDs. Courtesy of Columbia University.

augmentations placed in the virtual ether are shown on a variety of displays, such as head-mounted, handheld, and projected displays. Through such combinations of display types, the virtual ether combines the shared space with a Focus+Context display.

In the virtual ether, users are not restricted to a single display; rather, they can switch between displays or observe multiple displays at once. For example, a user can see a stationary display while using a see-through HMD or handheld display. This configuration can be used to show an overview map on a table display, while users control individual views shown in tracked first-person perspective on their mobile displays [Ullmer and Ishii 1997] [MacWilliams et al. 2003].

MultiFi [Grubert et al. 2015] implements a variant of the virtual ether with wearable displays—namely, HMDs and touch display (smartphone or smartwatch). A see-through HMD provides a context display for the higher-resolution touch display (Figure 8.27). The reference coordinate system is defined by the touch display. In the case of a smartwatch, the coordinate system is actually arm-referenced and supports use of the arm as an additional display surface. Alternatively, a world-referenced coordinate system can be used.

Figure 8.27   (top) Using icons on the lower arm, seen through a head-mounted display, as an extension of a wrist-worn display. (bottom) A smartphone picks up an icon from the lower arm. Courtesy of Jens Grubert.

Multiple Locales

A **multi-locale interface** differs from a shared space interface in that it does **not** use a common 3D coordinate system across multiple displays. Instead, a virtual object can appear in a different location on every display. This type of system is less useful for augmentations registered to concrete physical objects, but provides a lot of flexibility for arranging purely virtual objects or for augmenting generic tangibles.

Studierstube [Schmalstieg and Hesina 2002] allows a separate locale to be used on each display (Figure 8.28). For example, two HMD users can each bind the same virtual object to a handheld tangible object. Subsequently, every user can turn the tangible to obtain the desired viewpoint on the virtual object, without moving the head and without affecting the other user's view. Any changes made by one user to the virtual object are shared with the other user.

Another use of locales is the combination of an exocentric viewpoint and an egocentric viewpoint onto a virtual scene. Such a combination is a useful application of a Focus+Context

Figure 8.28   A user moves a mobile display (notebook) across multiple locales arranged side by side on a desk. Note how the notebook always shows the content of the same locale as the stationary display next to it. Courtesy of Gerd Hesina and Gerhard Reitmayr.

display, but cannot be conveniently navigated in a shared space, because any motion of the user always changes both viewpoints simultaneously. Decoupling the views into separate locales overcomes this problem. For example, a table display can show an overview map, while a wall display shows a first-person view of the virtual scene [Brown et al. 2003].

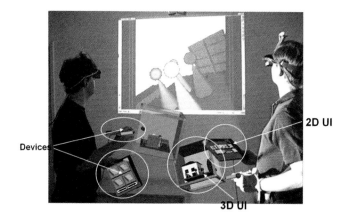

Figure 8.29   Concurrent first-person view seen on the wall projection, and third-person view seen through a head-mounted display. Courtesy of Gerd Hesina and Anton Fuhrmann.

Figure 8.30   The world-in-miniature shows an overview of an environment, while the first-person view shows labels directly in the world. Courtesy of Columbia University.

A three-dimensional overview of the scene, sometimes called a world-in-miniature [Stoakley et al. 1995] can also be shown in an HMD (Figure 8.29), while an exocentric is shown as a wall display [Schmalstieg et al. 2000] or by augmenting real-world objects directly (Figure 8.30) in an HMD [Bell et al. 2002].

Of course, any two locales can form a shared space, if the user so wishes. Changing locale associations over time allows users to work with spatially registered information in a shared space and later detach a locale from the shared space to use it on the go or at a different location.

Cross-View Interaction

Approaches relying on the coordinated multiple view principle are **implicitly** synchronized, in that an update to one view will immediately change all other views. In contrast, **cross-view interactions** provide **explicit** synchronization. For example, the user can drag an item from one view to the other.

This idea was originally proposed as **pick-and-drop** by Rekimoto [1997] for use with conventional 2D displays and input devices. The availability of spatial displays and, in particular, mobile displays allows for significantly better visual feedback during cross-view interaction, because a mobile display can show a visual representation of the dragged object throughout the interaction. For example, augmented surfaces [Rekimoto and Saitoh 1999] allow a user to move objects across adjacent displays, such as notebooks, tables, or wall displays. EMMIE [Butz et al. 1999] supports inter-display drag and drop via tracked input devices and facilitates placement of objects anywhere in the free space of a virtual ether, not just on surfaces. The cross-dimensional gestures described by Benko et al. [2005] allow an object to change dimensionality, so that it can move from a 2D table display to a 3D virtual ether above the table and back (Figure 8.31).

Figure 8.31 Cross-dimensional gestures can be used to pull an object out of a 2D touch surface and into the 3D space above it. Courtesy of Columbia University.

Lightspace [Wilson and Benko 2010] lets a user pick up virtual objects from surfaces, hold them in the hand, and place them onto other surfaces or hand them to other users. The underlying projector–camera system simply digitizes all objects in the environment, including the users, in real time and treats them as interactive surfaces. In this representation, locales are simply regions in space and not necessarily associated with any particular display.

Touch Projector [Boring et al. 2010] uses the built-in camera of a smartphone to track the pose of the smartphone relative to a wall display to create a virtual flashlight. By touching objects shown on the wall display in the live video on the smartphone screen, the objects on the wall display are remotely manipulated. Virtual Projection [Baur et al. 2012] uses a similar technical approach to simulate a handheld projector with a smartphone, which casts an interactive projection onto the wall display.

Haptic Interaction

We mentioned earlier that tangible objects or surfaces let AR benefit from passive haptic feedback at no additional effort. Unfortunately, it is much more challenging to add haptic feedback for **virtual objects.** Haptic displays are still expensive and brittle in this setting. The most established haptic display is an articulated arm with an end-effector that accepts a fingertip or a stylus, such as the Phantom[1] from Sensable. It has a limited working volume and displays haptic output for just a single point.

The main practical problem with using a haptic display in AR is that the display occludes other real objects in the field of view. Optical see-through displays will superimpose virtual objects semi-transparently on top of the user's perception of the real world. This approach can still be effective, but only when the virtual scene is interesting and the real-world lighting is adjusted such that just the user's hand (and not the haptic display) is illuminated.

Alternatively, a video see-through display offers the opportunity to replace the pixels occupied by the haptic device with arbitrary visual content (Figure 8.32) using a diminished reality approach (see Chapter 6). The user's hands and other real objects can be segmented and excluded from overpainting [Sandor et al. 2007]. The haptic device itself can be detected either through chroma-keying [Yokokohji et al. 1999] or by tracking the device itself [Cosco et al. 2009].

Multimodal Interaction

Until now, we have considered only individual means of interaction. Of course, humans actually use their senses and abilities simultaneously. In turn, contemporary computer interfaces combine multiple forms of input or output into **multimodal interaction.** The most commonly used

---

1. http://www.sensable.com/

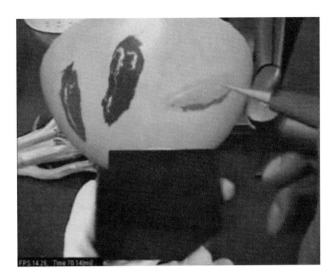

Figure 8.32 An example of haptic AR, letting the user paint on a virtual cup, with force feedback for the brush provided by a haptic arm. Courtesy of Christian Sandor.

input facilities beyond the keyboard and the mouse are speech, gestures, touch, gaze, head orientation, and body movements. Other forms of interaction, such as pen input or haptics, can be used as well.

A key idea of multimodal interfaces is to use multiple sensory channels together to trade one technique's weaknesses for another one's strengths. Ultimately, though, successful interpretation of multimodal input requires appropriate combination of the various input channels and mutual disambiguation—an action is fully defined through joint interpretation of the input channels. This has been the main area of scientific investigation vis-à-vis multimodal interfaces.

The quest for natural interfaces has led to a sustained interest in multimodal interaction. The pioneering work in this field was the Media Room [Bolt 1980], more commonly known as "Put-that-there." It allowed a user immersed in a VR environment to control object placement and other activities through a combination of gestures, gaze, and speech.

SenseShapes [Olwal et al. 2003] enhance the interpretation of multimodal input by computing statistical measures on geometric shapes attached to the user's body, such as a gaze or pointing volume. These measures describe properties of attained objects, such as the time the object remained inside the volume, the number of times the object entered and exited the volume, the distance to the user, or the amount of occlusion. The combination of these computed properties allows a disambiguation of the user's multimodal input, including speech [Kaiser et al. 2003].

If a particular application domain is known in advance, an important technique for the disambiguation of multimodal input is to complement sensor processing with domain knowledge—for example, a set of rules. Irawati et al. [2006] have demonstrated the ability to control an interior design application [Kato et al. 2000] simultaneously with gestures and speech. By temporally correlating gestures and speech utterances, their system reasons about the possible actions a user may intend. For example, dropping a piece of furniture is sensible only if the object can stand by itself and there is an empty space to support it. The system can also resolve positional statements with respect to the environment, such as "behind the table"—this will prompt the system to identify which table the user is looking at and to compute the area that is on the opposite side of the table with respect to the user's standpoint.

Heidemann et al. [2004] present a multimodal interaction framework that is capable of not only processing speech and gestures, but also learning to visually recognize objects in the environment and memorize them. In the volatile environments that are typical for AR, where objects continuously appear and disappear, recognition of novel objects can be a very important capability.

Conversational Agents

Humans have very rich means by which to communicate with one another, including through speech, gestures, eye contact, and other methods. Animated agents aim to leverage some properties of human communication so as to make interfaces more effective. An animated agent (sometimes called an embodied agent or interface agent) must have a visual representation and some level of autonomous intelligence. Intelligence in this context means that the agent can perceive and act upon its environment and that it can determine its behavior independently of the user and the environment.

Animated agents are frequently used to populate virtual worlds, and they are now commonplace in computer games. The most interesting approach for researchers in AR is to combine animated agents with multimodal input and output. With this strategy, the agent can obtain information by analyzing data from sensors, and provide its output through visual and audio displays. In particular, body posture, gesture analysis, and speech recognition are often used to drive the agent's simulated perception. If speech is used as means of interaction, the underlying mechanism is called an **embodied conversational agent**.

The relevance of animated agents for AR interfaces comes from the particular appeal that an embodied conversational agent has on a human user. An AR application can insert an agent into a physical environment, in which only the human user is present, thereby creating a feeling of "company." Humans seem to respond positively to this type of interface, despite their knowledge that the experience is computer generated.

For example, the ALIVE system described by Maes et al. [1997] provides a "magic mirror" environment, where the user sees herself digitally mirrored on a large screen. The video feed that drives the mirror is used for body posture analysis, yielding an estimate of the user's position in space and gestures made with hands and arms. Voice commands can also be provided. Various simulated creatures can be controlled by the user. The most popular example is a dog that has autonomous behaviors such as drinking or sleeping, but can also interact with the user—for example, by following orders or being petted.

The magic mirror metaphor prevents the user from physically entering the realm of the agent. Anabuki et al. [2000] argue that letting users and agents share the same physical environment directly is the most interesting and distinguishing feature of an AR agent. They have introduced Welbo, an animated creature observed in a see-through HMD (Figure 8.33). Welbo can express

Figure 8.33 Welbo is an animated agent that consults for the user in matters of interior decoration. Courtesy of Hiroyuki Yamamoto.

itself through speech synthesis, and recognizes the user's verbal instructions. It can act accord-ing to the user's commands—for example, by moving virtual furniture in a physical living room. It is aware of the physical environment and can, for example, avoid standing in the user's way.

Cavazza et al. [2003] combine AR agents with a storytelling engine. In their system, the user is cast into a particular role and can use body gestures and language commands to influence a story as it unfolds. MacIntyre et al. [2001] also consider AR for interactive storytelling. They propose a different representation of animated agents, not based on 3D rendered graphics, but rather on prerecorded video segments that are embedded into the real environment. Recording video entails working with human actors, who can provide a much richer spectrum of physical and verbal expression than that typically possible with computer animation. The disadvantage, of course, is that all behavioral sequences must be known in advance and cannot be computed on the fly.

The work by MacIntyre et al. [2001] uses optical see-through displays and, therefore, presents the video-based agents as partially transparent characters. As an appropriate setting, they pre-fer environments where ghostly appearances from the past are a plausible part of the storyline, such as a ghost in a graveyard or the former residents of a historical building. An extension in this line of work is AR Karaoke [Gandy et al. 2005], in which users are cast in a theatrical role and re-enact famous movie scenes along with virtual characters.

Several other researchers have incorporated animated agents in AR settings, exploring differ-ent types of applications. Balcisoy et al. [2001] employ virtual humans in AR as collaborative game partners. Vacchetti et al. [2003] use a virtual character to demonstrate the use of factory machinery in a training scenario. Schmeil and Broll [2007] describe MARA, an agent that follows the user around and acts as a personal secretary, such as by taking notes and by issuing remind-ers about dates and appointments.

Barakonyi et al. [2004b] argue that AR agents should be viewed as a part of a sentient or ubiquitous computing environment—in other words, a physical environment that is capable of responding to human-induced events in the most appropriate way. This has the implication that an agent can have multiple embodiments—purely virtual, purely real, or a mixture of both (Figure 8.34). The agent's behavior needs to be adaptive to make the best use of the environ-mental resources.

As an example, they present an agent-based system for guiding a user in the assembly of a self-driving LEGO robot. The robot itself is an agent that has multiple embodiments: the physical object and a virtual counterpart. Consider the task of attaching a wheel to the half-assembled robot. Before the wheel is attached to the robot body, a virtual representation of the wheel shows how to mount the physical wheel. After the wheel has been successfully attached, the virtual wheel is no longer required; instead, the physical wheel can be turned by means of the robot's motor unit, so that the user can verify that the wheel has been mounted correctly. To

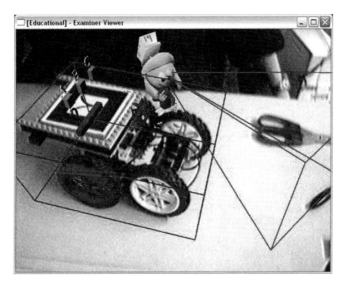

Figure 8.34 (top row) The AR Lego agent representing a vehicle can have different embodiments: real, augmented, or virtual. (bottom) Another agent, a cartoon character, instructs the user on the assembly of the vehicle. Courtesy of István Barakonyi.

achieve this style of interaction, the agent must be capable of switching among its multiple embodiments as appropriate.

Another example is a conversational agent that migrates among multiple displays to the most appropriate one. For example, a personal message might be delivered on a user's smartphone screen, while a public announcement might be made on a wall-mounted large-format display.

Summary

Interaction styles in AR are manifold, as they reflect the rich diversity of AR applications and setups. One common trait among all interaction techniques is the inclusion of the user's physical surrounding as part of the interface. The role of the physical environment can range from peripheral, when it is simply a backdrop augmented with computer-generated information, to central, when tangibles are used. Ideally, the affordances of the physical environment will be put to good use—for example, when physical surfaces or paper artifacts are augmented, or when haptic feedback is employed. The physical environment provides the frame of reference for multi-view interfaces, which allow users to establish different views into an augmented world. In addition, multimodal interaction can make AR richer and easier, and is a natural match for communicating with agents.

CHAPTER 9

MODELING AND ANNOTATION

Interaction with AR is exciting, but ultimately limited if only preexisting content is available. Modeling and annotation let AR users create new content that is spatially registered to the real world. Unlike preparing geometric and visual content in advance, in a setting that is detached from the task location, *situated* modeling provides the opportunity to work directly on location and, therefore, to verify that the input is truthful to the real world.

Modeling of geometry and appearance has many applications, both professional and personal. Computer-aided design (CAD) software is used to prepare models for architecture, transportation, mechanical and electrical engineering, movies, and games. More often than not, these models do not exist in isolation, but are supposed to fit into an existing environment. Given that traditional modeling is a desktop or drafting board activity, the work time of many professional modelers is split between the desktop computer and the location where the model belongs. This is equally true whether a physical object is ultimately deployed in the environment or not. For instance, a building should always fit its surroundings, independent of whether something is physically built or if an existing urban neighborhood is re-created for use in a computer game.

Moving back and forth between the desktop and the task location is tedious and inefficient. Not only is time spent on commuting and context switching, but, more importantly, effects of modeling changes on the environment are not immediately obvious. **Situated modeling** can overcome this gap by letting the user perform the modeling work directly at the task location.

Rather than determining a distance with a measuring tape and entering the result into CAD software, AR lets the user simply point out the dimensions in the real world. The results of this interaction are immediately visible and can be modified if they do not represent the desired state. In a simple example, the user might place a virtual object on top of a real surface and judge whether it fits. Situated modeling with AR has many possible applications, ranging from planning in architecture and construction, setup of technical facilities, product design, and interior decoration to recreational "sandbox" games, such as Minecraft. It includes any form of 3D reconstruction where a geometric model of existing physical artifacts is obtained.

In this chapter, we investigate modeling of geometric and appearance aspects, which yields only passive content that does not include any computed behavior. We begin with the manual acquisition of geometry and appearance, then examine semi-automatic methods for reconstruction. Additional sections deal with free-form modeling of nonplanar shapes and annotations; the latter associate a geometric shape with user-defined commentary. The specification of behavior in AR applications is discussed in Chapter 10.

Specifying Geometry

The fundamental problem of modeling is the specification of geometric primitives. In this section, we focus on simple polygonal geometry: points, planes, and volumes. While the resulting geometric entities are similar to the data structures in desktop CAD, the input techniques are different, owing to the need for physical motion in AR.

Points

Any spatial input by a human operator can always be categorized according to whether the relevant workspace is within arm's reach or whether the user operates at a distance, potentially outdoors, in an area where large distances must be covered. Within arm's reach, the easiest and most natural approach is certainly to let a user *point directly to the desired location*—for example, by using a tracked glove or stylus [Lee et al. 2002].

In most cases, however, operation at a distance will be required. Such an interaction is most commonly carried out by a variant of **raycasting**. That is, the user emits a ray into the environment, originating at a body part, either the head (gaze) or the hand. The **ray direction** is specified by the orientation of the body part alone or as the vector between two body parts (from head to hand or from hand to hand). A point can be determined by *specifying a second ray*, which intersects the first ray [Bunnun and Mayol-Cuevas 2008]. The point is then computed as the center of the minimal distance between these two rays, since exact intersection of two rays is usually not achievable in free-hand operation (Figure 9.1).

As an alternative to intersection, we can *specify the distance explicitly*. For example, a distance can be defined by moving the point along the using a "fishing reel" technique with a mouse wheel or a similar instrument [Bunnun and Mayol-Cuevas 2008] [Simon 2010]. Both methods for specifying a point along the ray expect the user subsequently to move away from the position where the ray was specified, so she can judge the distance input.

Another way to specify the third dimension for a point is to provide the user with an alternative perspective. For example, Wither et al. [2006] propose to let a user select a 2D position in an aerial image, which is retrieved based on the user's current GPS coordinate (Figure 9.2). This method is more convenient for outdoor use, when moving to a sufficiently distant location to cast a second ray would be tedious.

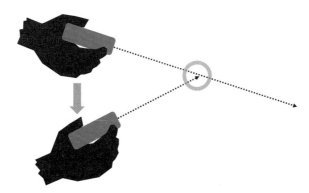

Figure 9.1   A three-dimensional point in free space can be specified by intersecting two rays.

Figure 9.2   Example annotation created by specifying two dimensions in the first-person view and the third dimension (distance) in a corresponding aerial image (insets in the lower-left corner). In this case, a region annotation is rendered as a wireframe bounding box.

A useful enhancement for any type of point specification is to provide automatic snapping to an existing point, line, or polygon, when the new location is sufficiently close.

Planes

While individual points by themselves are useful in AR as anchors for annotations, most geometric applications will involve planar structures [Piekarski and Thomas 2004]. Planes can be defined in a variety of ways (Figure 9.3). The most obvious method for defining arbitrary planes is to select three points. These points can, but need not, lie on a physical surface. For example, only two points may lie on the surface, while the third point defines the angle of the new plane relative to the surface. If the new plane is orthogonal to the existing one, a third point is not necessary. Note that without a physical surface, a new plane can be created from an existing free-space plane in a similar way.

If a gravity sensor is available, vertical planes can be defined by the user's viewing direction, and horizontal planes can be defined by specifying a single point for the height. Moreover, a

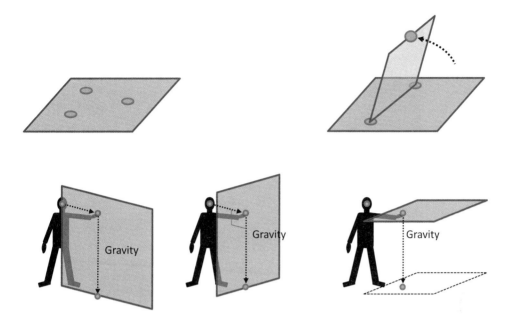

Figure 9.3   Five ways to specify a plane: (top left) Three points. (top right) Two points are reused from an existing plane, and a third point indicates the tilt. (bottom left) The plane is aligned with both the vector connecting the user's head and the gravity direction. (bottom middle) The plane is orthogonal to the vector connecting the user's head and hand and is aligned with the gravity direction. (bottom right) The plane contains the user's hand and is orthogonal to the gravity direction.

plane can be defined as parallel to an existing surface or plane by specifying the offset. This includes planes that are parallel to the viewing plane.

Volumes

Usually the specification of points and planes is just an intermediate step in a geometric modeling procedure, with the user being ultimately interested in *volumes*. The most straightforward way to arrive at such volumes is to connect points with edges to form polygons, and then to aggregate polygons to form volumes [Lee et al. 2002] [Simon 2010]. Depending on the complexity of the underlying object, this approach may be cumbersome and error-prone.

For these reasons, operations that generate a volumetric object in one step and ensure it is watertight and topologically valid are preferable. A simple approach would be to specify a box by indicating a base rectangle and a height. In general, **extrusion** is a popular approach for creating proper volumes [Baillot et al. 2001] [Piekarski and Thomas 2001] [Bunnun and Mayol-Cuevas 2008] [van den Hengel et al. 2009]. With a planar base shape (e.g., polygon or circle) and an indication of the height along the normal, an extruded shape (prism, pyramid, cylinder, or cone) can be created (Figure 9.4). Some systems also support rotational extrusion or mirroring.

Figure 9.4   The in-situ image-based modeling system JIIM lets a user outline polygonal surfaces directly in the keyframes of a SLAM map. Courtesy of Anton van den Hengel.

The modeling of more complex volume shapes is often approached with **constructive solid geometry**—that is, the combination of volumetric union, intersection, and difference. These operations can work on existing volumes (e.g., extrusions) or on sets of planes. Every plane defines a half-space, encompassing all points on the side of the positive normal vector. Intersecting the half-spaces shapes a volume by **space-carving**: Every plane removes a portion of the space, such that the desired volume is left (Figure 9.5). Specifying vertical and horizontal

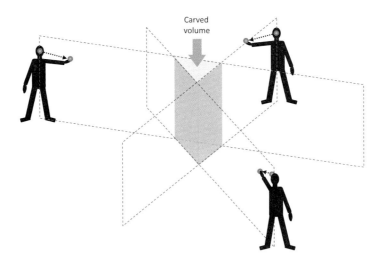

Figure 9.5   By specifying a number of working planes in viewing direction and intersecting the resulting half-spaces, a volume outline, such as given by a building, can be rapidly specified.

planes, as mentioned earlier, and intersecting their half-spaces is a useful method for modeling edifices and other large human-made objects [Piekarski and Thomas 2004].

Specifying Appearance

One distinct advantage of AR modeling over any other kind of geometric modeling is that the live video stream used in AR is a rich source of appearance information. In turn, surface textures for digitized real-world objects can be acquired on the fly using image-based modeling. Assuming the geometry of a polygon is known and the polygon is not tilted too dramatically away from the image plane, the polygon's texture can be directly acquired from the image [Lee et al. 2002]. Texture corruption from occlusions or specular reflections can be repaired by allowing the user to selectively replace portions of the texture with pixels from new camera images [van den Hengel et al. 2009].

Apart from appearance *acquisition*, designers are interested in appearance *modification*. Provided a phantom object is available, dynamic shader lamps [Bandyopadhyay et al. 2001] let a user paint with projected light on a real object (Figure 9.6). Initially, the object has an empty, transparent texture. Whenever the user applies "paint," the brush tip is transformed into local texture coordinates of the phantom object. The associated texture is filled with a color splat at the determined coordinate. The projection of the colored texture does not depend on the user's current point of view, because the projected information is constrained to lie on a physical surface.

Figure 9.6   A user painting with projected light on a canvas (foreground) and toy house (background). Courtesy of Michael Marner.

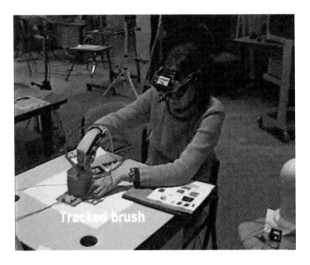

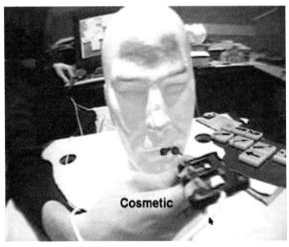

Figure 9.7   (top) A user wearing a head-mounted display paints on a real object with a tracked brush. (bottom) View of a styling application seen through an AR display. Courtesy of Raphael Grasset.

Grasset et al. [2005] show how a similar approach can be implemented using a video see-through display (Figure 9.7).

The AR airbrush technique [Marner et al. 2009] extends this idea by replacing the brush with a spray of particles. The farther the user holds the paint gun away from the surface, the wider the painted area is. By using a stencil in the nondominant hand, the user can constrain the deposit of paint particles on the surface (Figure 9.8). Just as with a real airbrush, a trained artist can move the paint gun and the stencil simultaneously to create smooth color gradients.

Figure 9.8   The AR Airbrush allows the user to deposit simulated paint on an object surface with a spray gun. Courtesy of Michael Marner.

Semi-automatic Reconstruction

Recent advances in online reconstruction now make it possible to acquire geometric models on the fly, while the user is exploring the environment. Even dense reconstruction is possible with a fast processor [Newcombe et al. 2011b] or a depth sensor [Newcombe et al. 2011a].

Unfortunately, the models obtained with automatic reconstruction are not immediately suitable for AR applications. On the one hand, these models often include unnecessary detail, requiring a lot of storage and processing power for rendering and physics. On the other hand, they lack semantic structure or meaning, so it is difficult to perform simple semantic operations such as the selection of one individual object.

To remedy these shortcomings, semi-automatic reconstruction is needed, in which an online reconstruction method (usually based on SLAM) provides the data for situated modeling operations. Note that we consider only ego-centric AR interfaces here, not desktop CAD using scanned geometry. We begin with approaches that use SLAM only with a monocular RGB camera.

The simplest approach uses SLAM to estimate **dominant planes** in the scene. The planes can be used for registration of virtual objects [Simon 2006] [Chekhlov et al. 2007] [Klein and Murray

2007] or to improve the registration results [Salas-Moreno et al. 2013]. An alternative approach is to detect vanishing points in the image, thereby establishing the ground plane and the main room orientation for supporting easy object placement [Nóbrega and Correia 2012].

Bunnun and Mayol-Cuevas [2008] described OutlinAR, the first system for modeling wireframe geometry during the mapping phase of SLAM. Simon [2010] has extended this approach by alternating between a modeling and a mapping phase. This separation gives the user more freedom of camera motion during the modeling phase.

Van den Hengel et al. [2009] describe JIIM, which lets the user model textured geometry from SLAM keyframes (Figure 9.4). JIIM also uses separate mapping and modeling phases. During modeling, the system presents keyframes as still images on a tablet computer, and the user draws polygonal outlines on top of the keyframes. The polygons are placed automatically at the depth of the underlying physical surfaces, estimated from the 3D information in the SLAM map.

Pan et al. [2009] describe ProFORMA, a method for semi-automatically reconstructing geometry and appearance of small handheld objects. They assume a stationary camera and require the user to turn the object in front of the camera. For every new view of the object, the object silhouette is determined using background subtraction, and probabilistic space carving is used to prune the tetrahedral volume, until the modeling is complete. The system also features situated visualizations for instructing the user how to best complete the modeling procedure (Figure 9.9).

Bastian et al. [2010] also focus on reconstructing small objects, but let the user move around the object rather than requiring the camera to remain stationary. After segmenting the object in the first keyframe based on user input, the object silhouette is traced through the image sequence and extracted with space carving.

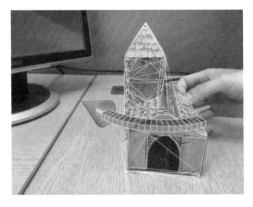 

Figure 9.9   ProFORMA incrementally captures the surface of an object turned in front of a stationary camera. The system can instruct the user what to do next by displaying directional arrows (left) and indicating incomplete surfaces (right). Courtesy of Qi Pan and Gerhard Reitmayr.

Figure 9.10   (top) A single-point laser range finder attached to an HMD. (bottom left) Partial segmentation of a foreground object based on a graph cut initialized with measurements from the laser range finder. (bottom right) Occlusion of a virtual statue computed using the foreground segmentation. Courtesy of Jason Wither.

With active depth sensors, it becomes much easier to obtain reliable geometric measurements, which greatly aids semi-automatic reconstruction methods. Wither et al. [2008] show that even a single-point laser range finder (Figure 9.10) is sufficient to facilitate the acquisition of environmental geometry outdoors. Unlike most structured light sensors, which work only indoors over short distances, a laser range finder delivers measurements over long distances. If it is rigidly registered to a video camera feed, the range measurement can be used to initialize an image-based segmentation. This operation is repeated multiple times for complex foreground objects. In a complementary approach, spreading interpolated depth values out in image space yields a coarse depth map of the environment. The depth map is useful for placing overlays and rendering correct occlusions.

Nguyen et al. [2013] demonstrate a similar setup for indoor reconstruction. Sparse input from the laser range finder is used to identify planar structures, such as walls, and to define their topological relationships. A constructive solid geometry approach merges this information in a volumetric model of the room structure.

 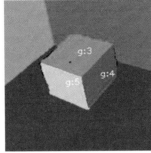 

Figure 9.11   (left) View of a simple scene from an RGBD sensor. (middle) Planes segmented from the depth image. (right) Geometric scene understanding detects straight edges, shown as yellow lines, and parallel planes, shown in the same color. Courtesy of Thanh Nguyen.

With enough geometric information, **scene understanding** based on computational analysis can be used as an additional tool for supporting modeling. Scene understanding often relies on statistical approaches and machine learning, which require large data sets. Consequently, most methods for scene understanding use offline reconstruction, followed by automated segmentation and classification of geometry. Scene understanding in real time is gradually becoming feasible, so it will likely be applicable to AR in the future. For instance, SLAM++ [Salas-Moreno et al. 2013] detects instances of known objects and builds a SLAM map incorporating complete objects. SemanticPaint [Valentin et al. 2015] allows users to scan an indoor environment with an RGB-D camera, while simultaneously segmenting the scene through simple touch gestures. Outdoors, the Semantic Paintbrush [Miksik et al. 2015] facilitates a similar functionality using passive stereo vision and a circling gesture with a laser pointer for interaction. In both cases, a dynamic machine learning process using a Conditional Random Field model continuously analyzes these online segmentations and labels new unseen parts of the environment accordingly.

Nguyen et al. [2015] describe a system for **structural modeling**, which computes high-level geometry with a low-polygon count from RGB-D SLAM information. This system extracts planes and analyzes the geometry of plane boundaries and plane-to-plane relationships such as incidence and orthogonality (Figure 9.11).

Free-Form Modeling

Traditional design methods for shape and appearance often involve making physical mockups and prototypes from malleable materials, such as clay, wood, or paper. AR can enhance the design process by combining digital design tools with physical objects. In this application area, the focus lies on creative freedom of expression, rather than on precise geometric input.

For example, Spacedesign [Fiorentino et al. 2002] lets a user sketch curves in space and fits free-form surfaces to an array of curves. Physical objects, such as mockup designs, can serve as a

Figure 9.12 A tracked hot wire cutter is used to simultaneously cut a physical foam piece and digitally compute the corresponding 3D shape for projector-based augmentation. Courtesy of Michael Marner.

reference. Another intuitive way of free-form modeling for volumes utilizes a spray of simulated foam particles [Jung et al. 2004]. Designers, however, may prefer established artistic techniques such as sculpting or sketching. For example, industrial designers use foam cutting as a rapid prototyping tool. This process builds on the practice of cutting a piece of foam with a hot wire cutter, until it assumes the desired shape. Marner and Thomas [2010] track the piece and the cutter and simulate the changes made to the piece's shape (Figure 9.12) to determine a phantom corresponding to the piece. They use a projector to augment the piece with additional information, such as an animation of the cuts already applied, the piece's interior structure, or a target shape.

Foam cutting has the disadvantage that it must be possible to create the desired shape in a physical sense. In contrast, AR-Jig [Anabuki and Ishii 2007] lets a user input a 2D curve with a tracked pin array (Figure 9.13). This pin array can be physically manipulated to represent the

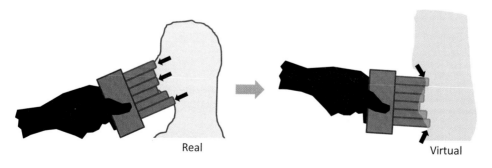

Real   Virtual

Figure 9.13 (left) AR-Jig can capture the curve of a real object. (right) The captured curve can be used for space carving on a virtual work piece.

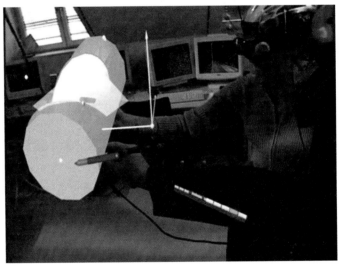

Figure 9.14 Construct3D allows free-form modeling of higher-order curved surfaces, such as the intersection of conics. Courtesy of Hannes Kaufmann.

desired curve—for example, by pressing it against a physical surface. With the curve-shaped tool, the user can carve a virtual volume or deform an object surface to match the curve.

AR can also support geometric modeling of higher-order structures—for example, to study mathematics [Kaufmann et al. 2000]. Students wearing HMDs can create advanced mathematical structures such as intersection curves of surfaces of revolution, and interactively modify their parameters using simple constraint modeling techniques (Figure 9.14).

Annotation

As we have seen, many compelling AR applications deal with geometry or appearance, but even more potential exists for associating the abundant abstract information with objects in our world through annotations of different kinds [Wither et al. 2009], which help users to understand and remember their environment better [Starner et al. 1997]. Sharing annotations with other users is a key requirement for social computing. Today's commercial AR browsers already let users contribute simple geo-referenced content, such as textual annotations. This concept has been branded "augment-able reality" by Rekimoto et al. [1998]. Once an object in the user's view is recognized, associated information, such as text, pictures, or audio clips, is brought to the user's attention. The user is not limited to purely passive consumption of the annotations, but rather can provide new information as needed—hence the term "augment-able." By depositing new annotations on a server indexed by location, this sharing of information becomes a collaborative effort.

In the real world, we cannot assume that tracking models for objects considered for annotation are already available. Therefore, before placing an annotation on an object, we must either reconstruct the object in 3D or, at a minimum, collect an image-based representation that makes it possible to reliably detect the annotated object or location at a later time. Such information can be obtained with SLAM techniques, similar in intention to the semi-automatic reconstruction approaches described earlier. The AR system captures the environment, and the user adds supplementary information in the form of annotations.

In indoor environments, a sparse map obtained by conventional SLAM can be used directly for the registration of annotations. Reitmayr et al. [2007] describe an approach where the user selects existing geometric features (squares, disks) in the environment and lets the system track these features (Figure 9.15). The automatic estimation of the features relieves the user from the burden of manually specifying surface geometry for the annotations.

Often, 3D annotations can conveniently be authored in 2D; in the case of AR annotations being issued via 2D sketches on video-see-through AR tablets, for example, by drawing an arrow or highlighting an object or part by circling it on the viewing plane [Gauglitz et al. 2014b]. Gesture-enhanced annotation interpretation and semi-automatic object segmentation in image or object space (acquired, for example, via SLAM) can disambiguate the 2D input and apply it to the 3D scene for correct interpretation from different viewpoints [Nuernberger et al. 2016].

As an outdoor application, Kim et al. [2007] have developed a system that lets users generate annotations on buildings in open environments. After establishing the user's current position relative to a building corner using a location in an aerial image together with mobile sensor information (GPS, compass, IMU), the building is tracked incrementally, and users can place the desired annotations on the image (Figure 9.16).

Figure 9.15   Semi-automatic annotation lets the user attach instructions, such as the directional arrows indicating maintenance operations, directly to features in a SLAM map. Courtesy of Gerhard Reitmayr, Ethan Eade, and Tom Drummond.

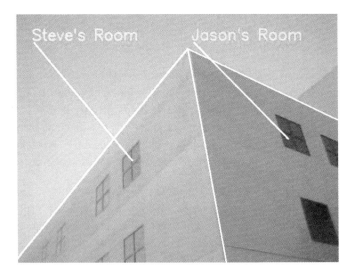

Figure 9.16   Live annotation attached during tracking a building corner. Courtesy of Sehwan Kim.

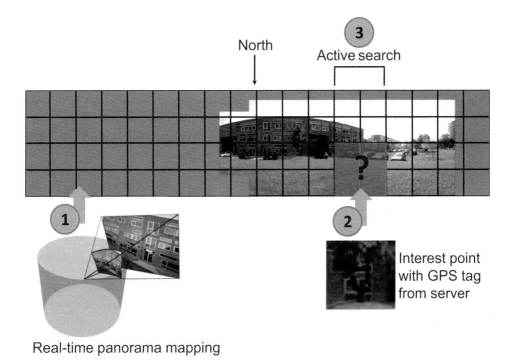

Real-time panorama mapping

Figure 9.17 Browsing annotations in surround panoramas: First, the user maps a partial panorama using a mobile client device. Second, the mobile client retrieves interest points based on the current GPS position. Third, the interest points are detected in the panorama, using the compass as a prior for active search.

A robust and scalable system for placing outdoor annotations anywhere can be built from the combination of mobile sensors and panoramic SLAM [Wagner et al. 2010]. During or after capturing a panorama, the user can select interest points in the environment and annotate them with text or audio clips [Langlotz et al. 2013]. The panoramas and the annotated locations are stored on a server, indexed by GPS coordinates. When another user wants to browse the annotations, a new panorama is built and compared to nearby panorama data sets stored on the server (Figure 9.17), using robust image matching [Langlotz et al. 2011] with the previously obtained sensor information (e.g., compass direction).

The motivation for organizing annotations using a combination of coarse positions and panoramas is that no prior knowledge of the environment is required and that all computations are extremely lightweight. If a three-dimensional city model is available, panoramas can be treated as ultra-wide-angle images for image-based matching with the city model [Arth et al. 2011]. In such an extended framework, annotations stored in absolute global coordinates can be used as well.

Summary

Modeling is an indispensable ingredient of AR interaction. In particular, modeling using a mobile interface has the intriguing property that one can compare the shape and appearance of the virtual image and the real image side by side, especially when re-creating existing physical structures. Perhaps inevitably, however, the reduced interaction capabilities of mobile devices make the precise specification of spatial input more difficult than in a desktop setting. Consequently, various techniques have been developed that assist a user in specifying geometric input. These input techniques typically require high-precision tracking, whereas free-form and annotation techniques can work with more relaxed requirements (but only because they are not intended to deliver a similar level of precision). Placing annotations will be an especially important concept for end-user modeling, if social AR is to become a mainstream medium.

CHAPTER 10

AUTHORING

While modeling deals with geometry and appearance, authoring is concerned with defining the semantics and the behavior of the application. Today, this activity still mostly takes place at the source code level. The reliance on programming as the sole AR authoring methodology limits developer productivity and prevents nonprogrammers, such as writers, designers, and artists, from taking an active role in the development of AR applications. This may affect the pace at which AR becomes a mainstream medium. In this chapter, we investigate strategies to improve this situation.

Particularly when AR is viewed more as a new medium and not so much as a new technology [MacIntyre et al. 2001], appropriately dealing with content becomes paramount. Hampshire et al. [2006] distinguish between *programming frameworks* and *content design frameworks* for AR. Low-level programming frameworks such as ARToolKit [Kato and Billinghurst 1999] expose basic AR functions, such as tracking. In contrast, high-level programming frameworks introduce building blocks for common concepts of AR applications, such as a scene graph. In the high-level category, both research frameworks, such as Studierstube [Schmalstieg et al. 2002] and DWARF [Bauer et al. 2001], and commercial frameworks, such as Vuforia,[1] are typically implemented in an object-oriented language.

In contrast to such programming frameworks (which are discussed in Chapter 14), this chapter discusses design frameworks, which deal with *content creation* for AR applications. With the right kind of content, an AR application can serve a variety of purposes. The most well-known content-driven applications may be computer games; indeed, AR games are an important use case for content-driven AR. However, there are many more compelling use cases, such as cultural education [Ledermann and Schmalstieg 2003], as exemplified in Figure 10.1, and assembly instructions, as illustrated in Figure 10.2.

Requirements of AR Authoring

Content creation requires understanding the unique properties of AR. A successful AR authoring solution must provide more than an attractive graphical user interface for an existing AR application framework.

Real-World Interfaces

One aspect that makes AR setups fundamentally different from other media is the presence of the real world in the user's perception of the application space—a feature that we have to take into account when structuring application space and interaction. Furthermore, the world is not just a passive container for the application's content; objects in the real world (e.g., furniture to assemble, real-world tools) are part of the application's user interface. In our conceptual model, we must address the different possibilities of relating application content to the real world. For example, physical elements must often be explicitly modeled as application objects, despite the fact that they will not be rendered graphically.

---

1. http://www.vuforia.com

Figure 10.1   Heidentor (heathen gate) is a Roman ruin from the 4th century, located in eastern Austria. The figure shows a scale model augmented with multimedia information. The user has selected the middle part with a red ray, causing a historic photograph to be displayed. Courtesy of Florian Ledermann.

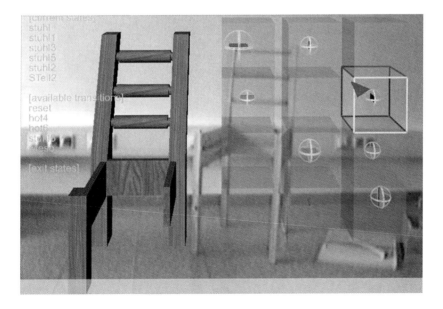

Figure 10.2   Do-it-yourself furniture assembly can be assisted by AR instructions. In this image, a virtual model is shown next to the chair to guide the user what to do next. Courtesy of Florian Ledermann.

Hardware Abstraction

A fundamental aspect of AR is the heterogeneity of hardware setups, devices, and interaction techniques that usually prohibits a "write once, run anywhere" approach or the development of standardized interaction toolkits. We need a strategy for hardware abstraction and an interaction concept that can be transparently applied to a wide range of input devices. By applying these abstractions, application portability can be improved, enabling applications to be developed on desktop workstations or in other test environments, instead of directly on the target AR system, which may be scarce or expensive to use.

An important requirement is that the framework should support the many possible combinations of input and output peripherals. In some cases, such as when working with mobile devices, it is also much more convenient to develop the application on a desktop computer, running it on the target system exclusively for evaluation, fine-tuning, and final deployment. Applications and their components should be reusable in different setups, and applications developed for one system should run on another setup, with little or no modification. For example, an application can be configured to run on a webcam-based home computer, as well as on a tracked see-through HMD.

Of course, the problem of platform incompatibility is not unique to AR. Consider the common problem of a mobile app that does not run on a particular type of smartphone. Even if hardware abstraction makes it possible to reuse an application on another device, serious usability problems may result. For example, an interface designed for a smartphone with a high-resolution screen may not work well when using an HMD. Despite these limitations, a good abstraction layer is always justified, as it can significantly ease the engineering of cross-platform solutions.

Authoring Workflow

Authoring benefits from existing tools and standards, providing interfaces for integrating these tools into a consistent workflow. The professional tools used by content creators and domain experts should be supported in the AR authoring process, removing the need to reimplement successful solutions in these areas.

As an example, let us assume that the programmatic building blocks for a particular application already exist. This leaves three main steps for the authoring. First, we must create multimedia assets. Second, we must link virtual and real entities—for example, by assigning 3D models to a target. Third, we must define entity behavior, by specifying what happens when the user interacts with objects in the environment. We leave out the preparation of the real world, such as the creation of appropriate physical artifacts, because this step cannot be achieved with digital technology, but rather requires traditional crafts such as stage design.

Obviously, such an authoring system cannot exist in isolation, but rather requires a runtime engine to execute the application and present the content. In particular, the runtime engine must allow us to control the spatial and temporal aspects of content creation.

To support a collaborative workflow and allow future reuse, it is also highly desirable to modu-larize applications. This applies not just to individual parts of an application's content, but also to abstract parts of the application, such as the storyboard, the interaction specifications, and the hardware description.

In this chapter, we first explore the elements that AR authoring is concerned with. Next, we describe how these elements are incorporated into stand-alone authoring solutions. The fol-lowing sections deal with modern approaches to authoring, which are often not stand-alone solutions, but rather use a plug-in approach or web technology.

Elements of Authoring

The two fundamental dimensions along which an application is organized are the temporal organization, which determines the visibility and behavior of the objects of the application over time, and the spatial organization, which determines the location and size of these objects in relation to the viewer. Such an overall structure bears some resemblance to conventional com-puter animation software. At the same time, some special considerations are required to make this approach work in AR applications (Figure 10.3).

Actors

We call the objects that make up an application's content actors. An actor may have a geomet-ric representation, such as a character that interacts with the user, but could also be a sound, or

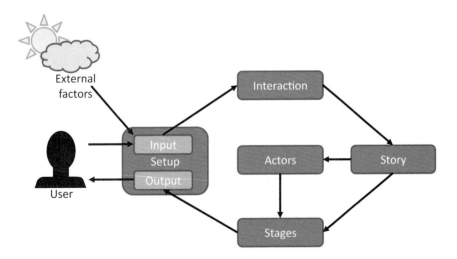

Figure 10.3   One way to look at authoring of AR experiences is using a theater metaphor. Based on a definition of setup for input and output, the authoring defines a story (application logic), driven by interaction and influencing actors arranged on stages.

a video clip, or even some abstract entity that controls the behavior of other actors. It is useful if actors can be nested, such that a single actor can control an entire group of other actors at once. Each actor should be an instance of a component (thereby allowing extension of the actor cast by adding new components) and have a collection of attributes that determine its behavior, if changed through timed events or as a result of user input.

Story

In computer animation, there is usually a chronological order of events, typically represented as a timeline. In contrast, interactive applications do not necessarily follow a chronological order. At any given moment, there will be a current **scene**, which determines which actors are visible and can be interacted with. Upon the satisfaction of certain conditions, the system advances to another scene. This unfolding of events and scene can be seen as a nonlinear story. It can be formally expressed as a finite state machine, where the current scene equals the currently activated state. Upon entering, executing, and leaving the scene, the properties of actors can be set or animated. For hierarchical control, it is also common to link one actor's properties to another actor.

Stages

The spatial organization of actors in an AR application differs from existing approaches in VR. In VR applications, typically a single scene is rendered for all users. In contrast, one of the specific strengths of AR systems is their ability to provide multiple users with different views on the world. Even in a single-user AR system, there may be several "realities" that are simultaneously viewed: the real world and corresponding registered computer-generated overlays, user interface elements such as heads-up displays or interaction panels, a world-in-miniature [Stoakley et al. 1995] for navigation, scenes rendered to a 2D texture for use as an information display, and so on.

To support this spatial multiplicity, the AR environment can be subdivided into spatial units that we call *stages*. It is convenient if authors can not only define spatial relationships of each state to the global world coordinates and to other stages, but also specify the rendering technique used (e.g., three-dimensional or as a texture on a flat surface) and the association of stages with certain physical displays (e.g., to provide "private" content for particular users).

Interactions

The simplest way to define an interactive behavior is to give the control over an actor property to the user. For this purpose, either direct manipulation (using a pointing device, a marker, or some other means) or a suitable virtual user interface element must be specified. Likewise, users should be able to trigger transitions between scenes by user interface elements, such as buttons, or by other means, such as by proximity to an actor. For convenience, it should be possible to test the basic interactions using a graphical user interface. Specification of more advanced interactions is usually enabled through a scripting language such as Python, C#, or JavaScript.

Setup

Flexibility in AR authoring requires separation of the application content from all aspects that depend on the actual system that the application will run on. Introducing a specific hardware description can provide a layer of abstraction that hides details of the underlying hardware from the user. Using different hardware descriptions, applications can be run on different hardware setups without changing their content.

Hardware specifics, such as calibration or networking parameters, can be configured using an existing device abstraction software framework, such as OpenTracker [Reitmayr and Schmalstieg 2001] or VRPN [Taylor et al. 2001]. The mapping from the hardware-dependent layer to the application must be sufficiently expressive to allow the application to make full use of hardware features such as tracking devices or displays. The general principle to achieve this utilization is to enumerate all hardware features, such as computers, displays, pointing, and interaction devices, stating suitable semantics for their use (e.g., head tracking versus hand tracking) via keywords. The application can refer indirectly to the hardware resources by specifying compatible keywords.

Stand-Alone Authoring Solutions

In this section, we describe a number of well-known examples of AR authoring systems and examine how well they address the design considerations outlined previously. We first look into AR authoring solutions using conventional desktop interaction. A desktop approach has the advantage that it can leverage established desktop interaction techniques, but it does not do justice to the immersive nature of AR. Therefore, we also give some examples of more experimental techniques that use AR interfaces directly for authoring, which we call authoring by performance.

Desktop Authoring

If a simple linear presentation is sufficient, a slideshow metaphor may be appropriate. For instance, PowerSpace [Haringer and Regenbrecht 2002] targets sequences of instructions presented as AR annotations of a physical scene—for example, in the automotive industry. It relies on a conventional slide editor (Microsoft PowerPoint) for quickly generating content for AR. The layout of graphical elements, which correspond to actors in AR, on top of a snapshot of the physical environment is done interactively inside the 2D slide editor. The result is exported to a 3D object format and further refined in the PowerSpace editor, which allows adjustment of the spatial arrangement of the actors as well as importing of 3D models. Clearly, the PowerSpace system is limited by the capabilities of PowerPoint and the linear slideshow concept, which does not accommodate different stages or nonlinear storytelling. Even so, PowerSpace can leverage people's proficiency in editing slides for achieving simple AR presentations with considerable efficiency.

The Situated Documentaries application developed at Columbia University runs on top of MARS, the mobile augmented reality system. Situated Documentaries are hypermedia narratives consisting of various multimedia elements, such as text, video and audio clips, and 3D models registered to the environment. These actors are bound to locations in an outdoor environment, which can be browsed by the user who is roaming the environment wearing MARS. The researchers developed a custom visual editor for Situated Documentaries [Höllerer et al. 1999a]. Situated Documentaries display geo-registered content when the user approaches a particular outdoor location, which implements the stage concept. However, authoring uses a desktop emulation, so authors do not have to move to physical places to manipulate objects registered there. A follow-up indoor/outdoor collaboration system added an indoor AR interface, operating on a world-in-miniature, as an authoring alternative for placement tasks [Höllerer et al. 1999b].

AMIRE (Authoring Mixed Reality) is a framework for creating AR applications from a dataflow of components. The AMIRE Authoring Wizard is able to create content for AR-based assembly instructions [Zauner et al. 2003]. To achieve that aim, it lets the user specify individual assembly steps and dependencies among the steps, leading to a tree-like structure. At runtime, this tree is linearized into a sequence of step-by-step instructions.

Similarly, the template-based authoring approach [Knöpfle et al. 2005] considers the authoring of a sequence of step-by-step instructions. Its developers specifically consider automotive maintenance procedures and provide a set of templates for creating the actors and interactions for such procedures. They estimate that with approximately 20–30 templates, 95% of all interactions in the given scope can be represented. Instantiating a template creates an ensemble of actors and interactions that are necessary for a particular work step. For example, the unfastening of an engine part using a screwdriver would involve a representation of the physical engine part, a virtual screwdriver, and a motion animation specifying the direction in which to turn the screwdriver.

The Augmented Reality Presentation and Interaction Language (APRIL) is a system for creating complex nonlinear AR experiences on top of the Studierstube system [Ledermann and Schmalstieg 2005]. It expresses nonlinear stories as concurrent hierarchical state machines [Beckhaus et al. 2004]. This choice allows a generic UML state chart editor to be repurposed as an AR authoring tool (Figure 10.4). APRIL supports multiple stages populated by actors and supports multiple users. It also provides arbitrary interactions and hardware abstraction through the use of the OpenTracker [Reitmayr and Schmalstieg 2005] device library.

Mohr et al. [2015] present a system that automatically transfers printed technical documentation, such as manuals and handbooks, to three-dimensional AR (Figure 10.5). Their system identifies the forms of instructions most frequently found in printed documentation, such as image sequences for assembly or maintenance, explosion diagrams, textual annotations, and arrows indicating motion. The analysis of the printed documentation works automatically,

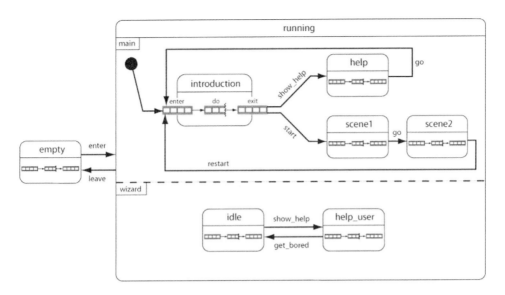

Figure 10.4   A UML state chart editor showing a part of an annotated state chart for an augmented reality tour using the APRIL framework. Courtesy of Florian Ledermann.

with minimal or no user input. The system requires only the documentation itself and a CAD model or 3D scan of the object described in the documentation. This makes the approach very practical for legacy objects, where only the object itself and the printed documentation exist. The output is a fully interactive AR application, presenting the information from the printed documentation in 3D, registered to the real object.

Authoring by Performance

If an AR interface is directly used to describe the content, we call the resulting solution authoring by *performance.*

The most obvious use of authoring by performance is to express animations involving real objects directly in the space in which they will be viewed later. 3D Puppetry [Held et al. 2012] is a prominent example. This system observes users playing with puppets and other objects, and captures the corresponding motions, which can be assembled into animation sequences. KinÊtre [Chen et al. 2012] takes a similar approach, but captures the motions of the users directly via skeleton tracking to transfer them to otherwise inanimate objects, such as a chair. The result looks similar to the animated household items from the Disney movie *Beauty and the Beast.*

Figure 10.5 A result of the retargeting of a printed instruction manual for a coffee maker to AR. (top) The avatar indicates which viewpoint the user should assume. (bottom) After the user moves to the indicated position, the door opens to reveal the brewing unit, shown in yellow. Courtesy of Peter Mohr.

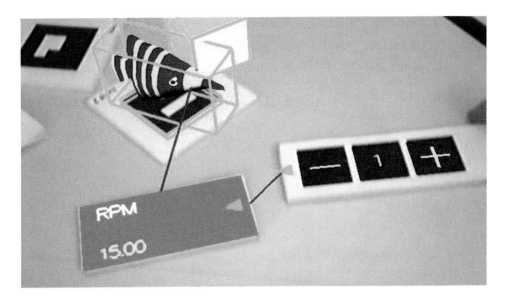

Figure 10.6   This sequence of screenshots from the framework for immersive authoring of tangible AR shows how to change the scale of a cube with an inspector widget and a keypad. Courtesy of Mark Billinghurst.

It is also possible to express application logic using immersive authoring. Lee et al. [2004] describe a tangible AR approach, which focuses on creating interactions between actors in the AR space in situ—that is, directly while immersed in the AR experience. To that aim, the system provides both *actor* markers and *tool* markers (Figure 10.6). The tool markers can be used to manipulate the content, such as to change scale and color. More complex behavior can be created by setting up a simple dataflow between properties of actors. For example, object visibility can be tied to the presence of a particular marker, to make objects appear based on the user's manipulation of that marker.

Plug-In Approaches

As AR is increasingly becoming a mainstream technology, experimental stand-alone authoring solutions, as presented in the last section, are being replaced by AR plug-ins for existing multimedia authoring and execution environments. Obviously, there is a large overlap between AR tools and general modeling tools (in particular, digital content creation tools and game engines). The maturity of existing modeling and animation software is a significant advantage that should not be overlooked. It can be leveraged by adding AR as a new target platform supported by the content creation software. This is relatively easy to achieve by using the built-in extension facilities that all of today's professional multimedia software packages have.

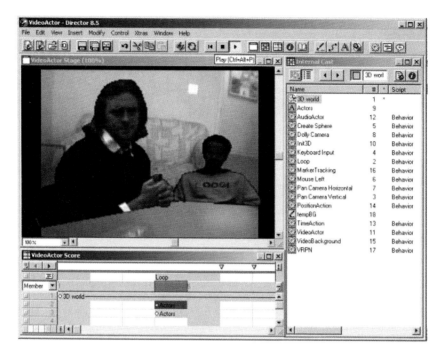

Figure 10.7   DART adds augmented reality authoring inside the Macromedia Director authoring environment. Courtesy of Blair Macintyre.

The trend-setter for the plug-in approach was the Designer's Augmented Reality Toolkit (DART) developed at Georgia Tech [MacIntyre et al. 2004b]: DART extends Macromedia Director, which was the premier authoring tool for multimedia applications in the early 2000s (Figure 10.7). DART allows designers who are already familiar with Director to quickly create compelling AR applications, often using sketches and videos, rather than 3D models, as a starting point. Macromedia Director provides nonlinear storytelling and a versatile scripting language, Lingo.

Macromedia Director's weak support for 3D graphics and the rise of competition in the form of web-based animation has led to the decline of the software platform, and with it, DART. Even so, the AR plug-in approach remains relevant [Gandy and MacIntyre 2014]. Prominent examples include the plug-ins for 3DS Max, Maya, and Google Sketchup [Terenzi and Terenzi 2011], and solutions that use the popular Unity3D game engine as a foundation, such as Qualcomm Vuforia,[2] Metaio Mobile SDK,[3] and TotalImmersion D'Fusion. Moreover, many noncommercial extensions are available for other multimedia tools such as Flash (e.g., FLARToolKit) and Processing.

---

2. Acquired by PTC in 2015.
3. Acquired by Apple in 2015.

Web Technology

In today's information systems, web technology has emerged as a leading vehicle to produce and consume multimedia information. The web has brought about a rich software environment of browsers, server frameworks, and content creation tools. Because of its dominance, web content is considered increasingly attractive to developers of AR browsers and AR tools, as it seems plausible that a lot of the work done on conventional web technologies might be leveraged and repurposed for AR.

Specifically, the most recent web standard HTML5 and its associated family of technologies are rapidly evolving toward a versatile application platform that addresses the fundamental needs of AR. Web technology promises to deliver AR experiences as part of an existing and widely available application framework, thereby achieving a good degree of platform independence. Placemarks known from the KML format popularized by Google Earth allow convenient storing of geo-referenced interest points. Cascading style sheets (CSS) can be used to separate content from appearance, and to provide custom control for the experience. CSS3 is already considering layout in three dimensions, which is a necessary prerequisite for effective AR layout. WebGL allows hardware-accelerated rendering of 3D graphics inside a web browser.

All of this is tied together by JavaScript, which has established itself as the ubiquitous programming language for web applications. Wrapping an AR framework with a JavaScript interface enables rapid AR development for web browsers. A large number of people have already been trained in web development, so adopting standard web formats for AR allows for drawing upon these existing skills in recruiting AR developers and content providers.

One of the most appealing properties of the web is that it decouples producers and consumers of multimedia information. Anybody can publish on a website, in a blog, on a Twitter account, or to an RSS feed without having to go through a central authority first. Users can subscribe to any number of these sources at their own discretion, and can combine the resulting information collection in an arbitrary way. In other words, users have access to a huge number of information **channels**. This idea of channels is important for scalable AR browsing, where users also subscribe to a number of AR channels providing placemarks and other AR content. The channel mechanism essentially provides a semantic filter, while proximity to the user's current location is used as a spatial filter. Together, the semantic and spatial filters can provide an efficient and effective way of managing information overload.

By using technologies such as client-side scripting, the distinction between "passive" content and "active" applications becomes blurred. Today, web development toolkits provide full control over the look and feel of the application. Various architectures for web applications are commonplace, including mobile code, which is executed at the client side. Application frameworks such as AJAX let part of the application code live on the client and part live on a server.

Figure 10.8   The Argon browser displays multiple channels of content defined through web technologies. Courtesy of Blair Macintyre.

An AR channel architecture must allow full control over the appearance of the content, even if it is displayed in parallel with other content. This can be done by rendering the content of each channel individually and then compositing the output. This approach does have a disadvantage: Multiple channels may compete for screen space or produce a cluttered display. Suitable strategies for view management that resolve such competition remain an open research topic.

The idea of web channels for AR was introduced with the Argon browser [MacIntyre et al. 2011]. It builds on a standard web browser engine (WebKit) to deliver rendering of HTML and KML content inside an AR display (Figure 10.8). Argon has significantly influenced the creation of the Augmented Reality Modeling Language (ARML), an XML dialect for web-based AR content [MacIntyre et al. 2013].

Summary

A new medium such as AR requires effort beyond overcoming technical difficulties before it is truly understood and becomes firmly established. One such effort is identifying and addressing the requirements that make AR unique and that must be addressed to make an AR-specific authoring solution successful. We have identified real-world interfaces, hardware abstraction, and authoring workflow tools as the most important requirements.

Beyond the basic requirements and the resulting technical questions, we have also looked at two recent trends in AR authoring—namely, solutions that introduce AR as a plug-in to existing multimedia and game engines, and solutions that leverage web technologies for AR. The richness of the features that these recent solutions inherit from their host environments may become an essential chance for AR authoring to succeed in a large community.

CHAPTER 11

NAVIGATION

AR navigation can enhance exploration of the real world, facilitate wayfinding, and support viewpoint control during the execution of real-world tasks. With its emphasis on a first-person viewpoint, AR can embed navigation support directly into a user's activities. However, designing augmentations so that they are truly supportive requires careful consideration. In this chapter, we discuss how AR can support exploration and discovery, visualize routes, and guide viewpoint adjustments. We also consider interfaces that combine multiple perspectives to provide overview and detail or transport a user to physically unreachable viewpoints.

Foundations of Human Navigation

Navigation—that is, moving in one's environment—encompasses **travel**, **wayfinding**, and **exploration**. Travel is the motor activity necessary to control one's position and orientation. Wayfinding is the higher-level cognition of a user, such as understanding one's current location, planning a path to another location, and updating a mental map of the environment. Exploration is concerned with understanding and surveying an unknown environment and its artifacts.

Wayfinding and exploration require acquiring *spatial knowledge* and structuring it into a mental map [Bowman et al. 2005] [Grasset et al. 2011]. Spatial knowledge can be acquired from various sources. Darken and Peterson [2001] distinguish between primary and secondary sources. The environment itself is the primary source: Humans continuously extract spatial information from their observations of the environment. All other sources, such as maps, pictures, and videos, are secondary sources. Secondary sources allow faster accumulation of spatial knowledge, but abstract representations can usually not match first-person experiences in terms of the accuracy of the mental map.

We organize spatial knowledge into the following categories [Lynch and Lynch 1960] [Siegel and White 1975]:

- **Landmarks** are prominent reference points in the environment, which are used by humans as hints on the environment's structure and the person's own location. Landmarks are remembered by their visual appearance, so it is important that they are unique and not easily confused. The most important landmarks are objects that can be seen from afar, but small local details can also serve as landmarks. Both view-dependent and view-independent landmarks are possible.

- **Routes** are sequences of actions needed to navigate from a given start point to a given end point. For every waypoint in between, the distance, the turns, and the ordering of landmarks are memorized. Other elements of the environment are often associated with a certain waypoint or segment of the route.

- **Nodes** are decision-making points, where users can choose among paths. Route planning and wayfinding decisions are usually made in relation to nodes.

- **Districts** are larger areas in the environment, such as parks or shopping boulevards.

- **Edges** partition the environment. For example, a road or a river requires special means or locations for crossing. What constitutes an edge depends on the context. For example, a pedestrian will classify a street as an edge, whereas a driver will classify a street as a route.

- **Survey knowledge** primarily consists of global spatial relationships between landmarks and routes. It develops over time, usually after repeated navigation in the environment or through secondary sources.

During navigational tasks, a user applies the various types of spatial knowledge depending on different frames of reference [Goldin and Thorndyke 1981]. **Ego-centric** tasks, such as estimating the orientation and distance to one's own body, require route knowledge. **Exo-centric** tasks, such as estimating distances between two faraway points in the environment, benefit from survey knowledge.

Because the available knowledge will vary, the key to successful navigation lies in resolving the transformation between the frame of reference for the spatial knowledge and the frame of reference for the task to be performed. The smaller the distance between the two frames of reference, the lower the burden on the user who must mentally transition between the two.

Exploration and Discovery

Fortunately, AR can provide navigation support in all reference frames. The most obvious use case is ego-centric exploration. Dynamic annotations displayed with an AR browser guide the user toward points of interest in the environment. The user can express personal preferences to inform the interest point selection.

The advantage of AR for exploration is twofold: (1) The user can perform the exploration faster, and (2) chances of identifying all relevant information are increased. The latter goal, which is sometimes referred to as **situation awareness**, is especially relevant in critical situations, such as search-and-rescue or military operations. In these cases, operators must continuously pay attention to their 3D environment without being distracted by operating an information device. A good example is the Battlefield Augmented Reality System developed by Julier et al. [2000], which provides information about the location of relevant elements (e.g., cars, tanks, or snipers). The location of these elements can change dynamically, so keeping the information in sight has significant advantages concerning awareness.

Exploration becomes *discovery* when the target object is not visible from the current point of view, at least not without moving a significant distance. We discussed visualization techniques aiding discovery in Chapter 7. Two important approaches to modify the user's view of the environment are X-ray visualization and scene deformation. X-ray visualization renders a part of the visible environment in a partially or fully transparent way to reveal hidden objects [Feiner and Seligmann 1992] [Avery et al. 2009] [Zollmann et al. 2010]. Deformations bend the environment to bring occluded [Veas et al. 2012b] or off-screen [Sandor et al. 2010b] parts into view or compress foreground objects to reveal occluded objects.

Route Visualization

Like exploration, wayfinding is an important navigation activity primarily performed in an ego-centric reference frame. A typical approach to support wayfinding in AR is to show a path as a continuous curve or a sequence of waypoints. The difference to conventional systems, such as in-car navigation, is that the path can be overlaid directly on top of the user's perception of the real environment. For example, Tinmith [Thomas et al. 1998] shows a waypoint sequence, with dynamic highlighting of the next waypoint as the user progresses. Signpost [Reitmayr and Schmalstieg 2004] lets the user choose a destination and dynamically shows a path visualization (Figure 11.1). The destination can also be another user, who can be followed or met halfway.

Wagner and Schmalstieg [2003] developed a successor, Indoor Signpost, for handheld devices. Their handheld interface points out doorways and superimposes an arrow pointing in the direction the user is supposed to go next (Figure 11.2).

Figure 11.1   The Signpost system lets an outdoor AR user follow a route consisting of waypoints (red cylinders). Courtesy of Gerhard Reitmayr.

Figure 11.2   The Indoor Signpost system highlights the next doorway along a path and shows a 3D arrow pointing in the direction of the final destination. Courtesy of Daniel Wagner.

Mulloni and Schmalstieg [2012] conducted a study comparing the use of AR and the use of a map for outdoor navigation. They found that users consulted an AR view mostly at the nodes of the route (i.e., for support at decision points), whereas they used the map continuously (Figure 11.3). This result suggests that navigation support is sufficient when a decision needs to be made, and that AR can provide an effective interface for this goal.

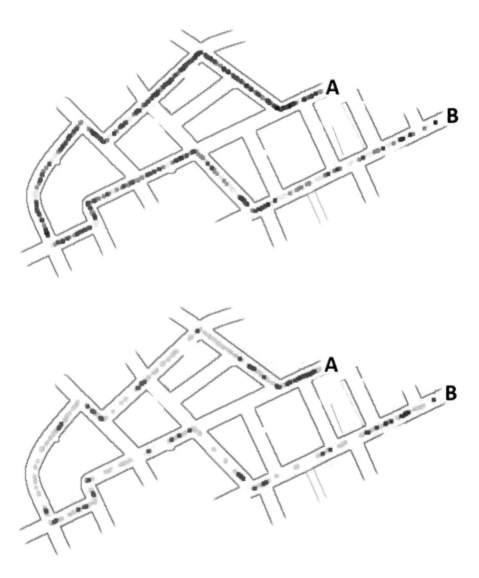

Figure 11.3 The plots show the number of users employing the navigation interface for every point along a route. Darker colors mean that more users were engaged with the interface. (top) With a conventional map interface, the usage is uniformly high along the entire path. (bottom) The AR interface was mostly used at nodes, when a decision needed to be made. Courtesy of Alessandro Mulloni.

Figure 11.4   (left) While the user walks, the route is visualized in VR. (middle) Once the user reaches a decision node, the whole path is shown aligned with the environment in AR. (right) After departing from the node, the display switches back to VR. Courtesy of Alessandro Mulloni.

A similar approach was taken for indoor navigation [Mulloni et al. 2012], a situation in which it is difficult to provide continuous localization. AR navigation at decision nodes, such as at crossings of hallways or at staircases, provides an effective tool for indoor navigation as well, if it is combined with route visualization in AR between nodes (Figure 11.4).

Viewpoint Guidance

While it might appear that, in small workspaces, a human easily obtains an overview of the environment and does not require any guidance, there are frequently occurring situations where AR can be beneficial. A target object may be outside the user's field of view, or it may be difficult to spot among many similar objects. Even more difficult than the problem of finding a target object may be the problem of finding a target viewpoint—for example, the viewpoint from which a particular photograph was taken [Bae et al. 2010]. In this section, we discuss both tasks: guiding a user toward a target object and guiding a user toward a target viewpoint.

Guidance Toward a Target Object

Target objects or waypoints that are out of sight are a frequently encountered problem in AR, especially given that many AR displays are plagued by a narrow field of view. In such cases, guidance is often provided by arrows or glyphs. These can take the form of a compass needle pointing the user in the right direction [Feiner et al. 1997] [Wagner and Schmalstieg 2003] or arrows near the border of the screen [Thomas et al. 1998]. Schinke et al. [2010] show that 3D arrows hinting at off-screen annotations are more effective for memorizing directions of target objects than 2D (top-down) radar maps.

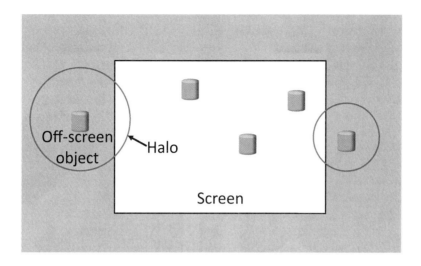

Figure 11.5   A halo is an arc with a curvature proportional to the distance of an object outside the screen.

Some more-advanced visual designs inform the user not only about the direction, but also about the distance and frequency of target objects. Halos [Baudisch and Rosenholtz 2003] are circles centered on the off-screen target object, with a radius such that the circle partially appears on the screen (Figure 11.5). The curvature of the visible arc can be intuitively related to the distance to the object.

The Context Compass [Suomela and Lehikoinen 2000] uses a narrow band across the top or bottom of the screen to display a vertically condensed cylindrical projection map of a target object covering a certain horizontal field of view (e.g., 110°) ahead. When a full 360° are displayed, this application is essentially a radar map with polar coordinates mapped cylindrically (Figure 11.6). The orientation always remains aligned with the display orientation, which means that visible objects appear in the center of the map. Elements that are not in the user's current field of view are indicated with icons on the sides of the overlay.

If the goal is not just general awareness of peripheral or out-of-sight objects, but the user should be guided toward a target object as fast as possible, then more screen real estate might deservedly be devoted to the guidance. A popular metaphor for informing and constraining the user's navigation is a **tunnel** (Figure 11.7). The outlines of a tunnel-like structure are displayed as a three-dimensional wireframe overlay. The perspective foreshortening of the structures conveys the path that the user must take without occupying too many pixels. As the user navigates through the tunnel, the portions already traversed disappear behind the user, while the details of the part ahead become more prominent. Biocca et al. [2006] introduced this design as the *attention funnel*, and empirically verified that it is more effective than visual

Figure 11.6   A context compass is a band at the bottom of the screen representing the possible directions. (left) An arrow overlay is visible. (right) The user can use the compass context to find the off-screen arrow. Courtesy of Alessandro Mulloni.

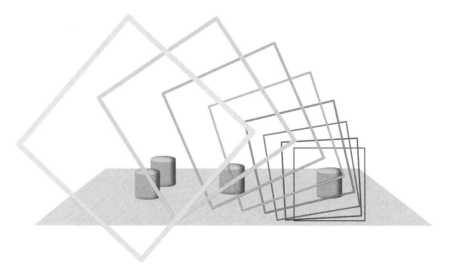

Figure 11.7   A tunnel visualization directs a user's attention toward a specific object at the tunnel's end.

highlighting of the target object. A user study showed that this visualization increases search speed, while decreasing cognitive effort. Schwerdtfeger and Klinker [2008] tested a modified tunnel design in a warehouse scenario for order picking and showed that it can improve performance in real-world tasks.

Shingu et al. [2010] discuss a conical tunnel for guiding the user toward a target point. The user must enter the cone and orient the camera such that a sphere centered on the target point is visible on the screen.

Hartl et al. [2014] discuss a system for verifying the authenticity of holograms on security documents, such as passports, with a mobile device. A specimen is tested by comparing observations with known views from the genuine hologram. To provide the observations, the user must point the camera toward the specimen from a set of given directions. Hartl et al. propose use of a "pie slice" interface, where directions are shown as a grid in polar coordinates superimposed in the plane of the specimen, with the target directions being highlighted (Figure 11.8). The pie slices can be seen as a minimalist version of a tunnel visualization, where only 2D endpoints are shown.

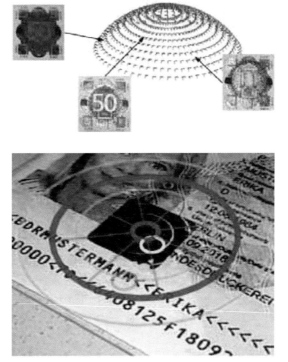

Figure 11.8 (top) The appearance of a hologram varies with the incident viewing direction. (bottom) The yellow circle directs the user toward a specific viewing direction, encoded as the angle and distance to the center of the pie slice visualization. Courtesy of Andreas Hartl.

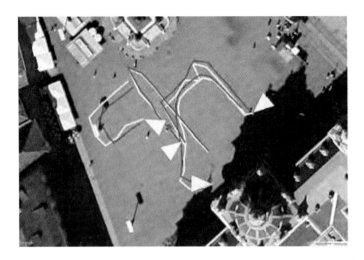

Figure 11.9 Yellow pyramid icons reveal the camera frusta corresponding to a sequence of images. Courtesy of Clemens Arth.

Sukan et al. [2014] observe that unless a target object is very small, there are usually many possibilities for observing it. Consequently, they propose the ParaFrustum, a generalized tunnel design that connects arbitrary look-from and look-at volumes for guiding the user to an acceptable view.

Guidance Toward a Target Viewpoint

Unlike guidance toward a target object, which is usually recognized once it is visible and the user's attention is drawn to it, a viewpoint does not have any physical appearance. Guiding a user toward a specific viewpoint can still be important—for example, to replicate photography when a contemporary update of a historic photograph is desired.

The most direct visualization of a desired viewpoint is a pyramid-shaped viewing frustum (Figure 11.9). This application has been proposed by Snavely et al. [2006] for navigating photo collections and by Sun et al. [2013] for accurate alignment of an ultrasonic probe.

Bae et al. [2010] suggest an indirect approach using directional arrows, similar to the ones used to point to off-screen targets, to let a user approach a desired viewpoint. When close enough to the target viewpoint, the user relies on a transparent rendering of the original photograph for precise alignment.

Multiple Perspectives

Overview and survey knowledge typically relies on an exo-centric perspective, such as that used by a map. As discussed in Chapter 8, ego-centric and exo-centric perspectives can be combined into a multi-view interface. In principle, consulting a map while immersed in an environment is an instance of such a combination. Digital maps are ubiquitously available on mobile devices and can be updated as the user is moving: Consider a car navigation system that shows a map of the user's vicinity aligned with the current orientation of the vehicle.

Simultaneous Multiple Perspectives

An ego-centric AR view can easily be combined with an exo-centric view, either by dedicating a portion of the screen to the exo-centric view or by overlaying the exo-centric view transparently over the ego-centric view (Figure 11.10). The latter approach exploits the fact that map information can often be rendered using just building footprints, interest points, and sparse textual labels. Transparent overlays can save screen space on displays with a narrow field of view.

Additional benefits are realized by linking the augmentations in the ego-centric and exo-centric views. Selection in one view leads to highlighting in the other view. The current position of the user is highlighted in the exo-centric view. The distance to an interest point in the map can be estimated [Wither and Höllerer 2005] by first identifying an interest point in the ego-centric view, then determining the distance from the user's location to the interest point in the exo-centric view (Figure 11.11). Route navigation can be conveniently planned by pointing out the destination in the exo-centric view, if it is not visible in the ego-centric view.

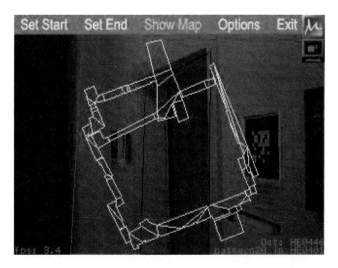

Figure 11.10   Overlaying a transparent layer combines two visualizations in one image: 3D AR overlaid on the video and a 2D map. Courtesy of Daniel Wagner.

Figure 11.11 With a top-down map, users can precisely determine the distance to various palm trees, also encoded in this experiment as the sizes of the virtual spheres in the ego-centric AR scene. Courtesy of Jason Wither.

Bell et al. [2002] propose an AR world-in-miniature (WIM), a 3D map that tilts toward a user wearing an HMD. As the user increasingly looks downward, the WIM rotates from a slightly tilted position to a straight top-down view. Reitmayr and Schmalstieg [2003] place a WIM in the user's hand (Figure 11.12), so that the user can access the WIM instantly, just by lifting the arm.

The X-ray visualization system of Bane and Höllerer [2004] allows the user to explore rooms in a building from a distance. The user first selects the target room and then triggers the display of an exo-centric virtual view of the selected room (Figure 11.13), called *Room in Miniature*.

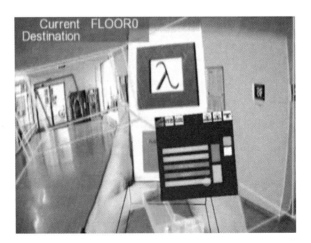

Figure 11.12 A world-in-miniature can be attached to a handheld or arm-mounted prop. Courtesy of Gerhard Reitmayr.

Figure 11.13   A remote maintenance scenario. (left) The user selects a room in a building in an ego-centric perspective. (right) The room is magnified and shown in an exo-centric perspective under the user's navigational control. The orange heat map depicts a temperature distribution.

Rather than showing an exo-centric view overlaid on an ego-centric view, Hoang and Thomas [2010] propose the opposite approach: They embed a zoomed-in view of a distant object detail into the normal ego-centric view. The zoomed view is obtained in real time using a camera with magnification lens. In contrast to a map or WIM, the overlay provides the detail, while the standard view provides the overview.

Transitional Interfaces

If insufficient screen real estate is available for showing multiple views, a **transitional interface** can be used. It relies on temporal—rather than spatial—separation to present multiple perspectives.

The term "transitional interface" was originally coined to describe interfaces that transport a user from an exo-centric AR view to an ego-centric VR view, essentially moving the user along the virtuality continuum (Figure 11.14). For example, Billinghurst et al. [2001] describe a system for transporting a user into the pages of a magic book as a narrative vehicle. Höllerer et al. [1999a] let a user transition into a surround-view immersive experience of a tunnel system underneath the user's physical location as part of an AR tour of a university campus' history.

Kiyokawa et al. [1999] let a user experience an architectural design from an ego-centric perspective after it has been created in an exo-centric view. In contrast, Mulloni et al. [2010] look at a transitional interface designed for providing an overview by moving from an ego-centric AR view to an exo-centric map view (Figure 11.15). The transition is achieved by smoothly moving between the viewpoint of the camera to a top-down viewpoint. The researchers evaluated their interface on a set of spatial search tasks and report that task performance of the transitional interface improves with increasing task complexity when the user strongly relies on overview.

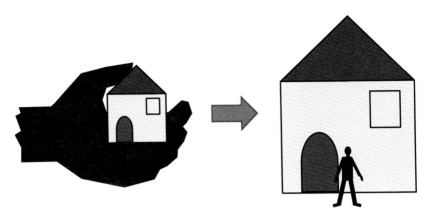

Figure 11.14   A transitional interface can take a user from an AR model into a life-size VR environment.

A similar effect can be overserved when transitioning to a panorama view, essentially simulating an ultra-wide-angle lens.

An alternative WIM representation can transition between ego-centric and exo-centric visualizations based on changes in the tracking quality. High quality tracking affords annotations and route information to be overlaid directly in the ego-centric view, while degraded tracking quality prompts the use of a WIM, which is displayed in a body-referenced coordinate system and therefore not affected by the lack of stable tracking [Höllerer et al. 2001b] [Bell et al. 2002].

Transitional interfaces are also useful if the user should experience a different ego-centric viewpoint—for example, a viewpoint that is difficult or inconvenient to reach. Sukan et al. [2012]

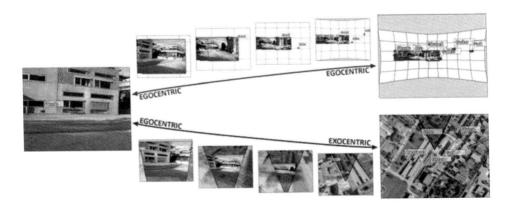

Figure 11.15   A zooming interface lets users seamlessly transition from an AR ego-perspective view to a panoramic view of the surroundings or to a map overview. Courtesy of Alessandro Mulloni.

propose a snapshot approach, in which the user first obtains static snapshot views of an environment in an AR mode and can then transition arbitrarily between those views in a VR mode.

Tatzgern et al. [2014a] propose an improved method for displaying the actual transitions. After obtaining a 3D scan of a static environment, the user can fly into the scene from a live AR view into an arbitrary VR view (Figure 11.16). This allows simple exploration of zoomed views (after they have been scanned with high resolution) or moving to occluded areas. For example, touching an object on the screen transports the user closer to this object until it fills the screen, and smoothly back after the user releases the touch screen.

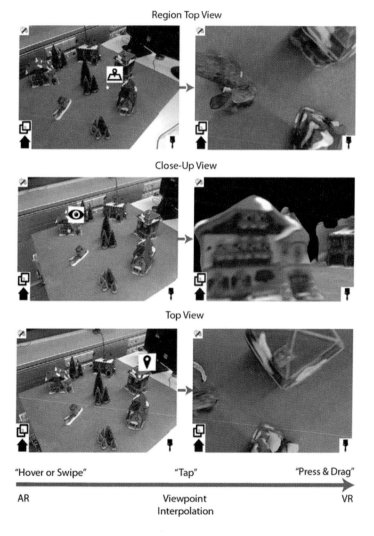

Figure 11.16   By touching an object in the live AR view (left), the user can trigger a transition to a magnified VR view from a top-down or frontal viewpoint. Courtesy of Markus Tatzgern.

Summary

Based on fundamental considerations of human navigation, we have discussed navigation using AR. Exploration can benefit from AR via increased situation awareness and discovery of hidden targets. Wayfinding can be supported by directly superimposing routes in an ego-centric AR view or by helping users at decision points. AR can also be used to supply various cues to let the user adjust a viewpoint so that a target object is observed or that a certain given view is obtained. Multiple perspective interfaces can provide overview and detail, either by spatial combination in a split screen or layered screen, or by transitioning from one view to the next.

CHAPTER 12

COLLABORATION

One of the greatest potential opportunities for AR is its use as a medium for communication. Collaborative AR enables multiple users to simultaneously experience an augmented environment. Indeed, AR offers unique opportunities for collaboration: In co-located situations, where multiple users are simultaneously present at the same location, AR can provide additional information concerning real-world artifacts that the users are discussing. For remote collaboration, which connects users who cannot be in the same location, AR can be used to communicate to one user information that another user wishes to share, without disrupting the first user's experience of the real environment.

Both categories of sharing have significant potential for enhancing collaboration [Lukosch et al. 2015]. In this chapter, we take a closer look at technologies and design strategies for using AR as a collaboration technology. We describe properties of collaborative AR systems, paying attention to physical and technical aspects as well as the relevant human factors. Based on these considerations, we describe approaches for co-located collaboration and for remote collaboration.

Properties of Collaboration Systems

Computer-supported cooperative work (CSCW) is not limited to AR, but can rely on any form of computer-based medium. A widely accepted categorization of CSCW uses a 2×2 classification, discriminating, on the one hand, the *temporal* aspects of collaboration and, on the other hand, the *spatial* aspects of collaboration [Rodden 1992]. In the temporal dimension, collaboration can involve multiple users *synchronously* (at the same time) or *asynchronously* (at different times and, therefore, independently of each other). In the spatial dimension, users can either be *co-located* (in the same place) or *remote* (in different places). Together, these 2×2 possibilities cover many possible forms of collaboration (Table 12.1).

Augmented reality is an interactive medium, so it is logical to primarily use it for synchronous collaboration, that is, enhancing the way collaborators can interact at the same time. An **AR shared space** enhances co-located collaboration: The collaborators meet in the same space, which is enhanced with spatially registered information via an AR display. In contrast, **AR telepresence** lets a user experience a live remote location.

Asynchronous AR is less frequently utilized. The most important use case in this category is the annotation of a physical environment by one user and later in situ browsing or editing of the annotations by another user. You might think of this application as a sort of virtual graffiti. The annotation activities happen in the same place (i.e., co-located), but do not happen at the same time. Asynchronous *remote* sharing of AR content is quite possible, but not specific to AR. Such an approach could be used for any kind of application where the content is of interest to more than one user and messages or notifications are being sent asynchronously.

In synchronous collaborative activities, we can distinguish between **communication space** and **task space** [Kiyokawa et al. 2002]:

Table 12.1 Categorization of Computer-Supported Cooperative Work in Relation to AR

	Co-located	Remote
Synchronous	AR shared space	AR telepresence
Asynchronous	AR annotating/browsing (in-situ)	Generic sharing

- The *communication space* is the space in which users exchange information. Communication demands that users can see and hear each other well. Normally, people engaged in a conversation look at each other's faces and observe each other's body language. Co-located situations usually do not require technical support for the communication space. In contrast, bridging the communication space of remote collaborators is the primary goal of all telecommunication systems.

- The *task space* is the space where the actual work is carried out. A real task space involves physical objects, while a virtual task space involves digital information (both 3D and non-3D).

The more strongly separated the communication and task spaces are, the more difficult it can become to alternate between communicating and performing a task [Ishii et al. 1994]. For example, consider two users sharing an office, with personal desktop computer screens facing in opposite directions. The co-workers must alternate between talking to each other and looking at their respective personal screens (which cannot be observed directly by the other user). Despite being co-present, they have only indirect means to refer to a joint task, unless they come together in front of one display. The lack of a **unified task and communication space** can be overcome with nontechnical means (e.g., huddling around one display) or technical means (e.g., desktop collaboration software) in co-located scenarios, but *must* be addressed with technical means in remote scenarios. If the two co-workers from this example work in different office buildings, they must rely, for instance, on a phone. These considerations suggest a number of scenarios for collaboration (Table 12.2).

AR shows its strength in unified space scenarios with "mixed" characteristics: A shared space combines a local (hence, *real*) communication space with a virtual task. A telepresence system combines a remote (hence, *virtual*) communication space with a real task.

Table 12.2 Classifying Communication and Task Space for Collaboration

Communication Space	Task Space	Unified Spaces	Example
Co-located	Real	No	Classroom lecturing
Co-located	Virtual	No	Joint work on one desktop computer
Remote	Real	No	Video conference
Remote	Virtual	No	Video conference with desktop sharing
Co-located	Real	Yes	Playing a real game of chess
Co-located	Virtual	Yes	**Shared space**
Remote	Real	Yes	**Telepresence**
Remote	Virtual	Yes	Immersive telepresence, online game

Co-located Collaboration

In a *shared space*, virtual augmentations can be arranged in between co-located users [Butz et al. 1999] [Benko et al. 2014]. If physical artifacts are present in the shared space, AR enables collaborators to annotate these artifacts with additional virtual information, which can be manipulated by either user. If purely virtual objects are present, users can still perceive them in the same location. For example, the simple conversational behavior of pointing to a particular object in the environment works both for real objects and for virtual objects.

We can distinguish collaborative applications by how they make use of the shared space. There are roughly three spatial categories. Fist, users can remain (relatively) stationary. Second, users can be mobile, but in just one confined location. Third, users may explore a larger area.

The primary advantage of applications that let users remain stationary is that tracking can be confined to a small working volume. Moreover, it is easy to keep the collaboration partner in view. Several applications for collaborative inspection of three-dimensional data have already been developed that use a simple stationary setup. The utility of these systems comes from the fact that virtual models can be viewed and discussed together.

Fuhrmann et al. [1998] describe a system for exploring three-dimensional surfaces that represent complex dynamic systems (Figure 12.1). They observe that compared to screen-based presentation, users are more engaged in understanding the three-dimensional structures.

Kato et al. [2000] describe an AR game of memory. Upon uncovering a game card with a marker on it, a 3D model is displayed. When placing two matching cards in close proximity, a special animation signals to the users that these cards form a pair (Figure 12.2). The marker recognition

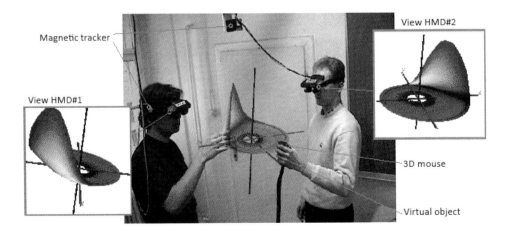

Figure 12.1   A shared space setup enables users wearing HMDs to establish an individual view on virtual objects, as with the mathematical visualization shown in the image. Courtesy of Anton Fuhrmann.

Figure 12.2 Users with HMDs playing a collaborative game of memory. Courtesy of Mark Billinghurst.

is executed independently for each user. Because the matching cards are predetermined, the triggering of the special animation is deterministic. In other words, no networking connection between the users' systems is necessary for collaborative play.

Kaufmann and Schmalstieg [2003] describe Construct3D, a 3D geometric construction tool specifically designed for mathematics and geometry education (Figure 12.3). The main goal is to develop a system for the improvement of spatial abilities and maximization of transfer of learning. With the AR system, students can actually walk around three-dimensional objects, which they previously had to calculate and construct with traditional (mostly, pen-and-paper) methods.

Teachers and students can assume different roles with Construct3D, supported by the system's capability to present private views. For example, the system can reveal a precomputed solution

Figure 12.3 Geometry education can benefit from being able to explore the geometric constructs in three dimensions. In this image, two students are trying to solve a problem involving tangential planes. Courtesy of Hannes Kaufmann.

to an exercise to the teacher, which students cannot see. The students can see only the initial description of the exercise and their own personal work (but not the work of other students).

Several systems let users wear HMDs while discussing a design review at a meeting table. For example, EMMIE [Butz et al. 1999], SeamlessDesign [Kiyokawa et al. 1999], MagicMeeting [Regenbrecht et al. 2002], and ARTHUR [Broll et al. 2004] all enable users to inspect architectural or mechanical models.

A more recent example, Mano-a-Mano [Benko et al. 2014], establishes a face-to-face device-less interaction for users freely moving in a room via dynamic spatial projection based on multiple projector–camera systems (with Kinect depth cameras). Perspectively correct three-dimensional augmentations are rendered in between the collaborating users.

Individual Displays and Views

In real-world tasks, collaboration is not a uniform activity, in which participants are continuously working together in close interaction. Instead, periods of individual work alternate with periods where results are shared and discussed [Gutwin and Greenberg 2000]. Thus, it is necessary that a collaborative environment support both individual and group work, requiring displays and views to address individual needs.

Personal displays not only afford an individual viewpoint per-user, but also let some users see an object or a piece of information that remains hidden from other users. Using an HMD as a personal viewing device enables users to assume an individual stereoscopic viewpoint on virtual objects. This capability is particularly beneficial when the geometric shape and arrangement of objects play roles in the scenario. Virtual objects can appear in arbitrary locations, such as in the air or on a table surface between meeting participants, thereby supporting a conveniently shaped task space.

Like an HMD, a handheld display is a personal viewing device. In principle, a handheld device can be viewed by multiple users simultaneously, which makes it somewhat less private than an HMD. Early work by Rekimoto [1996] demonstrated the collaborative use of handheld AR by means of tethered but mobile computer monitors with attached cameras. A small screen does not lend itself well to simultaneous viewing; moreover, given the availability of personal devices, users prefer to look on their own screen rather than sharing a screen [Morrison et al. 2011]. Fortunately, handheld devices such as smartphones are inexpensive, and supplying personal devices to every person in a group is an economically viable option.

As an alternative, large-format screens or projected displays are popular means of presenting virtual objects. Such a collaborative VR display can be seen as a restricted AR display, in which the real world (the occasional view onto the collaborators) is supplemented by the virtual content presented on the VR display. Stereo displays seen through lightweight shutter glasses afford some degree of mutual gaze awareness and eye contact. These displays cannot produce occlusions of real objects by virtual objects, however, and conventional stereo displays cannot present correct stereo images to more than one user. Presenting view-dependent stereo images to more than one tracked user requires special displays that are capable of multiplexing among multiple users, either in the time domain [Agrawala et al. 1997] or in the spatial domain [Kitamura et al. 2001] [Bimber et al. 2005] [Ye et al. 2010]. Group sizes for these displays are typically limited to four (or fewer) users, although recent advances combining time- and polarization-based multiplexing can accommodate six users [Kulik et al. 2011].

Multiple display types can be combined. For instance, the Visual Interaction Tool for Archeology (VITA) [Benko et al. 2004] is a system for letting a group of users explore data recorded from an archeological excavation. VITA can present an overview of the excavation site on a projected display, while an immersive HMD representation casts another user in the middle of the archeological site. AR can establish connections between different displays by allowing objects to be visualized while they are dragged out from or dropped on to physical displays of different types and sizes [Butz et al. 1999] [Rekimoto and Saitoh 1999]. When projectors are used to display information onto the physical world [Raskar et al. 2001] [Piper et al. 2002], the information display is confined to a physical surface, which limits the kind of AR content that can be shown. By comparison, view-dependent rendering for a head-tracked user can produce realistic 3D imagery that appears to exist away from surfaces [Jones et al. 2014].

Another collaborative experience using multiple display types is the magic book [Billinghurst et al. 2001], an interface that enables users to observe augmented book pages decorated with fiducial markers in the style of a pop-up book. The magic book uses HMDs as viewing devices, and the book can be observed by multiple users. The special feature of the magic book is that users can choose to fly into the book, changing their view from AR to immersive VR. One user can fly into the book, assuming an ego-centric viewpoint, while the other remains outside, assuming an exo-centric viewpoint. Users can see each other represented by avatars—a large head in the sky for the VR user and a doll-size avatar in the magic book for the AR user.

Sometimes it is desirable to afford users some degree of privacy. Users may be interested in hiding personal information, for example, or they may not wish to share unfinished work. If a physical display is shared by multiple users, hiding objects from other users is not possible. As a workaround, the display space can be subdivided into multiple areas—a public area, where collaborative viewing takes place, and private areas, which are intended only for individual users. In this case, social discretion is necessary to avoid getting in other users' way.

A better approach may be to let users explicitly make information public or retract it later. Butz et al. [1998] show how per-user displays can be configured to inspect and manipulate the privacy status of objects in a shared space (Figure 12.4). A **vampire mirror**, for example, reflects only objects that are publicly visible. A **privacy lamp** can be placed over a group of objects, with all objects illuminated by the lamp being hidden from public view.

Figure 12.4   A vampire mirror with selected objects (notepad and video tape icons) made private. Courtesy of Andreas Butz and Columbia University.

Gaze Awareness

One important limitation of using HMDs in collaborative applications is how well other users can be perceived. The visual quality of the real environment in a video see-through HMD is by no means equivalent to a user's direct perception of the real world. Consequently, users have a strongly diminished experience of other humans in the environment, which can, to some degree, affect communication. Moreover, direct gaze contact is precluded by the HMD's visor. In contrast, optical see-through HMDs provide a normal perception of the real world and some amount of eye contact, but usually render virtual objects semi-transparently and with poor contrast.

Several attempts have been made to recover gaze awareness for users wearing HMDs. In Miyasato's [1998] work on the eye-through HMD, a user's eyes are observed by inward-facing cameras inside the HMD and presented on small screens mounted to the front of the HMD. Takemura and Ohta [2002] present a rendering of the user's face overlaid onto the HMD as a vir-tual object. Tateno et al. [2005] enhance the communication of gaze by rendering stylized eyes.

In addition to direct reconstruction of gaze, it is possible to add synthetic cues concerning the gaze direction. A simple approach presented by Kiyokawa et al. [1998] is to render a line from the user's eye in the viewing direction. Given this explicit representation of the viewing direc-tion, the user need not look at the collaborator's face. Other potential representations include a cone or viewing frustum [Mogilev et al. 2002]. The use of an eye tracker makes it possible to further refine the estimate of the viewing direction [Novak et al. 2004].

Agile Collaboration in Shared Space

With a carefully optimized implementation, shared-space experiences can be realized that rely on relatively fast user motion in a small area. This advantage becomes most evident in games.

An early example was AR²Hockey [Ohshima et al. 1998], a two-user game of air hockey played on a real table, but with a virtual puck. Szalavári and colleagues [1998] presented a collaborative shared-space AR environment with tracked HMDs and handheld props. RV Border Guards [Ohshima et al. 1999] casts the user in the role of a space-age soldier fighting off aliens with a laser gun. Henrysson et al. [2005] describe an AR table tennis game played by two users with smartphones, with a fiducial marker on the table between them. In this application, the smartphone simultaneously acts as viewing device and tennis racket.

The Invisible Train [Pintaric et al. 2005] was the first collaborative AR game to be deployed on untethered handheld computers. In this game, users control multiple virtual toy trains driving on a network of wooden railway tracks (see Figure 1.11 in Chapter 1). The objective is to switch junctions in time to prevent train crashes (or, alternatively, to deliberately provoke them). The use of handheld computer affords a previously unseen amount of mobility and agility on the part of the users.

Mobile AR lets users move away from a confined area, so that physical movement can be leveraged as an element of the interaction or gameplay. The fact that a user encounters other people while on the move reintroduces social aspects from the real world, which are lost if users must stay inside a small workspace. An early example of such social roaming behavior, albeit not strictly an AR application, was *Pirates!* [Björk et al. 2001]. This game uses proximity sensors to determine that a user's handheld computer has entered a specific location, or that two pirates are sufficiently close to engage in a sea battle. It is played in a larger area, such as a conference center lobby. Researchers at the National University of Singapore have developed a series of games that make use of even larger areas in which players are moving [Cheok et al. 2002, 2003]. Games such as Niantic Labs' [2012] *Ingress* incorporate notions of AR on an even larger—worldwide—scale.

Mulloni et al. [2008] describe a location-based AR game entitled *Cows vs Aliens*, where users must interact with fiducial markers distributed throughout the gaming area, encompassing several adjacent rooms and hallways. In this game, users must try to guide their cows to safety, and an important game element is to preempt other players from accessing a particular fiducial marker to make their own moves first (Figure 12.5).

Morisson et al. [2011] describe *MapLens*, a system for collaborative use of augmented *mobile* maps. A group of outdoor users can observe augmentations on a paper map through their smartphones. This technology was field-tested in a scavenger hunt game played by teams of three users. From extensive observations, the researcher found that the map prompted a place-making behavior, where users would briefly stop and gather together around the map to check the augmented information (Figure 12.6). Given sufficiently robust tracking technology, these stops could be very brief, but were nonetheless essential for making joint decisions about how to proceed. If every user in the group was given a personal smartphone, multiple devices could be used in parallel, although there was usually one dominant user in the group. This user's device was the one primarily used for interaction with the augmented map.

Figure 12.5 In *Cows vs Aliens*, one player tries to slow down an opponent by covering the camera of the opponent's device with one hand, thereby preventing the opponent from interacting with the fiducial marker. Courtesy of Alessandro Mulloni.

Figure 12.6 Snapshots from the collaborative use of augmented maps in *MapLens*, a multiuser outdoor game played on smartphones. Courtesy of Ann Morrison.

Remote Collaboration

In terms of displays, remote collaboration has opposite characteristics to co-located collaboration: Only information that is explicitly shared and synchronized is visible to both parties. This restriction holds for all virtual objects, but more importantly remote users can see only those portions of a user's real environment that are being captured and transmitted to the remote site.

One of the first remote collaboration demonstrations featuring virtual augmentations was Myron Krueger's Videoplace Responsive Environment, proposed around 1972 and implemented in various incarnations between 1974 and the 1990s [Krueger et al. 1985]. Origi-nally conceived and implemented as a telecommunications environment, it combined silhou-ettes of participants with interactive computer graphics.

In all tele-collaboration environments, because users are not in the same place, it is likely that their physical situation and technical capabilities will differ as well. If two users have the same capabilities, their integration leads to symmetric collaboration. For example, in peer-to-peer conferencing, both users may have a smartphone. Asymmetric configurations are frequently found in the form of *remote expert* scenarios, where a mobile worker is tasked with an activity such as maintenance or construction, while a remote expert gives advice. The worker will prob-ably require hands-free operation and use only lightweight mobile hardware, while the remote expert may operate in a control center with more powerful stationary hardware, such as a desk-top computer with a large-format touchscreen. In such an asymmetric scenario, the additional resources of the remote expert should be used to provide the expert with improved situation awareness, compensating for the fact that the expert cannot directly perceive the task location.

Video Sharing

The primary mode of live transmission in remote collaboration is, of course, video streaming. In this sense, remote AR is similar to (or an extension of) *video conferencing*. In video conferencing, only objects and people in the camera's field of view are visible. If the camera does not cover the entire workspace, or if the user operating the camera fails to point at the location that is of interest to the remote user, communication value is diminished.

Professional video conferencing and surveillance systems use multiple cameras to obtain wide coverage of an environment. Of course, this approach leads to higher costs: Cameras must be placed, and network bandwidth for video streaming increases linearly with every camera. Most applications, especially mobile ones, will be able to afford just a single camera. We would like to place this camera such that its benefit is maximized. In a stationary environment, such as a desk or workbench, the camera might be placed overhead or at a raised position, overseeing the area.

In mobile applications, the user might wear the camera on a headband or helmet, or around the neck. Wearable cameras couple the camera's field of view to the user's motion. Thus, the local user actively decides which portion of the environment is transmitted to the remote user. The remote user may give feedback, such as via an audio channel, to direct the remote user to the location of interest. Alternatively, the remote user may invoke a freeze-frame or snapshot function to obtain a still image from the video, showing the relevant area. Doing so requires that the relevant area be viewed at least once. Moreover, a still frame can be only a temporary surrogate for live video, especially if changes to the environment are imminent.

Pure video conferencing cannot really be seen as video-based augmented reality, or *augmented virtuality*: In a standard video conference, no virtual objects are registered to the real world.

However, video conferencing can fairly easily be integrated or transformed into an AR experience. One way to do so is to use live texture mapping to project 2D video footage [Billinghurst et al. 1998a], possibly with the participant's head, torso, or body silhouette segmented from the background imagery, onto spatially arranged polygons (tracked, for example, by fiducial markers [Kato et al. 2001]). Minatani et al. [2007] have developed a system specifically designed for face-to-face tabletop remote collaboration in AR. Their approach uses video texture mapping, but relies on a single deformed billboard, which is shaped such that a user seated at a tabletop is optimally represented by a single billboard; in other words, the depth discrepancy between the user's head, upper body, and hands and the deformed billboard is minimal.

One can add further augmentations in image space by treating the video image as a canvas on which the user may draw, for example, using a mouse or touchscreen. As long as the video is stationary (requiring users of wearable cameras to stand still), dynamic augmentations can be established by drawing with very small technical effort. All that is required is transmitting the drawing updates in the feedback channel to the other user.

A useful extension is the use of *panoramas*. In Chapter 4, we saw how a panoramic view may be obtained over time by a user looking around and rotating a handheld camera device, while standing in one place. Chili [Jo and Hwang 2013] uses inexpensive orientation tracking with internal phone sensors to obtain the rotation and attach it to the transmitted video frame. This approach allows for spatial references in panoramic space. LiveSphere [Kasahara et al. 2014] uses a head-worn omnidirectional camera to transmit full panoramic video; with this system, the remote user's viewing direction is independent of the local camera motion, but a special camera device is required. Müller et al. [2016] describe how panoramas can be built from a video stream from a standard mobile phone by stitching them together in real time on the remote user's phone. Sharing of on-screen drawings registered to the panorama yields a simple but effective form of collaborative AR.

Video Sharing with Virtual Objects

AR video conferencing with the inclusion of virtual objects relies on a conventional video conference setting, which streams live video data over a network and processes the video to add various forms of AR cues. Barakonyi et al. [2004a] have developed an AR system in which the remote participants are shown in a 2D window. Users are able to add tracked 3D objects in the scene, which are manipulated by markers. The typical view for a participant consists of two windows. One window shows a mirrored view of the local user, allowing that user to control interaction with the handheld markers. The other window shows the remote participant. The video conferencing application not only streams the video, but also shares tracking information and the state of the 3D model with the remote site (Figure 12.7). In this way, the same AR view consisting of real and virtual elements can be shown on both sides.

As an application example, Barakonyi et al. [2004a] discuss a physician consulting with a colleague on a medical data set (Figure 12.8). Real-time rendering of volumetric data is computationally

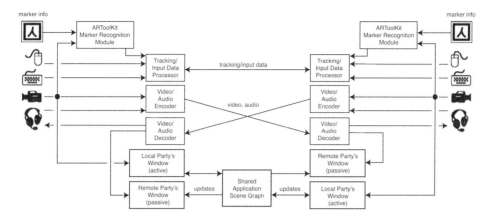

Figure 12.7   System overview of an AR video conferencing application. Besides the video stream, each side shares tracking information extracted from the video stream and updates it to a shared scene representation. This enables both sides to perform local AR rendering and compositing at the highest possible quality. Courtesy of István Barakonyi.

intensive, and streaming the results of the rendering as video is not desirable due to compression artifacts. Performing the volumetric rendering locally at each site and superimposing the result on the video image, however, yields the desired effect.

Yamamoto et al. [2008] suggest extending AR video collaboration from purely virtual objects to physical objects they call *tangible replicas*. With their approach, both users receive identical tracked objects. Manipulating one replica changes the other one as well. Many collaboration scenarios do not have the luxury of knowing in advance which objects will be required, which limits the general applicability of this approach.

Figure 12.8   Two physicians can collaborate by combining AR video conferencing with local, fast-volume rendering of medical data sets. Courtesy of István Barakonyi.

Video Sharing with Geometric Reconstruction

If wide-field-of-view or panoramic video is not sufficient to establish spatial awareness for the remote user, a combination of video sharing with geometric reconstruction can be considered. In Chapter 4, we saw that *simultaneous localization and mapping* (SLAM) can generate a three-dimensional scene representation from monocular video. Alternatively, one or more depth sensors can be used for faster and more robust capturing of geometry. This capability is particularly useful for moving objects such as the user's body, which cannot be captured in sufficient quality using monocular SLAM techniques.

Today's relative ease in capturing geometric models with depth sensors is built upon years of research exploration. The National Tele-Immersion Initiative, directed by Jaron Lanier [2001], supported research groups at initially eight and later four research universities in a three-year agenda (1997–2000) to drive network-engineering research for the not-for-profit research consortium Internet2. This initiative bundled existing research efforts on immersive tele-collaboration, including the vision for the Office of the Future [Raskar et al. 1998], and culminated in research demonstrations in 2000, which connected offices at the University of North Carolina–Chapel Hill, the University of Pennsylvania in Philadelphia, and the Advanced Network and Services branch in Armonk, New York, with 3D-reconstructed, 3D-augmented, tracked, interactive mixed reality [Towles et al. 2002]. While this research demonstration was realized with considerable custom hardware and software efforts, it represented a significant proof-of-concept step toward affordable commodity components supporting the same kind of experiences.

Combining geometric reconstruction with video sharing yields a system where the remote user is able to navigate the reconstructed environment and assume an arbitrary viewpoint without being constrained by the current point of view of the local user. Drawing annotations can be performed directly on the surfaces of the reconstructed geometry, making the feedback provided to the other user independent of the viewpoint.

An early system that made use of this idea was discussed by Reitmayr et al. [2007]. In this system, a worker with a mobile AR device streams video to the remote expert. Unlike the worker's mobile computer, the remote expert's workstation has the necessary computing power to generate a SLAM reconstruction from the received video. The remote expert can receive and annotate objects in the video stream. The annotations are attached to simple geometric features such as points, discs, and rectangles identified by the SLAM algorithm. Only the annotation placement in the coordinates of the worker's camera needs to be sent as feedback, so it can be overlaid on the worker's video stream.

Lee and Höllerer [2006] present a method for stabilizing live video from a moving camera in a video conference. The AR view is established by tracking 2D features in the video stream and estimating the homography of the dominant plane visible in the video. Both the local and remote participants can annotate such a planar physical meeting space with annotations that remain stable, even if the point of view changes to some degree.

Figure 12.9   Remote instruction for replacing the memory bank in a PC. The remote expert (right) can draw annotations directly into the mobile user's view. The live video feed is stabilized for the duration of the touch screen interaction while video updates continue, correctly projected onto the continuously updated model. Courtesy of Steffen Gauglitz.

The remote collaboration system developed by Gauglitz et al. [2014a] uses a SLAM system to identify the 3D position of feature points in the environment. The feature points are triangulated and texture mapped by projecting video keyframes from the estimated point of view of the camera. The resulting 3D model is a geometrically coarse, but visually detailed representation of the worker's environment (Figure 12.9). The remote expert can look at this model from an arbitrary viewpoint and annotate it using a touchscreen [Gauglitz et al. 2014b]. The systems developed by Adcock et al. [2013] and by Sodhi et al. [2013a] reconstruct the environment with a depth sensor, giving the remote expert access to a usable geometric model almost instantaneously. They use a Kinect sensor, which does not work outdoors.

Maimone and Fuchs [2012] discuss a telepresence system that uses several depth sensors to obtain a detailed geometric representation of the user's environment at real-time frame rates. Such a system requires space and effort to set up, but the rich 3D representation that it produces can realistically display participants engaged in full-body motion. Pejsa et al. [2016] focus on extracting the 3D capture of a local participant and plausibly projecting a live-sized virtual copy into the remote space.

Pointing and Gestures

Being able to provide spatial references through pointing or hand gestures has been identified as an important element of successful remote collaboration. Early work such as the Double-DigitalDesk by Wellner and Freeman [1993] transmitted video images of the user's hands operating on a desk. Bauer et al. [1999] presented empirical proof from a user study that, indeed, being able to point is an essential aspect of remote collaboration. Transmitting video of the user's hand allows not just pointing, but enables other forms of gesturing, such as conveying shapes, indicating distances with two hands, and showing motion trajectories [Fussell

Figure 12.10   (left) The stationary system records a user's pointing hand with cameras from multiple viewpoints. (right) The Hand of God appears in the mobile user's AR view, marking a particular location. Courtesy of Aaron Stafford and Bruce Thomas.

et al. 2004]. More recent work enables transmission of hand video for mobile workers [Alem et al. 2011] [Huang and Alem 2013].

If a video of the hands cannot be transmitted, a virtual pointer, such as a 2D or 3D arrow, can serve as a substitute for the pointing task [Chastine et al. 2008]. Alternatively, special hardware can be used. Kurata et al. [2004] describe a pan-tilt platform mounted on a worker's shoulder, equipped with a camera and laser pointer. This setup can be remote-controlled by the expert to change the field of view and mark objects in the environment with the laser beam. Ideally, virtual pointers and annotations should support the option of world-stabilization; that is, if desired, they should stay associated with linked physical locations in the remote collaborator's view, which requires tracking [Gauglitz et al. 2014b].

A 3D representation of hand gestures can be obtained with depth sensors [Sodhi et al. 2013a] or multiple cameras. Stafford et al. [2006] propose the "Hand of God" (HOG) for fostering the collaboration with a roaming user. It consists of a small cylindrical workspace equipped with multiple cameras that enable instant image-based capturing, transmission, and rendering of whatever is inside the workspace. The remote user sees a three-dimensional image-based rendering of whatever is put inside the workspace at a significantly enlarged scale—that is, several meters of actual height. A typical interaction is for the HOG user to place one hand inside the workspace to let an oversized hand appear in front of the remote user to point to a particular location (Figure 12.10). Another application is to put a sticky note with an annotation into the cylinder, which the remote user perceives as a large billboard.

Remote Collaboration with Agile Users

The HOG hints at the possibility of asymmetric remote collaboration with agile users, who are potentially roaming a wide area. For example, a stationary user might provide guidance or oversight for a mobile user acting as a scout. An early example of this kind of indoor–outdoor

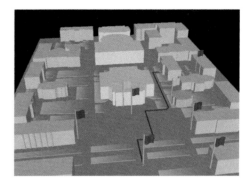

Figure 12.11 Collaboration of an outdoor user roaming a university campus (left, seen through an HMD) and a stationary user providing a path for the mobile user to follow (right, VR view). Courtesy of Columbia University.

collaboration was presented by Höllerer et al. [1999b]. In their application, an outdoor user roams the campus of Columbia University with a wearable AR system (Figure 12.11, left) and is connected to an indoor user. The indoor user employs either a desktop interface (Figure 12.11, right) or an immersive VR interface (with an HMD), in both cases showing a 3D map of the campus. The indoor user can communicate with the outdoor user and provide visual clues, such as suggested navigation paths and flags placed in the environment to mark objects of interest.

Summary

Augmented reality is suitable for various types of collaborative interfaces. It is a particularly powerful technology for synchronous collaboration, where the augmented real world is experienced and manipulated together by two or more users. The most natural approach is probably the idea of a shared space, where co-located AR users see the same real and virtual objects, but each user can assume an individual viewpoint. The power of this approach comes from the joint experience of virtual (or augmented) objects, without a particular need for sophisticated collaboration tools.

An equally important domain of collaborative AR is remote collaboration. On top of conventional video conferencing, AR views can be added by either introducing virtual or augmented objects or presenting remote users as video avatars. AR remote collaboration is also suitable for asymmetric scenarios, where one user captures live video or even a live geometric scene representation, and the other user provides feedback directly in the first user's view. This kind of setup is suitable for various kinds of scenarios involving remote expert consultation.

CHAPTER 13

SOFTWARE ARCHITECTURES

In this chapter, we take a closer look at the software architecture of AR systems. In terms of software technology, AR is a demanding application domain, bringing together components from a number of fields, each with its own set of challenges. The complexity of integrating diverse components into a single real-time application is shared by AR and VR. In addition, AR has further needs, such as integration with the real world and support for mobile computing styles, which make AR even more demanding than VR.

We start by analyzing general requirements, and then discuss a number of key approaches to software architecture in AR. Throughout the presentation, we use examples from various existing AR and VR systems, as these two domains often have similar requirements when it comes to software architecture.

As a typical foundation, AR builds on **distributed object systems.** In these systems, **dataflow approaches** are often used to orchestrate the communication and control, in particular for processing of input device data streams. Additionally, **scene graphs** are commonly used to describe the graphical aspects of AR applications. Finally, scripting languages and runtime reconfiguration facilities can improve the efficiency of AR application developers.

In this chapter, we begin by considering the requirements that motivate the solutions presented here. Well-designed software should be functionally correct, reliable, easily understandable, highly usable, efficient, and maintainable. Every piece of software with these attributes is likely to utilize architectural abstractions. We briefly discuss platform and user interface abstraction as the two most important bases for AR software, and then talk about reusability and extensibility, before focusing on distributed computing and one of the most important principles of real-time distributed mixed-reality software systems, **decoupled simulation.** In our discussion, we will repeatedly refer to the concept of **design patterns** [Gamma et al. 1995] [Buschmann et al. 1996] [Fowler 2003], which encapsulate principles of good software design.

First, however, we discuss one of the most distinctive characteristics of AR systems and the ensuing requirements on the software design: the fact that computing and interaction take place in the *physical world*, and therefore need to react and relate to it.

AR Application Requirements

One of the most distinctive features of AR systems is the fact that their user interfaces (UIs) involve the physical world. An augmented reality UI typically consists of both real and virtual objects, each potentially influencing information display and interaction possibilities. This leads to requirements regarding environment control, scene dynamics, display space management, real–virtual consistency, and semantic knowledge [Höllerer 2004].

Environment Control and Scene Dynamics

Augmented reality systems need to be able to react in real time to changes in user view pose and to the complexity and unpredictability of the real world. The UI for a desktop interface is comparatively static, whereas virtual reality interfaces, which are also real-time dynamic, can often adjust and arrange layouts slightly to optimize user interaction. AR interfaces have less flexibility, because the real world is generally not under the user's control. Assume an AR application requires an unobstructed view onto a physical object (e.g., a statue in a museum). This system needs to be prepared for (1) the user looking away from the statue; (2) an occluder, such as another visitor, coming in between the user and the statue; and (3) the appearance of the statue changing drastically because of real-world influences beyond the system's control (e.g., a spotlight illuminating the statue is turned off). Many real-world circumstances can be reasonably handled with strong general system defaults (e.g., robust tracking systems), world sensing (e.g., displays with lighting adaptation), and good user interface design (e.g., the system recognizing that a view may be suboptimal and guiding the user to improve it, if it cannot be corrected automatically). Even though AR systems must be able to react to real-world scene dynamics, AR screen composition should not change unduly [Bell et al. 2001], as unnecessary movement of annotations is known to be distracting.

Display Space

VR and AR share the trait of potentially unlimited display space surrounding the user, of which only a relatively small viewpoint window is visible at any time. The main difference is that, for AR, space is constrained by the real world. At the same time, AR affords many integration possibilities with real-world infrastructure. For example, AR systems can link up with many different displays and computational interfaces that exist in the physical world, such as billboards, wall displays, monitors, tablets, smartphones, and wearables. As a consequence, the AR system infrastructure must be able to function as part of a distributed computing environment.

Real–Virtual Consistency

People have learned through long years of experience—starting with early childhood, in fact— how to interact with the physical world. They have learned what to expect from, and how to use, desktop computers and, more recently, multi-touch–enabled smartphones and tablets (increasingly now from early childhood onward, as well). These more traditional computer plat-forms have defined their own UI logic, which is decoupled from the physical world, but borrows metaphors from it (e.g., flicking a scrollable view on a multi-touch device will give it a decelerat-ing motion that adheres roughly to the law of physics, assuming certain friction parameters). In VR, interfaces are not really standardized yet, and there is an opportunity to develop new UI standards, including the potential for "magic" user interfaces that go beyond naturalistic interactions [Bowman et al. 2006]. In AR, that potential also exists, but there is a much more stringent requirement to coordinate and reconcile user interaction and system output with the physical world. In general, the AR system needs to keep track of the states of interrelated physical and virtual objects, either to keep them consistent with each other or to purposefully break such consistency. As discussed in Chapter 7, this can go considerably beyond pure visual coherence (a topic covered in Chapter 6).

Semantic Knowledge

We have alluded several times to the relationships between physical and virtual objects. Often, these take the form of simple annotations, such as textual labels or hyperlinks attached to physical objects. They can also be much more elaborate, such as the programmed motion behavior of a virtual conversational agent [Anabuki et al. 2000] and its dynamic linkage to a certain area. It becomes clear that, for AR systems to make informed decisions about virtual object usage and placement, they need to establish semantic relationships between physical and virtual objects. To do so, they need information about the physical object, about the type of virtual augmentation, and about the relationship. Overall, then, sensing and interpreting the physical world is an increasingly important requirement for AR.

Physical Space

Another key difference of AR, compared to desktop and VR applications, is the use of physical locomotion. AR users commonly move about in the physical world. The size of the physical environments that users may traverse while experiencing AR puts stringent requirements on the supporting tracking technologies and the variability of the physical environments (e.g., urban canyons interfering with GPS signal reception). The potential use of different tracking technologies based on availability may lead to potentially large differences in tracking accuracy over time and space, which a good AR system should be prepared for and react to [MacIntyre and Coelho 2000] [Höllerer et al. 2001b].

Software Engineering Requirements

In addition to the requirements that AR software must fulfill to be able to operate in real-world conditions, the AR software must address requirements stemming from the engineering of complex software systems.

Platform Abstraction

Cross-platform compatibility is necessary to enable an AR application to run on any number of target systems, possibly featuring (among other things) a variety of operating systems, user interface toolkits, and graphics libraries. Platform independence avoids vendor lock-in and facilitates rapid adoption of new, more capable hardware, which is of particular importance in the rapidly changing market of mobile devices. Generally speaking, independence from a particular platform is a desirable property for all software. AR combines an unusually large variety of aspects, especially in relation to the heterogeneity of input and output devices, so this property is especially important in the AR realm. Applications should be aware of the current device configuration and be able to adapt themselves to maintain usability and effectiveness.

Platform independence also makes it easy to run a distributed AR application on an ensemble of computers with a heterogeneous software infrastructure. This flexibility can be useful if the application itself imposes any constraints. For example, device drivers for a certain input device may exist only on Windows, while existing code for a graphical application may run only on Linux. Rather than porting code from one platform to another, it may be easier to create a simple distributed system composed of a mixture of Windows and Linux systems, in particular, if the underlying AR platform lends itself to this approach.

Portability means that it should be possible to compile the source code of an AR application on any of the target platforms, with no—or only minimal—changes. This can be achieved by calling system-specific functions through an intermediate platform abstraction layer. A generic abstraction layer is often contained in VR/AR/game development platforms such as Unity [Hocking 2015], user interface toolkits such as Qt [Dalheimer 2002], and networking toolkits such as ACE [Schmidt and Huston 2001], and can be extended by the developer to cover all platform-specific needs of the AR system. When third-party libraries are employed, it is recommended to choose products that support all target platforms. If no such library exists, a single-platform library can be integrated as long as the overall system is designed so that it can still be used on other platforms, albeit without the specific capabilities provided by this library.

User Interface Abstraction

While basic platform abstraction is a very straightforward requirement, user interface abstraction is a conceptually more involved requirement of AR systems. Unlike desktop applications, which are always operated by mouse and keyboard and employ a standard WIMP (windows, icons, menus, pointers) paradigm, there is no single user interface paradigm for AR (see also Chapter 6). Consequently, it is desirable to achieve a certain degree of independence from a particular user interface style or device. This approach enables pieces of application logic to be developed without having to be concerned with AR user interface issues, as the UI may be difficult or inconvenient to operate and test while developing.

For example, suppose an application expects input from a wide-area tracking device. Not only might the actual choice of tracker be deferred until late in the development process, so as to take advantage of the latest hardware development, but it may also be more convenient for the developer to remain seated at the desk during testing, while simulating tracking input from a user roaming a large environment. Replacing input devices is a relatively simple approach to user interface abstraction, while replacing interaction techniques (which combine input with graphical or other feedback) is more complicated and may profoundly affect the user experience.

Reusability and Extensibility

The AR system should facilitate the reuse of software components. Reusability is a common goal of modern object-oriented programming languages, and fundamental reusability through abstraction in classes is trivial to accomplish. AR applications, however, have demands that go beyond that point. They are geared toward producing a novel kind of user experience, which typically requires a lot of incremental prototyping. Therefore, it is vital that software components can be rearranged and combined without writing too much glue code.

Likewise, the obvious requirement that software components should be extensible to customize their behavior should be addressed not only by specialization through subclassing (i.e., extending existing code), but also through the possibility of aggregating several components that act as building blocks for larger functional units. An architecture that lends itself to aggregation will prove to be more versatile.

Distributed Computing

As mentioned earlier, many AR applications will require some sort of distributed computing. This need may arise from the combination of multiple independent components, possibly executing on specialized hardware or platforms. Distributed computation is also necessary in scalable multiuser systems, where every user deploys an individual client computer connected to a common network. In any case, developers should be protected from the complexities of network programming as much as possible. The development of distributed applications should be as easy as the development of monolithic applications, or developers may refrain from using distribution.

This implies that the AR system must offer at least two features. First, it must provide a uniform communication mechanism for software components that makes communication over the network as easy as local communication. Note that the fundamental communication pattern in interactive systems is usually based on event passing rather than function calls, because event communication lends itself to extension through network message passing. Second, a convenient mechanism for the instantiation, runtime control, and debugging of a distributed system is necessary.

Decoupled Simulation

Decoupled simulation is a fundamental concept for distributed interactive systems and virtual (or augmented) environments. In this model, a system consists of at least two software components, which are concurrently executing with independent threads of control. Each component is responsible for simulating or maintaining a certain aspect of the environment and may execute at its own pace [Shaw et al. 1993]. Information concerning shared aspects of the environment is communicated from one component to another asynchronously, on a need-to-know basis.

For example, one component might be concerned with simulating objects' physics, while another component is responsible for drawing the three-dimensional scene. For smooth animation, drawing updates must occur at screen refresh rates and, therefore, need to occur more frequently than physics updates. Similarly, pose tracking and user interaction should be handled in separate threads, so that they don't unnecessarily slow down, or even block, drawing updates. The decoupled simulation model makes it simple to implement such a regimen. The decoupling of components also makes it easier to reconfigure and extend the overall system, because only local effects of changes must be considered.

Distributed Object Systems

Distributed object systems form the basic middleware on which state-of-the-art AR systems are based. General-purpose middleware (e.g., CORBA [Henning and Vinoski 1999], Java RMI [Grosso 2001], and ICE [Henning 2004]) is intended to raise the level of abstraction for platform independence and distributed computation. The fundamental concept introduced by distributed objects systems is objects—software components—that can be instantiated and operated anywhere in a network.

Communication between objects is facilitated either through remote method invocation or through message passing. The latter may be more appropriate for real-time systems governed by the decoupled simulation model, in which objects have independent threads of control and communicate asynchronously. Consequently, traditional object systems such as CORBA use relatively heavyweight objects, where each object owns a separate thread or even a separate process. In some other approaches, the basic objects in the system are more lightweight, and many objects share a thread.

If multiple threads of control exist—irrespective of whether the corresponding software objects are situated on the same host or on multiple hosts—the distinction between a main application and subordinate service objects becomes blurred. The user experience is a collaborative effort brought about by multiple software objects, some of which may directly interface with the human user, while others may operate in the background. Sometimes, one software object may assume a "master" role and create or destroy other software objects as needed. The absence of a dedicated application component also implies the use of an inversion of control pattern [Fowler 2003]: After setting up the distributed objects that constitute an application, the generation of events and forwarding of messages determines the behavior of the application, and no single object is in full control of all others.

An ensemble of distributed objects may be instantiated and wired for communication by a master object or startup facility. In the simplest case, the startup facility starts with an empty object store and uses its detailed knowledge about the overall architecture of the distributed application to create the ensemble of objects. After the initialization, each component in the ensemble commences operation locally, while communicating only with the peer objects it knows directly.

In a more realistic environment, this simple scheme using centralized knowledge is insufficient. For example, mobile AR makes it necessary to establish new communication links at runtime, when a new component comes into physical reach. In other cases, some components—for example, a device server—may execute continuously and offer their services to any suitable client over a potentially very long time. A startup facility is not at liberty to instantiate a new device server; instead, it must search for and bind to the existing one. In general, the existence and lifetime of any object can vary, and objects must be prepared to investigate the situation and dynamically adjust their behavior. This is a fundamental difference from programming in a single-host, single-process, or single-user environment.

Object Management

An important prerequisite to achieving such flexibility is the capacity of a runtime system or middleware for introspection—that is, the ability of the system to analyze its own structure, such as the typing of objects or components. In the simplest case, a pointer to a class or method can be converted into the name of a class or method given as a string, and vice versa. While newer programming languages such as Java and C# offer introspection support on a language level, AR systems are typically developed in traditional C++ for performance reasons, and introspection capabilities are on the level of the distributed object system. This can be done by introducing an interface definition language or by annotating the source code (e.g., via a preprocessor or precompiler).

With introspection, it becomes easy to create an object manager (or "broker" in CORBA), which is responsible for the objects in a distributed system: Objects are registered in a system-wide database maintained by the object manager, which contains details of an object's attributes and interfaces. Service objects can be discovered, and new connections can be established by querying the object manager for a particular object type or quality, with a network transparent handle to the desired object being returned in response. Oftentimes, this discovery is aided by a dedicated service localization protocol, such as SLP [Guttman 1999] or Bonjour [Cheshire and Krochmal 2006]. Objects can be created on remote hosts through factory methods [Gamma et al. 1995]. Introspection also enables object assemblies to be serialized and stored persistently or transmitted over the network.

The creators of some AR systems have chosen to implement only a local object manager and do not aim to provide application-transparent object distribution (i.e., uniform communication of local and remote objects). The advantage of this scheme is that a simple local object manager can be created from scratch in C++ with reasonable effort and there is no reliance on potentially heavyweight networking libraries. Examples of such architectures include AMIRE [Zauner et al. 2003] for AR and VR Juggler [Bierbaum et al. 2001] for traditional VR installations, such as a CAVE [Cruz-Neira et al. 1993].

Local object management can be easily extended with an explicit (nontransparent) distribution mechanism in the form of sender and receiver objects. The application programmer must set up these objects in pairs for explicit message passing across the network. This approach is ergonomic, if only a few static network communication paths are required, typically in combination with a dataflow architecture (see the "Dataflow" section later in this chapter). Several popular AR frameworks have chosen this approach, including Tinmith [Piekarski and Thomas 2003]. Another example from the VR field is AVANGO (also known as Avocado) [Tramberend 1999]. OpenTracker [Reitmayr and Schmalstieg 2005] is a library for managing dataflow from AR devices that also uses explicit networking. Avalon [Seibert and Dähne 2006] makes explicit networking more convenient by resolving the network location of a named destination automatically through Bonjour.

Building a runtime system for AR with fully transparent object distribution from scratch is a significant effort. Research pursuing this objective has relied on existing middleware implementations. For example, MORGAN [Ohlenburg et al. 2004] combines an object store built around CORBA with a publish–subscribe pattern for communication among the objects.

A more radical design is used in DWARF [Bauer et al. 2001]. DWARF is also a component-based distributed system built around CORBA, but does not use a conventional startup facility that relies on centralized knowledge of the overall application architecture and of the intercomponent communication needs. Instead, upon invocation, components (called services in DWARF) register their interfaces in terms of so-called needs and abilities at an object manager. This manager matches needs and abilities and connects suitable components at runtime in an opportunistic fashion. The application behavior emerges as a result of matching needs and abilities.

This approach has several theoretical advantages. Notably, the lifetime of the AR system is greatly extended, as the user can shut down and replace components at any time. This ability is particularly useful during active development, when the live system can be debugged and modified without ever having to perform a full system restart [MacWilliams et al. 2003]. The flexibility of DWARF is similarly useful for mobile AR applications, which can automatically adapt to a changing infrastructure. For example, a system component might monitor tracking accuracy and switch to a better tracking system once it becomes available. Similarly, the end user can plug modules together and benefit from new modules without having to modify the system configuration (a feature known as "plug and play" in consumer electronics). On the down side, DWARF's flexibility comes at the price of relatively high overhead through the CORBA-based communication and the continuous matching process. Without additional measures, the approach followed by DWARF does not scale very well in the number of concurrent objects.

Case Study: *SHEEP*

As an example of a multimodal system based on a distributed object architecture, we will discuss *SHEEP* [MacWilliams et al. 2003], a game for multiple users that uses DWARF services to achieve four simultaneous activities: visualization, tracking, interaction, and simulation of sheep. The application integrates several third-party libraries (e.g., for 3D graphics, tracking, and speech recognition) in the form of DWARF services.

Several views of a *SHEEP* pasture are shown in Figures 13.1 and 13.2. A projection table shows a top-down view of the scene, while HMDs with head tracking and tracked laptop screens present a first-person perspective. Moreover, a user with a personal digital assistant can pick a sheep from the pasture and see it on the handheld screen.

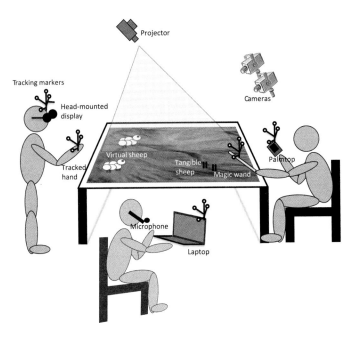

Figure 13.1   The physical setup of *SHEEP* consists of a projection table for multiple users, viewing devices such as head-mounted displays and laptops, and a variety of tracked devices.

The system architecture of *SHEEP* includes modules for tracking and calibration, presentation (VRML rendering and sound output), interaction (including collision detection involving tracked entities and speech recognition), and sheep simulation. Each group uses several services, and these services connect by expressing needs and abilities. It is possible to execute multiple instances of the same service in the distributed system. While the tracking service exists in a single instance and sends position updates to all interested components, user interface

Figure 13.2   (left) Two different impressions of the *SHEEP* pasture, one on the tabletop projection and the other on a laptop screen. (right) A user with a personal digital assistant picks up a sheep for closer inspection. Courtesy of Gudrun Klinker.

controller and VRML viewer services have as many instances as there are viewing devices. The largest group of services is associated with the sheep, each of which is represented by an individual sheep service.

An infrared tracking system from ART[1] delivers high-quality pose updates via a UDP data stream, which is converted into pose events understood by DWARF services. After calibration, the pose events are consumed by the other application services.

A flock simulation executes in a distributed fashion among the sheep represented by individual services. All sheep exchange their current pose, and this information is used to determine each sheep's movement. A sheep's goal is to stay near the herd, but avoid colliding with other sheep. The game also features a tracked physical sheep, which can be used to steer the herd to a particular location.

Viewer services connect to the sheep to display a representation of herd and pasture. Moreover, tracked views connect to the tracking service to update the virtual camera that determines the view whenever the user moves. Finally, the user interface controller collects user input, such as events from the speech recognition feature, and uses a simple state machine to determine appropriate reactions of the system to user input.

Dataflow

A component-based approach as detailed previously, be it local or distributed, is typically combined with dataflow, meaning a pipes-and-filters architecture [Buschmann et al. 1996]. AR applications employ a variety of input devices and facilities, which produce streaming data or discrete events, which we will collectively call *events*. An event usually passes through a series of steps before it triggers any effect perceived by the user. For example, events from position trackers are generated by hardware devices, read by device drivers, transformed to fit the requirements of the application, and transmitted over the network to other hosts. Different setups and applications may require different subsets and combinations of these steps, but the individual steps are commonly encountered in a wide range of applications. Examples of such common steps include geometric transformations and data fusion filters. Nevertheless, dataflow is not necessarily limited to devices or user input events. Any component in an application can generate new events and feed them into a dataflow system. For example, a physics simulation may generate events related to collision detection of real and virtual objects.

The main concept of a dataflow system is to break up the data manipulation into these individual steps and build a *dataflow graph* from these steps. The dataflow graph also abstracts from the details of accessing and manipulating the raw events by forming an architectural layer

---

1. http://www.ar-tracking.de/

between event producers and the application that consumes the events. The topology of a dataflow graph is usually a directed acyclic graph, as allowing events to be passed on in cycles is generally troublesome and not necessary.

Dataflow Graphs

In a dataflow graph, each unit of operation is called a *node*. Nodes are connected by directed edges to describe the direction of the flow. Each node can have multiple input and output ports. A port is a distinguished connection point for an edge; that is, the node can distinguish between events passing through different node ports. The output port of one node (the predecessor node) is connected to a compatible input port of another node (the successor node). This establishes the flow by defining directed edges in the graph. A node receiving a new event via one of its inputs computes a new update of its internal state and sends one or multiple new events out via its output ports. In some architectures, it is also permissible to connect one output port to multiple input ports or, conversely, to connect multiple output ports to one input port. Such fan-in or fan-out connections, which allow a more compact representation of a complex graph, can be handled by temporal multiplexing or demultiplexing of event propagation.

We distinguish three types of nodes:

- **Source nodes** have no input ports and receive their data values from external sources. Most source nodes encapsulate a device driver that accesses a particular input device. Other source nodes form bridges to self-contained systems, such as a visual tracking library. They can also retrieve data from the network or provide debugging input.

- **Filter nodes** are intermediate nodes with at least one input and one output port; they modify the values received from other nodes. Filter nodes receive values from other nodes. Upon receiving an update from one or more nodes, a filter node computes an update of its state, based on the collected data. Examples for filter nodes include geometric transformation filters (such as pre- or post-multiplication of a vector with a transformation matrix), logic operations on Boolean values such as those generated by button presses, signal filters for prediction, smoothing or noise removal, data selection, aggregation or fusion, conversion from one data space to another, and numeric truncation to a user-specified interval.

- **Sink nodes** have no output ports, but instead trigger effects of components outside of the dataflow. Sink nodes are similar to source nodes, but deliver data rather than receiving it. This includes delivering data to an application object that resides outside the dataflow graph, network transmission or multicasting to other hosts, logging to a file, and displaying console output.

Multimodal Interaction

Multimodal interaction requires that the dataflow system be capable of handling, mixing, and matching various types of data. In a simple implementation, like that widely used for embedding dataflow in scene graph libraries [Strauss and Carey 1992], events contain a single data item that has a type selected from a fixed—sometimes extensible—set of basic data types, such as Boolean, integer, string, or float3 vector. Input and output ports are likewise typed and accept only connections from compatible ports, possibly with some scheme for implicit type conversion. This scheme enables setting up a dataflow incorporating a mixture of event types, as long as the types are known a priori. Such a simple scheme cannot handle aggregate events, though. For example, a touchscreen may encode the (x, y) position of a tap operation together with the pressure of the tap. A marker tracking library may simultaneously track multiple markers and deliver the pose estimate together with an identifier discriminating the markers. These data items belong together, yet they cannot be mapped to any single basic data type.

To handle aggregate events, one option is to extend the system with a new basic type representing the aggregate information. Unfortunately, this kind of scheme can easily lead to a combinatorial explosion of very specialized data types. Moreover, such a specialization approach is not generally compatible with the reuse of existing nodes, which may understand only generic types. A more advanced approach is proposed in the OpenTracker library [von Spiczak et al. 2007]: Events are modeled as containers storing multiple typed key/value pairs. An event does not contain any specific key or type by default. A node can produce a new event, insert new key/value pairs into an existing event, or modify existing key/value pairs. Following a lazy type checking approach, a node receiving an event retrieves the desired attribute by key.

Runtime errors can occur if the required attribute is unavailable in the received event or if the attribute is not type compatible with the expected value. To avoid such errors, the application developer must ensure that suitable nodes are connected in the dataflow graph. In practice, runtime errors will occur only if the dataflow graph is composed in an incorrect way, so such errors are not a major concern.

Because this scheme induces more overhead for accessing the event data, events are passed on as call-by-reference rather than call-by-value, which avoids costly copying operations. There are some exceptions, however, where call-by-value cannot be used. Specifically, if the two connected nodes do not reside in the same address space or a fan-out is encountered, a deep copy of the event must be provided to the receiving end. If the event must be sent over the network, the type information contained in the event must be consulted to serialize the event.

Threads and Scheduling

There are two possibilities for how a node in a dataflow graph can operate, depending on which threads are set up: The node can wait to be called by a main thread, or it can operate with an independent thread of control. An independent thread of control is useful when decoupled simulation is desired—for example, when a device driver requires a blocking wait that would halt a single-threaded system entirely.

In contrast, assigning multiple nodes to a single main thread is more economical in terms of computational resources and gives the main thread control over the scheduling of the node updates. A main thread can choose from several scheduling strategies, depending on how temporal issues of events should be handled. We can distinguish push and pull strategies for this scheduling:

- The push strategy (Figure 13.3, top) simply forwards new events from predecessor nodes to successor nodes. To account for concurrency, every event must be time-stamped by the node that generated it. Subsequent nodes can react to temporal aspects of the data. For example, a prediction node will consider the time difference between subsequent events to update its output. Ideally, the scheduling algorithm should visit nodes in causal order, such that a node is visited only after all its predecessors have been visited. However, as long as all nodes are eventually visited, scheduling can occur in an arbitrary order, if it is acceptable that propagation of recent events can be delayed by several simulation cycles.

- In the pull strategy (Figure 13.3, bottom), successor nodes poll their predecessor nodes, supplying either a physical or logical time value as an argument. The pulling strategy is necessary for nodes that operate on groups of events, such as a windowed filter, or for nodes that operate on a given point in time, such as a prediction node.

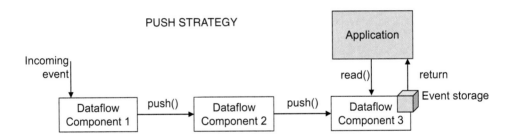

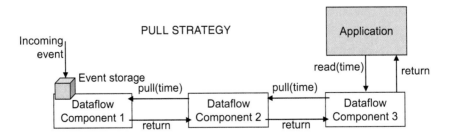

Figure 13.3   (top) The push strategy forwards the most recent event to a sink (buffer), where it can be immediately retrieved. (bottom) The pull strategy issues a recursive query, which can be parameterized by time, in the opposite direction of the dataflow.

To implement pulling, multiple events are queued at the edges of a graph. Again, all events must be timestamped, and the time supplied by the caller is used to select the desired entry from the queue, possibly requiring some temporal interpolation or even extrapolation. Because it induces more overhead, the pulling strategy is usually implemented only when necessary.

Case Study: Wearable Augmented Reality Setup

As an example, we consider one of the early wearable AR setups, designed around 2001 to be operated using OpenTracker [Reitmayr and Schmalstieg 2005]. The setup uses a notebook with a 1-GHz processor running Windows 2000. A Sony Glasstron see-through stereoscopic color HMD is used as an output device. The display is fixed to a helmet worn by the user, and an Inter-Sense InterTrax2 orientation sensor and a web camera for fiducial tracking of interaction props are mounted on the helmet. The computer is carried by the user in a backpack.

The main user interface is a pen-and-pad setup using a Wacom graphics tablet and its pen. Both devices are optically tracked by the camera using markers. The 2D position of the pen (provided by the Wacom tablet) is incorporated into the processing to provide more accurate tracking on the pad itself. Figure 13.4 shows an overview of the setup.

Tracking of the user and the interaction props is achieved by combining data from various sources. The OpenTracker component receives data about the user's head orientation from the InterTrax2 orientation tracker to provide a coordinate system with body-stabilized position and world-stabilized orientation.

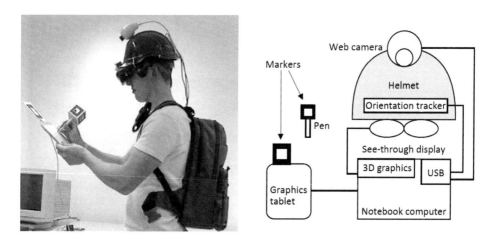

Figure 13.4 A wearable AR setup consisting of a backpack with a notebook, a head-mounted display fitted with inertial orientation tracker and camera, and a handheld tablet and stylus, which are also optically tracked using markers.

Within this coordinate system, the pen and pad are tracked using the video camera mounted on the helmet, with ARToolKit [Kato and Billinghurst 1999] being used to process the video information. Because the video camera and the HMD are fixed to the helmet, the transformation between the cameras and the user's coordinate system is fixed and determined in a calibration step.

The pad is equipped with one marker. This is enough for standard operation, where the user holds it within her field of view to interact with 2D user interface elements displayed on the pad. The pen, however, is equipped with a cube featuring a marker on the five free sides. This enables the user to track the pen in almost any position and orientation. Moreover, whenever the user touches the pad with the pen, the more accurate 2D information provided by the graphics tablet is used to set the position of the pen with respect to the tablet.

The dataflow graph describing the necessary data transformations is shown in Figure 13.5. The round nodes at the top are source nodes that encapsulate device drivers. The round nodes at the bottom are sinks that copy the resulting data to the AR software. Intermediate nodes receive events containing tracking data, transform it, and pass it downward. The relative transformation takes input from two different devices and interprets the location of one device relative to the location of the other (called the base).

In the figure, different shades of gray mark the paths through the graph that describe how the tracking data for different devices are processed. Relative transformations are marked by

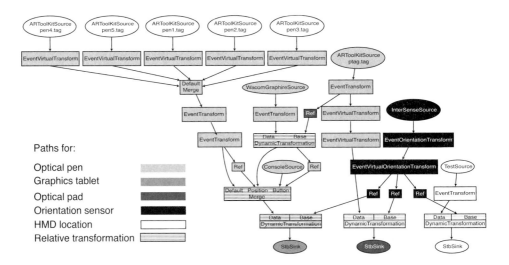

Figure 13.5 The dataflow graph of the tracking configuration for the mobile AR setup. Individual flows are indicated per source. The diagram was automatically generated from the configuration description. Courtesy of Gerhard Reitmayr.

hatching. For example, the optical pen path describes the five markers that are each transformed to yield the pen point location. The results are merged, then further transformed. After another merger with data from the graphics tablet, the data is once more transformed to the reference system established by the orientation sensor.

Similarly, the optical pad path describes the computation to obtain the location of the pad. As a side effect, the optical pad information is used at one step to transform the 2D information from the graphics tablet path to the actual pen position, which is subsequently merged with the pure optical information. Finally, the HMD location path is used to provide information about the head location. The TestSource node's task is to provide a constant value, which is then transformed by the orientation sensors.

Scene Graphs

We now turn our attention to scene graphs—a widely accepted data structure for representing and rendering graphical scenes, which forms the foundation of many graphics toolkits and game engines. Scene graphs grew out of the need to provide a high-level, object-oriented abstraction for the visual data contained in a scene to be rendered. Naïve data structures such as triangle lists that represent a one-to-one mapping of the drawing primitives passed to a procedural graphics library (such as OpenGL or DirectX) are not suitable for larger graphics projects, because they cannot represent higher-level objects with meaningful properties.

Instead of such a naïve data structure, a more sophisticated representation is required, which explicitly describes the objects contained in a scene together with their graphics attributes, thereby avoiding the duplicate database problem. That is, there should not be any need to store and maintain separate representations for object simulation and for drawing. A unified representation also lends itself to direct interaction in 3D, which is essential for many AR applications. This idea is summarized in Open Inventor's motto "Objects, not drawings" [Strauss and Carey 1992]. Scene graphs are important for AR because the objects contained in the scene graph can be used to model both virtual and real entities, enabling a unified treatment of both kinds.

Fundamentals of Scene Graphs

A scene graph is arranged as a directed acyclic graph, which is itself composed of nodes. Nodes are connected by directed edges, forming a hierarchy. This hierarchy models either geometric relationships (e.g., legs are attached to a table) or semantic relationships (e.g., all players of a team are grouped together). While these hierarchical relationships can usually be expressed as a tree, a directed acyclic graph is also allowed—that is, a node may have multiple predecessors. This allows the user to reuse subgraphs by referring to them from multiple places. For example, the wheels of a car can be represented by referring to the same node representing a single wheel four times, each time with different geometric transformations.

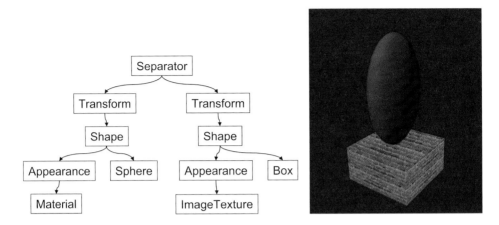

Figure 13.6   (a) A simple scene graph composed of a red ellipsoid and a box with a brick texture. (b) Screenshot of the geometric scene described by the scene graph.

Nodes are instances of a class, which determines their role in the scene. Leaf nodes correspond to geometric primitives, such as boxes, spheres, cones, or triangle meshes, or to other important objects in a graphical scene, such as lights and cameras. Interior nodes group their children. Property nodes such as color, texture, or geometric transformations can be represented by either interior or leaf nodes, depending on the semantics chosen by a particular scene graph library. For a simple example, consider Figure 13.6.

Every node is composed of attributes called fields. For example, a sphere node has fields for center and radius. Fields are themselves objects and capable of interacting with a runtime system, for example, by serialization or by participating as observables in an observer pattern [Gamma et al. 1995]. Based on the object-oriented capabilities offered by nodes and fields, the whole scene graph becomes self-descriptive (i.e., capable of reflection).

Scene graphs are processed by graph traversal—that is, by applying a visitor pattern [Gamma et al. 1994]. Usually the traversal proceeds in a depth-first order, moving from the scene graph root to the leaves of the scene graph. Traversal can be seen as the execution of a state machine, which accumulates state and triggers side effects as each node is visited and one of the node's virtual methods gets called. The most important traversal is the rendering traversal, which produces a view of the scene by invoking a render method for each node, which usually issues low-level graphics commands (OpenGL or DirectX). Other types of traversal include such diverse activities as frustum culling, bounding box computation, intersection with a ray, searching for certain node types, serialization into a file, and processing of device events.

Because a node can have multiple predecessors, it may be visited more than once during a given traversal. The reason for referring multiple times to the same node is that the same node should represent multiple distinct objects in the scene. To discriminate these scene objects, it is not sufficient to provide only a reference to a single node. Instead, an object is uniquely determined by providing a list of references—a path—to all nodes from the root to the node representing the object under consideration. For example, an application may query for the cumulative transformation from the root to a particular object by supplying a path.

Dependency Graph

Recall that the primary graph structure of a scene expresses a hierarchy that guides traversal. In most scene graphs, a secondary graph structure is also embedded. This so-called dependency graph expresses a dataflow, very similar to the dataflow discussed earlier. The dataflow in a scene graph is established between individual fields by a field connection. When two fields in the scene graph are connected by a field connection, any change made to the value of the source field is forwarded to the destination field. For example, a destination object could be set up to always assume the same color as a particular source object. In this way, portions of the scene graph that are spread apart in the primary scene graph structure can be wired to exhibit a common behavior.

Scene Graph Integration

Many different scene graph libraries have been developed, which cover a variety of design goals, such as optimal parallel rendering performance or compliance with the VRML or X3D standards. Given that scene graphs are the most convenient way to address the need for graphical rendering in an AR framework, most frameworks have adopted some form of scene graph. Even so, such integration is not trivially accomplished. Here, we briefly investigate the technical choices that must be made to achieve the integration of scene graphs into an AR framework.

A common approach is to embed the scene graph as a rendering component (i.e., a heavyweight object) of the AR framework (Figure 13.7, top). This choice is appropriate if the AR framework is already based on heavyweight (e.g., CORBA) objects, especially if an existing third-party scene graph should be integrated. For example, DWARF uses a VRML scene graph viewer as a component [Bauer et al. 2001], and MORGAN introduces a rendering component based on X3D [Ohlenburg et al. 2004]. Integrating an existing scene graph provides access to a potentially very rich set of graphics features, while avoiding duplication of work. However, it will usually not be possible to achieve very tight integration with the AR framework, because a third-party scene graph will introduce its own API, which may not fully harmonize with the AR framework's API. In particular, messages passed in the AR framework can be sent only to the rendering component, and not directly to individual nodes in the scene graph; the rendering component must act as a translator, which can lead to awkward software design.

Alternatively, if more fine-grained components are possible in the AR framework, a common approach is to link the scene graph to the dataflow in the AR framework by introducing a special node type in the scene graph that can send and receive dataflow messages as used by the AR framework (Figure 13.7, middle). This special dataflow node implements both the interface

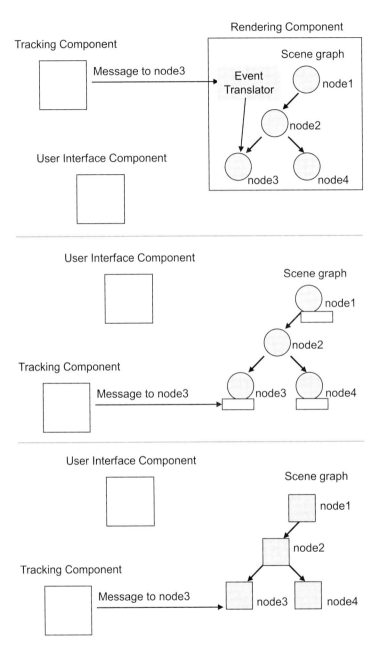

Figure 13.7   Three approaches to the integration of system-wide dataflow and scene graph systems. (top) A dedicated rendering component wrapping around a third-party scene graph needs to employ an event translator to forward messages from the dataflow network to the scene graph. (middle) The scene graph can be extended with special nodes or fields, which are able to communicate with dataflow components directly. (bottom) In a homogeneous architecture, the scene graph classes are derived from the dataflow classes, and scene graph and dataflow components can communicate seamlessly.

of scene graph nodes and the interface of dataflow objects. It thereby bridges the two systems in a more seamless way, which makes this approach very popular. Because only a new node must be implemented, this approach is also very compatible with third-party scene graphs. For example, Avalon [Seibert and Dähne 2006] embeds special nodes in a VRML scene graph based on OpenSG [Reiners et al. 2002], while Studierstube [Schmalstieg et al. 2002] embeds Open-Tracker nodes [Reitmayr and Schmalstieg 2005]. OSGAR [Coelho et al. 2004] combines Open-SceneGraph with dataflow from VRPN [Taylor et al. 2001]. Avango [Tramberend 1999] enables arbitrary field connections in a scene graph based on Performer [Rohlf and Helman 1994] to span over a network, thereby implementing a networked dataflow.

Messages from the dataflow network can be forwarded to the scene graph in many different ways. For example, the messages can be injected directly into a field, relayed by a publish–subscribe mechanism (i.e., nodes subscribe to certain events), or used as payload for a scene graph traversal (allowing for implementation of hierarchical filtering). The best approach depends on the particular needs of the application, although the direct injection into fields is the most commonly used option.

A third option is to implement a scene graph from scratch as a specialization of a hierarchical object system (Figure 13.7, bottom). For example, in the Tinmith system [Piekarski and Thomas 2003], all application data is arranged as objects in a hierarchical store, which makes it easy to address objects or groups of objects. The scene graph is simply a subgraph of the overall hierarchy, which is designated for rendering and composed of "renderable" objects. Dataflow among objects in Tinmith works in a fully unified fashion, because scene graph objects are also general objects adhering to a common interface.

Distributed Shared Scene Graph

Finally, we turn our attention to the distribution of scene graphs. As we have seen, dataflow systems can naturally support distributed applications, if the dataflow is permitted to cross the network. This idea can be applied to the dataflow in scene graphs—for example, by enabling field connections to cross the network. In the Avango system [Tramberend 1999], networked field connections provide the mechanism for multiuser or multiscreen applications. Every host in an ensemble of networked machines stores its own scene graph, but relevant shared data is linked through networked field connections, providing the desired synchronization across machine boundaries. A similar approach introduces special "network" nodes in a dataflow, such as in Avalon [Seibert and Dähne 2006] and OpenTracker [Reitmayr and Schmalstieg 2005]. Networked field connections are usually applied in a master–slave topology, where user input is directed to a master machine, and the slave machines are notified of updates via field connections.

In principle, field connections are sufficient to replicate full scene graphs. Every host can store a replica of the scene graph and connect all fields to the master copy via field connections. Unfortunately, this approach does not scale well, because an excessive number of field connections

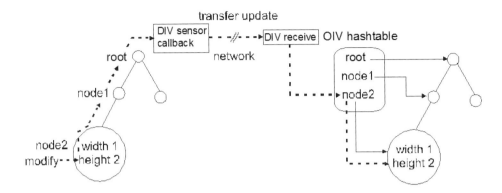

Figure 13.8   Example of a field update in a master–slave configuration. When a change is made to a field at the master ("height," in the example), the notification is propagated to an observer object. The observer sends the update over the network. At the slave, the message is decoded and the appropriate change is made to the replicated field in the scene graph.

is required. A more economic approach is provided by COTERIE [MacIntyre and Feiner 1998] and Distributed Open Inventor [Hesina et al. 1999]: In a nutshell, the scene graph is placed in a distributed shared memory, which is automatically synchronized across all replicas. From the application programmer's perspective, multiple hosts share a single common scene graph. Any operation applied to a part of the scene graph will be reflected by the other participating hosts. This synchronization happens in a way that is almost entirely transparent to the application programmer.

Internally, Distributed Open Inventor works as follows: Message passing is used to synchronize the scene graph replicas (Figure 13.8). An observer object is installed to monitor all changes to the replicated scene graph. When a modification is made, such as a value change on a field or a change in the scene graph topology, the observer detects this change and assembles an update message, which is then propagated to all other hosts that have a replica of the particular node or scene graph. Serialization of nodes and fields can be used to assemble update messages without predetermining a specific message protocol; instead, the node or field itself marshals or unmarshals the message payload. At the receiving end, a network listener decodes the message and applies the update to the replicated node. This simple approach can work either with a master–slave setup or with some form of causal or total ordering to achieve peer-to-peer synchronization if equal access for multiple users is required.

Developer Support

The software abstractions presented so far enable a skilled software developer to design and implement AR applications using very powerful building blocks. These powerful tools are highly complex, and wielding them is not necessarily easy in practice. For productive work, software developers need simple and error-tolerant support from the AR framework as well as rapid turnaround times. The latter consideration is of particular importance, because AR applications will rarely be implemented from a finished design; instead, iterative refinement with lots of prototyping—or "exploratory programming," as MacIntyre and Feiner [1996] call it—will be the preferred work style. These requirements prompt the adoption of scripting languages and runtime reconfiguration facilities.

Parameter Configuration

Many parameters can vary over the lifetime of an AR application. Important categories include the setup of the input and output devices; the content description of the application, especially the three-dimensional scene including real-world objects; and various aspects of the user interface, such as the available menu functions. Rather than hardcoding such parameters in the application or system source code, a better approach is to supply some form of configuration file.

The simplest form of configuration file is just a list of key/value pairs in a text file. Such a line-by-line configuration is usually the first attempt at structuring configuration when a new system or application is conceived. Its main appeal derives from its simplicity, which avoids the need for a sophisticated parser for the configuration files. All too quickly, though, an unordered collection of key/value pairs becomes unmanageable when multiple physical environments (such as a desktop simulation and a mobile AR setup) and multiple users with individual preferences come into play.

Declarative Scripting

A more powerful approach is to adopt a hierarchical description format alongside some form of markup language that supports syntactically distinguishing arguments given as plain text from meta-information such as parameter names. A hierarchical format can naturally express nested structures and lends itself to expressing scene graphs or dataflow graphs, which are often "almost" trees (i.e., there are only a few nodes with more than one parent), for which a special syntax for referencing must be used, when described in a linear textual form. Listing 13.1 is an example of a hierarchical scene graph.

The desire for online information systems to maintain a common representation that can be both understood by a human and processed by a machine has prompted the development of the eXtensible Markup Language (XML). The ease with which new XML dialects can be designed and the wide availability of XML parsing and processing tools have made XML very popular as a source format for configuration tools. For example, XML-based configuration formats are employed by OpenTracker [Reitmayr and Schmalstieg 2005], Tinmith [Piekarski and Thomas 2003], the X3D scene graph of MORGAN [Ohlenburg et al. 2004], and many others.

The description of the hierarchical structure of scene graphs and dataflow graphs largely determines the content and behavior of an application. It is more than merely a configuration

Listing 13.1 Textual Representation of VRML Model from Figure 13.6

```
#VRML V2.0 utf8
Separator {
  Transform {
    translation 0 1.5 0
    scale 0.5 1.5 1
    children[
      Shape {
        appearance Appearance {
          material Material { diffuseColor 0.8 0 0.2 }
        }
        geometry Sphere{ radius .5 }
      }
    ]
  }
  Transform {
    translation 0 0.5 0
    children [
      Shape {
        appearance Appearance {
          texture ImageTexture { url "brick.gif" }
        }
        geometry Box { size 1 0.5 1 }
      }
    ]
  }
}
```

aid, but rather should be seen as declarative scripting or programming. The hierarchical input description is effectively parsed into data structures of the AR framework, and interpreted by the AR runtime system. An important aspect of this runtime interpretation is the behavior built into nodes in a scene graph or dataflow graph. Each node can be seen as a small state machine, which changes its internal state when it receives events and which triggers resulting behaviors by setting its outputs. Through declarative scripting of a complex graph, larger state machines can be built from many individual nodes.

These state machines can be controlled by full-fledged programming languages. Several AR research prototypes have taken advantage of scripting languages that have close relationships with the field of artificial intelligence. Avango [Tramberend 1999], for example, provides a binding to Scheme, a functional programming language, for all of its objects. The choice of a functional language may be somewhat unusual for a systems-oriented application, but it enables convenient expression of both data structures and algorithms. The mobile AR research project at Columbia University has supported several scripting languages over the years, including the object-oriented distributed computing language Obliq [Najork and Brown 1995] [MacIntyre and Feiner 1998] as well as the rule-based JESS [Friedman-Hill 2003], a Java-based expert system scripting language with a LISP-like syntax. It was argued that the dynamic requirements of mobile AR systems, as discussed at the beginning of this chapter, make it necessary to actively manage the AR user interface through a real-time UI management system and that this could be done effectively using a real-time rule-based expert system infrastructure [Höllerer 2004].

Management of complex state machines originating from hierarchical declarative formats is a common concept explicitly used by various systems to craft an application execution model. For example, alVRed [Beckhaus et al. 2004] and APRIL [Ledermann and Schmalstieg 2005] are digital storytelling extensions for Avango [Tramberend 1999] and Studierstube [Schmalstieg et al. 2002], respectively. Their main design idea is to express a story as a nonlinear sequence of states, each associated with a specific VR or AR representation, which is itself composed of 3D multimedia content and interaction capabilities that enable a user to trigger transitions to a follow-up state. These runtime engines operate directly on an extended scene graph representation of the state machine. Other uses of scripted state machines are aimed at the prototyping of 3D interaction techniques through dataflow—for example, Unit [Olwal and Feiner 2004] or CUIML [Sandor and Reicher 2001].

Case Study: Augmented Reality Tour Guide

The Augmented Reality Tour Guide is an application that features a virtual animated character acting as a tour guide giving a tour of a university institute. The user wears a mobile AR setup with HMD (Figure 13.4). For indoor tracking, a head-mounted camera tracks markers placed onto walls of the building area. The markers make it possible to locate the user within this area, since the system knows their exact position in a precisely measured virtual model of the building that has been registered with its real counterpart.

The virtual tour guide character is placed into the reference frame of the real building (Figure 13.9). While walking around, the character provides assistance in finding selected destinations and provides location-specific explanations about the content of various rooms and people working in them using animation, 2D and 3D visual elements, and sound. Since the tour guide is aware of the building geometry, it appears to walk up real stairs and go through real doors and walkways.

The Tour Guide is realized using the Studierstube framework and two previously existing components, a navigation system capable of generating and visualizing indoor routes and an animated agent component. These two components were exposed to the APRIL scripting language, which uses state machines to describe sequences of events and actions.

The tour itself is modeled by the APRIL storyboard as a state engine. A small part of the complete state engine is shown in Figure 13.10. Individual stations of the guided tour are modeled as states, triggering linear presentations when the user arrives. The structure of the building and the different modes for the guided tour (linear or free mode) are modeled by transitions and superstates.

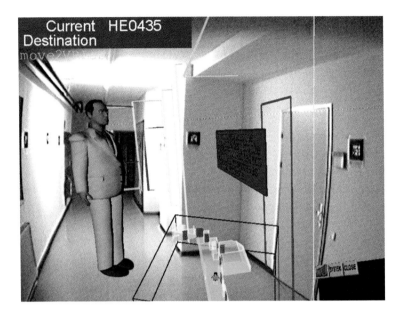

Figure 13.9 The indoor tour guide application view captured from the head-mounted display of a user wearing the mobile AR backpack system. A world-in-miniature view of the building model is shown, and location-dependent heads-up display overlay graphics are presented to the user as she roams the building. Courtesy of Florian Ledermann.

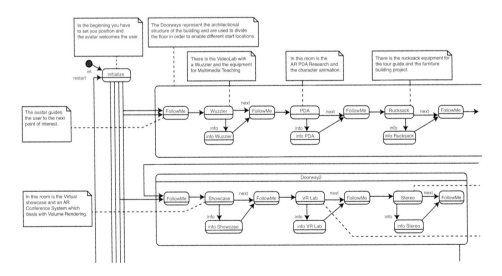

Figure 13.10 The story for the Tour Guide application is modeled as a hierarchical state machine, with places in the indoor environment as the main states. Courtesy of Florian Ledermann.

Procedural Scripting

If declarative scripting is not deemed sufficient to flexibly express and customize application logic, a procedural scripting language can be used. The expressive power of procedural languages is not generally greater than that of a declarative language. However, several of the declarative scripting languages described earlier were designed as a thin layer over the nodes in the scene graph or dataflow graph. As a consequence, they are relatively specialized and offer only a limited set of general computing capabilities.

A procedural language can be used either as the sole scripting facility of a VR or AR system, or in combination with a declarative scripting language. An example of a pure procedural solution is ImageTclAR [Owen et al. 2003], which relies on the Tcl language and a set of Tcl libraries such as ImageTcl. While ImageTclAR facilitates rapid prototyping through interpretation of Tcl code, it does not offer advanced architectural concepts such as dataflow, which means that application logic must be purely coded procedurally. Recently, a lot of development has occurred around newer scripting languages such as JavaScript Python, or Lua, or compiled ones, such as C#, which may be more familiar and convenient choices for today's programmers. A web-focused approach is taken by Argon, which incorporates WebKit into an AR browser and consequently enables the use of any web-related language (such as HTML, PHP, or JavaScript) to express content or behavior.

Most AR frameworks adopt procedural scripting to supplement a declarative mechanism, rather than replacing it. This approach is usually realized by setting up a mechanism to call a function given as interpreted script code from within the AR framework, so that the framework's inversion of control is not compromised by fully passing control over to the script code. For example, consider the PROTO construct in VRML, which embeds JavaScript in a custom node. For every event passed to the PROTO node, a user-defined JavaScript function is called. However, the purely local behavior possible inside a node imposes certain limits as to what such a scripting node can achieve. For example, it would be cumbersome or even impossible to search the whole scene graph for a particular data item from within a JavaScript function in a PROTO.

Mixed-Language Programming

A typical approach is to use scripting in combination with compiled-language programming: Time-critical and recurring features are implemented in C or C++, and then exposed through a custom scene graph or dataflow node or through a binding to a procedural scripting facility. The use of the new feature can conveniently be accessed through the scripting, so that the majority of development and testing of the actual application can be performed without the longer turnaround times imposed by the use of a compiler.

Runtime Reconfiguration

Finally, we take a look at the issue of runtime configuration. Recall that the main reason for developing a flexible, object-oriented architecture for AR frameworks is the intrinsic complexity of building unconventional user interfaces: If a wide variety of mechanisms and devices are combined into a single system, there is an increased risk—in particular, during development and debugging—that at least one of those components will malfunction or fail. The traditional way of separating application lifetime into separate phases for initialization and runtime operation is unsuitable for rapid prototyping, because it requires restarting the whole system every time a single problem occurs.

Instead, it is necessary to enable runtime reconfiguration of many, if not all, facilities in the AR framework. To meet this demand, the interfaces to system components must be designed so that a self-contained reinitialization can be triggered after a change occurs. For example, if an AR system is set up to provide dataflow from a particular tracking device to an application object, it should be possible to disconnect the tracking device, start up an alternative tracking device, and reconnect the dataflow from the new device to the application object. Achieving such flexibility at runtime can be tricky, because the developer cannot use many of the invariant assumptions concerning the system setup that are usually employed to keep the code simple. Nonetheless, it can pay off by making iterative development and runtime debugging significantly easier, especially in distributed environments.

The raw capability to reconfigure at runtime alone does not fully address the needs of the application developer. It is also necessary to expose the live system state for inspection and reconfiguration through an appropriate debugging interface, which allows for manipulating system intrinsics that are usually not available to the user. A key solution that offers fully general access to the system data comes from the clever use of reflection: If a runtime object system is capable of reflection, it can be used to enumerate system states automatically without much effort by the developer. The system can traverse the runtime object store and expose all items to a command line or graphical user interface.

For example, Tinmith [Piekarski and Thomas 2003] exposes its hierarchical objects store as an emulation of the network file system NFS. Using an NFS client on another host enables a developer to manipulate the object store using conventional UNIX file tools. In DWARF [MacWilliams et al. 2003], the dataflow of distributed objects can be visualized and modified at runtime using a proprietary graphical visualization tool. VjControl [Just et al. 2001] is a debugging front-end for the VR framework known as VR Juggler [Bierbaum et al. 2001]; it allows the developer to control VR Juggler's internal state over the network. A particularly elegant solution is proposed by Avalon [Seibert and Dähne 2006], which exposes its dataflow and scene graph through a webserver by automatically producing HTML pages that enable inspection and manipulation of the dataflow and scene graph. As a consequence, any web browser can be used for debugging. This solution has the advantage that it is highly versatile—in particular, when using mobile devices, where conventional debugging directly on the device is hard or impossible.

Choosing an AR Platform

In this chapter, we have described the software engineering principles behind successfully demonstrated AR platforms and projects. Many of today's successful AR software libraries do, in fact, exhibit these principles, or at least a good subset of them. But the question remains: Which libraries and system support tools should a software developer consult to find the best support for implementing new ideas? The answer, of course, depends on the specific needs of the developer. The supported hardware and software platforms are likely a key element to consider. The type and quality of tracking support is clearly another important decision factor. Also, content support is another significant decision factor: Because attractive and engaging content is an important aspect of many AR applications, many of today's development kits operate in conjunction with game engines, and the question of which engines are supported and which import options are available may influence the platform selection. Finally, the supported programming languages, runtime systems, and rapid prototyping tools are likely of high importance to developers.

The landscape of actively supported AR platforms and SDKs is changing rapidly. Many tools are available, including some supported by major industry players, such as PTI Vuforia, Google's Project Tango, or Microsoft's HoloLens platform. Apple made headlines in AR circles by purchasing the established AR platform provider Metaio in 2015. Another established AR solution and platform provider is Total Immersion, which developed the D'Fusion software. Many other libraries and toolkits exist. We give some pointers on this book's companion website.[2]

Summary

Software engineering for AR is very demanding because AR needs a complex real-time software infrastructure, which often also needs to support distributed operation. A number of key abstractions can be employed to address these challenges. One important concept is the use of a distributed object system based on dataflow. Such a pipes-and-filters architecture makes it possible for programmers to develop and test components in isolation, then string them together to create working applications. An additional benefit is that this approach naturally extends to a distributed system by enabling component connections to span multiple hosts in a network. Another important solution is the use of a hierarchical scene graph to model the virtual and real objects in the AR environment. By connecting scene graph and dataflow graph, a complete AR processing pipeline can be expressed using a graph-like structure. Moreover, the system architecture benefits greatly from the use of reflection: Apart from simplifying network transparency, reflection is instrumental in providing a binding to scripting languages for rapid prototyping, runtime inspection, and debugging of the object collection that constitutes the AR framework.

---

2. http://www.augmentedrealitybook.org

CHAPTER 14

THE FUTURE

We have entered the information age, and digital technology, which is largely freed from physical constraints, is progressing at an unprecedented pace. Moore's law, which originally predicted an exponential growth of transistor count in integrated circuits, has led to similar growth in the overall development of information technology.

The first major change in everyday life owed to information technology occurred in the 1980s, with the conversion of office work from analog to digital. Since the 1990s, many areas of private life, such as verbal communications, mail, photography, and music appreciation, have been altered in an irreversible way through information technology and the Internet. Over the subsequent years, social computing, mobile computing, and the cloud have made access to information universal.

This development is, in a way, predicted by Weiser's description of ubiquitous computing. When first made in 1991, Weiser's statement that there would be many computers per person might have seemed far-fetched and risky. Today, many people, not just information technology professionals, routinely carry many different devices with them when traveling, and integration with existing technology infrastructures, such as WiFi hotspots, wireless display connections to large-scale or shared displays, or even supermarket checkout stations is becoming more seamless.

But today's ubiquitous computing is not simply the calm computing that Weiser predicted. Rather, it sometimes seems as if there is now a dedicated smartphone app for every aspect of our life. Having the right app at hand for everything is already becoming tedious.

AR is a promising alternative. It could be used continuously—for example, with head-worn, body-worn, or spatial AR displays. Today, it is predominantly used in entertainment-related areas, such as gaming and advertising. Yet, massive commercial investments are also being devoted to the development of new VR and AR technologies that go beyond these application domains.

In this final chapter, we discuss a few areas where improvements are needed but substantial rewards from AR may be expected. With this discussion, we attempt to make a prediction of the future, at the risk of being proven wrong. The reader may decide, and, ultimately, time will tell.

What May Drive Business Cases

Commercial exploitation of AR cannot rely on just having proof-of-concept demonstrations. Paying customers require value for their money. In general, we can distinguish two use categories: professional and consumer.

Professional Users

For professional users, new technologies are potential tools for achieving a certain objective either faster (and, hence, cheaper) or with higher quality. In professional domains, it is acceptable to buy and use hardware, even if it is expensive, if the gains from using the new tool are believed to be sufficiently substantial. Even ergonomic limitations, such as the need to carry heavy equipment, can be tolerated in such a case. Consider, for example, the tools used by an engineer at a construction site or a surgeon in an operating theater.

At the same time, professional users expect reliability and continued profit from using the technology. A technology that works only 90% of the time may not be good enough. Professionals are also often reluctant to change if doing so means disrupting their established workflow. There must be a clear-cut advantage if the new tool is to be competitive.

Consequently, AR applications for the professional domain must be robust and well-tested. They may be expensive, require special hardware, or even be difficult to use (up to a certain point, if trainable), but they must provide substantial gains that cannot be achieved with traditional alternatives. In terms of software quality, this easily means a tenfold increase in the software engineering effort over the work invested in a research prototype. It may also require deep integration of the AR application with existing resources, such as enterprise information systems.

Consumers

For casual end consumers, the threshold for accepting a new technology is lower, as no lasting benefit is required for adoption. This makes AR attractive in the short term for purposes such as advertising and games, where an interesting and amusing experience is in itself the desired achievement. Of course, novelty effects and initial excitement quickly wear off and cannot compensate for shortcomings of the technology. Technology problems are exacerbated by the fact that in absence of a novel platform, which is hard to establish, AR for consumers must be a strict software-only solution delivered to devices the users already own. A consumer application must be very easy to use, require almost no training, and rely solely on additional peripheral devices, such as HMDs, in exceptional cases. Moreover, the expectations of the users concerning the quality of the content are very high. Users have come to expect the visual quality of today's premium movies and games everywhere, and this includes AR. They are not likely to be tolerant of jittery tracking and low-polygon models.

In both the professional and consumer categories, an application that relies on a conservative set of features combined with well-tuned technology and content will have a much better chance of succeeding in the marketplace than a radical, but unfinished product. In turn, it may take longer than expected for novel developments to enter the commercial domain. In particular, AR applications may depend on other infrastructure (e.g., online services for indoor maps) to be established before commercialization fully takes off.

An AR Developer's Wish List

Mobile computing is clearly a key enabling technology for AR. Mobile devices such as smartphones enable us to use substantial computational capabilities on the go. However, smartphones are multipurpose devices and must make difficult tradeoffs concerning size, weight, energy consumption, and—not to be forgotten—cost.

Many features that are technically possible are unlikely to appear in actual devices because they conflict with other more basic requirements. For example, battery life must not be overly affected by the addition of sensors, so new sensors can be integrated only after they have been tuned toward modest power consumption. Other product decisions are driven by cost, and can more easily be changed if sufficient demand is evident. For example, until recently smartphones had a single camera processor and could not provide video from the front-facing and back-facing cameras simultaneously. The main reason for this restriction was likely the cost for a second camera processor. Consequently, AR applications were unable to use both cameras for simultaneous tracking. Recent hardware generations have removed this restriction, apparently in response to demand for novel features regarding convenient capture of "selfie" pictures (such as a picture-in-picture feature in the camera app).

We envision several modifications that would make current mobile devices much more suitable for handheld AR on smartphones without severely affecting other device functions or increasing the cost significantly. The next step, head-worn AR, would simply be a matter of establishing a wireless connection to a headset equipped with appropriate sensors, while the smartphone can remain in one's pocket. Large companies such as Google (Project Tango) and Microsoft (HoloLens) are already pursuing some of these goals, but have not yet brought the results to a large-scale consumer market. The following considerations aim to provide some background for such applications and are independent of any specific product.

Low-Level Camera API

The camera module is usually completely self-contained and accessible only through high-level function calls intended for end-user applications. Control of the camera is indirect, and many camera settings, such as focus or white-balance, are not exposed and cannot be turned off. This is unfortunate for AR, which would significantly benefit from full control over the camera hardware. The Frankencamera project [Adams et al. 2010] has shown that low-level access to the camera is possible via bypassing the operating system, but this requires privileged access and defeats hardware abstraction. But even Frankencamera could not access the embedded image processor of the camera subsystem, which would be a valuable resource. Operating system vendors would be in a position to introduce a low-level API granting full control over the camera hardware.

Multiple Cameras

Miniature cameras are so cheap that multiple units can be built into mobile devices. Standard smartphones today provide one back-facing camera for photos and videos and another lower-resolution front-facing camera for video conferencing. Some vendors aim to go beyond that: The short-lived Amazon Fire phone (sold by Amazon between June 2014 and August 2015) sported four front-facing cameras for real-time face tracking. Multiple cameras can be used for stereo matching, although the maximum baseline between cameras mounted on a handheld device is rather small. Still, redundant images from multiple cameras can also be used in many applications relevant for AR, including metric reconstruction, light-field capture (with the side application of more convenient real-time surround-panoramas), as well as high-dynamic range imaging and other forms of computational photography.

Wide-Field-of-View Cameras

Cameras with a wide field of view capture more of the environment into a single picture. Lens optics supporting a wide field of view are more expensive and create conflicts with a compact casing design. However, they may provide essential input for image-based detection and tracking [Oskiper et al. 2015]. Real-time applications must work with the information that is fed to them, so high-quality sensors are crucial. The Microsoft HoloLens, for example, is predicted to use four environment-sensing cameras to cover a wide FOV, two on either side of the headset, in addition to a depth-sensing camera and a forward-oriented scene camera.

Sensors

After the relative success of the Microsoft Kinect, especially in AR/VR research communities, a wave of miniature depth sensors based on either structured light or time-of-flight principles has come under development. Commercial sensors, such as the Intel RealSense, already ship with mobile devices, and the Google Tango platform is expanding to an increasing number of devices. While the capabilities of these sensors vary widely, 3D sensing is an important addition to mobile AR. Obtaining a three-dimensional representation of the environment directly makes it possible to avoid a large amount of computation on the mobile device and can reduce energy consumption (although the sensor itself can draw significant amounts of power). More importantly, an AR system relying on a depth sensor does not have to worry as much about adverse environmental conditions affecting computer vision, such as poor lighting, which defeat processing of regular images. Thus, we expect that depth sensors, which were initially marketed as premium features for next-generation devices, will become commonplace soon.

Infrared sensing technology (for night vision and heat sensing) has improved significantly and technology miniaturization and price points are getting closer to a point where integration of such sensors into consumer devices might make sense. This would enable new AR applications in low-light surroundings (e.g., for navigation and collaboration).

Likewise, AR would benefit significantly from improved position and orientation sensors. Affordable RTK GPS technology and laser gyroscopes (as discussed in Chapter 3) would expand the arsenal of pose-sensing technologies and significantly improve the robustness of pose computations.

Unified Memory

Mobile devices usually have a unified memory architecture in the sense that the processor cores—CPU and GPU—share the available memory. However, this design is optimized toward low cost and low energy consumption. In practice, the available memory bandwidth must be shared between cores, and the shared memory architecture is not exposed to the application developer. This means that data must be explicitly copied between CPU and GPU, which is slow and wasteful. Data streams from the periphery, especially video data, cannot be forwarded to the GPU directly. Exposing a low-level interface to the unified memory architecture could avoid inefficient workarounds. Such a "bare metal" interface would be more difficult to program, and could potentially disrupt the stability of the operating system if used incorrectly. We believe that it would be smart to trust the developer's abilities more in this area.

Parallel Programming on the Mobile GPU

A general-purpose graphics processing unit (GPGPU) executes arbitrary programs in a massively parallel way. Mobile GPU designs have the same capabilities as their desktop counterparts, but do not support the full range of GPGPU programming languages. OpenCL is still in a scarcely available experimental state, while CUDA is available only on the latest mobile GPU generation of NVIDIA, which does not yet have a large user base. For numerical algorithms, such as image processing and stereo matching, a GPU typically surpasses a CPU by a large factor in performance. Even if the GPU cannot be loaded fully in a continuous manner because of thermal and energy constraints, having GPGPU abilities available on demand would make AR applications much more powerful. In the long term, energy requirements could be reduced by adding special functions in dedicated hardware to either the CPU or the GPU. We hold the opinion that developers should be given the opportunity of utilizing all available hardware, so that new important functions can be identified, before they go into dedicated hardware units.

Better Displays

More, and better, optical see-through head-mounted displays are becoming available, but the device that everybody desired is not among them yet. Recent research prototypes show possible directions for development in this area.

The first advancement that will significantly enhance AR experiences is a display with a **wide field of view.** Non-see-through displays, such as those from Oculus and HTC/Valve, offer more than a 90° field of view. In comparison, commercial optical see-through displays provide a less than 30° field of view. With such a narrow field of view, users must tediously move their head to precisely focus on a single object of interest, and they cannot make use of their peripheral vision. Designing AR experiences for "oversight," which features many augmentations to enhance a user's situation awareness, is not well supported, nor is the use of large-scale augmentations spanning a user's field of vision.

The limitations of today's display technologies have led to a narrow idea of AR as providing simple point-based annotations, such as labels, and small 3D objects. Instead, we may want to think about AR more like about VR in terms of immersion, only with the real world playing a more dominant role. It should be possible to stand in front of a life-sized architectural model of a planned building, in the exact spot where it is about to be built, and experience it in its entirety, with correct lighting and shadowing with regard to the real world. It should even be possible to enter such a building model, and appreciate it from the inside. High-end VR simulations of wide-field-of-view AR annotations, such as those for visually linking objects far apart in the field of regard [Ren et al. 2016], can already give an imposing impression of such novel capabilities. New optics designs may allow AR to take a big step forward (also see Chapter 2).

The bulky form factor of current HMDs is probably one of their biggest impediments to more widespread adoption. **Miniaturization** is therefore the second area where enhancement is needed. The idea of an AR contact lens may seem attractive. Unfortunately, as Hainich and Bimber [2011] convincingly argue, there are serious obstacles in the way of such a vision (size of the necessary optics, energy source, and also durability and health considerations). They concluded that actual contact lens displays are just mere speculation. Five years later, we are still confronted with the same technological obstacles regarding stand-alone contact-lens displays. However, as Chapter 2 discussed, recent developments in near-eye and light-field display technologies at least give hope for more lightweight (and hopefully stylish!) visor form-factors, potentially in combination with custom contact lenses for focus and filtering optics.

The third enhancement that would be of great value to AR and VR experiences alike is support for **varying focus.** With a conventional design, a display has a fixed focal distance. The difference between the distance of the simulated objects and the distance of the display makes perceiving stereoscopic images correctly difficult. Even with training, looking at this kind of display can be tiring. Displays supporting variable focus [Huang et al. 2015] or adaptable focus, as implied to be under development at AR startup Magic Leap, would offer a much more convenient viewing experience. Commercial solutions using light-field projections will require not only new hardware, but also changes to the computer graphics software, because stereoscopic image pairs must be replaced with a high-dimensional light-field representation [Wetzstein 2015]. The first commercial light-field displays will come in the form of personal near-eye displays, probably initially more bulky than audiences would like. Further down the road, pending a few technological breakthroughs, projective volumetric displays that can create lifelike 3D imagery in mid-air from miniature projectors potentially woven into our clothing, might present a more convenient social display alternative.

Taking AR Outdoors

Mobile AR means that a user is free to go anywhere. In practice, most commercial AR scenarios are still situated indoors, because it is significantly more difficult to take AR outdoors. If we want AR to become a breakthrough technology, it must work anywhere, *especially* outdoors. Image-based localization is the most challenging of the components important for outdoor AR. AR relying purely on built-in sensors such as GPS and inertial orientation tracking is delivering rather poor experiences, however, so we do not think this approach qualifies as outdoor AR in any meaningful and realistic sense. Consequently, there is a dire need for enhancements in several areas pertaining to outdoor localization (and, to a lesser degree, any form of wide-area localization).

Uncooperative Users

AR systems must be really simple to use. Users cannot be expected to be cooperative or master a learning curve on how to operate an AR device. They would like to take their device out of a pocket (or even better, use one they are already wearing), point it at a location deemed interesting and expect something to happen. Such a point-and-shoot approach will involve behavior that is notoriously difficult to handle. For example, users will make sudden quick motions and point the camera (responsible for computer vision) at unsuitable locations such as a white wall or the sky. A successful AR system will have to tolerate as many of these behaviors as it can. This will require robust methods of handling failure cases, which are likely to occur quite frequently. In particular, continuous reinitialization of the tracking, working with minimal latency and using several alternative methods (in case one should fail), will be necessary. This area is usually not yet handled well by today's commercial (or research) solutions.

Limited Device Capabilities

In the near future, localization must work directly on the device. Farming localization out to the cloud seems attractive, but currently incurs unacceptable latencies. Today's wireless networks are fast, but performance will vary tremendously depending on the actual outdoor location. We cannot expect network connectivity to always support remote procedure calls for real-time applications. Even so, this does not mean that no subdivision of work along the lines of a client–server system is possible. Asynchronous regimens, in which a server is invoked for prefetching data or performing background operations, while the client is generating the actual AR display with a steady frame rate, can be very useful. However, such asynchronous systems must tolerate a large variation in network latency and throughput via some form of graceful degradation of service quality. The user should always have some useful options left, even if the server is not responding promptly. This will require a rethinking of the AR application design as well, which may have multiple levels of operation depending on the state of the overall system. Needless to say, this need for concurrency within the AR system complicates system development.

Localization Success Rate

We need to use all tricks in the book to increase the localization success rate [Arth et al. 2009] [Arth et al. 2012] [Arth et al. 2015]. There are many techniques, but the ones that provide sufficient performance will typically excel at addressing a particular situation. Some can handle difficult viewing conditions robustly, whereas others can work with a minimal amount of input data (from either the model database or the life input streams). Typically, methods that rely on significant amounts of data or computation have higher success rates. This can, for example, mean that we have to search exhaustively rather than heuristically through a database, or that we employ dense rather than sparse feature tracking. We also want to use all capabilities of the device, including all sensors and computational units. New sensors, such as more accurate inertial and orientation sensors, depth sensors, and new computational units, such as GPGPU, are very helpful, but their use can increase energy consumption tremendously. Only the combination of all these options leads to a system that delivers an acceptable localization success rate in the wild. Obviously, this kind of solution implies a lot of software engineering complexity, even if powerful hardware can be assumed. Adjusting to a range of hardware capabilities, including those available in entry-level devices, is even more challenging.

In summary, many solutions for outdoor AR are available today, but it is not straightforward to leverage them. Addressing all challenges simultaneously requires extremely sophisticated software engineering, which by far exceeds the software complexity usually considered economically acceptable in the simple "app" universe of mobile devices. Besides client software, infrastructure in the form of cloud services must be built. We predict that several years of further development will be necessary before serious outdoor AR emerges.

Interfacing with Smart Objects

Many ideas originally proposed in the 1990s for ubiquitous computing are today making a reappearance under the term *Internet of Things* (IoT). This trend is fueled by the fact that more and more consumer electronics are controlled by a system-on-chip rather than by a more traditional microcontroller. Vendors, which have a constant need to distinguish their products from those offered by the competition, are using the programmability of the system-on-chip to add new functions via software. Wireless networking is one of these new functions—capable of turning an ordinary object into a smart object, connected to IoT. A similar trend can be observed in industry, where machines and facilities are organized into *cyber-physical systems*.

The novelty of IoT is that it provides the user with advanced control over the physical environment. Currently, though, it is unclear which type of user interface is suitable for this control task. First, there may be an overwhelming number of parameters to control, many of which are not easily understood by non-experts. Second, discovery services that allow a user to connect to unknown devices and services are not as easy to operate as they need to be to win widespread acceptance.

AR presents the opportunity of bringing direct manipulation, which we know from desktop computing, into an environment containing smart objects. Assume that the AR system is able to detect which objects the user is currently looking at or touching. The AR system can make contact with a target object via IoT and let the user take control of that object. This control can be carried out either directly, via a *tangible interface* for direct physical manipulation, or via a virtual interface. The latter is more appropriate if the target object is not stationary, if it is located at a distance, or if the desired span of control involves many objects at once.

This form of AR has several advantages over conventional tangible interaction. First, the amenability of a smart object to being controlled is conveyed visually, via an AR display. Second, the feedback from the control interaction can be presented in an AR display. Both advantages are especially important for smart objects that by themselves do not have sufficient abilities to present feedback—for example, because they are very small or lack a display.

Spatial arrangement of objects in the user's surroundings is one of the most important sources of context, but is barely exploited in current IoT approaches. Consider, for example, personal displays. Most people today own several displays: a TV set in the living room, a desktop or notebook computer, a smartphone, and a tablet. TV sets have Internet connections, and new cars have touchscreens. Smartwatches and displays built into glasses are receiving a lot of interest. Some of these displays are designed for interoperation. For example, we can control music playback from the smartphone on the car radio's touchscreen or forward text messages to a smartwatch. Second-screen applications show webpages that provide background information for TV shows currently on the air. However, current opportunities for such interoperation are sparse.

In the future, we would expect that every piece of information would be able to be redirected to any available display based on spatial proximity and simple user input. In fact, a growing number of research prototypes are already exploring this idea [Grubert et al. 2015]. Conversely, commercial vendors usually support interoperation only among their own product families, if at all. Progress in this area of interoperability has historically been slow, because it takes either a vertical systems integration approach that might establish a de facto standard (most affordable for an industrial player with a certain marketplace dominance) or potentially drawn-out negotiation of industry standards.

The same consideration applies to input. Given a description of spatial relationships in the environment, it is possible to infer many of the geometric relationships that are relevant for AR tracking and registration [Pustka et al. 2011]. For example, multiple tracking systems (e.g., two camera-tracking systems running on two users' smartphones) could be daisy-chained so that the pose of indirectly tracked objects is also made available to an AR application. Currently, there is no such interoperability among tracking systems, resulting in many lost opportunities.

Confluence of Virtual Reality and Augmented Reality

What happens down the line, when an AR system knows everything about our physical environment? Advances in 3D sensing and real-time reconstructing are amazing, delivering detailed models of our surroundings. With sufficient effort, we can generate synthetic views of digitized environments that are almost indistinguishable from an image taken with a video camera.

Eventually, scene acquisition will work instantaneously. This would allow us to deliver a perfect virtual reality experience based on the real world, effectively merging augmented reality and virtual reality into a high-quality augmented virtuality. We would no longer require different systems for AR and VR, but could transition between different levels of reality at will. Users could be in a different place instantaneously, or make arbitrary alterations to our real world.

Alan Turing devised the Imitation Game [Turing 1950], more commonly known as the *Turing Test*, in which a human engaged in a written conversation has to tell whether the replies are given by a fellow human or a computer. Soon, we may see an augmented virtuality experience pass the Visual Turing Test [Shan et al. 2013], in which a photo and a rendering are displayed side by side, and a human can no longer guess which is which. To do this reliably with moving imagery, however, is considerably more challenging, not even considering the real-time requirements of AR.

An even greater challenge might prove to be the realistic display of touch sensations. While AR will readily function without the implementation of force and tactile feedback, our discussion of multisensory AR in Chapter 2 showed that huge potential benefits could be gained through consideration of touch. The options range from worn or implanted equipment, as discussed in the next section on augmented humans, to the very futuristic vision of programmable matter [Goldstein et al. 2005] altering the physical environment in front of us at will.

Augmented Humans

The science fiction literature has popularized the idea of cybernetic organisms, or Cyborgs, which are part human and part machine. Many of these fictions are dystopian, with Cyborgs cast in the role of villains. Meanwhile, many ongoing technical developments aim at augmenting human perception and actions of ordinary humans.

Unlike smartphones, which are not designed for uninterrupted usage, wearable computers are meant to be a permanent part of our apparel, and may even be seen as extension of our bodies. A great advantage of wearable computers is that they are always available and efficient for interactions lasting only a very short duration, such as a fraction of a second. Such micro-interactions are not well addressed with devices that must be retrieved from the pocket first and that monopolize one's attention.

Of central importance in wearable computing is the placement of sensors and actuators. The most obvious place is the head, which is an appropriate venue for glasses, earphones, microphones, gaze trackers, and cameras aligned with the viewing direction. An HMD has the tremendous advantage over any other body-worn display in that the display always remains in view and can be checked with a glance, while the hands remain free. Head-worn electronics provide a significant improvement in privacy, because an observer can usually not tell which activities the user is engaged in. The wrist is a good position for wearing a smartwatch or a wristband. Wristbands can measure vital signals such as blood pressure or pulse, but can also house hand-gesture sensors.

Other body-signal sensors, which are now becoming popular for health and **quantified self** applications, may be placed in other body regions, such as across the chest. Inertial sensors, which are useful for step counting, but also for posture detection and activity recognition, can be placed all over the body. Similarly, vibrotactile actuators placed on the body can provide an ambient display without occupying the eyes and ears.

Electroencephalogram (EEG) devices are usually worn in the form of a cap on the skull. Even though inexpensive sensors, which are not in direct contact with the skin, exhibit comparatively limited performance, it is increasingly feasible to detect emotional state and brain activities with EEG. Brain–computer interface research has shown that simple "telekinesis" applications, in which we control our environment by thought, are within reach for ordinary users [Friedrich et al. 2013]. On the output side, deep brain stimulation technologies (which currently rely on invasive electrodes) have successfully been used to reduce symptoms in patients with tremor.

An important field where all of these technologies can come together for a worthwhile purpose is assisted living. Passive aids for the elderly or people with physical disabilities have been used for centuries, as in the case of spectacles. Electronic hearing aids are a more recent invention, but widespread. New technologies have plenty of potential for enhancing assisted living—not just for those who really need those technologies, but also for healthy individuals who seek convenience. Active reading assistance could be provided in an HMD, using video-based magnification or a text-to-speech function. Inertial sensors can detect if a wearer collapses and stops moving. Severely paralyzed patients are already relying on EEG to communicate.

All of these technologies, together with a sophisticated AR system, would certainly give a person Cyborg-like abilities without turning to extreme measures, such as wearing strength-enhancing exoskeletons (which do exist for military applications) or invasive embedding of sensors under the skin. At present, it is unclear which form of human augmentation will prove acceptable to society. Recent public reactions to early adopters wearing Google Glass in public demonstrated significant concern with the abuse potential of video surveillance. On the one hand, it seems that stealthy use of wearable electronics is perceived as much more problematic than the use of visible electronics, such as smartphones. On the other hand, we voluntarily reveal many details of our lives, such as our friends, our schedules, and even our precise where-abouts [Feiner 1999] to cloud services such as Google and Facebook (and less voluntarily to secret government services).

One might suspect that wearable technologies let these concerns bubble to the surface of public attention simply because they suddenly made them physically visible. Clearly, a social code of acceptable behavior of wearable computing must emerge. The principles of this social code must be established on the issue of data privacy itself, rather than on its user interface manifestations, such as AR.

AR as a Dramatic Medium

MacIntyre et al. [2001] argue that AR should progress from a technical capability to a narrative or dramatic medium, and that we must develop appropriate media forms for AR. According to these researchers, "Media forms can be thought of as sets of conventions and design elements that can be used by authors and developers to create meaningful experiences for their target users." In other words, even if we resolve all technical issues of AR (which is the main focus of this book), that achievement will not bring us any closer to successfully using AR as a dramatic medium, comparable to theater, movies, TV shows or, most recently, computer games.

New media do not have media forms per se; the conventions and practices must evolve with their use. Just as Orson Welles's film *Citizen Kane* is credited with establishing important stylistic conventions of modern cinematography, so the coming years will have to establish stylistic forms in AR storytelling. We can use Azuma's [1997] requirements for AR as hints for important characteristics of AR to take into account:

- AR combines real and virtual. Displaying virtual content anywhere in the physical environment yields rich dramatic capabilities.
- AR is spatially registered. This allows users to control the point of view of the experience.
- AR is interactive in real time. Even for experiences containing only passive virtual content, we always interact at least with the physical space.

As an example, consider the problem of narrative focus coming from free camera control. The user must be sufficiently motivated to point the camera on the character or object, which is important to drive the story forward. In computer games, first-person camera control is often replaced by scripted camera control in "cut scenes," which are non-interactive bits of the story. Unlike games, AR is not capable of taking away the camera control from the user. This may lead to the surprising conclusion that AR shares more dramatic conventions with a theater stage or an interactive museum installation than with movies or games.

AR as a Social Computing Platform

In addition to being a visualization tool or a dramatic medium, AR can be a communication tool. In that respect, it shares many characteristics with the World Wide Web, which progressed from a classic information system for passive consumers to a universal application platform and, even more importantly, to a social computing platform connecting billions of people with one another.

We may assume that, even if we manage to make mobile AR devices completely self-contained as far as processing is concerned, the content would still live in the cloud. This content may be provided by commercial suppliers, such as journalists [Höllerer et al. 1999a] or traffic authorities, but it may increasingly be created by other individuals in a social network. In addition to the thematic category, such as Twitter's "hashtag," the location or situation of the AR user will steer the content filtering. Photo websites such as flickr and Panoramio already allow filtering by geographic location, so social network users should be familiar with this idea. Yet AR would go beyond the simple application of this concept, as AR content would depend not just on a coarse geo-location, but on an exactly specified place—such as a particular person, a particular object, or even a particular part of an object. Advanced forms of meta-information will be necessary to let a user search efficiently through large quantities of data.

Markup languages to support this kind of content specification are already being developed. A minimal solution for AR markup can be achieved by rather straightforward transposing of concepts known from the Web to an AR situation [MacIntyre et al. 2013]: A real-world **artifact** (not necessarily a physical object) is **linked** to a piece of virtual **content**. Artifact, link, and content are the three axioms of AR markup. Layout of the content is driven by **styles,** which allow for the necessary flexibility in the spatial arrangement of the virtual content. **Localization** details are given as attributes of artifacts or content; this allows for more than one way to establish localization.

Like a web browser, an AR browser built on this kind of design can incorporate many content streams into one display. This is important, as we have a need to overcome the prevalent style of "AR apps," which monopolize the device and the user's attention. Just as many Facebook users dedicate some portion of their screen to the Facebook timeline as a kind of ambient display to observe as a background activity, so an AR browser can be "always on" and present contextual information from many sources, at the intensity desired by the user. AR researchers have searched far and long for the *killer app* [Navab 2004]. It may just be [Barba et al. 2012] that AR should instead become the killer *experience* that unifies our digital and physical universes.

Summary

The future is becoming the present, as you read these lines. Many of the opportunities mentioned in this chapter are very close to being released to mainstream audiences. While market success and widespread adoption depend on many factors and are notoriously hard to predict, this chapter has explored some areas where AR has already begun to conquer important business cases. AR will interface with the emerging Internet of smart objects. It will be adopted by humans who need assistance. It will be picked up by storytellers. It will be used as a social medium. All of these areas can (and do) exist independently of AR, but with AR, they can become so much more.

AR offers many fantastic opportunities, both for technology and design. We challenge you, the reader, to make a great contribution to its evolution!

REFERENCES

Abowd, G. D., Atkeson, C. G., Hong, J., Long, S., Kooper, R., and Pinkerton, M. (1997) Cyberguide: A mobile context-aware tour guide. *Wireless Networks* 3, 5, Springer, 421–433.

Adams, A., Talvala, E.-V., Park, S., Jacobs, D., Ajdin, B., Gelfand, N., Dolson, J., Vaquero, D., Baek, J., Tico, M., Lensch, H., Matusik, W., Pulli, K., Horowitz, M., and Levoy, M. (2010) The Franken-camera: An experimental platform for computational photography. *ACM Transactions on Graphics (Proceedings SIGGRAPH)* 30, 5, article 29.

Adcock, M., Anderson, S., and Thomas, B. (2013) RemoteFusion: Real time depth camera fusion for remote collaboration on physical tasks. In: *Proceedings of the ACM SIGGRAPH International Conference on Virtual-Reality Continuum and Its Applications in Industry (VRCAI)*, 235–242.

Agrawala, M., Beers, A.C., McDowall, I., Fröhlich, B., Bolas, M., and Hanrahan, P. (1997) The two-user responsive workbench. *Proceedings of the ACM SIGGRAPH Conference on Computer Graphics and Interactive Techniques*, 327–332.

Agusanto, K., Li, L., Chuangui, Z., and Sing, N. (2003) Photorealistic rendering for augmented reality using environment Illumination. *Proceedings of the IEEE and ACM International Symposium on Mixed and Augmented Reality (ISMAR)*, 208–216.

Airey, J. M., Rohlf, J. H., and Brooks, F. P. Jr. (1990) Towards image realism with interactive update rates in complex virtual building environments. *Proceedings of the ACM SIGGRAPH Symposium on Interactive 3D Graphics (I3D)*, 41–50.

Aittala, M. (2010) Inverse lighting and photorealistic rendering for augmented reality. *The Visual Computer* 26, 6, Springer, 669–678.

Alem, L., Tecchia, F., and Huang, W. (2011) HandsOnVideo: Towards a gesture based mobile AR system for remote collaboration. In: *Recent Trends of Mobile Collaborative Augmented Reality Systems*, Springer, 135–148.

Allen, B. D., Bishop, G., and Welch, G. (2001) Tracking: Beyond 15 minutes of thought. *ACM SIGGRAPH Course Notes 11*.

Anabuki, M., and Ishii, H. (2007) AR-Jig: A handheld tangible user interface for modification of 3D digital form via 2D physical curve. *Proceedings of the IEEE and ACM International Symposium on Mixed and Augmented Reality (ISMAR)*, 55–66.

Anabuki, M., Kakuta, H., Yamamoto, H., and Tamura, H. (2000) Welbo: An embodied conversational agent living in mixed reality space. *ACM SIGCHI Extended Abstracts on Human Factors in Computing Systems*, 10–11.

Arief, I., McCallum, S., and Hardeberg, J. Y. (2012) Realtime estimation of illumination direction for augmented reality on mobile devices. *Proceedings of the IS&T and SID Color and Imaging Conference*, 111–116.

Arth, C., Klopschitz, M., Reitmayr, G., and Schmalstieg, D. (2011) Real-time self-localization from panoramic images on mobile devices. *Proceedings of the IEEE International Symposium on Mixed and Augmented Reality (ISMAR)*, 37–46.

Arth, C., Mulloni, A., and Schmalstieg, D. (2012) Exploiting sensors on mobile phones to improve wide-area localization. *Proceedings of the International Conference on Pattern Recognition (ICPR)*, 2152–2156.

Arth, C., Pirchheim, C., Ventura, J., Schmalstieg, D., and Lepetit, V. (2015) Instant outdoor localization and SLAM initialization from 2.5D maps. *IEEE Transactions on Visualization and Computer Graphics (Proceedings ISMAR)* 21, 11, 1309–1318.

Arth, C., Wagner, D., Irschara, A., Klopschitz, M., and Schmalstieg, D. (2009) Wide area localization on mobile phones. *Proceedings of the IEEE International Symposium on Mixed and Augmented Reality (ISMAR)*, 73–82.

Arun, K. S., Huang, T. S., and Blostein, S. D. (1987) Least-squares fitting of two 3-D point sets. *IEEE Transactions on Pattern Analysis and Machine Intelligence* 9, 5, 698–700.

Auer, T., and Pinz, A. (1999) Building a hybrid tracking system: Integration of optical and magnetic tracking. *Proceedings of the International Workshop on Augmented Reality (IWAR)*, 13–22.

Avery, B., Piekarski, W., and Thomas, B. H. (2007) Visualizing occluded physical objects in unfamiliar outdoor augmented reality environments. *Proceedings of the IEEE and ACM International Symposium on Mixed and Augmented Reality (ISMAR)*, 285–286.

Avery, B., Sandor, C., and Thomas, B.H. (2009) Improving spatial perception for augmented reality X-ray vision. *Proceedings of IEEE Virtual Reality (VR)*, 79–82.

Azuma, R. T., (1997) A survey of augmented reality. *Presence: Teleoperators and Virtual Environments* 6, 4, MIT Press, 355–385.

Azuma, R., Baillot, Y., Behringer, R., Feiner, S., Julier, S., and MacIntyre, B. (2001) Recent advances in augmented reality. *IEEE Computer Graphics and Applications* 21, 6, 34–47.

Azuma, R. T., and Bishop, G. (1994) Improving static and dynamic registration in an optical see-through HMD. *Proceedings of the ACM SIGGRAPH Conference on Computer Graphics and Interactive Techniques*, 197–204.

Azuma, R., and Furmanski, C. (2003) Evaluating label placement for augmented reality view management. *Proceedings of the IEEE and ACM International Symposium on Mixed and Augmented Reality (ISMAR)*, 66–75.

Bachmann, E. R., and McGhee, R. B. (2003) Sourceless tracking of human posture using small inertial/magnetic sensors. *Proceedings of the IEEE International Symposium on Computational Intelligence in Robotics and Automation (CIRA)*, 822–829.

Bae, S., Agarwala, A., and Durand, F. (2010) Computational rephotography. *ACM Transactions on Graphics 29*, 3, article 24.

Baillot, Y., Brown, D., and Julier, S. (2001) Authoring of physical models using mobile computers. *Proceedings of the IEEE International Symposium on Wearable Computers (ISWC),* 39–46.

Bajura, M., and Neumann, U. (1995) Dynamic registration correction in augmented-reality systems. *Proceedings of the IEEE Virtual Reality Annual International Symposium (VRAIS),* 189–196.

Baker, S., and Matthews, I. (2004) Lucas-Kanade 20 years on: A unifying framework. *International Journal of Computer Vision* 56, 3, Springer, 221–255.

Balcisoy, S., Kallman, M., Torre, R., Fua, P., and Thalmann, D. (2001) Interaction techniques with virtual humans in mixed environments. *Proceedings of the International Symposium on Mixed Reality (ISMR),* 205–216.

Balogh, T., Kovács, P. T., and Megyesi, Z. (2007) HoloVizio 3D display system. *Proceedings of the International Conference on Immersive Telecommunications,* ICST, article 19.

Bandyopadhyay, D., Raskar, R., and Fuchs, H. (2001) Dynamic shader lamps: Painting on movable objects. *Proceedings of the IEEE and ACM International Symposium on Augmented Reality (ISAR),* 207–216.

Bane, R., and Höllerer, T. (2004) Interactive tools for virtual X-ray vision in mobile augmented reality. *Proceedings of the IEEE and ACM International Symposium on Mixed and Augmented Reality (ISMAR),* 231–239.

Banks, M. S., Kim, J., and Shibata, T. (2013) Insight into vergence–accommodation mismatch. *Proceedings of SPIE—International Society for Optical Engineering 8735.*

Barakonyi, I., Fahmy, T., and Schmalstieg, D. (2004a) Remote collaboration using augmented reality videoconferencing. *Proceedings of Graphics Interface,* 89–96.

Barakonyi, I., Psik, T., and Schmalstieg, D. (2004b) Agents that talk and hit back: Animated agents in augmented reality. *Proceedings of the IEEE and ACM International Symposium on Mixed and Augmented Reality (ISMAR),* 141–150.

Barba, E., MacIntyre, B., and Mynatt, E. D. (2012) Here we are! Where are we? Locating mixed reality in the age of the smartphone. *Proceedings of the IEEE* 100, 4, 929–936.

Baričević, D., Höllerer, T., Sen, P., and Turk, M. (2014) User-perspective augmented reality magic lens from gradients. *Proceedings of the ACM Symposium on Virtual Reality Software and Technology (VRST),* 87–96.

Baričević, D., Lee, C., Turk, M., Höllerer, T., and Bowman, D. A. (2012) A hand-held AR magic lens with user-perspective rendering. *Proceedings of the IEEE International Symposium on Mixed and Augmented Reality (ISMAR),* 197–206.

Barnum, P., Sheikh, Y., Datta, A., and Kanade, T. (2009) Dynamic seethroughs: Synthesizing hidden views of moving objects. *Proceedings of the IEEE International Symposium on Mixed and Augmented Reality (ISMAR),* 111–114.

Barron, J. T., and Malik, J. (2015) Shape, illumination, and reflectance from shading. *IEEE Transactions on Pattern Analysis and Machine Intelligence* 37, 8, 1670–1687.

Barsky, B. A., and Kosloff, T. J. (2008) Algorithms for rendering depth of field effects in computer graphics. *Proceedings of the WSEAS International Conference on Computers,* 999–1010.

Bastian, J., Ward, B., Hill, R., van den Hengel, A., and Dick, A. (2010) Interactive modelling for AR applications. *Proceedings of the IEEE International Symposium on Mixed and Augmented Reality (ISMAR),* 199–205.

Bau, O., and Poupyrev, I. (2012) REVEL: Tactile feedback technology for augmented reality. *ACM Transactions on Graphics (Proceedings SIGGRAPH)* 31, 4, article 89.

Baudisch, P., and Rosenholtz, R. (2003) Halo: A technique for visualizing off-screen objects. *Proceedings of the ACM SIGCHI Conference on Human Factors in Computing Systems (CHI),* 481–488.

Bauer, M., Bruegge, B., Klinker, G., MacWilliams, A., Reicher, T., Riss, S., Sandor, C., and Wagner, M. (2001) Design of a component-based augmented reality framework. *Proceedings of the IEEE and ACM International Symposium on Augmented Reality (ISAR),* 45–54.

Bauer, M., Kortuem, G., and Segall, Z. (1999) "Where are you pointing at?": A study of remote collaboration in a wearable videoconference system. *Proceedings of the IEEE International Symposium on Wearable Computers (ISWC),* 151–158.

Baur, D., Boring, S., and Feiner, S. (2012) Virtual Projection: Exploring optical projection as a metaphor for multi-device interaction. *Proceedings of the ACM SIGCHI Conference on Human Factors in Computing Systems (CHI),* 1693–1702.

Bay, H., Tuytelaars, T., and van Gool, L. (2006) SURF: Speeded up robust features. *Proceedings of the European Conference on Computer Vision (ECCV),* Springer, 404–417.

Beckhaus, S., Lechner, A., Mostafawy, S., Trogemann, G., and Wages, R. (2004) alVRed: Methods and tools for storytelling in virtual environments. *Proceedings Internationale Statustagung zur Virtuellen und Erweiterten Realität.*

Bederson, B. (1995) Audio augmented reality: A prototype automated tour guide. *ACM SIGCHI Conference Companion on Human Factors in Computing,* 210–211.

Bell, B., Feiner, S., and Höllerer, T. (2001) View management for virtual and augmented reality. *Proceedings of the ACM Symposium on User Interface Software and Technology (UIST),* 101–110.

Bell, B., Höllerer, T., and Feiner, S. (2002) An annotated situation-awareness aid for augmented reality. *Proceedings of the ACM Symposium on User Interface Software and Technology (UIST),* 213–216.

Bell, S., Bala, K., and Snavely, N. (2014) Intrinsic images in the wild. *ACM Transactions on Graphics (Proceedings SIGGRAPH)* 33, 4, article 159.

Benford, S., Greenhalgh, C., Reynard, G., Brown, C., and Koleva, B. (1998) Understanding and constructing shared spaces with mixed-reality boundaries. *ACM Transactions on Computer-Human Interaction* 5, 3, 185–223.

Benko, H., Ishak, E. W., and Feiner, S. (2004) Collaborative mixed reality visualization of an archaeological excavation. *Proceedings of the IEEE and ACM International Symposium on Mixed and Augmented Reality (ISMAR)*, 132–140.

Benko, H., Ishak, E. W., and Feiner, S. (2005) Cross-dimensional gestural interaction techniques for hybrid immersive environments. *Proceedings of IEEE Virtual Reality (VR)*, 209–216.

Benko, H., Jota, R., and Wilson, A. (2012) MirageTable: Freehand interaction on a projected augmented reality tabletop. *Proceedings of the ACM SIGCHI Conference on Human Factors in Computing Systems (CHI)*, 199–208.

Benko, H., Wilson, A. D., and Zannier, F. (2014) Dyadic projected spatial augmented reality. *Proceedings of the ACM Symposium on User Interface Software and Technology (UIST)*, 645–655.

Bier, E. A., Stone, M. C., Pier, K., Buxton, W., and DeRose, T. D. (1993) Toolglass and magic lenses: The see-through interface. *Proceedings of the ACM SIGGRAPH Conference on Computer Graphics and Interactive Techniques*, 73–80.

Bierbaum, A., Just, C., Hartling, P., Meinert, K., Baker, A., and Cruz-Neira, C. (2001) VR Juggler: A virtual platform for virtual reality application development. *Proceedings of IEEE Virtual Reality (VR)*, 89–96.

Billinghurst, M., Bowskill, J., Jessop, M., and Morphett, J. (1998a) A wearable spatial conferencing space. *Proceedings of the IEEE International Symposium on Wearable Computers (ISWC)*, 76–83.

Billinghurst, M., Kato, H., and Poupyrev, I. (2001) The MagicBook: A transitional AR interface. *Computers & Graphics 25*, Elsevier, 745–753.

Billinghurst, M., Weghorst, S., and Furness, T. A. (1998b) Shared space: An augmented reality approach for computer supported collaborative work. *Virtual Reality 3*, 1, Springer, 25–36.

Bimber, O., and Emmerling, A. (2006) Multifocal projection: A multiprojector technique for increasing focal depth. *IEEE Transactions on Visualization and Computer Graphics 12*, 4, 658–667.

Bimber, O., Emmerling, A., and Klemmer, T. (2005) Embedded entertainment with smart projectors. *IEEE Computer 38*, 1, 48–55.

Bimber, O., and Fröhlich, B. (2002) Occlusion shadows: Using projected light to generate realistic occlusion effects for view-dependent optical see-through displays. *Proceedings of the IEEE and ACM International Symposium on Mixed and Augmented Reality (ISMAR)*, 186–319.

Bimber, O., Fröhlich, B., Schmalstieg, D., and Encarnação, L. M. (2001) The virtual showcase. *IEEE Computer Graphics and Applications 21*, 6, 48–55.

Bimber, O., and Raskar, R. (2005) *Spatial Augmented Reality: Merging Real and Virtual Worlds.* AK Peters.

Biocca, F., Tang, A., Owen, C., and Xiao, F. (2006) Attention funnel: Omnidirectional 3D cursor for mobile augmented reality platforms. *Proceedings of the Hawaii International Conference on System Sciences*, 1115–1122.

Björk, S., Falk, J., Hansson, R., and Ljungstrand, P. (2001) Pirates! Using the physical world as a game board. *Proceedings of IFIP International Conference on Human Computer Interaction (INTERACT)*, 9–13.

Bleser, G., and Stricker, D. (2008) Advanced tracking through efficient image processing and visual-inertial sensor fusion. *Proceedings of IEEE Virtual Reality (VR)*, 137–144.

Blinn, J., and Newell, M. (1976) Texture and reflection in computer generated images. *Communications of the ACM* 19, 10, 542–546.

Blundell, B., and Schwartz, A. (1999) *Volumetric three-dimensional display systems*. Wiley.

Bolt, R. A. (1980) "Put-that-there": Voice and gesture at the graphics interface. *Proceedings of the ACM SIGGRAPH Conference on Computer Graphics and Interactive Techniques*, 262–270.

Boom, B., Orts-Escolano, S., Ning, X. X., McDonagh, S., Sandilands, P., and Fisher, R. B. (2013) Point light source estimation based on scenes recorded by a RGB-D camera. *Proceedings of the British Machine Vision Conference (BMVC)*.

Boring, S., Baur, D., Butz, A., Gustafson, S., and Baudisch, P. (2010) Touch projector: Mobile interaction through video. *Proceedings of the ACM SIGCHI Conference on Human Factors in Computing Systems (CHI)*, 2287–2296.

Bowman, D. A., Chen, J., Wingrave, C. A., Lucas, J., Ray, A., Polys, N., Li, Q., Haciahmetoglu, Y., Kim, J.-S., Kim, S., Boehringer, R., and Ni, T. (2006) New directions in 3D user interfaces. *International Journal of Virtual Reality* 5, 2, 3–14.

Bowman, D. A., Kruijff, E., LaViola, J. J., and Poupyrev, I. (2004) *3D User Interfaces: Theory and Practice*. Addison-Wesley.

Bowman, D. A., and McMahan, R. P. (2007) Virtual reality: How much immersion is enough? *IEEE Computer* 40, 7, 36–43.

Boyd, S., and Vandenberghe, L. (2004) *Convex Optimization*. Cambridge University Press.

Bränzel, A., Holz, C., Hoffmann, D., Schmidt, D., Knaust, M., Lühne, P., Meusel, R., Richter, S., and Baudisch, P. (2013) GravitySpace: Tracking users and their poses in a smart room using a pressure-sensing floor. *ACM SIGCHI Extended Abstracts on Human Factors in Computing Systems*, 2869–2870.

Braun, A., and McCall, R. (2010) User study for mobile mixed reality devices. *Proceedings of the Joint Virtual Reality Conference*, EUROGRAPHICS Association, 89–92.

Breen, D. E., Whitaker, R. T., Rose, E., and Tuceryan, M. (1996) Interactive occlusion and automatic object placement for augmented reality. *Computer Graphics Forum* 15, 3, Wiley-Blackwell, 11–22.

Broll, W., Lindt, I., Ohlenburg, J., Wittkämper, M., Yuan, C., Novotny, T., Fatah gen. Schieck, A., Mottram, C., and Strothmann, A. (2004) ARTHUR: A collaborative augmented environment for architectural design and urban planning. *Journal of Virtual Reality and Broadcasting* 1, 1.

Brown, L. D., Hua, H., and Gao, C. (2003) A widget framework for augmented interaction in SCAPE. *Proceedings of the ACM Symposium on User Interface Software and Technology (UIST)*, 1–10.

Bryson, S. (1992) Measurement and calibration of static distortion of position data from 3D trackers. *Proceedings of the SPIE Conference on Stereoscopic Displays and Applications*, 244–255.

Buchmann, V., Nilsen, T., and Billinghurst, M. (2005) Interaction with Partially Transparent Hands and Objects. *Proceedings of the Australasian Conference on User interfaces, Australian Computer Society*, 12–17.

Buehler, C., Bosse, M., McMillan, L., Gortler, S., and Cohen, M. (2001) Unstructured lumigraph rendering. *Proceedings of the ACM SIGGRAPH Conference on Computer Graphics and Interactive Techniques*, 425–432.

Buker, T. J., Vincenzi, D. A., and Deaton, J. E. (2012) The effect of apparent latency on simulator sickness while using a see-through helmet-mounted display: Reducing apparent latency with predictive compensation. *Human Factors* 54, 2, Sage Publications, 235–249.

Bunnun, P., and Mayol-Cuevas, W. W. (2008) OutlinAR: An assisted interactive model building system with reduced computational effort. *Proceedings of the IEEE and ACM International Symposium on Mixed and Augmented Reality (ISMAR)*, 61–64.

Burgess, D. A. (1992) Techniques for low cost spatial audio. *Proceedings of the ACM Symposium on User Interface Software and Technology (UIST)*, 53–59.

Buschmann, F., Meunier, R., Rohnert, H., Sommerlad, P., and Stal, M. (1996) *Pattern-Oriented Software Architecture, Volume 1, A System of Patterns*. Wiley.

Butz, A., Beshers, C., and Feiner, S. (1998) Of vampire mirrors and privacy lamps: Privacy management in multi-user augmented environments. *Proceedings of the ACM Symposium on User Interface Software and Technology (UIST)*, 171–172.

Butz, A., Höllerer, T., Feiner, S., MacIntyre, B., and Beshers, C. (1999) Enveloping users and computers in a collaborative 3D augmented reality. *Proceedings of the International Workshop on Augmented Reality (IWAR)*, 35–44.

Cakmakci, O., and Rolland, J. (2006) Head-worn displays: A review. *Journal of Display Technology* 2, 3, IEEE/OSA, 199–216.

Calonder, M., Lepetit, V., Strecha, C., and Fua, P. (2010) BRIEF: Binary robust independent elementary features. *Proceedings of the European Conference on Computer Vision (ECCV)*, Springer, 778–792.

Cao, X., and Foroosh, H. (2007) Camera calibration and light source orientation from solar shadows. *Computer Vision and Image Understanding* 105, 1, Elsevier, 60–72.

Cao, X., and Shah, M. (2005) Camera calibration and light source estimation from images with shadows. *Proceedings of the IEEE Conference on Computer Vision and Pattern Recognition (CVPR)*, 923–928.

Card, S. K., Mackinlay, J. D., and Shneiderman, B. (1999) *Readings in Information Visualization: Using Vision to Think*. Morgan Kaufmann Publishers.

Caudell, T. P., and Mizell, D. W. (1992) Augmented reality: An application of heads-up display technology to manual manufacturing processes. *Proceedings of the Hawaii International Conference on System Sciences,* 659–669.

Cavazza, M., Martin, O., Charles, F., Mead, S., and Marichal, X. (2003) Interacting with virtual agents in mixed reality interactive storytelling. In: *Intelligent Virtual Agents*, Springer, 231–235.

Chan, L., Müller, S., Roudaut, A., and Baudisch, P. (2012) CapStones and ZebraWidgets: Sensing stacks of building blocks, dials and sliders on capacitive touch screens. *Proceedings of the ACM SIGCHI Conference on Human Factors in Computing Systems (CHI),* 2189–2192.

Chastine, J., Nagel, K., Zhu, Y., and Hudachek-Buswell, M. (2008) Studies on the effectiveness of virtual pointers in collaborative augmented reality. *IEEE Symposium on 3D User Interfaces (3DUI),* 117–124.

Chekhlov, D., Gee, A. P., Calway, A., and Mayol-Cuevas, W. (2007) Ninja on a plane: Automatic discovery of physical planes for augmented reality using visual SLAM. *Proceedings of the IEEE and ACM International Symposium on Mixed and Augmented Reality (ISMAR),* 1–4.

Chen, J., Izadi, S., and Fitzgibbon, A. (2012) KinÊtre: Animating the world with the human body. *Proceedings of the ACM Symposium on User Interface Software and Technology (UIST),* 435–444.

Chen, J., Turk, G., and MacIntyre, B. (2008) Watercolor inspired non-photorealistic rendering for augmented reality. *Proceedings of the ACM Symposium on Virtual Reality Software and Technology (VRST),* 231–234.

Chen, Q., and Koltun, V. (2013) A simple model for intrinsic image decomposition with depth cues. *IEEE International Conference on Computer Vision (ICCV),* 241–248.

Cheok, A. D., Fong, S. W., Goh, K. H., Yang, X., Liu, W., and Farzbiz, F. (2003) Human Pacman: A sensing-based mobile entertainment system with ubiquitous computing and tangible interaction. *Proceedings of the ACM SIGCOMM Workshop on Network and System Support for Games,* 106–117.

Cheok, A. D., Yang, X., Ying, Z. Z., Billinghurst, M., and Kato, H. (2002) Touch-Space: Mixed reality game space based on ubiquitous, tangible, and social computing. *Journal of Personal and Ubiquitous Computing* 6, 5–6, Springer, 430–442.

Cheshire, S., and Krochmal, M. (2006) DNS-based service discovery. *IETF Internet Draft.*

Coelho, E. M., MacIntyre, B., and Julier, S. J. (2004) OSGAR: A scene graph with uncertain transformations. *Proceedings of the IEEE and ACM International Symposium on Mixed and Augmented Reality (ISMAR),* 6–15.

Cohen, M. F., Wallace, J., and Hanrahan, P. (1993) *Radiosity and realistic image synthesis*. Academic Press Professional.

Collins, C. C., Scadden, L. A., and Alden, A. B. (1977) Mobile studies with a tactile imaging device. *Proceedings of the Conference on Systems and Devices for the Disabled.*

Cosco, F. I., Garre, C., Bruno, F., Muzzupappa, M., and Otaduy, M. A. (2009) Augmented touch without visual obtrusion. *Proceedings of the IEEE International Symposium on Mixed and Augmented Reality (ISMAR)*, 99–102.

Craft, B., and Cairns, P. (2005) Beyond guidelines: What can we learn from the visual information seeking mantra? *Proceedings of IEEE Information Visualization (InfoVis)*, 110–118.

Crivellaro, A., and Lepetit, V. (2014) Robust 3D tracking with descriptor fields. *Proceedings of the IEEE Conference on Computer Vision and Pattern Recognition (CVPR)*, 3414–3421.

Crow, F .C. (1977) Shadow algorithms for computer graphics. *Proceedings of the ACM SIGGRAPH Conference on Computer Graphics and Interactive Techniques*, 242–248.

Cruz-Neira, C., Sandin, D. J., and DeFanti, T. A. (1993) Surround-screen projection-based virtual reality: The design and implementation of the CAVE. *Proceedings of the ACM SIGGRAPH Conference on Computer Graphics and Interactive Techniques*, 135–142.

Cummings, J., Bailenson, J., and Fidler, M. (2012) How immersive is enough? A foundation for a meta-analysis of the effect of immersive technology on measured presence. *Proceedings of the Conference of the International Society for Presence Research.*

Curless, B., and Levoy, M. (1996) A volumetric method for building complex models from range images. *Proceedings of the ACM SIGGRAPH Conference on Computer Graphics and Interactive Techniques*, 303–312.

Cutting, J. E., and Vishton, P. M. (1995) Perceiving layout and knowing distances: The integration, relative potency, and contextual use of different information about depth. In: W. Epstein and S. Rogers, eds., *Handbook of Perception and Cognition, Vol. 5: Perception of Space and Motion.* Academic Press, 69–117.

Dabove, P., and Petovello, M. (2014) What are the actual performances of GNSS positioning using smartphone technology? *Inside GNSS* 9, 6, Gibbons Media and Research, 34–37.

Dalheimer, M. K. (2002) *Programming with Qt.* O'Reilly Media.

Darken, R. P., and Peterson, B. (2001) Spatial orientation, wayfinding, and representation. In: K. Stanney, ed., *Handbook of Virtual Environment Technology*, CRC Press, 467–491.

Davison, A. J., Reid, I. D., Molton, N. D., and Stasse, O. (2007) MonoSLAM: Real-time single camera SLAM. *IEEE Transactions on Pattern Analysis and Machine Intelligence* 29, 6, 1052–1067.

Debevec, P. (1998) Rendering synthetic objects into real scenes. *Proceedings of the ACM SIGGRAPH Conference on Computer Graphics and Interactive Techniques*, 189–198.

Debevec, P. (2005) A median cut algorithm for light probe sampling. *ACM SIGGRAPH Course Notes 6.*

Debevec, P. E., and Malik, J. (1997) Recovering high dynamic range radiance maps from photographs. *Proceedings of the ACM SIGGRAPH Conference on Computer Graphics and Interactive Techniques*, 369–378.

DiVerdi, S., and Höllerer, T. (2006) Image-space correction of AR registration errors using graphics hardware. *Proceedings of IEEE Virtual Reality (VR)*, 241–244.

DiVerdi, S., Wither, J., and Höllerer, T. (2008) Envisor: Online environment map construction for mixed reality. *Proceedings of IEEE Virtual Reality (VR)*, 19–26.

Dorfmüller, K. (1999) An optical tracking system for VR/AR-applications. *Proceedings of the Eurographics Workshop on Virtual Environments (EGVE)*, Springer, 33-42.

Doucet, A., de Freitas, N., and Gordon, N., eds. (2001) *Sequential Monte Carlo Methods in Practice.* Springer.

Drettakis, G., Robert, L., and Bugnoux, S. (1997) Interactive common illumination for computer augmented reality. *Proceedings of the Eurographics Workshop on Rendering Techniques*, 45–56.

Drummond, T., and Cipolla, R. (2002) Real-time visual tracking of complex structures. *IEEE Transactions on Pattern Analysis and Machine Intelligence* 24, 7, 932–946.

Durrant-Whyte, H. F. (1988) Sensor models and multisensor integration. *International Journal of Robotics Research* 7, 6, Sage Publications, 97–113.

Eisemann, E., Wimmer, M., Assarsson, U., and Schwartz, M. (2011) *Real-time shadows*. CRC Press.

Elmqvist, N. (2011) Distributed user interfaces: State of the art. In: Gallud, J., Tesoriero, R., Penichet, V., eds., *Distributed User Interfaces*, Springer, 1–12.

Emoto, M., Niida, T., and Okano, F. (2005) Repeated vergence adaptation causes the decline of visual functions in watching stereoscopic television. *Journal of Display Technology* 1, 2, IEEE/OSA, 328–340.

Engel, J., Schöps, T., and Cremers, D. (2014) LSD-SLAM: Large-scale direct monocular SLAM. *Proceedings of the European Conference on Computer Vision (ECCV)*, Springer, 834–849.

Enomoto, A., and Saito, H. (2007) Diminished reality using multiple handheld cameras. *Proceedings of the ACM and IEEE International Conference on Distributed Smart Cameras*, 251–258.

Everitt, C., and Kilgard, M. J. (2002) Practical and robust stenciled shadow volumes for hardware-accelerated rendering. arXiv preprint cs/0301002.

Faugeras, O. (1993) *Three-Dimensional Computer Vision: A Geometric Viewpoint*. MIT Press.

Feiner, S. K. (1999) The importance of being mobile: Some social consequences of wearable augmented reality systems. *Proceedings of the International Workshop on Augmented Reality (IWAR)*, 145–148.

Feiner, S., MacIntyre, B., and Seligmann, D. (1993a) Knowledge-based augmented reality. *Communications of the ACM 36*, 7, 53–62.

Feiner, S., MacIntyre, B., Haupt, M., and Solomon, E. (1993b) Windows on the world: 2D windows for 3D augmented reality. *Proceedings of the ACM Symposium on User Interface Software and Technology (UIST)*, 145–155.

Feiner, S., MacIntyre, B., Höllerer, T., and Webster, A. (1997) A touring machine: Prototyping 3D mobile augmented reality systems for exploring the urban environment. *Proceedings of the IEEE International Symposium on Wearable Computers (ISWC)*, 74–81.

Feiner, S. K., and Seligmann, D. D. (1992) Cutaways and ghosting: Satisfying visibility constraints in dynamic 3D illustrations. *The Visual Computer* 8, 5-6, Springer, 292–302.

Fiala, M. (2010) Designing highly reliable fiducial markers. *IEEE Transactions on Pattern Analysis and Machine Intelligence* 32, 7, 1317–1324.

Fiorentino, M., de Amicis, R., Monno, G., and Stork, A. (2002) Spacedesign: A mixed reality workspace for aesthetic industrial design. *Proceedings of the IEEE and ACM International Symposium on Mixed and Augmented Reality (ISMR)*, 86–94.

Fischer, J., Bartz, D., and Straßer, W. (2004) Occlusion handling for medical augmented reality using a volumetric phantom model. *Proceedings of the ACM Symposium on Virtual Reality Software and Technology (VRST)*, 174–177.

Fischer, J., Bartz, D., and Straßer, W. (2005) Stylized augmented reality for improved immersion. *Proceedings of IEEE Virtual Reality (VR)*, 195–202.

Fischer, J., Bartz, D., and Straßer, W. (2006) Enhanced visual realism by incorporating camera image effects. *Proceedings of the IEEE and ACM International Symposium on Mixed and Augmented Reality (ISMAR)*, 205–208.

Fischer, J., Haller, M., and Thomas, B. (2008) Stylized depiction in mixed reality. *International Journal of Virtual Reality* 7, 4, 71–79.

Fischer, J., Huhle, B., and Schilling, A. (2007) Using time-of-flight range data for occlusion handling in augmented reality. *Proceedings of the Eurographics Conference on Virtual Environments (EGVE)*, 109–116.

Fischler, M., and Bolles, R. (1981) Random sample consensus: A paradigm for model fitting with applications to image analysis and automated cartography. *Communications of the ACM* 24, 6, 381–395.

Fitzmaurice, G. W. (1993) Situated information spaces and spatially aware palmtop computers. *Communications of the ACM* 36, 7, 38–49.

Fitzmaurice, G. W., Ishii, H., and Buxton, W. A. S. (1995) Bricks: Laying the foundations for graspable user interfaces. *Proceedings of the ACM SIGCHI Conference on Human Factors in Computing Systems (CHI)*, 442–449.

Fjeld, M., and Voegtli, B. M. (2002) Augmented chemistry: An interactive educational workbench. *Proceedings of the IEEE and ACM International Symposium on Mixed and Augmented Reality (ISMAR)*, 259–321.

Fournier, A., Gunawan, A. S., and Romanzin, C. (1993) Common illumination between real and computer generated scenes. *Proceedings of Graphics Interface*, 254–262.

Fowler, M. (2002) *Patterns of Enterprise Application Architecture*. Addison-Wesley.

Foxlin, E. (1996) Inertial head-tracker sensor fusion by a complementary separate-bias Kalman filter. *Proceedings of the IEEE Virtual Reality Annual International Symposium (VRAIS)*, 184–194.

Foxlin, E. (2005) Pedestrian tracking with shoe-mounted inertial sensors. *IEEE Computer Graphics and Applications* 25, 6, 38–46.

Foxlin, E., Altshuler, Y., Naimark, L., and Harrington, M. (2004) FlightTracker: A novel optical/inertial tracker for cockpit enhanced vision. *Proceedings of the IEEE and ACM International Symposium on Mixed and Augmented Reality (ISMAR)*, 212–221.

Foxlin, E., Harrington, M., and Pfeifer, G. (1998) Constellation: A wide-range wireless motion-tracking system for augmented reality and virtual set applications. *Proceedings of the ACM SIGGRAPH Conference on Computer Graphics and Interactive Techniques*, 372–378.

Foxlin, E., and Naimark, L. (2003) VIS-tracker: A wearable vision-inertial self-tracker. *Proceedings of IEEE Virtual Reality (VR)*, 199–206.

Franke, T. A. (2013) Delta light propagation volumes for mixed reality. *Proceedings of the IEEE International Symposium on Mixed and Augmented Reality (ISMAR)*, 125–132.

Franke, T. A. (2014) Delta voxel cone tracing. *Proceedings of the IEEE International Symposium on Mixed and Augmented Reality (ISMAR)*, 39–44.

Friedman-Hill, E. J. (2003) *Jess in Action: Java Rule-Based Systems*. Manning Publications.

Friedrich, E. V. C., Neuper, C., and Scherer, R. (2013) Whatever works: A systematic user-centered training protocol to optimize brain-computer interfacing individually. *PLoS One* 8, 9, e76214.

Frisby, J. P., and Stone, J. V. (2010) *Seeing: The Computational Approach to Biological Vision*. MIT Press.

Fuhrmann, A., Hesina, G., Faure, F., and Gervautz, M. (1999) Occlusion in collaborative augmented environments. *Computers & Graphics* 23, 6, Elsevier, 809–819.

Fuhrmann, A., Löffelmann, H., Schmalstieg, D., and Gervautz, M. (1998) Collaborative visualization in augmented reality. *IEEE Computer Graphics and Applications* 18, 4, 54–59.

Fuhrmann, A., Schmalstieg, D., and Purgathofer, W. (2000) Practical calibration procedures for augmented reality. *Proceedings of the Eurographics Workshop on Virtual Environments (EGVE)*, 3–12.

Fung, J., and Mann, S. (2004) Using multiple graphics cards as a general purpose parallel computer: Applications to computer vision. *Proceedings of the IEEE International Conference on Pattern Recognition (ICPR)*, 805–808.

Funkhouser, T., Jot, J.-M., and Tsingos, N. (2002) "Sounds good to me!" Computational sound for graphics, virtual reality, and interactive systems. *ACM SIGGRAPH 2002 Course Notes*.

Furness, T. (1986) The super cockpit and its human factors challenges. *Proceedings of the Human Factors Society Annual Meeting*, 48–52.

Fussell, S., Setlock, L., Yang, J., Ou, J., Mauer, E., and Kramer, A. (2004) Gestures over video streams to support remote collaboration on physical tasks. *Human–Computer Interaction* 19, 3, 273–309.

Gabbard, J., Swan, J. E. II, and Hix, D. (2006) The effects of text drawing styles, background textures, and natural lighting on text legibility in outdoor augmented reality. *Presence: Teleoperators and Virtual Environments* 15, 1, MIT Press, 16–32.

Gabbard, J. L., Swan, J. E. II, Hix, D., Si-Jung Kim, and Fitch, G. (2007) Active text drawing styles for outdoor augmented reality: A user-based study and design implications. *Proceedings of IEEE Virtual Reality (VR)*, 35–42.

Gamma, E., Helm, R., Johnson, R., and Vlissides, J. (1994) *Design Patterns: Elements of Reusable Object-Oriented Software.* Addison-Wesley.

Gandy, M., and MacIntyre, B. (2014) Designer's augmented reality toolkit, ten years later: Implications for new media authoring tools. *Proceedings of the ACM Symposium on User Interface Software and Technology (UIST)*, 627–636.

Gandy, M., MacIntyre, B., Presti, P., Dow, S., Bolter, J., Yarbrough, B., and O'Rear N. (2005) AR karaoke: Acting in your favorite scenes. *Proceedings of the IEEE and ACM International Symposium on Mixed and Augmented Reality (ISMAR)*, 114–117.

Gauglitz, S., Höllerer, T., and Turk, M. (2011) Evaluation of interest point detectors and feature descriptors for visual tracking. *International Journal of Computer Vision* 94, 3, Springer, 335–360.

Gauglitz, S., Nuernberger, B., Turk, M., and Höllerer, T. (2014a) World-stabilized annotations and virtual scene navigation for remote collaboration. *Proceedings of the ACM Symposium on User Interface Software and Technology (UIST)*, 449–459.

Gauglitz, S., Nuernberger, B., Turk, M., and Höllerer, T. (2014b) In touch with the remote world: Remote collaboration with augmented reality drawings and virtual navigation. *Proceedings of the ACM Symposium on Virtual Reality Software and Technology (VRST)*, 197–205.

Gauglitz, S., Sweeney, C., Ventura, J., Turk, M., and Höllerer, T. (2014c) Model estimation and selection towards unconstrained real-time tracking and mapping. *IEEE Transactions on Visualization and Computer Graphics* 20, 6, 825–838.

Genc, Y., Tuceryan M., and Navab, N. (2002) Practical solutions for calibration of optical see-through devices. *Proceedings of the IEEE and ACM International Symposium on Mixed and Augmented Reality (ISMAR)*, 169–175.

Georgel, P., Schroeder, P., Benhimane, S., Hinterstoisser, S., Appel, M., and Navab, N. (2007) An industrial augmented reality solution for discrepancy check. *Proceedings of the IEEE and ACM International Symposium on Mixed and Augmented Reality (ISMAR)*, 111–115.

Getting, I. (1993) The global positioning system. *IEEE Spectrum* 30, 12, 36–47.

Gibson, S., Cook, J., Howard, T., and Hubbold, R. (2003) Rapid shadow generation in real-world lighting environments. *Proceedings of the Eurographics Symposium on Rendering Techniques*, Springer, 219–229.

Goldin, S., and Thorndyke, P. (1981) *Spatial Learning and Reasoning Skill.* RAND Corporation.

Goldstein, E. (2009) *Sensation and Perception.* Cengage Learning.

Goldstein, S. C., Campbell, J. D., and Mowry, T. C. (2005) Programmable matter. *IEEE Computer* 38, 6, 99–101.

Gordon, G., Billinghurst, M., Bell, M., Woodfill, J., Kowalik, B., Erendi, A., and Tilander, J. (2002) The use of dense stereo range data in augmented reality. *Proceedings of the IEEE and ACM International Symposium on Mixed and Augmented Reality (ISMAR)*, 14–23.

Grasset, R., Gascuel, J.-D., and Schmalstieg, D. (2005) Interactive mediated reality. *Proceedings of the Australasian User Interface Conference*, Australian Computer Society, 21–29.

Grasset, R., Mulloni, A., Billinghurst, M., and Schmalstieg, D. (2011) Navigation Techniques in Augmented and Mixed Reality: Crossing the Virtuality Continuum. *Handbook of Augmented Reality* (ed. Borko Furht), Springer, 379–408.

Grasset, R., Tatzgern, M., Langlotz, T., Kalkofen, D., and Schmalstieg, D. (2012) Image-driven view management for augmented reality browsers. *Proceedings of the IEEE International Symposium on Mixed and Augmented Reality (ISMAR)*, 177–186.

Grassia, F. S. (1998) Practical parameterization of rotations using the exponential map. *Journal of Graphics Tools* 3, 3, Taylor & Francis, 29–48.

Greger, G., Shirley, P., Hubbard, P. M., and Greenberg, D. P. (1998) The irradiance volume. *IEEE Computer Graphics and Applications* 18, 2, 32–43.

Grosch, T. (2005) Differential photon mapping: Consistent augmentation of photographs with correction of all light paths. *Proceedings of Eurographics 2005 Short Papers*.

Grosch, T., Eble, T., and Müller, S. (2007) Consistent interactive augmentation of live camera images with correct near-field illumination. *Proceedings of the ACM Symposium on Virtual Reality Software and Technology*, 125–132.

Grosso, W. (2001) *Java RMI*. O'Reilly & Associates.

Gruber, L., Richter-Trummer, T., and Schmalstieg, D. (2012) Real-time photometric registration from arbitrary geometry. *Proceedings of the IEEE International Symposium on Mixed and Augmented Reality (ISMAR)*, 119–128.

Gruber, L., Ventura, J., and Schmalstieg, D. (2015) Image-space illumination for augmented reality in dynamic environments. *Proceedings of IEEE Virtual Reality (VR)*, 127–134.

Grubert, J., Heinisch, M., Quigley, A., and Schmalstieg, D. (2015) MultiFi: Multi fidelity interaction with displays on and around the body. *Proceedings of the ACM SIGCHI Conference on Human-Computer Interaction (CHI)*, 3933–3942.

Grundhöfer, A., Seeger, M., Hantsch, F., and Bimber, O. (2007) Dynamic adaptation of projected imperceptible codes. *Proceedings of the IEEE and ACM International Symposium on Mixed and Augmented Reality (ISMAR)*, 181–190.

Guttman, E. (1999) Service location protocol: Automatic discovery of IP network services. *IEEE Internet Computing* 3, 4, 71–80.

Gutwin, C., and Greenberg, S. (2000) The mechanics of collaboration: Developing low cost usability evaluation methods for shared workspaces. *Proceedings of the IEEE International Workshops on Enabling Technologies: Infrastructure for Collaborative Enterprises*, 98–103.

Haber, R. B., and McNabb, D. A. (1990) Visualization idioms: A conceptual model for scientific visualization systems. *Proceedings of IEEE Visualization*, 74–93.

Hainich, R. R. (2009) *The End of Hardware: Augmented Reality and Beyond*. BookSurge Publishing.

Hainich, R. R., and Bimber, O. (2011) *Displays—Fundamentals and Applications*. CRC Press.

Hallaway, D., Feiner, S., and Höllerer, T. (2004) Bridging the gaps: Hybrid tracking for adaptive mobile augmented reality. *Applied Artificial Intelligence* 18, 6, Taylor & Francis, 477–500.

Halle, M. W. (1994) Holographic stereograms as discrete imaging systems. *Proceedings of the IS&T/SPIE International Symposium on Electronic Imaging: Science and Technology*, International Society for Optics and Photonics, 73–84.

Haller, M., Drab, S., and Hartmann, W. (2003) A real-time shadow approach for an augmented reality application using shadow volumes. *Proceedings of the ACM Symposium on Virtual Reality Software and Technology (VRST)*, 56–65.

Haller, M., Landerl, F., and Billinghurst, M. (2005) A loose and sketchy approach in a mediated reality environment. *Proceedings of the International Conference on Computer Graphics and Interactive Techniques in Australasia and South East Asia*, ACM Press, 371–379.

Haller, M., and Sperl, D. (2004) Real-time painterly rendering for MR applications. *Proceedings of the International Conference on Computer Graphics and Interactive Techniques in Australasia and South East Asia*, ACM Press, 30–38.

Hampshire, A., Seichter, H., Grasset, R., and Billinghurst, M. (2006) Augmented reality authoring: Generic context from programmer to designer. *Proceedings of the Australian Conference on Computer-Human Interaction*, ACM Press, 409–412.

Hara, K., Nishino, K., and Ikeuchi, K. (2003) Determining reflectance and light position from a single image without distant illumination assumption. *Proceedings of the IEEE International Conference on Computer Vision (ICCV)*, 560–567.

Hara, K., Nishino, K., and Ikeuchi, K. (2008) Mixture of spherical distributions for (single-view) relighting. *IEEE Transactions on Pattern Analysis and Machine Intelligence* 30, 1, 25–35.

Haringer, M., and Regenbrecht, H. T. (2002) A Pragmatic Approach to Augmented Reality Authoring. *Proceedings of the IEEE and ACM International Symposium on Mixed and Augmented Reality (ISMAR)*, 237–245.

Harris, C., and Stephens, M. (1988) A combined corner and edge detector. *Proceedings of the Alvey Vision Conference*, 147–152.

Harrison, C., Benko, H., and Wilson, A. D. (2011) OmniTouch: Wearable multitouch interaction everywhere. *Proceedings of the ACM Symposium on User Interface Software and Technology (UIST)*, 441–450.

Hartl, A., Arth, C., and Schmalstieg, D. (2014) AR-based hologram detection on security documents using a mobile phone. *Proceedings of the International Symposium on Visual Computing (ISVC)*, Springer, 335–346.

Hartley, R., and Zisserman, A. (2003) *Multiple View Geometry in Computer Vision*. Cambridge University Press.

Hartmann, K., Ali, K., and Strothotte, T. (2004) Floating labels: Applying dynamic potential fields for label layout. *Proceedings of Smart Graphics*, Springer, 101–113.

Hartmann, W., Zauner, J., Haller, M., Luckeneder, T., and Woess, W. (2003) Shadow catcher: A vision based illumination condition sensor using ARToolKit. *IEEE International Workshop on ARToolkit*, 44–45.

Heidemann, G., Bax, I., and Bekel, H. (2004) Multimodal interaction in an augmented reality scenario. *Proceedings of the ACM International Conference on Multimodal Interfaces (ICMI)*, 53–60.

Heilig, M. L. (1962) Sensorama simulator. US patent no. 3050870.

Heilig, M. L. (1992) El cine del futuro: The cinema of the future. *Presence: Teleoperators and Virtual Environments* 1, 3, 279–294.

Held, R., Gupta, A., Curless, B., and Agrawala, M. (2012) 3D puppetry: A kinect-based interface for 3D animation. *Proceedings of the ACM Symposium on User Interface Software and Technology (UIST)*, 423–434.

Henderson, S. J., and Feiner, S. (2009) Evaluating the benefits of augmented reality for task localization in maintenance of an armored personnel carrier turret. *Proceedings of the IEEE International Symposium on Mixed and Augmented Reality (ISMAR)*, 135–144.

Henderson, S., and Feiner, S. (2010) Opportunistic tangible user interfaces for augmented reality. *IEEE Transactions on Visualization and Computer Graphics 16*, 1, 4–16.

Henning, M. (2004) A new approach to object-oriented middleware. *IEEE Internet Computing* 8, 1, 66–75.

Henning, M., and Vinoski, S. (1999) *Advanced CORBA Programming with C++*. Addison-Wesley.

Henrysson, A., Billinghurst, M., and Ollila, M. (2005) Face to face collaborative AR on mobile phones. *Proceedings of the IEEE and ACM International Symposium on Mixed and Augmented Reality (ISMAR)*, 80–89.

Herling, J., and Broll, W. (2010) Advanced self-contained object removal for realizing real-time diminished reality in unconstrained environments. *Proceedings of the IEEE International Symposium on Mixed and Augmented Reality (ISMAR)*, 207–212.

Herling, J., and Broll, W. (2012) PixMix: A real-time approach to high-quality diminished reality. *Proceedings of the IEEE International Symposium on Mixed and Augmented Reality (ISMAR)*, 141–150.

Hesina, G., Schmalstieg, D., Fuhrmann, A., and Purgathofer, W. (1999) Distributed Open Inventor: A practical approach to distributed 3D graphics. *Proceedings of the ACM Symposium on Virtual Reality Software and Technology (VRST)*, 74–81.

Hightower, J., and Borriello, G. (2001) Location systems for ubiquitous computing. *IEEE Computer* 34, 8, 57–66.

Hill, A., Schiefer, J., Wilson, J., Davidson, B., Gandy, M., and MacIntyre, B. (2011) Virtual transparency: Introducing parallax view into video see-through AR. *Proceedings of the IEEE International Symposium on Mixed and Augmented Reality (ISMAR)*, 239–240.

Hillaire, S., Lecuyer, A., Cozot, R., and Casiez, G. (2008) Using an eye-tracking system to improve camera motions and depth-of-field blur effects in virtual environments. *Proceedings of IEEE Virtual Reality (VR)*, 47–50.

Hilliges, O., Kim, D., Izadi, S., and Weiss, M. (2012) HoloDesk: Direct 3D interactions with a situated see-through display. *Proceedings of the ACM SIGCHI Conference on Human Factors in Computing Systems (CHI)*, 2421–2430.

Hoang, T. N., and Thomas, B. H. (2010) Augmented viewport: An action at a distance technique for outdoor AR using distant and zoom lens cameras. *Proceedings of the IEEE International Symposium on Wearable Computers (ISWC)*, 1–4.

Hocking, J. (2015) *Unity in Action: Multiplatform Game Development in C# with Unity 5.* Manning Publications.

Hoff, W. A., Lyon, T., and Nguyen, K. (1996) Computer vision-based registration techniques for augmented reality. *Proceedings of Intelligent Robots and Control Systems XV, Intelligent Control Systems and Advanced Manufacturing*, SPIE, 538–548.

Hoffman, D. M., Girshick, A. R., Akeley, K., and Banks, M. S. (2008) Vergence–accommodation conflicts hinder visual performance and cause visual fatigue. *Journal of Vision* 8, 3, article 33.

Höllerer, T. H. (2004) User interfaces for mobile augmented reality systems. *Dissertation, Computer Science Department*, Columbia University.

Höllerer, T., and Feiner, S. (2004) Mobile augmented reality. In: Karimi, H., and Hammad, A., eds., *Telegeoinformatics: Location-Based Computing and Services*, Taylor & Francis.

Höllerer, T., Feiner, S., Hallaway, D., Bell, B., Lanzagorta, M., Brown, D., Julier, S., Baillot, Y., and Rosenblum, L. (2001a) User interface management techniques for collaborative mobile augmented reality. *Computers & Graphics 25*, 5, Elsevier, 799–810.

Höllerer, T., Feiner, S., and Pavlik, J. (1999a) Situated documentaries: Embedding multimedia presentations in the real world. *Proceedings of the IEEE International Symposium on Wearable Computers (ISWC)*, 79–86.

Höllerer, T., Feiner, S., Terauchi, T., Rashid, G., and Hallaway, D. (1999b) Exploring MARS: Developing indoor and outdoor user interfaces to a mobile augmented reality system. *Computers & Graphics 23*, 6, Elsevier, 779–785.

Höllerer, T., Hallaway, D., Tinna, N., and Feiner, S. (2001b) Steps toward accommodating variable position tracking accuracy in a mobile augmented reality system. *Proceedings of the International Workshop on Artificial Intelligence in Mobile Systems (AIMS)*, 31–37.

Holloway, R. L. (1997) Registration error analysis for augmented reality. *Presence: Teleoperators and Virtual Environments* 6, 4, MIT Press, 413–432.

Holman, D., Vertegaal, R., Altosaar, M., Troje, N., and Johns, D. (2005) Paper windows: Interaction techniques for digital paper. *Proceedings of the ACM SIGCHI Conference on Human Factors in Computing Systems (CHI)*, 591–599.

Hong, J. (2013) Considering privacy issues in the context of Google Glass. *Communications of the ACM* 56, 11, 10–11.

Horn, B. K. P. (1987) Closed-form solution of absolute orientation using unit quaternions. *Journal of the Optical Society of America A* 4, 4, 629–642.

Huang, F.-C., Luebke, D., and Wetzstein, G. (2015) The light field stereoscope: Immersive computer graphics via factored near-eye light field displays with focus cues. *ACM Transactions on Graphics (Proceedings SIGGRAPH)* 34, 4, article 60.

Huang, W., and Alem, L. (2013) HandsInAir: A wearable system for remote collaboration on physical tasks. *Companion of the ACM Conference on Computer Supported Cooperative Work*, 153–156.

Hughes, J. F., van Dam, A., McGuire, M., Sklar, D. F., Foley, J. D., Feiner, S. K., and Akeley, K. (2014) *Computer Graphics: Principles and Practice*, 3rd ed., Addison-Wesley.

Hwang, J., Yun, H., Suh, Y., Cho, J., and Lee, D. (2012) Development of an RTK-GPS positioning application with an improved position error model for smartphones. *Sensors* 12, 10, MDPI, 12988–13001.

Ikeda, T., Oyamada, Y., Sugimoto, M., and Saito, H. (2012) Illumination estimation from shadow and incomplete object shape captured by an RGB-D camera. *Proceedings of the International Conference on Pattern Recognition (ICPR)*, 165–169.

Inami, M., Kawakami, N., Sekiguchi, D., Yanagida, Y., Maeda, T., and Tachi, S. (2000) Visuo-haptic display using head-mounted projector. *Proceedings of IEEE Virtual Reality (VR)*, 233–240.

Inami, M., Kawakami, N., and Tachi, S. (2003) Optical camouflage using retro-reflective projection technology. *Proceedings of the IEEE and ACM International Symposium on Mixed and Augmented Reality (ISMAR)*, 348–349.

Irawati, S., Green, S., Billinghurst, M., Duenser, A., and Ko, H. (2006) "Move the couch where?": Developing an augmented reality multimodal interface. *Proceedings of the IEEE and ACM International Symposium on Mixed and Augmented Reality (ISMAR)*, 183–186.

Irie, K., McKinnon, A. E., Unsworth, K., and Woodhead, I. M. (2008) A technique for evaluation of CCD video-camera noise. *IEEE Transactions on Circuits and Systems for Video Technology* 18, 2, 280–284.

Irschara, A., Zach, C., Frahm, J.-M., and Bischof, H. (2009) From structure-from-motion point clouds to fast location recognition. *Proceedings of the IEEE Conference on Computer Vision and Pattern Recognition (CVPR)*, 2599–2606.

Isard, M., and Blake, A. (1998) CONDENSATION: Conditional density propagation for visual tracking. *International Journal of Computer Vision* 29, Springer, 5–28.

Ishii, H., Kobayashi, M., and Arita, K. (1994) Iterative design of seamless collaboration media. *Communications of the ACM* 37, 8, 83–97.

Ishii, H., and Ullmer, B. (1997) Tangible bits: Towards seamless interfaces between people, bits and atoms. *Proceedings of the SIGCHI Conference on Human Factors in Computing Systems (CHI)*, ACM Press, 234–241.

Ishii, M., and Sato, M. (1994) A 3D spatial interface device using tensed strings. *Presence: Teleoperators and Virtual Environments* 3, 1, MIT Press, 81–86.

Itoh, Y., and Klinker, G. (2014) Interaction-free calibration for optical see-through head-mounted displays based on 3D eye localization. *IEEE Symposium on 3D User Interfaces (3DUI)*, 75–82.

Itti, L., Koch, C., and Niebur, E. (1998) A model of saliency-based visual attention for rapid scene analysis. *IEEE Transactions on Pattern Analysis and Machine Intelligence* 20, 11, 1254–1259.

Iwai, D., Mihara, S., and Sato, K. (2015) Extended depth-of-field projector by fast focal sweep projection. *IEEE Transactions on Visualization and Computer Graphics (Proceedings VR)* 21, 4, 462–470.

Iwata, H., Yano, H., Uemura, T., and Moriya, T. (2004) Food simulator: A haptic interface for biting. *Proceedings of IEEE Virtual Reality (VR)*, 51–57.

Jachnik, J., Newcombe, R. A., and Davison, A. J. (2012) Real-time surface light-field capture for augmentation of planar specular surfaces. *Proceedings of the IEEE International Symposium on Mixed and Augmented Reality (ISMAR)*, 91–97.

Jacobs, K., and Loscos, C. (2004) Classification of illumination methods for mixed reality. *Computer Graphics Forum* 25, 1, 29–51.

Jacobs, K., Nahmias, J.-D., Angus, C., Reche, A., Loscos, C., and Steed, A. (2005) Automatic generation of consistent shadows for augmented reality. *Proceedings of Graphics Interface*, 113–120.

Jacobs, M. C., Livingston, M. A., and State, A. (1997) Managing latency in complex augmented reality systems. *Proceedings of the ACM SIGGRAPH Symposium on Interactive 3D Graphics (I3D)*, 49–55.

Jarusirawad, S., Hosokawa, T., and Saito, H. (2010) Diminished reality using plane-sweep algorithm with weakly-calibrated cameras. *Progress in Informatics* 7, National Institute of Informatics, Japan, 11–20.

Jensen, H. W. (1995) Importance driven path tracing using the photon map. *Eurographics Workshop on Rendering*, Springer, 326–335.

Jeon, S., and Choi, S. (2009) Haptic augmented reality: Taxonomy and an example of stiffness modulation. *Presence: Teleoperators and Virtual Environments* 18, 5, MIT Press, 387–408.

Jo, H., and Hwang, S. (2013) Chili: Viewpoint control and on-video drawing for mobile video calls. *ACM SIGCHI Extended Abstracts on Human Factors in Computing Systems*, 1425–1430.

Jones, A., McDowall, I., Yamada, H., Bolas, M., and Debevec, P. (2007) Rendering for an interactive 360° light field display. *ACM Transactions on Graphics (Proceedings SIGGRAPH)*, 26, 3, article 40.

Jones, B. R., Benko, H., Ofek, E., and Wilson, A. D. (2013) IllumiRoom: Peripheral projected illusions for interactive experiences. *Proceedings of the ACM SIGCHI Conference on Human Factors in Computing Systems (CHI)*, 869–878.

Jones, B. R., Sodhi, R., Campbell, R. H., Garnett, G., and Bailey, B. P. (2010) Build your world and play in it: Interacting with surface particles on complex objects. *Proceedings of the IEEE and ACM International Symposium on Mixed and Augmented Reality (ISMAR),* 165–174.

Jones, B., Sodhi, R., Murdock, M., Mehra, R., Benko, H., Wilson, A., Ofek, E., MacIntyre, B., Raghuvanshi, N., and Shapira, L. (2014) RoomAlive: Magical experiences enabled by scalable, adaptive projector-camera units. *Proceedings of the ACM Symposium on User Interface Software and Technology (UIST)*, 637–644.

Julier, S., Baillot, Y., Brown, D., and Lanzagorta, M. (2002) Information filtering for mobile augmented reality. *IEEE Computer Graphics and Applications* 22, 5, 12–15.

Julier, S., Baillot, Y., Lanzagorta, M., Brown, D., and Rosenblum, L. (2000) BARS: Battlefield augmented reality system. *NATO Symposium on Information Processing Techniques for Military Systems*, 9–11.

Julier, S. J., and Uhlmann, J. K. (2004) Unscented filtering and nonlinear estimation. *Proceedings of the IEEE* 92, 3, 401–422.

Jung, H., Nam, T., Lee, H., and Han, S. (2004) Spray modeling: Augmented reality based 3D modeling interface for intuitive and evolutionary form development. *Proceedings of the International Conference on Artificial Reality and Tele-Existence (ICAT)*.

Just, C., Bierbaum, A., Hartling, P., Meinert, K., Cruz-Neira, C., and Baker, A. (2001) VjControl: An advanced configuration management tool for VR Juggler applications. *Proceedings of IEEE Virtual Reality (VR)*, 97–104.

Kainz, B., Hauswiesner, S., Reitmayr, G., Steinberger, M., Grasset, R., Gruber, L., Veas, E., Kalkofen, D., Seichter, H., and Schmalstieg, D. (2012) OmniKinect: Real-time dense volumetric data acquisition and applications. *Proceedings of the ACM Symposium on User Interface Software and Technology (UIST)*.

Kaiser, E., Olwal, A., McGee, D., Benko, H., Corradini, A., Li, X., Cohen, P., and Feiner, S. (2003) Mutual disambiguation of 3D multimodal interaction in augmented and virtual reality. *Proceedings of the ACM International Conference on Multimodal Interfaces (ICMI)*, 12–19.

Kakuta, T., Oishi, T., and Ikeuchi, K. (2005) Shading and shadowing of architecture in mixed reality. *Proceedings of the IEEE and ACM International Symposium on Mixed and Augmented Reality (ISMAR)*, 200–201.

Kalkofen, D., Mendez, E., and Schmalstieg, D. (2007) Interactive focus and context visualization in augmented reality. *Proceedings of the IEEE and ACM International Symposium on Mixed and Augmented Reality (ISMAR)*, 191–200.

Kalkofen, D., Sandor, C., White, S., and Schmalstieg, D. (2011) Visualization techniques for augmented reality. In: Furht, B., ed., *Handbook of Augmented Reality*, Springer, 65–98.

Kalkofen, D., Tatzgern, M., and Schmalstieg, D. (2009) Explosion diagrams in augmented reality. *Proceedings of IEEE Virtual Reality (VR)*, 71–78.

Kalkusch, M., Lidy, T., Knapp, M., Reitmayr, G., Kaufmann, H., and Schmalstieg, D. (2002) Structured visual markers for indoor pathfinding. *Proceedings of the IEEE International Workshop on ARToolKit*.

Kalman, R. E. (1960) A new approach to linear filtering and predictive problems. *Transactions of the ASME: Journal of Basic Engineering* 82, 34–45.

Kameda, Y., Takemasa, T., and Ohta, Y. (2004) Outdoor see-through vision utilizing surveillance cameras. *Proceedings of the IEEE and ACM International Symposium on Mixed and Augmented Reality (ISMAR)*, 151–160.

Kán, P., and Kaufmann, H. (2012a) High-quality reflections, refractions, and caustics in augmented reality and their contribution to visual coherence. *IEEE International Symposium on Mixed and Augmented Reality (ISMAR)*, 99–108.

Kán, P., and Kaufmann, H. (2012b) Physically-based depth of field in augmented reality. *Proceedings of Eurographics short papers*.

Kán, P., and Kaufmann, H. (2013) Differential irradiance caching for fast high-quality light transport between virtual and real worlds. *Proceedings of the IEEE International Symposium on Mixed and Augmented Reality (ISMAR)*, 133–141.

Kanbara, M., and Yokoya, N. (2004) Real-time estimation of light source environment for photorealistic augmented reality. *Proceedings of the International Conference on Pattern Recognition (ICPR)*, 911–914.

Kaplanyan, A., and Dachsbacher, C. (2010) Cascaded light propagation volumes for real-time indirect illumination. *Proceedings of the ACM SIGGRAPH Symposium on Interactive 3D Graphics and Games (I3D)*, 99–107.

Karsch, K., Hedau, V., Forsyth, D., and Hoiem, D. (2011) Rendering synthetic objects into legacy photographs. *ACM Transactions on Graphics (Proceedings SIGGRAPH Asia)* 30, 6, article 157.

Karsch, K., Sunkavalli, K., Hadap, S., Carr, N., Jin, H., Fonte, R., Sittig, M., and Forsyth, D. (2014) Automatic scene inference for 3D object compositing. *ACM Transactions on Graphics* 33, 3, article 32.

Kasahara, S., Nagai, S., and Rekimoto, J. (2014) LiveSphere: Immersive experience sharing with 360 degrees head-mounted cameras. *Proceedings of the Adjunct Publication of the ACM Symposium on User Interface Software and Technology (UIST)*, 61–62.

Kato, H., and Billinghurst, M. (1999) Marker tracking and HMD calibration for a video-based augmented reality conferencing system. *Proceedings of the International Workshop on Augmented Reality (IWAR)*, 85–94.

Kato, H., Billinghurst, M., Morinaga, K., and Tachibana, K. (2001) The effect of spatial cues in augmented reality video conferencing. *Proceedings of HCI International*, Lawrence-Erlbaum.

Kato, H., Billinghurst, M., Poupyrev, I., Imamoto, K., and Tachibana, K. (2000) Virtual object manipulation on a table-top AR environment. *Proceedings of the IEEE and ACM International Symposium on Augmented Reality (ISAR)*, 111–119.

Kaufmann, H., and Schmalstieg, D. (2003) Mathematics and geometry education with collaborative augmented reality. *Computers & Graphics* 27, 3, Elsevier, 339–345.

Kaufmann, H., Schmalstieg, D., and Wagner, M. (2000) Construct3D: A virtual reality application for mathematics and geometry education. *Education and Information Technologies* 5, 4, 263–276.

Keller, A. (1997) Instant radiosity. *Proceedings of the ACM SIGGRAPH Conference on Computer Graphics and Interactive Techniques*, 49–56.

Kerl, C., Sturm, J., and Cremers, D. (2013) Dense visual SLAM for RGB-D cameras. *Proceedings of the IEEE/RSJ International Conference on Intelligent Robot Systems*, 2100–2106.

Kholgade, N., Simon, T., Efros, A., and Sheikh, Y. (2014) 3D object manipulation in a single photograph using stock 3D models. *ACM Transactions on Graphics (Proceedings SIGGRAPH)* 33, 4, article 127.

Kijima, R., and Ojika, T. (1997) Transition between virtual environment and workstation environment with projective head mounted display. *Proceedings of IEEE Virtual Reality (VR)*, 130–137.

Kim, S., DiVerdi, S., Chang, J. S., Kang, T., Iltis, R., and Höllerer, T. (2007) Implicit 3D modeling and tracking for anywhere augmentation. *Proceedings of the ACM Symposium on Virtual Reality Software and Technology (VRST)*, 19–28.

Kimura, H., Uchiyama, T., and Yoshikawa, H. (2006) Laser produced 3D display in the air. *ACM SIGGRAPH 2006 Emerging Technologies*, 20.

Kitamura, Y., Konishi, T., Yamamoto, S., and Kishino, F. (2001) Interactive stereoscopic display for three or more users. *Proceedings of the ACM SIGGRAPH Conference on Computer Graphics and Interactive Techniques*, 231–240.

Kiyokawa, K. (2007) An introduction to head mounted displays for augmented reality. In: Haller, M., Billinghurst, M., and Thomas, B. H., eds., *Emerging Technologies of Augmented Reality*, IGI Global, 43–63.

Kiyokawa, K. (2012) Trends and vision of head mounted display in augmented reality. *Proceedings of the International Symposium on Ubiquitous Virtual Reality (UbiVR)*, IEEE Press, 14–17.

Kiyokawa, K., Billinghurst, M., Campbell, B., and Woods, E. (2003) An occlusion capable optical see-through head mount display for supporting co-located collaboration. *Proceedings of the IEEE and ACM International Symposium on Mixed and Augmented Reality (ISMAR)*, 133–141.

Kiyokawa, K., Billinghurst, M., Hayes, S. E., Gupta, A., Sannohe, Y., and Kato, H. (2002) Communication behaviors of co-located users in collaborative AR interfaces. *Proceedings of the IEEE and ACM International Symposium on Mixed and Augmented Reality (ISMAR)*, 139–148.

Kiyokawa, K., Iwasa, H., Takemura, H., and Yokoya, N. (1998) Collaborative immersive workspace through a shared augmented environment. *Proceedings of the SPIE Intelligent Systems in Design and Manufacturing,* 2–13.

Kiyokawa, K., Takemura, H., and Yokoya, N. (1999) SeamlessDesign: A face-to-face collaborative virtual/augmented environment for rapid prototyping of geometrically constrained 3-D objects. *Proceedings of the IEEE International Conference on Multimedia Computing and Systems*, 447–453.

Klein, G., and Drummond, T. (2004) Sensor fusion and occlusion refinement for tablet-based AR. *Proceedings of the IEEE and ACM International Symposium on Mixed and Augmented Reality (ISMAR)*, 38–47.

Klein, G., and Murray, D. (2007) Parallel tracking and mapping for small AR workspaces. *Proceedings of the IEEE and ACM International Symposium on Mixed and Augmented Reality (ISMAR)*, 225–234.

Klein, G., and Murray, D. (2008) Improving the agility of keyframe-based SLAM. *Proceedings of the European Conference on Computer Vision (ICCV)*, Springer, 802-815.

Klein, G., and Murray, D. W. (2010) Simulating low-cost cameras for augmented reality compositing. *IEEE Transactions on Visualization and Computer Graphics* 16, 3, 369–380.

Knecht, M., Traxler, C., Mattausch, O., Purgathofer, W., and Wimmer, M. (2010) Differential instant radiosity for mixed reality. *Proceedings of the IEEE International Symposium on Mixed and Augmented Reality (ISMAR)*, 99–107.

Knecht, M., Traxler, C., Purgathofer, W., and Wimmer, M. (2011) Adaptive camera-based color mapping for mixed-reality applications. *Proceedings of the IEEE International Symposium on Mixed and Augmented Reality (ISMAR)*, 165–168.

Knecht, M., Traxler, C., Winklhofer, C., and Wimmer, M. (2013) Reflective and refractive objects for mixed realty. *IEEE Transactions on Visualization and Computer Graphics,* 19, 4, 576–582.

Knöpfle, C., Weidenhausen, J., Chauvigne, L., and Stock, I. (2005) Template based authoring for AR based service scenarios. *Proceedings of IEEE Virtual Reality (VR)*, 249–252.

Knorr, S. B., and Kurz, D. (2014) Real-time illumination estimation from faces for coherent rendering. *Proceedings of the IEEE International Symposium on Mixed and Augmented Reality (ISMAR)*, 113–122.

Kohler, I. (1962) Experiments with goggles. *Scientific American* 206, 62–72.

Kölsch, M., Turk, M., Höllerer, T., and Chainey, J. (2004) Vision-based interfaces for mobility. *Proceedings of the IEEE International Conference on Mobile and Ubiquitous Systems: Networking and Services (Mobiquitous)*, 86–94.

Korkalo, O., Aittala, M., and Siltanen, S. (2010) Light-weight marker hiding for augmented reality. *Proceedings of the IEEE International Symposium on Mixed and Augmented Reality (ISMAR)*, 247–248.

Kosara, R., Hauser, H., and Gresh, D.L. (2003) An interaction view on information visualization. *Eurographics State of the Art Reports*.

Krauss, L. M. (1995) *The Physics of Star Trek*. Basics Books.

Kress, B., and Starner, T. (2013) A review of head-mounted displays (HMD) technologies and applications for consumer electronics. *Proceedings of SPIE Defense, Security, and Sensing*, International Society for Optics and Photonics, 87200A.

Kronander, J., Banterle, F., Gardner, A., Miandji, E., and Unger, J. (2015) Photorealistic rendering of mixed reality scenes. *Computer Graphics Forum* 34, 2, 643-665.

Krueger, M. W. (1991) *Artificial Reality II,* 2nd ed., Addison-Wesley.

Krueger, M. W., Gionfriddo, T., and Hinrichsen, K. (1985) VIDEOPLACE: An artificial reality. *ACM SIGCHI Bulletin* 16, 4, 35–40.

Kulik, A., Kunert, A., Beck, S., Reichel, R., Blach, R., Zink, A., and Fröhlich, B. (2011) C1x6: A stereoscopic six-user display for co-located collaboration in shared virtual environments. *ACM Transactions on Graphics (Proceedings SIGGRAPH Asia)* 30, 6, article 188.

Kummerle, R., Grisetti, G., Strasdat, H., Konolige, K., and Burgard, W. (2011) G2o: A general framework for graph optimization. *Proceedings of the IEEE International Conference on Robotics and Automation (ICRA)*, 3607–3613.

Kurata, T., Sakata, N., Kourogi, M., Kuzuoka, H., and Billinghurst, M. (2004) Remote collaboration using a shoulder-worn active camera/laser. *Proceedings of the IEEE International Symposium on Wearable Computers (ISWC)*, 62–69.

Kurz, D., and BenHimane, S. (2011) Inertial sensor-aligned visual feature descriptors. *Proceedings of the IEEE Conference on Computer Vision and Pattern Recognition (CVPR),* 161–166.

Lagger, P., and Fua, P. (2006) Using specularities to recover multiple light sources in the presence of texture. *Proceedings of the IEEE International Conference on Pattern Recognition (CVPR)*, 587–590.

LaMarca, A., Chawathe, Y., Consolvo, S., Hightower, J., Smith, I., Scott, J., Sohn, T., Howard, J., Hughes, J., Potter, F., Tabert, J., Powledge, P., Borriello, G., Schilit, B. (2005) Place Lab: Device positioning using radio beacons in the wild. *Proceedings of the International Conference on Pervasive Computing*, Springer, 116–133.

Land, E. H., and Mccann, J. J. (1971) Lightness and retinex theory. *Journal of the Optical Society of America* 61, 1, 1–11.

Langlotz, T., Degendorfer, C., Mulloni, A., Schall, G., Reitmayr, G., and Schmalstieg, D. (2011) Robust detection and tracking of annotations for outdoor augmented reality browsing. *Computers & Graphics* 35, 4, Elsevier, 831–840.

Langlotz, T., Regenbrecht, H., Zollmann, S., and Schmalstieg, D. (2013) Audio stickies: Visually-guided spatial audio annotations on a mobile augmented reality platform. *Proceedings of the Australian Conference on Computer-Human Interaction,* 545–554.

Lanier, J. (2001) Virtually there. *Scientific American* 284, 4, 66–75.

Lanman, D., and Luebke, D. (2013) Near-eye light field displays. *ACM Transactions on Graphics (Proceedings SIGGRAPH)* 32, 6, 1–10, article 11.

Ledermann, F., Reitmayr, G., and Schmalstieg, D. (2002) Dynamically shared optical tracking. *Proceedings of the IEEE International Workshop on ARToolKit.*

Ledermann, F., and Schmalstieg, D. (2003) Presenting past and present of an archaeological site in the virtual showcase. *Proceedings of the International Symposium on Virtual Reality, Archeology, and Intelligent Cultural Heritage,* 119–126.

Ledermann, F., and Schmalstieg, D. (2005) APRIL: A high level framework for creating augmented reality presentations. *Proceedings of IEEE Virtual Reality (VR),* 187–194.

Lee, C., DiVerdi, S., and Höllerer, T. (2007) An immaterial depth-fused 3D display. *Proceedings of the ACM Symposium on Virtual Reality Software and Technology (VRST),* 191–198.

Lee, G. A., Nelles, C., Billinghurst, M., and Kim, G.J. (2004) Immersive authoring of tangible augmented reality applications. *Proceedings of the IEEE and ACM International Symposium on Mixed and Augmented Reality (ISMAR),* 172–181.

Lee, J., Hirota, G., and State, A. (2002) Modeling real objects using video see-through augmented reality. *Presence: Teleoperators and Virtual Environments* 11, 2, MIT Press, 144–157.

Lee, K., Zhao, Q., Tong, X., Gong, M., Izadi, S., Lee, S., Tan, P., and Lin, S. (2012) Estimation of intrinsic image sequences from image+depth video. *Proceedings of the European Conference on Computer Vision (ECCV),* Springer, 327–340.

Lee, T., and Höllerer, T. (2006) Viewpoint stabilization for live collaborative video augmentations. *Proceedings of the IEEE and ACM International Symposium on Mixed and Augmented Reality (ISMAR),* 241–242.

Lee, T., and Höllerer, T. (2007) Handy AR: Markerless inspection of augmented reality objects using fingertip tracking. *Proceedings of the IEEE International Symposium on Wearable Computers (ISWC),* 83–90.

Lee, T. and Höllerer, T. (2008) Hybrid feature tracking and user interaction for markerless augmented reality. *Proceedings of IEEE Virtual Reality (VR),* 145–152.

Leibe, B., Starner, T., Ribarsky, W., Wartell, Z., Krum, D., Singletary, B., and Hodges, L. (2000) The perceptive workbench: Toward spontaneous and natural interaction in semi-immersive virtual environments. *Proceedings of IEEE Virtual Reality (VR),* 13–20.

Leigh, S., Schoessler, P., Heibeck, F., Maes, P., and Ishii, H. (2014) THAW: Tangible interaction with see-through augmentation for smartphones on computer screens. *Proceedings of the Adjunct Publication of the ACM Symposium on User Interface Software and Technology (UIST)*, 55–56.

Lensing, P., and Broll, W. (2012) Instant indirect illumination for dynamic mixed reality scenes. *Proceedings of the IEEE International Symposium on Mixed and Augmented Reality (ISMAR)*, 109–118.

Lepetit, V., and Berger, M.-O. (2000) Handling occlusion in augmented reality systems: A semi-automatic method. *Proceedings of the IEEE and ACM International Symposium on Augmented Reality (ISMAR)*, 137–146.

Lepetit, V., and Fua, P. (2005) Monocular model-based 3D tracking of rigid objects: A survey. *Foundations and Trends in Computer Graphics and Vision* 1, 1, Now Publishers, 1–89.

Lepetit, V., Berger, M., and Lorraine, L. (2001) An intuitive tool for outlining objects in video sequences: Applications to augmented and diminished reality. *Proceedings of the International Symposium on Mixed Reality (ISMR)*, 159–160.

Leykin, A., and Tuceryan, M. (2004) Determining text readability over textured backgrounds in augmented reality systems. *Proceedings of the IEEE and ACM International Symposium on Mixed and Augmented Reality (ISMAR)*, 436–439.

Li, H., and Hartley, R. (2006) Five-point motion estimation made easy. *Proceedings of the IEEE International Conference on Pattern Recognition (ICPR)*, 630–633.

Li, Y., Snavely, N., Huttenlocher, D., and Fua, P. (2012) Worldwide pose estimation using 3D point clouds. *Proceedings of the European Conference on Computer Vision (ECCV)*, Springer, 15–29.

Lincoln, P., Welch, G., Nashel, A., State, A., Ilie, A., and Fuchs, H. (2010) Animatronic shader lamps avatars. *Proceedings of IEEE Virtual Reality (VR)*, 225–238.

Lindeman, R. W., Noma, H., and de Barros, P. G. (2007) Hear-through and mic-through augmented reality: Using bone conduction to display spatialized audio. *Proceedings of the IEEE and ACM International Symposium on Mixed and Augmented Reality (ISMAR)*, 173–176.

Lindeman, R. W., Page, R., Yanagida, Y., and Sibert, J. L. (2004) Towards full-body haptic feedback. *Proceedings of the ACM Symposium on Virtual Reality Software and Technology (VRST)*, 146–149.

Liu, H., Darabi, H., Banerjee, P., and Liu, J. (2007) Survey of wireless indoor positioning techniques and systems. *IEEE Transactions on Systems, Man, and Cybernetics, Part C: Applications and Reviews* 37, 6, 1067–1080.

Liu, S., Cheng, D., and Hua, H. (2008) An optical see-through head mounted display with addressable focal planes. *Proceedings of the IEEE and ACM International Symposium on Mixed and Augmented Reality (ISMAR)*, 33–42.

Liu, Y., and Granier, X. (2012) Online tracking of outdoor lighting variations for augmented reality with moving cameras. *IEEE Transactions on Visualization and Computer Graphics* 18, 4, 573–580.

Livingston, M. A., Gabbard, J. L., Swan, J. E. II, Sibley, C. M., and Barrow, J. H. (2013) Basic perception in head-worn augmented reality displays. In: Huang, W., Alem, L., and Livingston, M., eds., *Human Factors in Augmented Reality Environments.* Springer, 35–65.

Loomis, J. M., Golledge, R. G., and Klatzky, R. L. (1998) Navigation system for the blind: Auditory display modes and guidance. *Presence: Teleoperators and Virtual Environments* 7, 2, MIT Press, 193–203.

Loomis, J., Golledge, R., and Klatzky, R. (1993) Personal guidance system for the visually impaired using GPS, GIS, and VR technologies. *Proceedings of the Conference on Virtual Reality and Persons with Disabilities.*

Looser, J., Grasset, R., and Billinghurst, M. (2007) A 3D flexible and tangible magic lens in augmented reality. *Proceedings of the IEEE and ACM International Symposium on Mixed and Augmented Reality (ISMAR)*, 51–54.

Lopez-Moreno, J., Garces, E., Hadap, S., Reinhard, E., and Gutierrez, D. (2013) Multiple light source estimation in a single image. *Computer Graphics Forum* 32, 8, 170–182.

Loscos, C., Frasson, M.-C., Drettakis, G., and Walter, B. (1999) Interactive virtual relighting and remodeling of real scenes. *IEEE Transactions on Visualization and Computer Graphics* 6, 4, 329–340.

Löw, J., Ynnerman, A., Larsson, P., and Unger, J. (2009) HDR light probe sequence resampling for realtime incident light field rendering. *Proceedings of the Spring Conference on Computer Graphics*, 43–50.

Lowe, D. G. (1999) Object recognition from local scale-invariant features. *Proceedings of the International Conference on Computer Vision (ICCV)*, 1150–1157.

Lowe, D. G. (2004) Distinctive image features from scale-invariant keypoints. *International Journal of Computer Vision* 60, 2, 91–110.

Lucas, B., and Kanade, T. (1981) An iterative image registration technique with an application to stereo vision. *Proceedings of the International Joint Conference on Artificial Intelligence (IJCAI)*, 674–679.

Lukosch, S., Billinghurst, M., Alem, L., and Kiyokawa, K. (2015) Collaboration in augmented reality. *Computer Supported Cooperative Work (CSCW)* 24, 6, 515–525.

Lynch, K., and Lynch, M. (1960) *The Image of the City.* MIT Press.

Ma, C., Suo, J., Dai, Q., Raskar, R., and Wetzstein, G. (2013) High-rank coded aperture projection for extended depth of field. *IEEE International Conference on Computational Photography (ICCP)*, 1–9.

Ma, Y., Soatto, S., Kosecka, J., and Sastry, S.S. (2003) *An Invitation to 3-D Vision: From Images to Geometric Models.* Springer Verlag.

MacIntyre, B., Bolter, J. D., and Gandy, M. (2004a) Presence and the aura of meaningful places. *International Workshop on Presence.*

MacIntyre, B., Bolter, J. D., Moreno, E., and Hannigan, B. (2001) Augmented reality as a new media experience. *Proceedings of the IEEE and ACM International Symposium and Augmented Reality (ISAR)*, 29–30.

MacIntyre, B., and Coelho, E. M. (2000) Adapting to dynamic registration errors using level of error (LOE) filtering. *Proceedings of the IEEE and ACM International Symposium on Augmented Reality (ISAR)*, 85–88.

MacIntyre, B., Coelho, E. M., and Julier, S. (2002) Estimating and adapting to registration errors in augmented reality systems. *Proceedings of IEEE Virtual Reality (VR)*, 73–80.

MacIntyre, B., and Feiner, S. (1996) Language-level support for exploratory programming of distributed virtual environments. *Proceedings of the ACM Symposium on User Interface Software and Technology (UIST)*, 83–94.

MacIntyre, B., and Feiner, S. (1998) A distributed 3D graphics library. *Proceedings of the ACM SIGGRAPH Conference on Computer Graphics and Interactive Techniques*, 361–370.

MacIntyre, B., Gandy, M., Dow, S., and Bolter, J. (2004b) DART: A toolkit for rapid design exploration of augmented reality experiences. *Proceedings of the ACM Symposium on User Interface Software and Technology (UIST)*, 197–206.

MacIntyre, B., Hill, A., Rouzati, H., Gandy, M., and Davidson, B. (2011) The Argon AR web browser and standards-based AR application environment. *Proceedings of the IEEE International Symposium on Mixed and Augmented Reality (ISMAR)*, 65–74.

MacIntyre, B., Rouzati, H., and Lechner, M. (2013) Walled gardens: Apps and data as barriers to augmenting reality. *IEEE Computer Graphics and Applications* 33, 3, 77–81.

Mackay, W. E. (1998) Augmented reality: Linking real and virtual worlds: A new paradigm for interacting with computers. *Proceedings of the Working Conference on Advanced Visual Interfaces,* ACM Press, 13–21.

Mackay, W., and Fayard, A.-L. (1999) Designing interactive paper: Lessons from three augmented reality projects. *Proceedings of the International Workshop on Augmented Reality (IWAR)*, 81–90.

MacWilliams, A., Sandor, C., Wagner, M., Bauer, M., Klinker, G., and Brügge, B. (2003) Herding sheep: Live system development for distributed augmented reality. *Proceedings of the IEEE and ACM International Symposium on Mixed and Augmented Reality (ISMAR),* 123–132.

Madsen, C. B., and Laursen, R. (2007) A scalable GPU based approach to shading and shadowing for photorealistic real-time augmented reality. *Proceedings of the International Conference on Graphics Theory and Applications*, 252–261.

Madsen, C. B., and Nielsen, M. (2008) Towards probe-less augmented reality. *Proceedings of the International Conference on Graphics Theory and Applications*, 255–261.

Maes, P., Darrell, T., Blumberg, B., and Pentland, A. (1997) The ALIVE system: Wireless, full-body interaction with autonomous agents. *Multimedia Systems* 5, 2, 105–112.

Maimone, A., and Fuchs, H. (2012) Real-time volumetric 3D capture of room-sized scenes for telepresence. *Proceedings of the 3DTV Conference*.

Maimone, A., Lanman, D., Rathinavel, K., Keller, K., Luebke, D., and Fuchs, H. (2014) Pinlight displays. *ACM Transactions on Graphics (Proceedings SIGGRAPH)* 33, 4, article 20.

Mann, S. (1997) Wearable computing: A first step toward personal imaging. *IEEE Computer* 30, 2, 25–32.

Mann, S. (1998) Humanistic intelligence: WearComp as a new framework for intelligent signal processing. *Proceedings of the IEEE* 86, 11, 2123–2151.

Mariette, N. (2007) From backpack to handheld: The recent trajectory of personal location aware spatial audio. *Proceedings of the International Digital Arts and Culture Conference.*

Mark, W. R., McMillan, L., and Bishop, G. (1997) Post-rendering 3D warping. *Proceedings of the ACM SIGGRAPH Symposium on Interactive 3D Graphics (I3D)*, 7–16.

Marner, M. R., and Thomas, B. H. (2010) Augmented foam sculpting for capturing 3D models. *Proceedings of the IEEE Symposium on 3D User Interfaces (3DUI)*, 63–70.

Marner, M. R., Thomas, B. H., and Sandor, C. (2009) Physical-virtual tools for spatial augmented reality user interfaces. *Proceedings of the IEEE International Symposium on Mixed and Augmented Reality (ISMAR)*, 205–206.

Marr, D. (1982) *Vision: A Computational Investigation into the Human Representation and Processing of Visual Information.* MIT Press.

Mashita, T., Yasuhara, H., Plopski, A., Kiyokawa, K., and Takemura, H. (2013) In-situ lighting and reflectance estimations for indoor AR systems. *Proceedings of the IEEE International Symposium on Mixed and Augmented Reality (ISMAR)*, 275–276.

Matsukura, H., Yoneda, T., and Ishida, H. (2013) Smelling screen: Development and evaluation of an olfactory display system for presenting a virtual odor source. *IEEE Transactions on Visualization and Computer Graphics* 19, 4, 606–615.

Matsushita, N., Hihara, D., Ushiro, T., Yoshimura, S., Rekimoto, J., and Yamamoto, Y. (2003) ID CAM: A smart camera for scene capturing and ID recognition. *Proceedings of the IEEE and ACM International Symposium on Mixed and Augmented Reality (ISMAR)*, 227–236.

May-raz, E., and Lazo, D. (2012) *Sight: A Futuristic Short Film.* YouTube, accessed March 2016.

Mazuryk, T., Schmalstieg, D., and Gervautz, M. (1996) Zoom rendering: Improving 3-D rendering performance with 2-D operations. *International Journal of Virtual Reality* 2, 2, 1–8.

Mei, X., Ling, H., and Jacobs, D.W. (2009) Sparse representation of cast shadows via L1-regularized least squares. *Proceedings of the IEEE International Conference on Computer Vision (ICCV)*, 583–590.

Meilland, M., Barat, C., and Comport, A. I. (2013) 3D high dynamic range dense visual SLAM and its application to real-time object re-lighting. *Proceedings of the IEEE International Symposium on Mixed and Augmented Reality (ISMAR)*, 143–152.

Mendez, E., Feiner, S., and Schmalstieg, D. (2010) Focus and context by modulating first order salient features for augmented reality. *Proceedings of Smart Graphics*, Springer, 232–243.

Mendez, E., Kalkofen, D., and Schmalstieg, D. (2006) Interactive context-driven visualization tools for augmented reality. *Proceedings of the IEEE and ACM International Symposium for Mixed and Augmented Reality (ISMAR)*, 209–218.

Meyer, K., Applewhite, H. L., and Biocca, F. A. (1992) A survey of position trackers. *Presence: Teleoperators and Virtual Environments* 1, 2, MIT Press, 173–200.

Michael, K., and Michael, M. G. (2013) *Uberveillance and the Social Implications of Microchip Implants*. IGI Global.

Mikolajczyk, K., and Schmid, C. (2004) Scale and affine invariant interest point detectors. *International Journal of Computer Vision* 60, 1, 63–86.

Mikolajczyk, K., and Schmid, C. (2005) A performance evaluation of local descriptors. *IEEE Transactions on Pattern Analysis and Machine Intelligence* 27, 10, 1615–1630.

Miksik, O., Torr, P. H. S., Vineet, V., Lidegaard, M., Prasaath, R., Nießner, M., Golodetz, S., Hicks, S. L., Pérez, P., and Izadi, S. (2015) The semantic paintbrush: Interactive 3D mapping and recognition in large outdoor spaces. *Proceedings of the ACM SIGCHI Conference on Human Factors in Computing Systems (CHI)*, 3317–3326.

Milgram, P., and Kishino, F. (1994) A taxonomy of mixed reality visual displays. *IEICE Transactions on Information Systems E77-D*, 12, 1321–1329.

Minatani, S., Kitahara, I., Kameda, Y., and Ohta, Y. (2007) Face-to-face tabletop remote collaboration in mixed reality. *Proceedings of the IEEE and ACM International Symposium on Mixed and Augmented Reality (ISMAR)*, 43–46.

Mine, M. R., Brooks, F. P. Jr., and Sequin, C. H. (1997) Moving objects in space: Exploiting proprioception in virtual-environment interaction. *Proceedings of the ACM SIGGRAPH Conference on Computer Graphics and Interactive Techniques*, 19–26.

Mistry, P., and Maes, P. (2009) SixthSense: A wearable gestural interface. *ACM SIGGRAPH Asia Sketches*.

Miyasato, T. (1998) An eye-through HMD for augmented reality. *Proceedings of the IEEE International Symposium on Robot and Human Interactive Communication*.

Mogilev, D., Kiyokawa, K., Billinghurst, M., and Pair, J. (2002) AR pad: An interface for face-to-face AR collaboration. *ACM CHI Extended Abstracts on Human Factors in Computing Systems*, 654–655.

Mohr, P., Kerbl, B., Kalkofen, D., and Schmalstieg, D. (2015) Retargeting technical documentation to augmented reality. *Proceedings of the ACM SIGCHI Conference on Human–Computer Interaction (CHI)*, 3337–3346.

Moreels, P., and Perona, P. (2007) Evaluation of features, detectors and descriptors based on 3D objects. *International Journal of Computer Vision* 73, 3, 263–284.

Morrison, A., Mulloni, A., Lemmelae, S., Oulasvirta, A., Jacucci, G., Peltonen, P., Schmalstieg, D. and Regenbrecht, H. (2011) Collaborative use of mobile augmented reality with paper maps. *Computers & Graphics* 35, 4, Elsevier, 789–799.

Müller, J., Langlotz, T., and Regenbrecht, H. (2016) PanoVC: Pervasive telepresence using mobile phones. *Proceedings of the IEEE International Conference on Pervasive Computing.*

Mulloni, A., Dünser, A., and Schmalstieg, D. (2010) Zooming interfaces for augmented reality browsers. *Proceedings of the ACM International Conference on Human–Computer Interaction with Mobile Devices and Services (MobileHCI)*, 161–169.

Mulloni, A., Ramachandran, M., Reitmayr, G., Wagner, D., Grasset, R., and Diaz, S. (2013) User friendly SLAM initialization. *Proceedings of the IEEE International Symposium on Mixed and Augmented Reality (ISMAR)*, 153–162.

Mulloni, A., and Schmalstieg, D. (2012) Enhancing handheld navigation systems with augmented reality. *Proceedings of the International Symposium on Service-Oriented Mapping.*

Mulloni, A., Seichter, H., and Schmalstieg, D. (2012) Indoor navigation with mixed reality world-in-miniature views and sparse localization on mobile devices. *Proceedings of the International Working Conference on Advanced Visual Interfaces*, ACM Press, 212.

Mulloni, A., Wagner, D., and Schmalstieg, D. (2008) Mobility and social interaction as core gameplay elements in multi-player augmented reality. *Proceedings of the International Conference on Digital Interactive Media in Entertainment and Arts (DIMEA)*, 472–478.

Mynatt, E. D., Back, M., Want, R., Baer, M., and Ellis, J. B. (1998) Designing audio aura. *Proceedings of the ACM SIGCHI Conference on Human Factors in Computing Systems (CHI)*, 566–573.

Naimark, L., and Foxlin, E. (2002) Circular data matrix fiducial system and robust image processing for a wearable vision-inertial self-tracker. *Proceedings of the Symposium on Mixed and Augmented Reality (ISMAR)*, 27–36.

Najork, M. A., and Brown, M. H. (1995) Obliq-3D: A high-level, fast-turnaround 3D animation system. *IEEE Transactions on Visualization and Computer Graphics* 1, 2, 145–175.

Nakaizumi, F., Noma, H., Hosaka, K., and Yanagida, Y. (2006) SpotScents: A novel method of natural scent delivery using multiple scent projectors. *Proceedings of IEEE Virtual Reality (VR)*, 207–214.

Nakamae, E., Harada, K., Ishizaki, T., and Nishita, T. (1986) A montage method: The overlaying of the computer generated images onto a background photograph. *Proceedings of the ACM SIGGRAPH Conference on Computer Graphics and Interactive Techniques*, 207–214.

Narumi, T., Kajinami, T., Nishizaka, S., Tanikawa, T., and Hirose, M. (2011a) Pseudo-gustatory display system based on cross-modal integration of vision, olfaction and gustation. *Proceedings of IEEE Virtual Reality (VR)*, 127–130.

Narumi, T., Nishizaka, S., and Kajinami, T. (2011b) Augmented reality flavors: Gustatory display based on edible marker and cross-modal interaction. *Proceedings of ACM SIGCHI Conference on Human Factors in Computing Systems (CHI)*, 93–102.

Navab, N. (2004) Developing killer apps for industrial augmented reality. *IEEE Computer Graphics and Applications* 24, 3, 16–20.

Navab, N., Heining, S.-M., and Traub, J. (2010) Camera augmented mobile C-arm (CAMC): Calibration, accuracy study, and clinical applications. *IEEE Transactions on Medical Imaging* 29, 7, 1412–1423.

Newcombe, R. A., Izadi, S., Hilliges, O., Molyneaux, D., Kim, D., Davison, D., Kohli, P., Shotton, J., Hodges, S., Fitzgibbon, A. (2011a) KinectFusion: Real-time dense surface mapping and tracking. *Proceedings of the IEEE International Symposium on Mixed and Augmented Reality (ISMAR)*, 127–136.

Newcombe, R. A., Lovegrove, S. J., and Davison, A. J. (2011b) DTAM: Dense tracking and mapping in real-time. *Proceedings of the IEEE International Conference on Computer Vision*, 2320–2327.

Newman, J., Bornik, A., Pustka, D., Echtler, F., Huber, M., Schmalstieg, D., Klinker, G. (2007) Tracking for distributed mixed reality environments. *Proceedings of the IEEE Virtual Reality Workshop on Trends and Issues in Tracking for Virtual Environments*.

Newman, J., Ingram, D., and Hopper, A. (2001) Augmented reality in a wide area sentient environment. *Proceedings of the International Symposium on Augmented Reality (ISAR)*, 77–86.

Nguyen, T., Grasset, R., Schmalstieg, D., and Reitmayr, G. (2013) Interactive syntactic modeling with a single-point laser range finder and camera. *Proceedings of the IEEE International Symposium on Mixed and Augmented Reality (ISMAR)*, 107–116.

Nguyen, T., Reitmayr, G., and Schmalstieg, D. (2015) Structural modeling from depth images. *IEEE Transactions on Visualization and Computer Graphics (Proceedings ISMAR)*, 21, 11, 1230–1240.

Niantic. (2012) *Ingress. The game.* https://www.ingress.com. Accessed March 2016.

Nishino, K., and Nayar, S. K. (2004) Eyes for relighting. *ACM Transactions on Graphics* 23, 3, 704–711.

Nistér, D. (2004) An efficient solution to the five-point relative pose problem. *IEEE Transactions on Pattern Analysis and Machine Intelligence* 26, 6, 756–777.

Nistér, D., Naroditsky, O., and Bergen, J. (2004) Visual odometry. *Proceedings of the IEEE Computer Society Conference on Computer Vision and Pattern Recognition (CVPR)*, 652–659.

Nistér, D., and Stewenius, H. (2006) Scalable recognition with a vocabulary tree. *Proceedings of the IEEE Computer Society Conference on Computer Vision and Pattern Recognition (CVPR)*, 2161–2168.

Nóbrega, R., and Correia, N. (2012) Magnetic augmented reality: Virtual objects in your space. *Proceedings of the International Working Conference on Advanced Visual Interfaces (AVI)*, ACM Press, 332–335.

Novak, V., Sandor, C., and Klinker, G. (2004) An AR workbench for experimenting with attentive user interfaces. *Proceedings of the IEEE and ACM International Symposium on Mixed and Augmented Reality (ISMAR)*, 284–285.

Nowrouzezahrai, D., Geiger, S., Mitchell, K., Sumner, R., Jarosz, W., and Gross, M. (2011) Light factorization for mixed-frequency shadows in augmented reality. *Proceedings of the IEEE International Symposium on Mixed and Augmented Reality (ISMAR)*, 173–179.

Nuernberger, B., Lien, K.-C., Höllerer, T., and Turk, M. (2016) Interpreting 2D gesture annotations in 3D augmented reality. *Proceedings of the IEEE Symposium on 3D User Interfaces (3DUI)*, 149–158.

Oberweger, M., Wohlhart, P., and Lepetit, V. (2015) Hands deep in deep learning for hand pose estimation. *Proceedings of the Computer Vision Winter Workshop (CVWW)*, 21–30.

Ohlenburg, J., Herbst, I., Lindt, I., Fröhlich, T., and Broll, W. (2004) The MORGAN framework: Enabling dynamic multi-user AR and VR projects. *Proceedings of the ACM Symposium on Virtual Reality Software and Technology (VRST)*, 166–169.

Ohshima, T., Satoh, K., Yamamoto, H., and Tamura, H. (1998) AR2 hockey: A case study of collaborative augmented reality. *Proceedings of the IEEE Virtual Reality Annual International Symposium (VRAIS)*, 268–275.

Ohshima, T., Yamamoto, H., and Tamura, H. (1999) RV-Border Guards: A multi-player entertainment in mixed reality space. Poster. *Proceedings of the International Workshop on Augmented Reality (IWAR)*.

Oishi, T., and Tachi, S. (1995) Methods to calibrate projection transformation parameters for see-through head-mounted displays. *Presence: Teleoperators and Virtual Environments* 5, 1, MIT Press, 122–135.

Okabe, T., Sato, I., and Sato, Y. (2004) Spherical harmonics vs. Haar wavelets: Basis for recovering illumination from cast shadows. *Proceedings of the IEEE Conference on Computer Vision and Pattern Recognition (CVPR)*, 1, 50–57.

Okumura, B., Kanbara, M., and Yokoya, N. (2006) Augmented reality based on estimation of defocusing and motion blurring from captured images. *Proceedings of the IEEE and ACM International Symposium on Mixed and Augmented Reality (ISMAR)*, 219–225.

Olwal, A., Benko, H., and Feiner, S. (2003) SenseShapes: Using statistical geometry for object selection in a multimodal augmented reality system. *Proceedings of the IEEE and ACM International Symposium on Mixed and Augmented Reality (ISMAR)*, 300–301.

Olwal, A., and Feiner, S. (2004) Unit: Modular development of distributed interaction techniques for highly interactive user interfaces. *Proceedings of the International Conference on Computer Graphics and Interactive Techniques in Australasia and South East Asia (GRAPHITE)*, 131–138.

Oskiper, T., Samarasekera, S., and Kumar, R. (2012) Multi-sensor navigation algorithm using monocular camera, IMU and GPS for large scale augmented reality. *Proceedings of the IEEE International Symposium on Mixed and Augmented Reality (ISMAR)*, 71–80.

Oskiper, T., Sizintsev, M., Branzoi, V., Samarasekera, S., and Kumar, R. (2015) Augmented reality binoculars. *IEEE Transactions on Visualization and Computer Graphics* 21, 5, 611–623.

Owen, C., Tang, A., and Xiao, F. (2003) ImageTclAR: A blended script and compiled code development system for augmented reality. *Proceedings of the ISMAR Workshop on Software Technology in Augmented Reality Systems (STARS)*.

Ozuysal, M., Fua, P., and Lepetit, V. (2007) Fast keypoint recognition in ten lines of code. *Proceedings of the IEEE Conference on Computer Vision and Pattern Recognition (CVPR)*, 1–8.

Pan, Q., Reitmayr, G., and Drummond, T. (2009) ProFORMA: Probabilistic feature-based on-line rapid model acquisition. *Proceedings of the British Machine Vision Conference (BMVC)*, 1–11.

Park, Y., Lepetit, V., and Woo, W. (2009) ESM-Blur: Handling and rendering blur in 3D tracking and augmentation. *Proceedings of the IEEE International Symposium on Mixed and Augmented Reality (ISMAR)*, 163–166.

Parker, S. G., Bigler, J., Dietrich, A., Friedrich, H., Hoberock, J., Luebke, D., McAllister, D., McGuire, M., Morley, K., Robison, A., and Stich, M. (2010) OptiX: A general purpose ray tracing engine. *Proceedings of SIGGRAPH, ACM Transactions on Graphics (Proceedings SIGGRAPH)* 29, 4, Article 66.

Pausch, R., Proffitt, D., and Williams, G. (1997) Quantifying immersion in virtual reality. *Proceedings of the ACM SIGGRAPH Conference on Computer graphics and Interactive Techniques (SIGGRAPH)*, 13–18.

Pejsa, T., Kantor, J., Benko, H., Ofek, E., and Wilson, A.D. (2016) Room2Room: Enabling life-size telepresence in a projected augmented reality environment. *Proceedings of the ACM Conference on Computer Supported Cooperative Work (CSCW)*, 1716–1725.

Pessoa, S., Moura, G., Lima, J., Teichrieb, V., and Kelner, J. (2010) Photorealistic rendering for augmented reality: A global illumination and BRDF solution. *Proceedings of IEEE Virtual Reality (VR)*, 3–10.

Petersen, N., and Stricker, D. (2009) Continuous natural user interface: Reducing the gap between real and digital world. *Proceedings of the IEEE International Symposium on Mixed and Augmented Reality (ISMAR)*, 23–26.

Pick, S., Hentschel, B., Tedjo-Palczynski, I., Wolter, M., and Kuhlen, T. (2010) Automated positioning of annotations in immersive virtual environments. *Proceedings of the Eurographics Conference on Virtual Environments & Joint Virtual Reality (EGVE–JVRC)*, 1–8.

Piekarski, W., and Thomas, B. H. (2001) Tinmith-Metro: New outdoor techniques for creating city models with an augmented reality wearable computer. *Proceedings of the IEEE International Symposium on Wearable Computers,* 31–38.

Piekarski, W., and Thomas, B. H. (2002) Tinmith-Hand: Unified user interface technology for mobile outdoor augmented reality and indoor virtual reality. *Proceedings of IEEE Virtual Reality (VR)*, 287–288.

Piekarski, W., and Thomas, B. H. (2003) An object-oriented software architecture for 3D mixed reality applications. *Proceedings of the IEEE and ACM International Symposium on Mixed and Augmented Reality (ISMAR)*, 247–256.

Piekarski, W., and Thomas, B. H. (2004) Augmented reality working planes: A foundation for action and construction at a distance. *Proceedings of the IEEE and ACM International Symposium on Mixed and Augmented Reality (ISMAR)*, 162–171.

Pierce, J. S., Forsberg, A. S., Conway, M. J., Hong, S., Zeleznik, R. C., and Mine, M. R. (1997) Image plane interaction techniques in 3D immersive environments. *Proceedings of the ACM SIGGRAPH Symposium on Interactive 3D Graphics (I3D)*, 39–43.

Pilet, J., Geiger, A., Lagger, P., Lepetit, V., and Fua, P. (2006) An all-in-one solution to geometric and photometric calibration. *Proceedings of the IEEE and ACM International Symposium on Mixed and Augmented Reality (ISMAR)*, 69–78.

Pinhanez, C. S. (2001) The everywhere displays projector: A device to create ubiquitous graphical interfaces. *Proceedings of the International Conference on Ubiquitous Computing (UbiComp)*, Springer, 315–331.

Pintaric, T., and Kaufmann, H. (2008) A rigid-body target design methodology for optical pose-tracking systems. *Proceedings of the ACM Symposium on Virtual Reality Software and Technology (VRST)*, 73–76.

Pintaric, T., Wagner, D., Ledermann, F., and Schmalstieg, D. (2005) Towards massively multi-user augmented reality on handheld devices. *Proceedings of the International Conference on Pervasive Computing*, Springer, 208–219.

Piper, B., Ratti, C., and Ishii, H. (2002) Illuminating clay: A 3-D tangible interface for landscape analysis. *Proceedings of the ACM SIGCHI Conference on Human Factors in Computing Systems (CHI)*, 355–362.

Pirchheim, C., Schmalstieg, D., and Reitmayr, G. (2013) Handling pure camera rotation in keyframe-based SLAM. *Proceedings of the IEEE International Symposium on Mixed and Augmented Reality (ISMAR)*, 229–238.

Plopski, A., Itoh, Y., Nitschke, C., Kiyokawa, K., Klinker, G., and Takemura, H. (2015) Practical calibration of optical see-through head-mounted displays using corneal imaging. *IEEE Transactions on Visualization and Computer Graphics (Proceedings VR)* 21, 4, 481–490.

Poupyrev, I., Tan, D. S., Billinghurst, M., Kato, H., Regenbrecht, H., and Tetsutani, N. (2002) Developing a generic augmented-reality interface. *IEEE Computer* 35, 3, 44–50.

Pustka, D., Huber, M., Waechter, C., Echtler, F., Keitler, P., Newman, J., Schmalstieg, D., Klinker, G. (2011) Ubitrack: Automatic configuration of pervasive sensor networks for augmented reality. *IEEE Pervasive Computing* 10, 3, 68–79.

Quan, L., and Lan, Z. (1999) Linear N-point camera pose determination. *IEEE Transactions on Pattern Analysis and Machine Intelligence* 21, 8, 774–780.

Rakkolainen, I., DiVerdi, S., Olwal, A., Candussi, N., Höllerer, T., Laitinen, M., Piirto, M., and Palovuori, K. (2005) The interactive FogScreen. *ACM SIGGRAPH 2005 Emerging Technologies*, article 8.

Ramamoorthi, R., and Hanrahan, P. (2001) A signal-processing framework for inverse rendering. *Proceedings of the ACM SIGGRAPH Conference on Computer Graphics and Interactive Techniques*, 117–128.

Raskar, R. (2004). Spatial augmented reality. Keynote, *Symposium on Virtual Reality (SVR)*.

Raskar, R., Welch, G., Cutts, M., Lake, A., Stesin, L., and Fuchs, H. (1998) The office of the future: A unified approach to image-based modeling and spatially immersive displays. *Proceedings of the ACM SIGGRAPH Conference on Computer Graphics and Interactive Techniques,* 179–188.

Raskar, R., Welch, G., Low, K.-L., and Bandyopadhyay, D. (2001) Shader lamps: Animating real objects with image-based Illumination. *Proceedings of the Eurographics Workshop on Rendering Techniques,* Springer, 89–102.

Regan, M., and Pose, R. (1994) Priority rendering with a virtual reality address recalculation pipeline. *Proceedings of the ACM SIGGRAPH Conference on Computer Graphics and Interactive Techniques,* 155–162.

Regenbrecht, H., Wagner, M. T., and Baratoff, G. (2002) MagicMeeting: A collaborative tangible augmented reality system. *Virtual Reality* 6, 3, Springer, 151–166.

Reiners, D., Voß, G., and Behr, J. (2002) OpenSG: Basic concepts. *Proceedings of the OPENSG Symposium.*

Reitmayr, G., and Drummond, T. (2006) Going out: Robust model-based tracking for outdoor augmented reality. *Proceedings of the ACM and IEEE International Symposium on Mixed and Augmented Reality (ISMAR),* 109–118.

Reitmayr, G., Eade, E., and Drummond, T. (2005) Localisation and interaction for augmented maps. *Proceedings of the IEEE and ACM International Symposium on Mixed and Augmented Reality (ISMAR),* 120–129.

Reitmayr, G., Eade, E., and Drummond, T. W. (2007) Semi-automatic annotations in unknown environments. *Proceedings of the IEEE and ACM International Symposium on Mixed and Augmented Reality (ISMAR),* 67–70.

Reitmayr, G., and Schmalstieg, D. (2001) An open software architecture for virtual reality interaction. *ACM Symposium on Virtual Reality Software and Technology (VRST),* 47–54.

Reitmayr, G., and Schmalstieg, D. (2003) Location based applications for mobile augmented reality. *Proceedings of the Australasian User Interface Conference (AUIC),* Australian Computer Society, 65–73.

Reitmayr, G., and Schmalstieg, D. (2004) Collaborative augmented reality for outdoor navigation and information browsing. *Proceedings of the Symposium on Location Based Services and TeleCartography,* 31–41.

Reitmayr, G., and Schmalstieg, D. (2005) OpenTracker: A flexible software design for three-dimensional interaction. *Virtual Reality* 9, 1, Springer, 79–92.

Rekimoto, J. (1996) Transvision: A hand-held augmented reality system for collaborative design. *Proceedings of the ACM International Conference on Virtual Systems and Multi-Media (VSMM),* 31–39.

Rekimoto, J. (1997) Pick-and-drop: A direct manipulation technique for multiple computer environments. *Proceedings of the ACM Symposium on User Interface Software and Technology (UIST),* 31–39.

Rekimoto, J. (1998) Matrix: A realtime object identification and registration method for augmented reality. *Proceedings of the 3rd Asia Pacific Conference on Computer–Human Interaction*, 63–68.

Rekimoto, J., Ayatsuka, Y., and Hayashi, K. (1998) Augment-able reality: Situated communication through physical and digital spaces. *Proceedings of the IEEE International Symposium on Wearable Computers*, 68–75.

Rekimoto, J., and Nagao, K. (1995) The world through the computer: Computer augmented interaction with real world environments. *Proceedings of the ACM Symposium on User Interface Software and Technology (UIST)*, 29–36.

Rekimoto, J., and Saitoh, M. (1999) Augmented surfaces: A spatially continuous work space for hybrid computing environments. *Proceedings of the ACM SIGCHI Conference on Human Factors in Computing Systems (CHI)*, 378–385.

Rekimoto, J., Ullmer, B., and Oba, H. (2001) DataTiles: A modular platform for mixed physical and graphical interactions. *Proceedings of the ACM SIGCHI Conference on Human Factors in Computing Systems* (CHI), 269–276.

Ren, D., Goldschwendt, T., Chang, Y., and Höllerer, T. (2016) Evaluating wide-field-of-view augmented reality with mixed reality simulation. *Proceedings of IEEE Virtual Reality (VR)*, 93–102.

Ribo, M., Lang, P., Ganster, H., Brandner, M., Stock, C., and Pinz, A. (2002) Hybrid tracking for outdoor augmented reality applications. *IEEE Computer Graphics and Applications* 22, 6, 54–63.

Richardt, C., Stoll, C., Dodgson, N.A., Seidel, H.-P., and Theobalt, C. (2012) Coherent spatio-temporal filtering, upsampling and rendering of RGBZ videos. *Computer Graphics Forum* (*Proceedings Eurographics*) 31, 2, 247–256.

Ritschel, T., Grosch, T., and Seidel, H.-P. (2009) Approximating dynamic global illumination in image space. *Proceedings of the ACM SIGGRAPH Symposium on Interactive 3D Graphics and Games (I3D)*, 75–82.

Robinett, W., and Holloway, R. (1992) Implementation of flying, scaling and grabbing in virtual worlds. *Proceedings of the ACM SIGGRAPH Symposium on Interactive 3D Graphics (I3D)*, 189–192.

Robinett, W., Tat, I., and Holloway, R. (1995) The visual display transformation for virtual reality. *Presence: Teleoperators and Virtual Environments* 4, 1, 1–23.

Rodden, T. (1992) A survey of CSCW systems. *Interacting with Computers* 3, 3, Elsevier, 319–353.

Rohlf, J., and Helman, J. (1994) IRIS Performer: A high performance multiprocessing toolkit for real-time 3D Graphics. *Proceedings of the ACM SIGGRAPH Conference on Computer Graphics and Interactive Techniques*, 381–394.

Rolland, J. P., Biocca, F., Hamza-Lup, F., Ha, Y., and Martins, R. (2005) Development of head-mounted projection displays for distributed, collaborative, augmented reality applications. *Presence: Teleoperators and Virtual Environments* 14, 5, 528–549.

Rolland, J. P., and Cakmakci, O. (2009) Head-worn displays: The future through new eyes. *Optics & Photonics News*, April, 20–27.

Rolland, J. P., Davis, L. D., and Baillot, Y. (2001) A survey of tracking technologies for virtual environments. In: Barfield, W., and Caudell, T., eds., *Fundamentals of Wearable Computers and Augmented Reality*. Lawrence Erlbaum Associates, 67–112.

Rong, G., and Tan, T.-S. (2006) Jump flooding in GPU with applications to Voronoi diagram and distance transform. *Proceedings of the ACM SIGGRAPH Symposium on Interactive 3D Graphics and games (I3D)*, 130, 109–116.

Rosten, E., and Drummond, T. (2006) Machine learning for high-speed corner detection. *Proceedings of the European Conference on Computer Vision (ECCV)*, Springer, 430–443.

Rosten, E., Reitmayr, G., and Drummond, T. (2005) Real-time video annotations for augmented reality. *Proceedings of the International Symposium on Visual Computing (ISVC)*, 294–302.

Saito, T., and Takahashi, T. (1990) Comprehensible rendering of 3-D shapes. *Proceedings of the ACM SIGGRAPH Conference on Computer Graphics and Interactive Techniques*, 197–206.

Salas-Moreno, R. F., Newcombe, R. A., Strasdat, H., Kelly, P. H. J., and Davison, A. J. (2013) SLAM++: Simultaneous localisation and mapping at the level of objects. *Proceedings of the IEEE Conference on Computer Vision and Pattern Recognition (CVPR),* 1352–1359.

Sandor, C., Cunningham, A., Barbier, S., Eck, U., Urquhart, D., Marner, M. R., Jarvis, G., Rhee, S. (2010a) Egocentric space-distorting visualizations for rapid environment exploration in mobile mixed reality. *Proceedings of IEEE Virtual Reality (VR)*, 47–50.

Sandor, C., Cunningham, A., Dey, A., and Mattila, V.-V. (2010b) An augmented reality X-ray system based on visual saliency. *Proceedings of the IEEE International Symposium on Mixed and Augmented Reality (ISMAR).* 27–36.

Sandor, C., and Reicher, T. (2001) CUIML: A language for the generation of multimodal human–computer interfaces. *Proceedings of the European UIML Conference.*

Sandor, C., Uchiyama, S., and Yamamoto, H. (2007) Visuo-haptic systems: Half-mirrors considered harmful. *Proceedings of the Joint EuroHaptics Conference, Symposium on Haptic Interfaces for Virtual Environment and Teleoperator Systems, and World Haptics*, 292–297.

Sapiezynski, P., Stopczynski, A., Gatej, R., and Lehmann, S. (2015) Tracking human mobility using WiFi signals. *PloS ONE* 10, 7, e0130824.

Sato, I., Sato, Y., and Ikeuchi, K. (1999) Acquiring a radiance distribution to superimpose virtual objects onto a real scene. *IEEE Transactions on Visualization and Computer Graphics* 5, 1, 1–12.

Satoh, K., Hara, K., Anabuki, M., Yamamoto, H., and Tamura, H. (2001) TOWNWEAR: An outdoor wearable MR system with high-precision registration. *Proceedings of the International Symposium on Mixed Reality (ISMR)*, 210–211.

Sattler, T., Leibe, B., and Kobbelt, L. (2011) Fast image-based localization using direct 2D-to-3D matching. *Proceedings of the IEEE International Conference on Computer Vision (ICCV)*, 67–674.

Sattler, T., Leibe, B., and Kobbelt, L. (2012) Improving image-based localization by active correspondence search. *Proceedings of the European Conference on Computer Vision (ECCV)*, 752–765.

Sawhney, N., and Schmandt, C. (2000) Nomadic radio: Speech and audio interaction for contextual messaging in nomadic environments. *ACM Transactions on Computer–Human Interaction* 7, 3, 353–383.

Schall, G., Mendez, E., Kruijff, E., Veas, E., Junghanns, S., Reitinger, B., and Schmalstieg, D. (2008) Handheld augmented reality for underground infrastructure visualization. *Journal of Personal and Ubiquitous Computing* 13, 4, Springer, 281–291.

Schall, G., Wagner, D., Reitmayr, G., Taichmann, E., Wieser, M., Schmalstieg, D., and Hofmann-Wellenhof, B. (2009) Global pose estimation using multi-sensor fusion for outdoor augmented reality. *Proceedings of the IEEE International Symposium on Mixed and Augmented Reality (ISMAR)*, 153–162.

Schinke, T., Henze, N., and Boll, S. (2010) Visualization of off-screen objects in mobile augmented reality. *Proceedings of the ACM International Conference on Human Computer Interaction with Mobile Devices and Services (MobileHCI)*, 313–316.

Schmalstieg, D., Encarnação, L. M., and Szalavari, Z. (1999) Using transparent props for interaction with the virtual table. *Proceedings of the ACM SIGGRAPH Symposium on Interactive 3D Graphics (I3D)*, 147–154.

Schmalstieg, D., Fuhrmann, A., and Hesina, G. (2000) Bridging multiple user interface dimensions with augmented reality. *Proceedings of the IEEE and ACM International Symposium on Augmented Reality (ISAR)*, 20–29.

Schmalstieg, D., Fuhrmann, A., Hesina, G., Szalavári, Z., Encarnação, L. M., Gervautz, M., and Purgathofer, W. (2002) The Studierstube augmented reality project. *Presence: Teleoperators and Virtual Environments* 11, 1, MIT Press, 33–54.

Schmalstieg, D., Fuhrmann, A., Szalavri, Z., and Gervautz, M. (1996) Studierstube: An environment for collaboration in augmented reality. *Proceedings of the Workshop on Collaborative Virtual Environments (CVE)*, 37–48.

Schmalstieg, D., and Hesina, G. (2002) Distributed applications for collaborative augmented reality. *Proceedings of IEEE Virtual Reality (VR)*, 59–66.

Schmeil, A., and Broll, W. (2007) MARA: A mobile augmented reality-based virtual assistant. *Proceedings of IEEE Virtual Reality (VR)*, 267–270.

Schmidt, D. C., and Huston, S. D. (2001) *C++ Network Programming. Volume I: Mastering Complexity with ACE and Patterns.* Addison-Wesley.

Schneider, P., and Eberly, D. (2003) *Geometric Tools for Computer Graphics*. Morgan Kaufmann Publishers.

Schönfelder, R., and Schmalstieg, D. (2008) Augmented reality for industrial building acceptance. *Proceedings of IEEE Virtual Reality (VR)*, 83–90.

Schowengerdt, B. (2010) Near-to-eye display using scanning fiber display engine. *SID Symposium Digest of Technical Papers* 41, 1, Paper 57.1, 848–851.

Schowengerdt, B. T., and Seibel, E. J. (2012) Multifocus displays. In: Chen, J., Cranton, W., and Fihn, M., eds., *Handbook of Visual Display Technology*. Springer, Berlin/Heidelberg, Germany, 2239–2250.

Schwerdtfeger, B., and Klinker, G. (2008) Supporting order picking with augmented reality. *Proceedings of the IEEE International Symposium on Mixed and Augmented Reality (ISMAR)*, 91–94.

Seah, S. A., Martinez Plasencia, D., Bennett, P. D., Karnik, A., Otrocol, V. S., Knibbe, J., Cockburn, A., and Subramanian, S. (2014) SensaBubble: A chrono-sensory mid-air display of sight and smell. *Proceedings of the ACM Conference on Human Factors in Computing Systems (CHI)*, 2863–2872.

Searle, C. L., Braida, L. D., Davis, M. F., and Colburn, H. S. (1976) Model for auditory localization. *Journal of the Acoustical Society of America* 60, 5, 1164–1175.

Seibert, H., and Dähne, P. (2006) System architecture of a mixed reality framework. *Journal of Virtual Reality and Broadcasting* 3, 7, urn:nbn:de:0009-6-7774.

Seo, B.-K., Lee, M.-H., Park, H., and Park, J.-I. (2008) Projection-based diminished reality system. *Proceedings of the International Symposium on Ubiquitous Virtual Reality*, IEEE Press, 25–28.

Shan, Q., Adams, R., Curless, B., Furukawa, Y., and Seitz, S. M. (2013) The Visual Turing Test for scene reconstruction. *Proceedings of the IEEE International Conference on 3D Vision (3DV)*, 25–32.

Shaw, C., Green, M., Liang, J., and Sun, Y. (1993) Decoupled simulation in virtual reality with the MR toolkit. *ACM Transactions on Information Systems* 11, 3, 287–317.

Shi, J., and Tomasi, C. (1994) Good features to track. *Proceedings of the IEEE Conference on Computer Vision and Pattern Recognition (CVPR)*, 593–600.

Shingu, J., Rieffel, E., Kimber, D., Vaughan, J., Qvarfordt, P., and Tuite, K. (2010) Camera pose navigation using augmented reality. *IEEE International Symposium on Mixed and Augmented Reality (ISMAR)*, 271–272.

Shneiderman, B. (1996) The eyes have it: A task by data type taxonomy for information visualizations. *Proceedings of the IEEE Symposium on Visual Languages,* 336–343.

Siegel, A., and White, S. (1975) The development of spatial representations of large-scale environments. *Advances in Child Development and Behavior* 10, Academic Press, 9–55.

Siltanen, S. (2006) Texture generation over the marker area. *Proceedings of the IEEE and ACM International Symposium on Mixed and Augmented Reality (ISMAR)*, 253–254.

Simon, G. (2006) Automatic online walls detection for immediate use in AR tasks. *Proceedings of the IEEE and ACM International Symposium on Mixed and Augmented Reality*, 39–42.

Simon, G. (2010) In-situ 3D sketching using a video camera as an interaction and tracking device. *Proceedings of Eurographics Short Papers*.

Skrypnyk, I., and Lowe, D. (2004) Scene modelling, recognition and tracking with invariant image features. *Proceedings of the IEEE and ACM International Symposium on Mixed and Augmented Reality (ISMAR)*, 110–119.

Slater, M. (2003) A note on presence terminology. *Presence Connect* 3.

Sloan, P.-P., Kautz, J., and Snyder, J. (2002) Precomputed radiance transfer for real-time rendering in dynamic, low-frequency lighting environments. *ACM Transactions on Graphics (Proceedings SIGGRAPH)* 21, 3, 527–536.

Snavely, N., Seitz, S. M., and Szeliski, R. (2006) Photo tourism: Exploring photo collections in 3D. *ACM Transactions on Graphics (Proceedings SIGGRAPH)* 25, 3, 835–846.

Sodhi, R. S., Jones, B. R., Forsyth, D., Bailey, B. P., and Maciocci, G. (2013a) BeThere: 3D mobile collaboration with spatial input. *Proceedings of the ACM SIGCHI Conference on Human Factors in Computing Systems (CHI)*, 179–188.

Sodhi, R., Poupyrev, I., Glisson, M., and Israr, A. (2013b) AIREAL: Interactive tactile experiences in free air. *ACM Transactions on Graphics (Proceedings SIGGRAPH)* 32, 4, article 134.

Song, H., Grossman, T., Fitzmaurice, G., Guimbretière, F., Khan, A., Attar, R., and Kurtenbach, G. (2009) PenLight: Combining a mobile projector and a digital pen for dynamic visual overlay. *Proceedings of the ACM SIGCHI Conference on Human Factors in Computing Systems (CHI)*, 143–152.

Song, J., Sörös, G., Pece, F., Fanello, S. R., Izadi, S., Keskin, C., and Hilliges, O. (2014) In-air gestures around unmodified mobile devices. *Proceedings of the ACM Symposium on User Interface Software and Technology (UIST)*, 319–329.

Spence, R. (2007) *Information Visualization: Design for Interaction*. Pearson Education.

Spindler, M., Martsch, M., and Dachselt, R. (2012) Going beyond the surface: Studying multi-layer interaction above the tabletop. *Proceedings of the SIGCHI Conference on Human Factors in Computing Systems (CHI)*, 1277–1286.

Spohrer, J. C. (1999) Information in places. *IBM Systems Journal* 38, 4, 602–628.

Stafford, A., Piekarski, W., and Thomas, B. H. (2006) Implementation of god-like interaction techniques for supporting collaboration between outdoor AR and indoor tabletop users. *Proceedings of the IEEE and ACM International Symposium on Mixed and Augmented Reality (ISMAR)*, 165–172.

Starner, T., Mann, S., Rhodes, B. J., Levine, J., Healey, J., Kirsch, D., Picard, R. W., and Pentland, A. (1997) Augmented reality through wearable computing. *Presence: Teleoperators and Virtual Environments* 6, 4, MIT Press, 386–398.

State, A., Chen, D. T., Tector, C., Brandt, A., Ohbuchi, R., Bajura, M., and Fuchs, H. (1994) Observing a volume rendered fetus within a pregnant patient. *Proceedings of IEEE Visualization*, 364–368.

State, A., Hirota, G., Chen, D. T., Garrett, W. F., and Livingston, M. A. (1996a) Superior augmented reality registration by integrating landmark tracking and magnetic tracking. *Proceedings of the ACM SIGGRAPH Conference on Computer Graphics and Interactive Techniques (SIGGRAPH)*, 429–438.

State, A., Keller, K. P., and Fuchs, H. (2005) Simulation-based design and rapid prototyping of a parallax-free, orthoscopic video see-through head-mounted display. *Proceedings of the IEEE and ACM International Symposium on Mixed and Augmented Reality (ISMAR)*, 28–31.

State, A., Livingston, M. A., Garrett, W. F., Hirota, G., Whitton, M. C., Pisano, E. P., and Fuchs, H. (1996b) Technologies for augmented reality systems: Realizing ultrasound-guided needle biopsies. *Proceedings of the ACM Conference on Computer Graphics and Interactive Techniques (SIGGRAPH)*, 439–446.

Stauder, J. (1999) Augmented reality with automatic illumination control incorporating ellipsoidal models. *IEEE Transactions on Multimedia* 1, 136–143.

Stein, T., and Décoret, X. (2008) Dynamic label placement for improved interactive exploration. *Proceedings of the ACM International Symposium on Non-Photorealistic Animation and Rendering (NPAR)*, 15–21.

Steptoe, W., Julier, S., and Steed, A. (2014) Presence and discernability in conventional and non-photorealistic immersive augmented reality. *Proceedings of the IEEE International Symposium on Mixed and Augmented Reality (ISMAR)*, 213–218.

Stewénius, H., Engels, C., and Nistér, D. (2006) Recent developments on direct relative orientation. *ISPRS Journal of Photogrammetry and Remote Sensing* 60, 4, 284–294.

Stoakley, R., Conway, M. J., and Pausch, R. (1995) Virtual reality on a WIM: Interactive worlds in miniature. *Proceedings of the ACM SIGCHI Conference on Human Factors in Computing Systems (CHI)*, 265–272.

Strauss, P. S., and Carey, R. (1992) An object-oriented 3D graphics toolkit. *Proceedings of the ACM Conference on Computer Graphics and Interactive Techniques (SIGGRAPH)*, 341–349.

Sugano, N., Kato, H., and Tachibana, K. (2003) The effects of shadow representation of virtual objects in augmented reality. *Proceedings of the IEEE and ACM International Symposium on Mixed and Augmented Reality (ISMAR)*, 76–83.

Sukan, M., Elvezio, C., Oda, O., Feiner, S., and Tversky, B. (2014) ParaFrustum: Visualization techniques for guiding a user to a constrained set of viewing positions and orientations. *Proceedings of the ACM Symposium on User Interface Software and Technology (UIST)*, 331–340.

Sukan, M., Feiner, S., Tversky, B., and Energin, S. (2012) Quick viewpoint switching for manipulating virtual objects in hand-held augmented reality using stored snapshots. *Proceedings of the IEEE International Symposium on Mixed and Augmented Reality (ISMAR)*, 217–226.

Sun, S.-Y., Gilbertson, M., and Anthony, B. W. (2013) Computer-guided ultrasound probe realignment by optical tracking. *Proceedings of the IEEE International Symposium on Biomedical Imaging (ISBI)*, 21–24.

Suomela, R., and Lehikoinen, J. (2000) Context compass. *Proceedings of the International Symposium on Wearable Computers (ISWC)*, 147–154.

Supan, P., Stuppacher, I., and Haller, M. (2006) Image based shadowing in real-time augmented reality. *International Journal of Virtual Reality* 5, 3, 1–7.

Sutherland, I. E. (1965) The ultimate display. *Proceedings of the Congress of the International Federation of Information Processing (IFIP)*, 506–508.

Sutherland, I. E. (1968) A head-mounted three dimensional display. *Proceedings of the AFIPS Fall Joint Computer Conference, Part I*, 757–764.

Sweeney, C., Fragoso, V., Höllerer, T., and Turk, M. (2014) gDLS: A scalable solution to the generalized pose and scale problem. *Proceedings of the European Conference on Computer Vision (ECCV)*, Springer, 16–31.

Szalavári, Z., Eckstein, E., and Gervautz, M. (1998) Collaborative gaming in augmented reality. *Proceedings of the ACM Symposium on Virtual Reality Software and Technology (VRST)*, 195–204.

Szalavári, Z., and Gervautz, M. (1997) The personal interaction panel: A two-handed interface for augmented reality. *Computer Graphics Forum (Proceedings Eurographics)* 16, *3*, 335–346.

Szeliski, R. (2006) Image alignment and stitching: A tutorial. *Foundations and Trends in Computer Graphics and Vision* 2, 1, Now Publishers, 1–104.

Szeliski, R. (2010) *Computer Vision: Algorithms and Applications*. Springer.

Takacs, G., Xiong, Y., Grzeszczuk, R., Xiong, Y., Chen, W.-C., Bismpigiannis, T., Grzeszczuk, R., Pulli, K., and Girod, B. (2008) Outdoors augmented reality on mobile phone using loxel-based visual feature organization. *Proceedings of the ACM International Conference on Multimedia Information Retrieval (MIR)*, 427–434.

Takemura, M., and Ohta, Y. (2002) Diminishing head-mounted display for shared mixed reality. *Proceedings of the IEEE and ACM International Symposium on Mixed and Augmented Reality (ISMAR)*, 149–156.

Tallon, L., and Walker, K. (2008) *Digital technologies and the museum experience: Handheld guides and other media*. AltaMira Press.

Tamura, H. (2000) What happens at the border between real and virtual worlds: The MR project and other research activities in Japan. *Proceedings of the IEEE and ACM International Symposium on Augmented Reality (ISAR)*, xii–xv.

Tamura, H., Yamamoto, H., and Katayama, A. (2001) Mixed reality: Future dreams seen at the border between real and virtual worlds. *IEEE Computer Graphics and Applications* 21, 6, 64–70.

Tan, H. Z., and Pentland, A. (2001) Tactual displays for sensory substitution and wearable computers. In: Barfield, W., and Caudell, T., eds., *Fundamentals of Wearable Computers and Augmented Reality*. Lawrence Erlbaum Associates, 579–598.

Tanaka, K., Kishino, Y., Miyamae, M., Terada, T., and Nishio, S. (2008) An information layout method for an optical see-through head mounted display focusing on the viewability. *Proceedings of the IEEE and ACM International Symposium on Mixed and Augmented Reality*, 139–142.

Tateno, K., Takemura, M., and Ohta, Y. (2005) Enhanced eyes for better gaze-awareness in collaborative mixed reality. *Proceedings of the IEEE and ACM International Symposium on Mixed and Augmented Reality (ISMAR)*, 100–103.

Tatzgern, M., Orso, V., Kalkofen, D., Jacucci, G., Gamberini, L., and Schmalstieg, D. (2016) Adaptive information density for augmented reality displays. *Proceedings of IEEE Virtual Reality (VR)*.

Tatzgern, M., Grasset, R., Kalkofen, D., and Schmalstieg, D. (2014a) Transitional augmented reality navigation for live captured scenes. *Proceedings of IEEE Virtual Reality (VR)*, 21–26.

Tatzgern, M., Kalkofen, D., Grasset, R., and Schmalstieg, D. (2014b) Hedgehog labeling: View management techniques for external labels in 3D space. *Proceedings IEEE Virtual Reality (VR)*, 27–32.

Tatzgern, M., Kalkofen, D., and Schmalstieg, D. (2010) Multi-perspective compact explosion diagrams. *Computers & Graphics* 35, 1, Elsevier, 135–147.

Taylor, R. M., Hudson, T. C., Seeger, A., Weber, H., Juliano, J., and Helser, A. T. (2001) VRPN: A device-independent, network-transparent VR peripheral system. *Proceedings of the ACM Symposium on Virtual Reality Software and Technology (VRST)*, 55–61.

Teh, J. K. S., Cheok, A. D., Peiris, R. L., Choi, Y., Thuong, V., and Lai, S. (2008) Huggy pajama: A mobile parent and child hugging communication system. *Proceedings of the International Conference on Interaction Design and Children (IDC)*, ACM Press, 250–257.

Terenzi, A. and Terenzi, G. (2011) Towards augmented reality design: The case for the AR plugins. *Proceedings of the IEEE ISMAR Workshop on Authoring Solutions for Augmented Reality*.

Thomas, B., Demczuk, V., Piekarski, W., Hepworth, D., and Gunther, B. (1998) A wearable computer system with augmented reality to support terrestrial navigation. *Proceedings of the IEEE International Symposium on Wearable Computers (ISWC)*, 168–171.

Tomasi, C., and Kanade, T. (1991) Detection and tracking of point features. Shape and motion from image streams: A factorization method—Part 3. *Technical Report CMU-CS-91-132, School of Computer Science*, Carnegie Mellon University.

Tomioka, M., Ikeda, S., and Sato, K. (2013) Approximated user-perspective rendering in tablet-based augmented reality. *Proceedings of the IEEE International Symposium on Mixed and Augmented Reality (ISMAR)*, 21–28.

Towles, H., Chen, W., Yang, R., Kum, S., Fuchs, H., Kelshikar, N., Mulligan, J., Daniilidis, K., Holden, L., Zeleznik, R. C., Sadagic, A., and Lanier, J. (2002) 3D tele-collaboration over Internet2. *International Workshop on Immersive Telepresence (ITP)*, ACM Press.

Tramberend, H. (1999) Avocado: A distributed virtual reality framework. *Proceedings of IEEE Virtual Reality (VR)*, 14–21.

Treisman, A. M., and Gelade, G. (1980) A feature-integration theory of attention. *Cognitive Psychology* 12, 1, 97–136.

Triggs, B., McLauchlan, P., Hartley, R., and Fitzgibbon, A. (2000) Bundle adjustment: A modern synthesis. In: Triggs, B., Zisserman, A., and Szeliski, R., eds., *Vision Algorithms: Theory and Practice*. Springer, 298–372.

Tsai, R. Y. (1986) An efficient and accurate camera calibration technique for 3D machine vision. *Proceedings of the IEEE Conference on Computer Vision and Pattern Recognition*, 364–374.

Tsai, R. Y. and Lenz, R. K. (1989) A new technique for fully autonomous and efficient 3D robotics hand/eye calibration. *IEEE Journal of Robotics and Automation* 5, 3, 345–358.

Tsetserukou, D., Sato, K., and Tachi, S. (2010) ExoInterfaces: Novel exosceleton haptic interfaces for virtual reality, augmented sport and rehabilitation. *Proceedings of the ACM Augmented Human International Conference (AH)*, article 1.

Tsumura, N., Dang, M. N., and Miyake, Y. (2003) Estimating the directions to light sources using images of eye for reconstructing 3D human face. *Color Imaging Conference*, Society for Imaging Science and Technology, 77–81.

Tuceryan, M., Genc, Y., and Navab, N. (2002) Single-point active alignment method (SPAAM) for optical see-through HMD calibration for augmented reality. *Presence: Teleoperators and Virtual Environments* 11, 3, MIT Press, 259–276.

Turing, A. M. (1950) Computing machinery and intelligence. *Mind*, LIX, 236, 433–460.

Uchiyama, S., Takemoto, K., Satoh, K., Yamamoto, H., and Tamura, H. (2002) MR platform: A basic body on which mixed reality applications are built. *Proceedings of the International Symposium on Mixed and Augmented Reality (ISMAR)*, 246–320.

Ullmer, B., and Ishii, H. (1997) The metaDESK: Models and prototypes for tangible user interfaces. *Proceedings of the ACM Symposium on User Interface Software and Technology (UIST)*, 223–232.

Umeyama, S. (1991) Least-squares estimation of transformation parameters between two point patterns. *IEEE Transactions on Pattern Analysis and Machine Intelligence* 13, 4, 376–380.

Underkoffler, J., and Ishii, H. (1998) Illuminating light: An optical design tool with a luminous-tangible interface. *Proceedings of the ACM SIGCHI Conference on Human Factors in Computing Systems (CHI)*, 542–549.

Underkoffler, J., and Ishii, H. (1999) Urp: A luminous-tangible workbench for urban planning and design. *Proceedings of the ACM SIGCHI Conference on Human Factors in Computing Systems (CHI)*, 386–393.

Vacchetti, L., Lepetit, V., Papagiannakis, G., Ponder, M., and Fu, P. (2003) Stable real-time interaction between virtual humans and real scenes. *Proceedings of the International Conference on 3D Digital Imaging and Modeling (3DIM)*, 449–456.

Valentin, J., Vineet, V., Cheng, M-M., Kim, D., Shotton, J., Kohli, P., Nießner, M., Criminisi, A., Izadi, S., and Torr, P. (2015) SemanticPaint: Interactive 3D labeling and learning at your fingertips. *ACM Transactions on Graphics (Proceedings SIGGRAPH)* 34, 5, Article 154.

van den Hengel, A., Hill, R., Ward, B., and Dick, A. (2009) In situ image-based modeling. *Proceedings of the IEEE International Symposium on Mixed and Augmented Reality (ISMAR)*, 107–110.

Veas, E., Grasset, R., Ferencik, I., Grünewald, T., and Schmalstieg, D. (2012a) Mobile augmented reality for environmental monitoring. *Personal and Ubiquitous Computing* 17, 7, Springer, 1515–1531.

Veas, E., Grasset, R., Kruijff, E., and Schmalstieg, D. (2012b) Extended overview techniques for outdoor augmented reality. *IEEE Transactions on Visualization and Computer Graphics* 18, 4, 565–572.

Veas, E., Mulloni, A., Kruijff, E., Regenbrecht, H., Schmalstieg, D. (2010) Techniques for view transition in multiview outdoor environments. *Proceedings of Graphics Interface,* Canadian Information Processing Society, 193–200.

Ventura, J., Arth, C., Reitmayr, G., and Schmalstieg, D. (2014a) Global localization from monocular SLAM on a mobile phone. *IEEE Transactions on Visualization and Computer Graphics* 20, 4, 531–539.

Ventura, J., Arth, C., Reitmayr, G., and Schmalstieg, D. (2014b) A minimal solution to the generalized pose-and-scale problem. *Proceedings of IEEE Computer Vision and Pattern Recognition (CVPR)*, 422–429.

Viega, J., Conway, M., Williams, G., and Pausch, R. (1996) 3D magic lenses. *Proceedings of the ACM Symposium on User Interface Software and Technology (UIST)*, 51–58.

Vinnikov, M., and Allison, R. S. (2014) Gaze-contingent depth of field in realistic scenes. *Proceedings of the ACM Symposium on Eye Tracking Research and Applications (ETRA)*, 119–126.

von Spiczak, J., Samset, E., DiMaio, S., Reitmayr, G., Schmalstieg, D., Burghart, C., and Kikinis, R. (2007) Multimodal event streams for virtual reality. *Proceedings of the SPIE Conference on Multimedia Computing and Networking (MMCN)*, SPIE 6504-0M.

Wagner, D., Langlotz, T., and Schmalstieg, D. (2008a) Robust and unobtrusive marker tracking on mobile phones. *Proceedings of the IEEE and ACM International Symposium on Mixed and Augmented Reality,* 121–124.

Wagner, D., Mulloni, A., Langlotz, T., and Schmalstieg, D. (2010) Real-time panoramic mapping and tracking on mobile phones. *Proceedings of IEEE Virtual Reality (VR)*, 211–218.

Wagner, D., Reitmayr, G., Mulloni, A., Drummond, T., and Schmalstieg, D. (2008b) Pose tracking from natural features on mobile phones. *Proceedings of the IEEE and ACM International Symposium on Mixed and Augmented Reality,* 125–134.

Wagner, D., Reitmayr, G., Mulloni, A., and Schmalstieg, D. (2009) Real time detection and tracking for augmented reality on mobile phones. *IEEE Transactions on Visualization and Computer Graphics,* 16, 3, 355–468.

Wagner, D., and Schmalstieg, D. (2003) First steps towards handheld augmented reality. *Proceedings of the IEEE Symposium on Wearable Computers (ISWC)*, 127–135.

Wagner, D., and Schmalstieg, D. (2007) ARToolKitPlus for pose tracking on mobile devices. *Proceedings of the Computer Vision Winter Workshop (CVWW)*.

Walsh, J. A., von Itzstein, S., and Thomas, B. H. (2013) Tangible agile mapping: Ad-hoc tangible user interaction definition. *Proceedings of the Australasian User Interface Conference (AUIC)*, Australian Computer Society, 139, 3–12.

Wang, Y., and Samaras, D. (2006) Estimation of multiple illuminants from a single image of arbitrary known geometry. *Proceedings of the European Conference on Computer Vision (ECCV)*, Springer, 272–288.

Want, R., Hopper, A., Falcao, V., and Gibbons, J. (1992) The Active Badge location system. *ACM Transactions on Information Systems* 10, 1, 91–102.

Ward, G. J., Rubinstein, F. M., and Clear, R. D. (1988) A ray tracing solution for diffuse interreflection. *Proceedings of the ACM SIGGRAPH Conference on Computer Graphics and Interactive Techniques*, 85–92.

Watson, B. A., and Hodges, L. F. (1995) Using texture maps to correct for optical distortion in head-mounted displays. *Proceedings of the IEEE Virtual Reality Annual International Symposium (VRAIS)*, 172–178.

Weir, P., Sandor, C., Swoboda, M., Nguyen, T., Eck, U., Reitmayr, G., and Dey, A. (2013) BurnAR: Involuntary heat sensations in augmented reality. *Proceedings of IEEE Virtual Reality (VR)*, 43–46.

Weiser, M. (1991) The computer for the 21st century. *Scientific American* 265, 3, 94–104.

Welch, G., and Bishop, G. (1995) An introduction to the Kalman filter. Technical Report 95-041, University of North Carolina, Chapel Hill, Updated: July 2006.

Welch, G., and Bishop, G. (1997) SCAAT: Incremental tracking with incomplete information. *Proceedings of the ACM SIGGRAPH Conference on Computer Graphics and Interactive Techniques*, 333–344.

Welch, G., and Bishop, G. (2001) An introduction to the Kalman filter. *ACM SIGGRAPH Course Notes*.

Welch, G., Bishop, G., Vicci, L., Brumback, S., Keller, K., and Colucci, D. (2001) High-performance wide-area optical tracking: The HiBall tracking system. *Presence* 10, 1, 1–21.

Welch, G., and Foxlin, E. (2002) Motion tracking: No silver bullet, but a respectable arsenal. *Computer Graphics and Applications* 22, 6, 24–38.

Wellner, P. (1993) Interacting with paper on the DigitalDesk. *Communications of the ACM* 36, 7, 87–96.

Wellner, P., and Freemann, S. (1993) The DoubleDigitalDesk: Shared editing of paper documents. Technical Report EPC-93-108, Xerox Research Centre Cambridge Laboratory, Cambridge, UK.

Wetzstein, G. (2015) Why people should care about light field displays. *SID Information Display* 31, 2, 22–28.

White, S., and Feiner, S. (2009a) SiteLens: Situated visualization techniques for urban site visits. *Proceedings of the ACM SIGCHI Conference on Human Factors in Computing Systems (CHI)*, 1117–1120.

White, S., Feiner, S., and Kopylec, J. (2006) Virtual vouchers: Prototyping a mobile augmented reality user interface for botanical species identification. *Proceedings on the IEEE Symposium on 3D User Interfaces (3DUI)*, 119–126.

White, S., Feng, D., and Feiner, S. (2009b) Interaction and presentation techniques for shake menus in tangible augmented reality. *IEEE International Symposium on Mixed and Augmented Reality (ISMAR)*, 39–48.

Wigdor, D., Forlines, C., Baudisch, P., Barnwell, J., and Shen, C. (2007) LucidTouch: A see-through mobile device. *Proceedings of the ACM Symposium on User Interface Software and Technology (UIST)*, 269–278.

Williams, L. (1978) Casting curved shadows on curved surfaces. *Proceedings of the ACM SIGGRAPH Conference on Computer Graphics and Interactive Techniques*, 270–274.

Wilson, A. D., and Benko, H. (2010) Combining multiple depth cameras and projectors for interactions on, above and between surfaces. *Proceedings of the ACM Symposium on User Interface Software and Technology (UIST)*, 273–282.

Wilson, A. D., Benko, H., Izadi, S., and Hilliges, O. (2012) Steerable augmented reality with the beamatron. *Proceedings of the ACM Symposium on User Interface Software and Technology (UIST)*, 413–422.

Wither, J., Coffin, C., Ventura, J., and Höllerer, T. (2008) Fast annotation and modeling with a single-point laser range finder. *IEEE International Symposium on Mixed and Augmented Reality (ISMAR)*, 65–68.

Wither, J., Diverdi, S., and Höllerer, T. (2006) Using aerial photographs for improved mobile AR annotation. *IEEE International Symposium on Mixed and Augmented Reality (ISMAR)*, 159–162.

Wither, J., DiVerdi, S., and Höllerer, T. (2007) Evaluating display types for AR selection and annotation. *IEEE International Symposium on Mixed and Augmented Reality (ISMAR)*, 95–98.

Wither, J., DiVerdi, S., and Höllerer, T. (2009) Annotation in outdoor augmented reality. *Computers & Graphics,* 33, 6, Elsevier, 679–689.

Wither, J., and Höllerer, T. (2005) Pictorial depth cues for outdoor augmented reality. *Proceedings of the IEEE International Symposium on Wearable Computers (ISWC)*, 92–99.

Wloka, M. M. (1995) Lag in multiprocessor virtual reality. *Presence: Teleoperators and Virtual Environments* 4, 1, MIT Press, 50–63.

Wloka, M. M., and Anderson, B. G. (1995) Resolving occlusion in augmented reality. *Proceedings of the ACM SIGGRAPH Symposium on Interactive 3D Graphics (I3D)*, 5–12.

Woo, G., Lippman, A., and Raskar, R. (2012) VRCodes: Unobtrusive and active visual codes for interaction by exploiting rolling shutter. *Proceedings of the IEEE International Symposium on Mixed and Augmented Reality (ISMAR)*, 59–64.

Xiao, R., Harrison, C., and Hudson, S.E. (2013) WorldKit: Rapid and easy creation of ad-hoc interactive applications on everyday surfaces. *Proceedings of the ACM SIGCHI Conference on Human Factors in Computing Systems (CHI)*, 879–888.

Yamada, T., Yokoyama, S., Tanikawa, T., Hirota, K., and Hirose, M. (2006) Wearable olfactory display: Using odor in outdoor environment. *Proceedings of IEEE Virtual Reality (VR)*, 199–206.

Yamamoto, S., Tamaki, H., Okajima, Y., Bannai, Y., and Okada, K. (2008) Symmetric model of remote collaborative MR using tangible replicas. *Proceedings of IEEE Virtual Reality (VR)*, 71–74.

Ye, G., State, A., and Fuchs, H. (2010) A practical multi-viewer tabletop autostereoscopic display. *Proceedings of the IEEE International Symposium on Mixed and Augmented Reality (ISMAR)*, 147–156.

Yii, W., Li, W. H., and Drummond, T. (2012) Distributed visual processing for augmented reality. *Proceedings of the IEEE International Symposium on Mixed and Augmented Reality (ISMAR)*, 41–48.

Yokokohji, Y., Hollis, R. L., and Kanade, T. (1999) WYSIWYF display: A visual/haptic interface to virtual environment. *Presence: Teleoperators and Virtual Environments* 8, 4, MIT Press, 412–434.

Yoshida, T., Jo, K., Minamizawa, K., Nii, H., Kawakami, N., and Tachi, S. (2008) Transparent cockpit: Visual assistance system for vehicle using retro-reflective projection technology. *Proceedings of IEEE Virtual Reality (VR)*, 185–188.

You, S., and Neumann, U. (2001) Fusion of vision and gyro tracking for robust augmented reality registration. *Proceedings of IEEE Virtual Reality (VR)*, 71–78.

Zauner, J., Haller, M., Brandl, A., and Hartman, W. (2003) Authoring of a mixed reality assembly instructor for hierarchical structures. *Proceedings of the IEEE International Symposium on Mixed and Augmented Reality (ISMAR)*, 237–246.

Zhang, Z. (2000) A flexible new technique for camera calibration. *IEEE Transactions on Pattern Analysis and Machine Intelligence 22*, 11, 1330–1334.

Zheng, F., Schmalstieg, D., and Welch, G. (2014) Pixel-wise closed-loop registration in video-based augmented reality. *Proceedings of the IEEE International Symposium on Mixed and Augmented Reality (ISMAR)*, 135–143.

Zokai, S., Esteve, J., Genc, Y., and Navab, N. (2003) Multiview Paraperspective Projection Model for Diminished Reality. *Proceedings of the IEEE International Symposium on Mixed and Augmented Reality (ISMAR)*, 217–226.

Zollmann, S., Hoppe, C., Langlotz, T., and Reitmayr, G. (2014) FlyAR: Augmented reality supported micro aerial vehicle navigation. *IEEE Transactions on Visualization and Computer Graphics* 20, 4, 560–568.

Zollmann, S., Kalkofen, D., Mendez, E., and Reitmayr, G. (2010) Image-based ghostings for single layer occlusions in augmented reality. *Proceedings of the IEEE International Symposium on Mixed and Augmented Reality (ISMAR)*, 19–26.

INDEX

Numbers

2D
> annotations, 325
> establishing 3D point from 2D observations, 136–137
> radar maps in navigation guidance, 350

3D
> ability of AR to produce 3D views, 25
> annotations, 325
> in AR games, 27
> combining 3D tracking with 3D scanning, 106
> establishing 3D point from 2D observations, 136–137
> tracking, 87
> using 3D scanners in construction and industry, 14
> volumetric displays and, 58

3D Puppetry, authoring by performance, 337

3DOF. *See also* Degrees of freedom (DOF)
> in gyroscope, 102
> in linear accelerometers, 104
> in measurement systems, 92

3DS Max plug-in, for authoring, 340

6DOF. *See also* Degrees of freedom (DOF)
> complementary sensor fusion, 117
> in measurement systems, 92
> Perspective-n-Point (PnP) problem, 146–147
> tracking/manipulating rigid objects, 280

A

Aberrations. *See also* Distortions, 55

Absolute measurements, versus relative, 93

Absolute orientation
> alignment of two tracking systems, 188
> in multiple-camera infrared tracking, 137–138

Abstraction
> hardware abstraction, 332
> platform abstraction, 382–383
> UI abstraction, 383

Accelerometers, mobile sensors for tracking, 103–104

Accommodation. *See also* Focus
> in multifocal display, 46
> at various distances, 45

Accommodation-vergence conflict, 45–46, 64, 69

Accuracy, of measurements, 95

Acquisition stage, of VST pipeline, 197–198

Active illumination, in optical tracking, 107

Active light probes, 208

Active searches
> incremental tracking technique, 150–151
> zero-normalized cross-correlation and, 152–153

Active sources, signals, 92

Actors, authoring elements, 333–334

Advertising, examples of use of AR, 25–27

Agile displays, as output modality, 274–276

Agile projectors, 275

A-GPS. *See* Assisted GPS

Airbrush, in specifying appearance, 318–319

AIREAL prototype, extrinsic haptic displays and, 36

AiRScouter (Brother), retinal scanning displays, 65

AJAX, producing/consuming multimedia information, 341

Albedo constant
> in diffuse reflectance, 214
> double shadowing problem and, 222–223

ALIVE system, conversational agents, 307

alVRed, for declarative scripting, 403

Amazon Fire Phone, user-tracking systems with, 184

AMIRE. *See* Authoring Mixed Reality

Angles, in determining location, 91

Annotations
> collaboration and, 325–327
> image-guided placement, 252–253
> labeling, 248–249
> legibility, 253–254
> optimization techniques, 249–250
> overview of, 248
> temporal coherence, 250–252
> use in navigation guidance, 350

Antiradiance, 225

Appearance
> free-form modeling, 322
> specifying, 317–319

Applications
> AR examples, 13, 23, 24
> AR software requirements, 380–382
> benefits of modularization, 333
> hardware abstraction and, 332

APRIL. *See* Augmented Reality Presentation and Interaction Language

AR²Hockey, agile collaboration in shared space, 369

Architecture. *See* Software architectures

Argon
> procedural scripting, 405
> web channels in Argon browser, 342

AR-Jig, for free-form modeling, 323–324

REGISTER YOUR PRODUCT at informit.com/register

Access Additional Benefits and SAVE 35% on Your Next Purchase

- Download available product updates.

- Access bonus material when applicable.

- Receive exclusive offers on new editions and related products.
  (Just check the box to hear from us when setting up your account.)

- Get a coupon for 35% for your next purchase, valid for 30 days. Your code will
  be available in your InformIT cart. (You will also find it in the Manage Codes
  section of your account page.)

Registration benefits vary by product. Benefits will be listed on your account page
under Registered Products.

InformIT.com–The Trusted Technology Learning Source

InformIT is the online home of information technology brands at Pearson, the world's foremost
education company. At InformIT.com you can

- Shop our books, eBooks, software, and video training.
- Take advantage of our special offers and promotions (informit.com/promotions).
- Sign up for special offers and content newsletters (informit.com/newsletters).
- Read free articles and blogs by information technology experts.
- Access thousands of free chapters and video lessons.

Connect with InformIT–Visit informit.com/community

Learn about InformIT community events and programs.

the trusted technology learning source

Addison-Wesley • Cisco Press • IBM Press • Microsoft Press • Pearson IT Certification • Prentice Hall • Que • Sams • VMware Press

ALWAYS LEARNING · PEARSON